The Path of the Masters

HUZUR MAHARAJ
BABA SAWAN SINGH JI
1858—1948

Dedication
to
Maharaj Sawan Singh Ji

There is a story to the effect that shortly before the assassination of President Lincoln, a Negro man came to him, bringing his twelve-year-old son. With tears streaming down his face, the man fell upon his knees before the Great Emancipator and said, "Master Lincoln, I am only a poor slave, and all I have is this boy of mine. But my heart is full of love and gratitude for all you have done for me and my people. It is not much I can offer, but I want to give to you this boy and myself as your servants for life. We will serve you gladly as your slaves, bound to you only by the bonds of love."

The case is similar with me now. All I have is this child of mine —this book—and myself. But I offer them both to you, my beloved Emancipator!

Julian Johnson

THE
PATH
OF
THE
MASTERS

The Science of Surat Shabd Yoga

The Yoga of the Audible Life Stream

Julian Johnson, M.A., B.D., M.D.

RADHA SOAMI SATSANG BEAS
PUNJAB, INDIA

Published by

S. L. Sondhi, Secretary
Radha Soami Satsang Beas
P.O. Dera Baba Jaimal Singh
Dist. Amritsar   143204
Punjab, India

First edition (printed in France)	2,000 copies	1939
Second edition (reprint in U.S.A.)	2,000 copies	1951
Third edition (revised)	1,000 copies	1957
Fourth edition (reprint in U.S.A.)	1,000 copies	1958
Fifth edition	2,000 copies	1963
Sixth edition	3,000 copies	1965
Seventh edition	3,000 copies	1969
Eighth edition (revised)	5,000 copies	1972
Ninth edition	5,000 copies	1974
Tenth edition	5,000 copies	1975
Eleventh edition	7,000 copies	1977
Twelfth edition	8,000 copies	1980
Thirteenth edition (revised)	12,000 copies	1985
Fourteenth edition	12,000 copies	1988

Printed at India Offset Press, Maya Puri Phase-I, New Delhi-110 064

Contents

Dedication   iii
Preface to the Thirteenth Edition   xiii
Preface to the Eighth Edition   xv
Preface to the Third Edition   xvii
Preface   xix
Author's Foreword   xxxv

Chapter One

THE PHILOSOPHICAL BACKGROUND

1. The Noble Birthright of Man   5
2. Man's First Duty—To Know Himself   8
3. The New Social Order   10
4. A Great Spiritual Awakening   12
5. No Democratic Government Known   17

Chapter Two

A REVIEW OF WORLD RELIGIONS: THEIR MEANING AND ANALYSIS

1. The Spiritual Plight of Mankind   21
2. Does the Remedy Cure the Disease?   25
3. The Religions of China   31
4. What Is the Meaning of Tao?   34
5. The Zoroastrian Faith   37
6. Buddhism in India   45
7. An Unnecessary Sacrifice   47
8. Islam, the Religion of Mohammed   52
9. The Bhagavad Gita   59
10. Quotations From the Gita   61
11. The Yoga of the Gita   66
12. The Four Vedas of the Hindus   70
13. An Epitome of Vedic Philosophy   74
14. The Yoga of Patanjali   79

15. Jesus Christ and the Christian Religion   83
16. Teachings Emphasized by Jesus   85
17. Paul, the Founder of Christianity   89
18. The Substance of the Teachings of Jesus   92
19. The Church Needs a Living Master   99
20. Theosophy   103
21. Christian Science as a Religion   110
22. Modern Spiritualism   114
23. The Rosicrucians   119
24. The Jewish Religion   123
25. The Sikh Religion of India   135
26. The Basic Elements of All Religions   138
27. Love, the Essence of Religion   141
28. Key to the Analysis of Religions   146
29. Guarding One's Own Mental Processes   149
30. Analyzing Religious Movements   154

Chapter Three

THE MASTERS AND THEIR DUTIES

1. Who and What Are the Masters?   157
2. What Is a Genuine Master?   159
3. The Master More Than Super-Man   165
4. The Master and the Supreme One   168
5. Time Limit of the Master's Work   171
6. How Shall We Recognize a Master?   175
7. Objective Indices of Mastership   178
8. Very Difficult to Find a Master   181
9. Positive Knowledge Versus Beliefs   183
10. The Duties of the Masters   185
11. Why Surrender to a Master   188
12. The Masters' Change of Policy   190
13. The Function of the Spiritual Master   193

Chapter Four

THE CREATION AND ORDER
OF THE UNIVERSE

1. The Cosmogony of the Masters   199
2. The Four Grand Divisions of Nature   201

3. Sat Desh, the Highest Region — 205
4. Brahmanda, the Second Grand Division — 207
5. Anda, the Lowest of the Heavens — 209
6. The Grand Division of Pinda — 210

Chapter Five

GOD AND THE GRAND HIERARCHY
OF THE UNIVERSE

1. The Perplexing Question of God — 213
2. A Word of Caution to Scientists — 217
3. Who or What Is God? — 220
4. Names of the Supreme Being — 221
5. Monotheism, Polytheism, Monism and Pantheism — 229
6. The Grand Hierarchy of the Universe — 232
7. The Negative Power — 237

Chapter Six

ANALYSIS OF MAN:
THE PSYCHOLOGY OF THE MASTERS

1. The New-Old Psychology — 242
2. What Is the Real Man? — 245
3. The Several Parts of Man — 247
4. The Analysis of Mind — 252
5. The Four Antashkarans — 255
6. A New Force Enters the Mind — 264
7. The Five Perversions of Mind — 267
   Kam — 269
   Krodh — 271
   Lobh — 274
   Moh — 276
   Ahankar — 278
8. Antidotes to the Deadly Five — 281

Chapter Seven

KARMA AND REINCARNATION

1. What Is Karma? — 283
2. Karma Binds the World Together — 286

3. What Is Reincarnation? 289
4. Metempsychosis, a Bitter Pill 294
5. Reincarnation Explains Much 298
6. What Happens After Death 301
7. How to Do Karmaless Actions 306
8. Karma and the Vegetable Diet 309
9. Reincarnation and Social Reconstruction 312
10. Karma and the Nature of Evil 317
11. Love, the Passkey to the Kingdom 320

Chapter Eight

THE EXISTENCE OF HIGHER WORLDS

1. A New Concept of the Universe 324
2. Quotations From Prominent Christians 327
3. Inner Experiences Analyzed 333
4. Inner Experiences of Mediums 335
5. Inner Experiences of the Masters 338

Chapter Nine

THE MICROCOSMIC CENTERS IN MAN

1. Man Himself a Microcosm 339
2. The Microcosmic Centers 343
3. The Meaning of Going Within 346
4. The Release of the Kundalini 347

Chapter Ten

MENTAL PREPARATION FOR
THE GREAT WORK

1. A Flawless Morality 350
2. The Next Step Is Viveka 351
3. The Christ Attitude of Mind 355
4. The Gita Ideal of Discipleship 356
5. Vairagya, the Next Step on the Path 357
6. The Final Destruction of Desire 361
7. That Which Kills Desire 364

Chapter Eleven

THE AUDIBLE LIFE STREAM:
THE SOURCE OF ALL BEING

1. The Central Fact in Santon ki Shiksha   368
2. Names of the Supreme Logos   370
3. What Is the Audible Life Stream?   373
4. The Life Stream Can Be Heard   376
5. The Sufi Idea of the Divine Vadan   378
6. The Only Means of Spiritual Liberation   384
7. New Birth Through the Shabd   385
8. Shams-i-Tabriz on the Life Stream   389
9. Science of the Masters—In Six Words   391

Chapter Twelve

THE GREAT WORK OF THE MASTERS:
WHAT THEY ACTUALLY DO

1. The Scientific Yoga of the Saints   395
2. Demonstrating Truth for Oneself   400
3. What Does This Science Offer?   402
4. The Surat Shabd Yoga   407
5. The Technology of This Yoga   415
6. Passing "The Gates of Death"   417
7. Evolution and the Final Goal   425

Glossary   433
Index   445
Local Addresses   453
Books on this Science   457

Preface to the Thirteenth Edition

FIRST PUBLISHED IN 1939, this book is now in its thirteenth printing, which attests to its continuing popularity over the years. It is gratifying to know that Western readers have found in it a complete guide to the teachings of the Saints; it has appealed to educated seekers of Truth everywhere because it discusses the Sant Mat philosophy in great depth.

In explaining the philosophy and its relationship to the many religious systems of the world, the author has used a number of Sanskrit and Hindi terms. For ease of reading, these terms are italicized only the first time they appear, and are defined in the Glossary.

A small change has been made in the format of the book. Originally, *The Path of the Masters* was published in a large size, which was subsequently reduced to bring it into uniformity with our other publications. Beginning with this edition, the book is being presented once again in the slightly larger size, for the convenience of the reader. A new index has also been prepared.

We wish to thank Wayne and Miriam Caravella for their work in connection with this edition, including preparation of the press copy, design, and seeing the book through the press; Bonnie Fields for preparing the index; and Louise Hilger for her usual loving guidance and overall supervision.

S. L. Sondhi
Secretary

Radha Soami Satsang Beas
Punjab, India
February 1985

Preface to the Eighth Edition

THIS BOOK, which deals so exquisitely with the science of the Audible Life Stream, the Voice of Silence, or the Ageless Wisdom, has over the years had a very special appeal. It has been reprinted several times, as well as translated into a number of languages. Many a communication comes in every year from almost every part of the world—even the remotest of corners—where a seeker has happened to get access to the book and has ultimately found himself at the feet of the Master. The book has someway or somehow met the basic need of the individual, the material thirst of his mind, and the deep longing of his soul. One feels as if a spiritual legacy reposed in the book is making the rounds and fulfilling itself in many ways.

With a view to conforming the book's size to our other books, it has been from the seventh edition onward reduced to 22½ × 14 cms. from the original 25 × 16½ cms.

Mr. J. S. White of the American International School, New Delhi, has kindly done the editing and proofreading of this edition, and we are greatly beholden to him for his labor of love for the Master.

K. L. Khanna
Secretary

Radha Soami Satsang Beas
Punjab, India

January 1972

Preface to the Third Edition

THIS BOOK is now well known to the West and is almost a classic on Sant Mat in English. In fact, it has been instrumental in guiding many seekers to the Path of the Masters.

Dr. Johnson was a man of parts, and besides being a distinguished surgeon, was also an artist, scholar, pilot, and an ordained minister of the church, and had been in India before, as a missionary.

He could not, however, rest satisfied with orthodox religion and church dogmas. His soul longed for Truth and firsthand experience. He felt keenly that no departed Intelligence, however great, could be a substitute for a living Teacher. But where was one to be found?

His quest was soon rewarded, and the guiding forces brought him to the feet of the Great Master, whose picture adorns the first page of this book. At his feet this apt pupil imbibed the principles of Sant Mat at firsthand, and under his supervision and guidance he practised devotion and meditation; and this spiritual intercourse went on uninterruptedly thenceforth.

Though he was the recipient of considerable attention and grace, he did not accept things blindly and would quite often say, with a half-suppressed smile, to his satsangi friends in private conversation, "I am from Missouri."[1] And herein lies the great value of the book.

Being a man of strong conviction and penetrating judgment, he has expressed himself rather strongly here and there, but it is all in good faith. True to his profession, he has not hesitated to carry on the operation, simply to spare the feelings of the patient. Had he lived longer, he might have softened some of his expres-

---

1. An American expression that means, in effect, "Prove to me that what you are saying is true."

sions, but he was snatched away from us while the book was yet in the press.

The Great Master, who inspired this book, is no more, and his successor, Sardar Bahadur Jagat Singh Maharaj, has also joined him on the other side after finishing his work. The steady demand for the book, however, continues and has necessitated a new edition. The present Master, Maharaj Charan Singh Ji, perhaps on account of my previous associations with the learned author, has kindly entrusted to me the duty of revising and editing the book where necessary, before sending it to the press. In doing this, while I have taken note of the suggestions and criticisms, my aim has been not to mar the character and main trend of the book. May it continue to serve as a beacon light to all those struggling on the Path!

Grateful acknowledgments are due to Mrs. Madelene Mutter for kindly correcting grammatical and typographical errors; to Mr. Harvey H. Myers, Col. C. W. Sanders and Dr. Pierre Schmidt for several corrections and useful suggestions; to Mr. and Mrs. P. Fripp, who happened to be visiting Dera at this time, for the considerable pains they took in revising and correcting the Index and for their help in going through the proofs; and last, but not the least, to Shri R. D. Ahluwalia and Rai Sahib Munshi Ram for kindly going through the manuscript with me and helping me in the difficult task of editing the book.

Jagmohan Lal

Radha Soami Satsang Beas
Punjab, India
April 1957

MAHARAJ CHARAN SINGH JI

It behooves us, wrapped—so to speak—in a kind of icy immobility, not to turn aside from all the tremors of our individual being in our efforts to perceive a world from which we are to be banished, and which is possible of contemplation only by an impersonal intelligence. On the contrary, it is by the very effort of our daily struggle to acquire the most acute consciousness of this perpetual debate with ourself in which our 'Me' constitutes itself, that we are ushered into the very heart of this Reality.

We moderns are so busy studying the external world that we have to a great extent forgotten to study the internal world. We worry about the cure of our aches and pains, our asthma and rheumatism, and take no thought for the cure of our feverish desires and unworthy ambitions.

It is strange that though all must tread the path of life, so few know whither they are going!

> How little do we know that which we are!
> How less that, we may be!
>
> —BYRON

We wander from the cradle to the tomb, yet know not our true destination, which is not the tomb but rather the discovery of our 'Super-Self'.

For long ages we have accepted the tradition of the existence of two worlds: one, the world of appearances; the other, the world of existences; and have assumed that as the knowledge of things always means our linking them to our being, the appearances alone are accessible to us. But it is a mistake to imagine that back of those appearances there are real things perceivable to a more penetrating gaze, for a spectator can only behold the thing he contemplates from without. Everything therefore is necessarily an appearance. In fact, reality can only be attained within and not without ourselves. Man should turn his gaze within in order to begin that most marvelous of all explorations, since happiness comes only from within.

'The divine strain' hums all around us, yet we are of so gross a nature that we hear it not! Only by entering into the divine

Preface

None is poor, O Bhikha;
Every one hath got rubies in his bundle.
But how to open the knot he doth not know
And therefore is he a pauper!
—BHIKHA (an Indian Saint)

NO PROBLEM OF GREATER or of more moving import confronts man than that of possible awareness of his own consciousness, the deep significance of the place he occupies in the world as a whole, and of the Purpose he should first discover and then pursue.

This consciousness of Self[1] is the primal metaphysical experience, which, whilst causing one to penetrate into one's innermost being, at the same time causes one to penetrate into the universe. We cannot behold this universe as we could some spectacle before our eyes, for we ourselves are part of it; we aid in its formation; we are—as it were—fellow actors in a kind of drama, the variations of which depend on our subjective life which expresses its manifold incidents. Our affective states are not to be considered as mere accidents, of interest to no one but ourselves, to which the universe remains impassive, for thereby we penetrate into its intimacy and participate in the innermost workings of its life and gain the revelation of its mystery. —LAVELLE

Human science is peripheric and essentially centrifugal; it makes a study of the visible part of the sensible world, the surface upon which—so to speak—thought reflects itself upon itself. Spiritual science is, on the contrary, essentially centripetal; it studies the internal thought from internal planes, thence to deeper and deeper ones, approaching nearer and nearer the Absolute from which all life proceeds and which is the one and the only Reality.

1. Self, called by Brunton "Overself" and by Graham Howe "I" and "Me."

silence and closing our ears to the world of illusions can we catch the celestial melody, or else we are but yielding to the illusions of our imagination and reaping bitter misery.

The discovery of 'Self' is first of all an act of inward retirement; it is what is termed the going in. "We penetrate then"—says Lavelle—"into an invisible world; but this discovery occasions anguish and it is presumptuous to march to the conquest of this inner world without very definite directions, very precise counsels—hence the absolute necessity of a Master. 'Whoever goeth on a pilgrimage needeth a pilgrim for the way, be he a Hindu, a Turk or an Arab' (*Maulana Rum*). Then the outward universe withdraws and fades away as does the most beautiful scenery when the play is too dramatic, but soon we experience the joy of the revelation; the universe is now no longer an object outside of ourselves, an enigma to be solved; we no longer contemplate it from without, but from within. Its secret is our secret. This discovery, far from causing us a sense of misery, becomes a source of confidence and of light and we soon begin to suffer when we refuse to draw from this well! So then, after having lived long in the world as a stranger, he who takes refuge in solitude perceives a new world welcoming him and by-and-by obtains the direct perception of superior planes."

In the mystery of solitary intimacy—*magna solitudo*—the individual and the Supreme Being behold each other face to face, for the former returns to his original Self. "It is"—says Hegel—"in the very heart of my own subjectivity that I discover true reality and not in the motley spectacle displayed to my eyes. It is contradictory to seek for existence outside of myself, since outside of this Self I can find only an appearance for me; but I must seek for it in the very depth of my being, since I, at least, participate in existence."

To understand this truth does not demand violence; it needs only an inward reverence and a willing 'ear'. Truth reveals itself only to those who seek and love it. The great purpose of spiritual training is the absolute Union with the primordial Self.

This regeneration, *this second birth,* is what Christian theologians have called "the descent of the Holy Ghost." The inner illumination is united to an infinite love for the Divine—this inner flame, this simultaneous love and knowledge which, when born, rises and grows, until finally through a kind of impersonal ecstasy our whole being is kindled with a supreme desire for 'union'. (We call 'impersonal' that state of intuition in which our thought is no longer divided into a thinking subject and an external world, but rather the outer world is abolished by its integration in our personal consciousness. Our personal consciousness is by no means nullified. Nirvana is not the abolition of personality; on the contrary, it is the completeness of personality.)

"The summit of Reality can only be realized within oneself," said Buddha. A great Sufi Master adds that "the source of truth is within and he Himself is the object of his realization"; and according to Schopenhauer, *The essential to life's happiness resides in what one has in one's Self.* Verily the principal source of human bliss comes from within, *from the very depth of one's being."*

We cannot hope to possess other true riches than those we already *bear within us,* and we should use them and not neglect them, but they are, alas! so familiar to us that they no longer appear of any value; and we pursue other tawdry chattels whose possession is denied us. We are so weak that the world is sometimes obliged to rebuff us to cause us to detach ourselves from the world.

The kingdom of heaven is in the heart of those who realize God, and the whole purpose of life is to make God a reality. "Verily, it is simpler to find a way to heaven than to find one's way on earth" *(Hazrat Inayat Khan).* And how true is this sentence of the Bible: *"The kingdom of heaven is within you!"*

But how are we to discover this kingdom? Is this not the main object of philosophy as well as of religion? The former, alas, in spite of the numerous chairs where it is taught and the many writings of the greatest philosophers, has not proved to be the source at which the inquirer may quench his thirst. In the first place, philosophy is the appanage of an 'elite' and appeals mostly to the intellect, the mind. It is a dry subject. Furthermore, philosophizing has been going on for ages. Thousand and one arguments and theories have been put forth, but only lip-say are these—as the

Indian Saints say—for they have no life and our knowledge of God hath not advanced even an inch! But we have religion. Alas, concerning the latter, we fully agree with the opinion of Kerneiz: "Religion, to the masses, means one of the most redoubtable instruments of servitude of the human mind, and the founding of a new religion, however excellent it may be, is but to found a new prison in which to confine the spirit." The consolations religions afford are most platonic and the number steadily increases of those who nowadays can no longer believe or find any satisfaction in religion, for lack of manifest proofs and on account of the flagrant hypocrisy of so many false prophets or of their militant followers.

Nevertheless, the existence of this science of the unknown— the science of the soul, we might say—is a fact and sooner or later all will ardently yearn for it. Some advanced individuals claim a knowledge of it, but those who approach this discovery realize that it is the appanage of an extremely limited number.

Up to the present the Occident had never been granted the privilege of having the revelations of the Sages of this world in everyday language. Heretofore, the philosophical and spiritual teachings were veiled, and that is why such teachings were classified as *esoteric*, knowable only to a limited number of the initiated. This initiation was gained through secret revelations, allegorical and symbolic writings possible of interpretation only by those possessing the key and the direct teaching of the Master to his disciple. Uninitiated mortals were unable to penetrate the *arcanum*, so that only the advanced spiritual souls could grasp the imagery of the language, the divulgation of which was prohibited and the meaning of which without the key was impossible of interpretation.

Rare indeed are the Westerners possessing 'the knowledge', and this is but right, for the Sages of this world considered it useless to cast "pearls before swine" and to deliver the lucubrations of sterile discussion of this *enfant terrible* called 'the mind'— to nonprepared Egos—directions, counsels, precepts, truths and lines of conduct for spiritual ascension.

Heretofore, it was the privilege of a particular class of society to penetrate into spiritual secrets. However, such knowledge has degrees and starts from the simplest counsels to attain the profoundest truths, enabling the future disciple to grasp the Truth through his own personal experience; it is nevertheless true that the first steps and certain more advanced stages, known already to the priesthood, were safeguarded in a veiled form, in the secret books of the various religions of the world.

Life refuses to yield up or to display its sublimest secret to the slothful. If you wish to discover the depth of its meaning, why then, you must break up the fallow ground and prepare to search for it, and the place to seek it is within, for its treasures will neither be found outside of one's being nor can five senses lay hold on them. Are, then, the methods of the yogis hidden?

> Does a Raja strew his jewels on the highway in a public display? No, he hides them in the deep treasure-chambers, in the vaults of his palace. The knowledge of the Science of 'Self' is one of the greatest treasures a man can discover and possess. Is he forthwith to offer it in the bazaars for all and sundry? Let all who desire to attain and to lay hold of this treasure first ardently long for and then seek it. That is the only way, and it is the right way. Knowledge is hidden in order to ward off the superficial curious enquirer, the mentally unprepared and perhaps also the spiritually unworthy.   —BRAMA

The following questions and topics are set forth and explained in this book in modern, simple and clear language:

What is religion? What are its promises and its bestowals? Monotheism, Polytheism, Monism, Pantheism. The statement concerning the main religious movements of the East and of the West. The value of ceremonies, rites and sacred books. What is God? What are his Names? The great spiritual hierarchies. The superior planes and high regions. The spiritual guides of the past and present time. The role of the Masters. True and false 'Guru'; how to recognize them. The way to realize union with the Supreme Being. The various stages to be passed through by those who are willing to tread the pathway of the Master. How to become a disciple. Asceticism. The esoteric constitution of the human being. The chakras. Kundalini. The problem of desire. The five perversions, or passions, and their antidotes. The diverse karmas. Reincarnation and metempsychosis. Death and after death. The various yogas. The importance of the Audible Life Stream. In short, all that concerns 'the science of the Masters'.

The author has most satisfactorily adhered to the rule of Aristotle, viz.: "To write well, express yourself in the common language of the people, but think like a wise man." Here is a collection of spiritual wealth of the East revealed to the dazzled gaze of the West. Here we are not dealing with vain promises such as are given in most of the so-called philosophical societies and in so many books which lead to nothing and nowhere. Nor does one hear when at last nearing the long sought-for goal: "Oh, this is not for you, you are not advanced enough, it is a secret," and where "the Soul flies away, just at the very moment when we seem to hold its gleaming splendor in our hands and all we are left with is one more dead butterfly to add to our molding collection" *(Sri Krishna Prem)*. No, from beginning to end it sets forth plainly the path to be trodden in order to reach the highest goal, 'the Supreme Union'.

Formerly it was considered a violation to divulge the secret of the inner path according to the yogis. This secret was only to be revealed after having sustained the most difficult and rigid tests and countertests. This is quite natural where the Patanjali system is concerned because of the dangers of the tests submitted to by the *chelas*.[1] In this exposition of *Santon ki Shiksha*, contrary to so many yogas, dangers and difficulties do not beset the disciple at any step in the course of his spiritual practices.

"One reason this book is written now"—says the author— "at the express command of a Great Master, is to give to all who may possibly be able to recognize its value some understanding of the priceless truth of the Masters of all ages. The ancient screen of profound secrecy is now removed. There is no longer any need for such secrecy. It was not many centuries ago that no Saint

---

1. For ease of reading, Hindi and Sanskrit terms are italicized only the first time they appear, and are defined in the Glossary.

could speak openly, except at the peril of his own life. The method of the Saints expressed here is so safeguarded in itself that no harm can result from giving it out to the whole world, provided it be guarded from any abuse or misuse."

There is nowadays an incredible number of books written to build a bridge between the Orient and the Occident; there are innumerable books about yogas published in countless languages, written by either Orientals who came to the Occident to familiarize themselves with its trend of thought or else by Occidentals who essayed to penetrate the Eastern spirit.

The publication is not an adaptation from others' thoughts but verily a revelation for all concerned. Neither is it a question of race or religious current to be adapted to suit the one or the other, nor is it the search for points of mutual understanding. No, it is indeed the very basis of Religion, the revelation of a great mystery: the knowledge of our true origin and how once more to find the Father's home as did the prodigal son of yore, and this through the scientific self-experimental process that every sincere soul can verify for himself.

The highway to be trodden is here traced, and we can repeat the sentence of the Sufi Master, " The supreme purpose of life is to make God a reality"; for this purpose, "give us all you have and we shall give you all we possess!" Do not the Masters teach that every gift offered by us without any thought of compensation is already returned to us?

This book is not written with a view to satisfying curiosity or to please the mind or the imagination, but rather to quench the thirst of the true, sincere and humble seeker. Mental acrobatics, tortuous, complicated philosophical gymnastics are not requisite, nor is there any necessity to pore for hours over a page or an extract in order to ascertain the author's meaning.

The plain truth is too simple for the seeker after complexity, looking for things he cannot understand. The intellect creates its own problems and then makes itself miserable trying to solve them! Truth always expresses itself with the greatest simplicity. *Simplex veri sigillum!*

The writing and publishing of this book have the approval of and are in accordance with the express wish of the Great Master whose life and teachings have inspired these pages. However, as Dr. Johnson wrote, "The Master himself must not be held responsible for any inaccuracy or other imperfections in this volume. The writer alone is responsible for these; he makes no claims for himself and takes no credit whatsoever."

To practice yoga out of curiosity, in search of new sensations or in order to gain psychic power, is a mistake which is punished with futility, neurosis or even worse. None should seek initiation into the mysteries from unworthy motives, for disaster would surely result.   —BRUNTON

Are we to believe without proofs? Is blind faith indispensable? Theoretically, he who perceives in himself the call of the Absolute should be supposed to quit everything: situation, family, friends, in order to answer this call, as in the "come and follow me" of the Bible. But in the Occident there is no place whither to resort to embrace a particular philosophical discipline. There is no place in our society for the *sannyasi*.

The method exposed in these pages does not in any way require the seeker to leave everything and start out as a pilgrim with sandals and pack, in order to submit to endless tortures and tests! No, the part of the true adept consists in remaining in his usual surroundings and *there* to earn his living in a situation permitting him to live a simple, honest and decent life. It is therefore in the smoke of the battle of daily life that he has to make his way.

The battle of life must be won and not run away from. Origen's act of self-castration did not enable him to attain that state that Hindu tradition terms *brahmacharya*, and rigid isolation in a mountain cave will not bring about that inner detachment from the passing show of things which is the soil in which alone the flower of true wisdom can grow.   —SRI KRISHNA PREM

Is it possible amid the agitation of our modern life to adhere to any spiritual discipline? The author's answer is categorically affirmative. "The escape from one's surroundings can only be through isolation or flight. Certain people take refuge in *themselves*. So they find solitude in the midst of the crowd" *(Dr. Alexis Carrel).* "You can"—says Marcus Aurelius—"at any time you like retire *into yourself*. There is no retreat more quiet, more peaceful and less restless for man than the one that he finds *in his own soul.*"

The perfecting required by the disciple must be gained there where his karma has placed him. But he must progressively learn the value of renunciation of perishable things and find, even in success and terrestrial happiness, that bitter savor by which he recognizes he is but an exile in the world, and to experience even in the sweetest hours the poignant homesickness for a lost native land. Then it is, he realizes the fact that one can begin to hear only when the ears are shut, and that when the eyes are closed one at last can see, as "he who depends upon his eyes for sight, his ears for hearing and his mouth for speech, he is still dead" *(Hazrat Inayat Khan).*

The author plainly sets forth, without any circumvolution, the necessity for every being seeking for truth, first to ardently desire it, then to search for a Master, *a living Master.*

> Now, truth is never a thing that one finds but it is always taught us by somebody. But it is essential that this teaching should not oppress us, but rather should it restore our 'Self', it should reveal to us our liberty as well as the very meaning of our existence. —LAVELLE

And this is precisely what is realized through the Surat Shabd Yoga. This yoga is also called *Ananda Yoga*—the yoga of happiness and bliss—or again, *the Yoga of the Master.* It is founded on this cardinal and primordial notion of the *Sound,* the *Word.* Remember the magical scene that Goethe placed in the beginning of his *Faust;* his hero took for his text: "In the beginning was the Word." The light reveals the world: it was created by the Word. To see is to discover the work of creation. To hear is to have a sense of complicity with the Creator.

This divine melody—'this heavenly *Bani*'—is the hyphen

Whilst writing these lines we are deeply grieved in thinking of the author so recently departed in the middle of the preparation of this publication, leaving us the heavy responsibility of correcting the proofs of this book for which he worked with so much ardor and love.

But our promise of modest collaboration will not have been given in vain. This task has not been accepted blindly but on account of the immediate pledge to satisfy our 'reasoning reason'. First, we read with delight and interest his work describing his meeting with the living Master, then his autobiography; finally, after much mutual correspondence we were able to meet him and discuss every possible question concerning the very substance of this work.

What interests us is that the author was an Occidental, nay, an American, not a dreamer but a practical man who was first a Baptist Minister, for many years preaching the Gospel. Then he went to India as a missionary; oh, the irony, to bring to the Hindus the spiritual revelation of the Occident! He who went to teach, learned with awe of his ignorance and was soon overwhelmed in ascertaining the narrowness of the teaching he had received, in comparison to the incomparable riches of India concerning spiritual and philosophical matters.

Dr. Johnson could no longer bear to teach and preach to those toward whom he felt more and more a pupil rather than a teacher, and so he decided to return to America. But soon the narrow-mindedness of his coreligionists obliged him to leave this intolerant and petty atmosphere. Then he followed a postgraduate course of theology at the University of Chicago and was deeply impressed by the broad-minded attitude and spirit of his professors. But more and more his mind was dwelling on all the things he lacked, and this feeling of spiritual emptiness became so acute that he gave up his theological career and began to study medicine, achieving brilliant success. He then established himself as a surgeon and became so skillful that very quickly he acquired a large practice and a hospital where he was continually operating. He had his private motorcars and even his own airplanes. He was one of the first American amateur pilots. The foregoing is to satisfy the critics and to show how thoroughly he was equipped in various practical domains, having besides a broad general culture.

His work, however, did not satisfy him as he felt the uselessness of this superactive yet purposeless life, and his constant preoccupation was to discover at any price a definite spiritual direction, and above all *a living Master* who would be able to lead him to it.

One day he discovered the Master who could reveal to him what he exposes today in these memorable pages. He gave up all that he possessed—airplanes, motorcars, his house, the hospital, properties, patients—all his material comfort acquired by hard work, and went back again to India, but this time as a humble disciple.

———————

To write a book is to tell oneself one's secrets, but through it, the reader must feel that he is discovering his own; this is the author's desire.

In a first volume,[1] Dr. Johnson described his impressions after spending four years 'at the feet of the Master'. He then settled in India, this time not to teach but to learn.

Dr. Johnson, the minister who preached, the physician at the head of a hospital and its staff, and one who gave orders, became the humble adept freed from all the baggage of the past, in order to acquire 'the knowledge'. There the sick or crippled Indian brothers and sisters were given the advantage of his professional capacities. He treated and operated free of charge. And there on the bank of the river Beas, at the feet of the Master, he wrote this work which today constitutes his spiritual legacy, the first of its kind revealed to the Occident.

In the course of our stay in India we had the privilege of discussing with him personally all the questions dealt with in this

———————

1. Julian Johnson, *With a Great Master in India* (Beas, India: Radha Soami Satsang Beas, 1982). Originally published, 1934.

volume and we render homage of deep gratitude to his unselfish and disinterested efforts, to his perfect uprightness, rectitude and probity, to his tolerance and his untiring goodness. Dr. Johnson was a scholar of philosophy as well as of literature; he was also a man trained in scientific disciplines, precious token for every Occidental mind.

He received us with open hands, not to take but to give. His warm, benevolent and most generous hospitality, and the acquaintance with the Master he discovered in the north of India on the bank of this sacred river (from which at sunrise the impressive profile of the Himalayas is to be seen), all this will remain in the very depth of our heart as the most moving, happy and blissful experience.

"God speaks to the ears of every heart, but it is not every heart that hears Him"; nevertheless, he who seeks, finds—sooner or later—and to everyone is given the meeting he deserves. It is the destiny of every being to germinate in the dark—as the germ of wheat—and to die in the light. But this death, far from being an annihilation, is in reality 'a new birth'!

> *The prophet said: God saith to me—*
> *I do not live high or low at all;*
> *I live in the heart of the devotee.*
> *If thou desirest Me,*
> *Then seek Me from his heart.*
> *The Mosque is inside the Saints,*
> *And there resideth God for the homage of all.*
>
> —MAULANA RUM[1]

He who has found Him, seeks no more; the riddle is solved, desire gone, he is at peace. Having approached from everywhere that which is everywhere whole, he passes into the whole.

—BRUNTON[2]

---

1. Quoted in *Mysticism, the Spiritual Path* by Lekh Raj Puri (Beas, India: Radha Soami Satsang Beas, 1964). Originally published, 1938.
2. Paul Brunton, *A Search in Secret India* (New York, Weiser: 1981), paper edition. Reference from 6th edition.

Pilgrim who treadest the Mystic Path, if thou searchest humbly and sincerely, thou wilst find in Santon ki Shiksha—this Voice of the Silence—the resolution of the great Enigma and the perfect union with the Supreme Being from whom thou issuest.

Dr. Pierre Schmidt

Geneva, Switzerland
October 1939

The Author's Foreword

THE SUBJECT MATTER of this book is so important, so far-reaching and revolutionary, that the task of presenting it properly appears to be an undertaking beyond the powers of any ordinary man. The writer realizes his lack of complete competency. But the message of the Masters had to be given to the world at this time, in the English language, and no one appeared who was better qualified. To have evaded the responsibility would have been to shirk a plain duty. After years of careful study, in close association with the Great Master, besides much time spent with advanced and learned disciples of the Master, this duty was assigned to me as if by common consent.

I wish to record my obligations and thanks to those noble souls who have given so much help, and who have been to me personally a very great inspiration. They all reflect the light of the Masters. They all go to make up that grand galaxy of spiritual luminaries pointing the starry way to higher worlds beyond all stars. These men are not only learned in the lore of this Path, but they are quite familiar with the various systems of Indian philosophy and religion; and hence are able to make intelligent discrimination between all of them and this Path of the Masters. They themselves have chosen this Path not blindly but in full light of knowledge. With their collaboration, this work has been carried forward to completion.

It must be said here, as well as in the heart of this book, that this is not another phase of 'Hindu philosophy'. Neither is it Vedantism. It is none of the schools and cults of India. This is not a cult, nor is it even a religion, in the historic sense of that term. What is it? *It is a scientific method of entering and realizing the kingdom of heaven while still living here in the human body.* That is the sum and the substance of this book. Is that too much to expect? No. It can be done, and this book points the Way. That is the great work of all the Masters and Saints of all ages. In this book, for the first time in history, the complete story of the Masters' scientific Path is given to the world in the English language, by one who was born among the English-speaking people. It is, therefore, written from the Western viewpoint. The Master now wishes to meet the demands of that ever-growing number of students who will not be satisfied with formal and ceremonial religion. In this age of scientific achievement, the Master wishes to offer a spiritual system of 'self-realization' and of 'God-realization' which meets every demand of science. For the first time a definite method or science is given to the English-speaking world, which shows the aspiring and yearning soul just how to enter and possess that kingdom of heaven spoken of by all prophets and all religions. Many books give hints, but they describe no definite method by which anyone may rise to the highest heavens during this life. Most of them cannot do so, because they themselves have neither the knowledge nor the method. Only the Masters have it, and this is the first time that they felt that the time was ripe for a general distribution of such a large portion of their science.

For centuries men have been told that they themselves are the temples of God. But they have not been shown how to enter those temples and there to meet God. This system offers the method. It gives the key to that temple. It bids the student open the door and enter. Ever since the earliest men began to speculate concerning what lies out beyond death, mankind has stood silent at the graves of its loved ones, shuddering at 'the dark unknown'. But to the Masters and their students there is no 'dark unknown'. They know what comes after death, as well as they know any ordinary fact of this life. How? Because the Master and his advanced students are able at will to pass through the gates of death, to see what is there, and then return to normal life at any time and as often as they wish. Thus they have, while still living in the body, conquered the last enemy.

Ever since men began to think, slowly awakening from the prehistoric lethargy into which they had sunk, they have found themselves drifting with the tides, helpless victims of a thousand ills, driven by apparently blind forces, obstructed and harassed at every turn, wounded and bleeding, heartsick and weary; and there has been but precious little they could do to change the situation. Who has not realized his inability to cope with the thousand and one enemies constantly besetting his path? But the Masters and their disciples are not so helpless. They are not like the chaff driven by the winds. A Master is a Master indeed. He controls life and death, and he holds the forces of Nature in his hand as a mechanic manipulates his machine. Life to the Masters holds no unsolved problems; death to them has no terrors. To them the future is an open book, and joy goes with them all the day long, like the sweet chime of bells. Since all the world is seeking happiness, here is the Royal Road to happiness. It is *el Camino Real* of the Masters.

This book is not an encyclopedia of Oriental philosophy. Hence, but few quotations are given from the sacred books or so-called authorities. If the student felt any obligation to accept these 'authorities', he would not need this book. A short resume of the different religions is given for the sake of comparison. The best features of each religion or system are given and then an effort has been made to show just where and how the science of the Masters transcends them all and accomplishes something which no other system does. Each philosophy or religion is given credit for fulfilling a need in the day and country when and where it was given out. Each religion usually runs its course and becomes obsolete. One difficulty has been that no religion is willing to acknowledge the fact when it is dead. Only the moral precepts of all religions— which are essentially the same in them all, remain as universal truth. Even these are subject to considerable change as the ages pass. But beyond all of them, the science of the Masters stands out like the majestic peak of Everest, defying the storms of the centuries. And this is so because the science of the Masters is a universal science. It is not limited to any one country or time. Neither is it for any one group of people but for all mankind.

These are some of the facts which this book attempts to elucidate. We do not believe any apology is required for the manner of stating this science. Demonstrated facts of any science may be stated in positive language. Even though the statement may appear dogmatic, yet it is not really so. Dogma is a declaration of opinion which the writer assumes to be fact, but concerning which he has no definite knowledge. But if a man should assert with Euclid that the square formed on the hypotenuse of a right angle triangle is equal to the sum of the squares formed on the other two sides, he is not stating a dogma, he is stating a fact which any mathematician may demonstrate for himself. The case is similar with the facts given out by the Masters. They tell only what they *know,* and they know because they themselves have demonstrated everything they teach. If we give to the world in this book some of the findings of the Masters, we are not giving out opinions nor dogmas nor theories. And this is why we must make certain statements which, on their surface, may appear dogmatic. In no instance is the mere opinion of this writer ever given, except where it is definitely stated as his opinion and nothing else.

The volume of this teaching is given out as the findings of the great Masters, and the reader is referred to their writings for verification of all that is given here. Their writings are mostly in Hindi and Sanskrit, but they can be read. Also, there is at least one great Master now living in the flesh, at whose feet this writer has had the inestimable privilege of sitting as an humble student for many years past.[1] Some of us believe that he is the greatest of all Masters known to history, and we have for this opinion what to us appears good and sufficient evidence. However, this is only an opinion, because we have not personally seen all of the great Masters of history. Be that as it may, he is a living exemplar of all that is taught in this book. Concerning these things, he speaks as one having authority, and not as the pundits. He has not only read them in a book, he has experienced them in his own life and he knows their reality.

We may refer to such great Masters of the past as Shams-i-Tabriz and Maulana Rum of Persia; and in more recent times, Kabir Sahib, Tulsidas, Guru Nanak and his nine successors; and still more recently, Soami Ji, Baba Jaimal Singh, and Sawan

---

1. The author is referring here to Maharaj Sawan Singh Ji, who passed on in 1948. He was succeeded by Maharaj Jagat Singh Ji. The present living Master is Maharaj Charan Singh Ji.

Singh Maharaj of Beas, who is the living Master. Many others might be mentioned, scattered all through history. But their names would not be known to many of the readers of this book, and so they would carry no weight of authority. Of course, many students will ask: What about Buddha and Jesus Christ? Also, Zarathustra and Mohammed? Were they Masters of the highest order? Happily we are not called upon to pass judgment upon their degrees of mastership. However, let us accept them as Masters and give them all love and honor. It would have been a joy to know them. To meet any spiritual man or woman, even of the yogi degree, is no small good fortune.

Personally, I feel so grateful for the privilege of associating with even a disciple of the Great Master that I would be willing to be his servant, if occasion required. This is because I have some little idea of what a real Master is. A story is told of Shiva, which well illustrates this point. Walking through a jungle, he suddenly stopped, and while gazing at a large stone, tears began to run down his face. When asked why he wept, he replied: "Ten thousand years ago a real Saint sat upon this rock, and just to think, I was not here to see him!" It is only those who have known a Master who can appreciate a Master. So let us never speak lightly of any spiritual teacher or Master. Let us revere any advanced soul, past or present. All honor and love and praise to them. They are the salt of the earth. Their lives radiate the sweet perfume, wafted down through the centuries, to purify the air of history.

But there is one vital point of importance which must never be overlooked when we are discussing the Masters of the past. That is the fact that the real work of the Master on this earth plane lasts only during his individual lifetime, and ends with the end of that life. The Master assumes human form in order to do a particular work which he could not do without human form. This being so, how can he do that work after leaving the human form? This is only common sense. Even the Supreme Being himself could not do the work of a Master on this plane, unless he took human form. This is not because the Supreme himself is limited, but because we are limited. We cannot receive what he wishes to give, except through a human body.

This is one of the tragic mistakes of history. Millions of people today imagine themselves followers of some dead Master. But such a thing is quite impossible. Can a woman marry a dead man and live with him? Can a dead doctor give medicine? Can a dead judge decide a case at law? The relationship existing between Master and disciple is a personal one. It involves vastly more than a few instructions that might be given in a book. Instructions in some code of ethics is not what men need. They require the personal aid of a living Master.

If anyone imagines himself a disciple of a dead Master, he only deceives himself. He may revere the memory of a Master or read his writings. He may feel in his heart love and veneration for him. He may be willing to die for the honor of his name. But he can never be a real initiate of that Master. He must look to a living Master if he wishes to enter the Path of the Masters. Without a living Master, no one can ever go beyond the uncertain influence of a ceremonial religion. The benefits of such religion are problematical.

Those who insist that one religion is as good as another, or that one road to heaven is as good as any other road, are many. And they are right, as far as they go. Among all the religions of the world, there is very little that anyone can boast of as superior to all others. Each one generally imagines he is right and that all others are wrong. Suppose all roads lead to heaven, as truly as all roads led to Rome. There was only one Rome, but there are many heavens. Vast numbers of them, one above another, the higher one more beautiful and more extensive than the one below it. Now, suppose all roads lead to the lowest heaven—all roads leading from this physical plane. That does not imply that all roads lead to the higher regions. Those vast heavens stretch away to unimaginable distances. And the higher heavens are known only to the higher Masters. The lower ones are known to the yogis and masters of the lower degrees. If the lower roads lead to the lower heavens, there are higher roads that lead to the higher heavens, and these are known only to the great Masters. Consequently, if the student wishes to go to the highest of them, he must seek out a real Master to show him the way and help him to walk upon that Path.

And here is the essential point of difference between the Path of the Masters and that of all religions and so-called masters of inferior degrees. The disciple must take his choice whom he will follow, the real Master who goes to the highest regions, or the yogi who goes to the lower regions. For it is a fact well understood by occultists that no one can go higher than his Master. It is with the greatest satisfaction that we are able to offer in this book some glimpses of the Path that leads to the highest achievements.

If you ask how we know that Path leads to regions higher than that of any other system, I will answer that the evidence is based upon experience. It is not a theory or a belief. If those different systems set forth their claims, and a disciple of the Masters goes inside and traverses all regions mentioned by those systems, and then goes on to some region far beyond anything they ever dreamed of, is that not sufficient evidence? One student of the Master here was conversing with a follower of another religion who claimed superiority of his own lord and his own religion. The disciple replied that she had many times seen the lord of the other party and had passed by him on her way to higher regions. Is this not sufficient proof of the superiority of the Path of the Masters? Of course, it is not possible to present this proof to the external senses. But to such as have gone higher, it is conclusive. The disciple of the higher Path *knows*, while the religionist of other schools, never having gone up, simply guesses.

Once a lady asked the Great Master how he knew that there was not some higher region or some Path to a higher region than anything known to him? He replied, "Very well, if anyone can show me the way to anything higher than that known to the Saints, I shall gladly go with him!"

I must call attention here to the one thing that, above all, distinguishes this system from others—its central theme and the vital content of this book. It is *the Audible Life Stream*. It is the most important fact of the entire universe, and yet it is not well known to any of the world religions or systems of thought except the

Masters'. How this amazing fact has ever come about in history is not easy to tell. Without this factor in religion and philosophy, everything else is barren and useless by comparison. To bring this great fact to the attention of the thinking world is the most revolutionary and important announcement that has been made to the world in a hundred centuries. The fact that the Creator himself can actually be heard vibrating through all space in musical vibrations of the most enchanting quality, is a fact of supreme importance, and especially so when it is known that by following this enchanting music anyone may rise to the extreme heights of spiritual attainment. Is there anything else of comparable value?

We hope the reader will keep this amazing fact in mind throughout his study of this book. It is the one thing of supreme value in the book. It is to make this great fact known that the book has been written. It should be always and everywhere known that without this one thing of supreme importance, no philosophy and no religion has any actual value. At the same time, let no one complain that this is merely a dogmatic assertion. It is not so. This is a fact which has been abundantly proved by the Masters. The entire thesis of this book is an attempt to elucidate this great truth.

We may call attention to Chapter Two, in which a brief review of world religions has been given. This chapter is intended to meet the requirements of certain students. If different types of students do not find this chapter necessary or important in their studies, they may omit it and go direct to that section which deals with pure *Santon ki Shiksha,* 'the teachings of the Masters'. At least, they may do this at the first reading, and then go back, if they like, to that section which constitutes a comparative study. It is believed, however, that this section will be of value to all students who wish to make a thorough study of the Master's system.

Every effort has been made to make this book as scientifically and historically accurate as possible. If the critic finds too many statements which emphasize this point, he will forgive us, I hope. It is an extremely important point. H. P. Blavatsky once said, speaking of her Eastern masters: "They showed us that by combining science with religion, the existence of God and the immortality of man's spirit may be demonstrated like a problem in

Euclid." And this is literally true. It is exactly what the Masters and their disciples are doing all the time. All men will acknowledge the importance of this demonstration, provided it can actually be made. But the great Masters have made it, and they have been making it for many thousands of years in India and other countries. Among them the spiritual Path was actually marked out, and scientifically marked out, vast eons of time before our ancestors had emerged from primeval savagery. That the bulk of the Indian population appears now in a state of retrogression has nothing to do with the above historical fact. Masters still live and demonstrate their science in India.

Many intimate things intended for disciples alone, and which only initiates will find of value, are omitted from this volume. This is not because the Masters wish to withhold anything of value from any honest student, but it is because some of those things would be of no use to the uninitiated and might result in confusion and misunderstanding. Hence, they are omitted here. Until one has become an initiate himself, and has made a little headway on the Path, there are many things which appear so astounding and revolutionary, so unlike all that the Western people have been accustomed to believe as established facts in psychology and religion, that they will be inclined to cast them aside as unbelievable. But when one has gone a little distance on the Path of the Masters, he accepts these things with great joy because he has positive proof of them and is able to see their rationale and their great beauty. The strong food of an adult laborer cannot be given to an infant; neither can a man who never left the ground step into an airplane and take it through the skies with skill and precision. Philosophy and religion must come to the consumer in such doses as he can assimilate.

If the modern scientist objects that we are trying to extend the field of science beyond its legitimate scope, let him remember that science has been for centuries extending its bounds, enlarging its fields of operation. Why should we try now to limit it? Shall we deny that exact knowledge may be had concerning the soul and the life after death? Why should we so handicap our investigations? It were no part of wisdom to do so. Let all science remain free. It has fought with ecclesiasticism for centuries to gain the freedom it now enjoys. Shall science itself now turn and attempt to circumscribe its own activities? Shall it try to curb its own investigations? It cannot be so.

Sir Arthur Eddington said: "I am not sure that the mathematician understands this world of ours better than the poet and the mystic." Science should never become conceited. Why may we not treat of heaven and hell in mathematical terms? Sir James Jeans admits in his *Mysterious Universe* that science is not yet in contact with ultimate reality. And Professor Max Mueller said: "Who are the blind? They who cannot see the inner worlds!" Some go so far as to say that ultimate reality is beyond the ken of man. But that is a bold assumption, and is unbecoming to a scientist in these days of superachievements. It is then the aim and purpose of this book to take the hand of science and introduce it to ultimate reality. Does this sound like vain presumption? Nay, it is not so. Today there are living men, not one but many, who are in conscious contact with ultimate reality.

One living mystic says, "True religion consists in developing that attitude of mind which ultimately results in seeing one infinite existence prevailing throughout the universe, thus finding the same divinity in both art and science." This is the higher ideal of science. Why limit science to the test tube and microscope? Real science finds its ultimate domain in those broader and more beautiful worlds where only the mind and soul may enter, after being purified from the dross of materiality.

Ouspensky has written a book in which he attempts to place side by side with scientific discoveries many spiritual realities. Thus he aims to show their proper relationships. That there is a very definite relation between the spiritual and the material should be understood as a fundamental premise of all investigations. How far Ouspensky has succeeded is a question. But the idea is a noble one. He might have done better if he had been in possession of the knowledge of the Masters concerning spiritual realities. He was a noble scientist himself. But he had to acknowledge that after his most diligent explorations into the various fields of science he always found himself brought up against a blank wall. His *A New Model of the Universe* is only another attempt to explain that of which the writers themselves are entirely ignorant. Some are shrewder guessers than others.

It is only when a man begins to rise above the world of sense that he actually begins to *know*. The *Tertium Organum* of Ouspensky presumes to be a "key to the enigmas of the Universe." But a man in possession of the knowledge of the Masters has that key, in fact. Doubt not that such a key exists. Every Master has it, and he offers it without money and without price to any sincere student. The science of the Masters is the only system in the world which offers a definite and scientific Anthroposophy. Rudolph Steiner made a noble endeavor to discover such a science. He had some light but it is a pity that Steiner had not the clear vision of a real Master. Let us thank him and bless his memory, however, for the good work he did in calling the attention of the world to some of the higher truths. Doubtless he did much to prepare the way for a nobler science.

Any doctrine which is to gain a lasting hold upon the thought of mankind or touch their lives to any degree must not only appeal to the emotions, but it must carry a spiritual uplift that will change the lives of its advocates. This is the great weakness of the prevailing religions. Their advocates do not in their lives demonstrate any great superiority over their fellowmen who do not accept that religion. Not only so, but that doctrine which is to establish itself in the inner lives of the people must also have a definite appeal to the intellect. Gone are the days when thinking people will accept anything on the authority of a book or a priest. It must satisfy rational intelligence. It is just here where the science of the Masters makes its strongest appeal to mankind at large. It is rational. It is scientific.

Last of all, let us say, if the reader's impulses are sufficiently altruistic and he wishes above all to be of service to mankind, especially to those whom he loves, he can follow no wiser course than to qualify as a master scientist on this Path. No matter if it takes him five, ten, or twenty years to qualify, it will pay him well.

He will actually save time. For one who is well qualified in this master science can do more for humanity in one day than he could otherwise do in twenty years as an ordinary man. With assurance and high hopes we therefore send out this volume on its mission of love.

The Master, the Audible Life Stream, and spiritual liberation during this lifetime—these three constitute the substance of this book.

The Path
of the
Masters

This book is a comprehensive statement of Santon ki Shiksha, or Sant Mat, the teachings of the great spiritual Masters. After living with such a Master for almost seven years, the author gives an outline of Surat Shabd Yoga, the Yoga of the Audible Life Stream, which is the scientific system through which the Masters attain the highest degree of spiritual development.

Chapter One

THE PHILOSOPHICAL BACKGROUND

---

1. The Noble Birthright of Man

JUDGING purely from the trend of present-day events, noting the deep undercurrents of thought—religious, philosophical, scientific—it is the opinion of this writer that within three centuries from now *the science of the Masters* will prevail over the whole world. Not, indeed, accepted by everyone or even a majority; but it will constitute the dominant stream of thought and it will be generally acknowledged as the king of the sciences. By that time a high ethical standard of conduct will be adopted everywhere as a wholesome reaction from the present chaos in morals and standards. This will come about by a universal increase in knowledge and an enlightened conscience. At that time the best there is in all systems of religion and philosophy will be separated from the worthless, as wheat from the chaff, and a new social order will be established upon the foundation of rational and scientific demonstration. As flowers and fruit adorn and glorify the plant, so upon this new intellectual, ethical and social foundation a great spiritual evolution will take place. This spiritual quickening will not be caused by the new social order, but will itself become the fountainhead of the new order. Spirituality is not the flower or the fruit of ethics and of social reconstruction, but sound ethics and a just social order are good soil out of which spirituality may spring up, when vitalized by the showers of living water. It will be the function of the Masters and their spiritual science to supply those living waters by connecting men with the Audible Life Stream.

This is the age of the intellect, but we are approaching the dawn of the age of the spirit. That spiritual evolution will then be explained in terms of the science of the Masters. Is this a bold assumption? We think not. It is a rational calculation. This is the age of science—at least its beginning. For even science will merge its supreme glory in that age when spirit shall be enthroned. Soul and intellect should sit side by side upon the throne of world empire. Theological speculation is dead, or is about to breathe its last. Even the most religious care but little for dogma and metaphysical dissertations. They are searching for Reality, for something solid upon which to rest their tired feet. They are looking for reality in the realms of religion and the spiritual just as surely as they are looking for it in agriculture and trade. The scientific spirit must eventually lead mankind to adopt the scientific method in religion. And there is but one scientific method in religion. There never has been but one. There never can be but one. That is the method of Nature, the method of the Masters. There is but *one* universal God, and there has been but one way to approach Him, and that is the method established by the Creator himself. This method cannot be altered or substituted by man.

There will be congestions and fevers, when the bloodstreams of the nations will become impure. There will be years of stagnation and decades of intense activity. There will be moments of wild delirium. There will be the dark days of war and the bright periods of peace. There will be retrogression and advance, but the retrogression will be only seeming, only temporary. In reality, the world will move on slowly but steadily toward the new Golden Age. Of course, that new *Sat Yuga*[1] is yet many millennia distant. But the darkest days of this *Kal Yuga*—the Iron Age—have already passed. We need not be discouraged if a few stormy years intervene, when sections of the world will be war-torn by the most violent social eruptions known to history. When these terrible

---

1. For ease of reading, Hindi and Sanskrit terms are italicized only the first time they appear, and are defined in the Glossary.

days have passed, all nations—chastened, cleansed and reorganized—will return to sanity and will settle down to a more steady advance. Only by bitter experience can man learn the folly of fratricidal strife. It is utterly unthinkable that men will go on committing suicide by wholesale slaughter, even under the sway of mob psychology.

When the happy days of sound sense and scientific reconstruction shall dawn, the human race shall move with quickened pace toward the era of light. In that new civilization the spiritual science of the Masters will be the guiding star. In truth, this great science will be, and is now, the fountain source of all world civilization—though the world doesn't know it. But this science will come into its own by a general recognition, when men shall become sufficiently awakened to profit by it.

Nothing which is written here is to be construed as a prophecy. It is only an expression of the author's private convictions based upon a careful study of history and the obvious trend of present-day events. It is believed that these convictions are shared by a great number of men who have studied the situation. One thing we must not forget. The Supreme Will must prevail in world affairs. We need not worry. The whole world cannot go to the devil, because the Infinite One is guiding its destiny.

Nations and individuals are still rushing about trying to sell their birthright for a mess of pottage. They are so eager to achieve sense-gratification. They know not their true inheritance. They go on digging in the earth for worms, when gold and diamonds lie under their doorsteps. Man has not yet arrived on his planet, although he thinks he has. That being which imagines himself man, which builds houses and writes books, is only man in the process of becoming. That being who goes about calling himself 'Homo Sapiens' is only a suggestion, a promise, of what is to come. In offering this book to the world, giving for the first time a comprehensive statement of the Masters' science in the English tongue, the main purpose of the writer is to help fulfill this promise. At present the idea that man has already arrived is *the great illusion*. But that he will arrive in due time is the finest vision of the prophet. To prepare the way for his arrival, in ever-increasing numbers, is the dominating thought of the friends of man.

All men are born to an inheritance far above and beyond their wildest flights of fancy. The Masters sometimes compare the soul to a beautiful queen who wanders away from her palace. Her mind becomes clouded. She lays aside her royal robes, clothes herself in rags, and becomes an associate of dirty sweepers, the lowest of the low. This is a correct picture of the situation in respect to all souls, except those who have become really enlightened by contact with a Master. They have all descended from their original home in the kingdom of light. They are children of the King of kings. But they have lost all knowledge of their origin and of their noble inheritance. Their minds have grown clouded, their perceptions dulled, and now they have not the least idea of their innate powers and possibilities. Wandering about for ages in these lowlands of *maya*, they drag out a miserable existence surrounded by filth and darkness.

2. Man's First Duty—To Know Himself

It was, therefore, extremely appropriate that the ancient sages pointed out man's first and primary duty. The Greek philosophers said, in substance: *"Worship the gods, if you must; but your first duty is to find out who and what you are yourself."* So they wrote over the doors of their temples, *"Gnothe Seauton"*—Know Thyself. And that is today the first command of the modern Masters. To know oneself, however, in the meaning of that phrase as given by the great Masters, is a very different thing from the meaning given it by the modern psychologist. This fact will become apparent to the reader as he advances into this book. So long as man believes himself to be only a worm of the dust, limited and bound by the physical, he will remain so. But he is only limited and bound because he chooses to remain so. When a man gets but a glimpse of what he really is now, and especially of what he may yet become by a little effort, that knowledge will give him the greatest possible inspiration.

Men are extremely proud of their intellectual achievements, and indeed they are considerable. But lying latent in man's brain is a capacity one million times greater than he is now using. Great scientists[1] now assert that the average man of today uses only about one-millionth part of his brain cells. This is an amazing thing. What were those cells put there for? What then would happen, what could man not do, if he should once awaken to his possibilities and begin to use his brain at full capacity? Who can envision such an awakening? Take the average skilled machinist, not to mention the men of greater brain capacity and education —multiply his brain action by one million, and then populate the world with such men. Truly, the real man has not yet arrived.

If we but make note of only a few of the achievements of modern intelligence during the last half-century, we may begin to catch glimpses of human possibilities. We are amazed to discover such gigantic and revolutionary changes in the earth as the diastrophic records show hidden away in subterranean rocks. But a more amazing phenomenon presents itself to the student when he takes note of the current records, during his own lifetime, proving that greater changes have taken place during the last half-century in the daily life of man than in all the preceding centuries since the time of Christ. Progress has taken to the airplane. It doesn't walk anymore. It travels at three or four hundred miles per hour, and that will soon be exceeded. Yet all of the modern achievements of man in science and invention, in control of the earth itself and Nature's forces, are as nothing when compared with what man may do when he comes consciously into his inheritance. The accomplishments of the mind, gigantic as they may now appear, are as the play of little children when compared to the possible triumph of the liberated soul. If every brain in the world were working at full capacity, even then the achievements of the intellect would be as nothing when compared to what may be done by mind and soul working together under the full light of spiritual illumination. When man has subjugated his passions, brought his mind under the control of spirit, when soul stands unfettered and undimmed, it is then and then only that he will begin to get some idea of his exalted birthright.

The world has always gazed with awe upon a miracle. But to

1. See Alexis Carrel, M. D., *Man the Unknown* (New York: Harper, 1935).

the highly developed man, the Master, miracles are like the play of children, as when a child blows bubbles. The real Master can manipulate the forces of Nature as a mechanic manipulates the levers of his machine. He is master of those forces. They must obey him. He is no longer a helpless drifter in Nature's vortex. But how fallen from his high estate is the average man! How pitiable his plight! Bent as a twig by every breeze that blows, a prey to every hostile creature that crosses his path, a victim of poverty, disease, pain, death, he doesn't know that he is a god clothed in rags! He is master of the universe, going about begging a crust of bread. He is a king, prostrated before his own servants. He is a prisoner, walled in by his own ignorance. Would he be free? He has only to walk out of his self-constructed prison: "None holds ye, but yourself," says the noble Buddha.

3. The New Social Order

Science is the keynote of this age of the intellect. Science is the *magnum opus* of this age. It may almost be said to be the habit of the age. It is the vogue. The practical or applied sciences are daily becoming more popular. To science, men are turning more and more for the solution of all of their material problems. A little more than three hundred years ago Sir Nicholas Bacon gave to modern science her firstborn son, in the days when Elizabethan England was in the zenith of her greatness. When that son, Francis Bacon, became Lord Chancellor, he was already recognized as a philosopher. In him was thus early embodied the synthesis of world thought. He then laid the foundations of modern science.

The great Renaissance of learning began with Roger Bacon, almost three hundred years before Francis Bacon. The torch of genius was then taken up by Leonardo da Vinci. It was thrown into the sky by Copernicus and Galileo. Their bold stand, in spite of ecclesiastical suppression, gave hope to the timid spirit of the age. The research of Gilbert and Vesalius called out the slumbering genius of pre-Reformation days, and then came Francis Bacon to call together the training school of Europe. It was a time of general awakening from the dark night of medieval ignorance.

Savonarola and Luther, John Knox and the Wesleys, came into the general stir not so much to inculcate science but to awaken the stupefied spirit. At about the same time, in sleepy old India, Kabir Sahib and Guru Nanak were doing the same thing. They were trying to quicken the religious and spiritual instincts. In America the pilgrims were at that time too busy fighting the Indians and building themselves homes to bother much about new concepts in religion and science. That came later. It was an era when the whole world was just beginning to sit up and take notice. Nevertheless, it was the birth period of modern scientific thought.

Science has always had to contend with three powerful obstacles to its progress, each of which was almost insurmountable. These three are *Monarchism, Priestcraft* and *Popular Ignorance.* Slowly and steadily science has been obliged to fight every step of its way against these three. Can anyone explain this obtrusive phenomenon of history? Science is today almost universally recognized as a great friend of man. Religion is supposed to be a friend of man, and yet the two have been in deadly conflict during nearly the entire period of known history. But science has had one strong ally in philosophy. The function of philosophy has been to take up the findings of science and give them a place in rational thought. In this respect the services to mankind of such men as Bacon, Spinoza, Voltaire, Emerson, Berkeley, Kant, Hegel, Spencer, Schopenhauer and even of Nietzsche, have all been of incalculable value to the genius of science in its battles for freedom.

Darwin gave to the world a method of study. But philosophy has already said too much about evolution. Now, thanks to the light that could not be dimmed, monarchism is dead. There is not a single vestige of it left on earth in its old form. We need not take too seriously the phases of modern dictatorship. They will soon pass as chilly autumn winds. They are by-products of a passing age.

The second enemy of progress, priestcraft, is now almost an absurd anachronism. H. G. Wells calls it "a funny old thing." It still exists in an anemic form, but time and science will finish it ere long. There remains now but one of the formidable three— popular ignorance—to block the progress of science, and even that is slowly passing away. In a recent tour of the world, this writer was amazed to find in almost every village of the remote corners of the globe that the English language is carrying the rudiments of enlightenment and establishing schools where the elementary sciences are being taught. Truly, this is the age of science, the dawn of universal enlightenment.

4. A Great Spiritual Awakening

To the discerning student one thing more is apparent in this general forward movement of world enlightenment. It is the fact that along with scientific education there is a parallel current of spiritual awakening. The student has to look a little deeper to see this. It is not on the surface like the scientific wave and it has not affected so many people as the other. But today it is a tremendous force in the world. There was a time when Darwinism threatened to sweep all philosophy into the muddy stream of animal biology. Men were about to overlook the fact that souls existed. But again that light, which no superficial speculation could dim for long, has emerged from the fogs and now it daily grows brighter. Materialism no longer sits upon her throne unchallenged.

When Henri Bergson entered the arena of modern thought, he at once did something to smash the mechanistic theory of the universe and to see in the world a complex whole, throbbing with light and life. 'Creative Evolution' was to him not an orderly universe evolving out of chaos by the blind impulses of physical force, but a thing of life and beauty and, above all, a thing of soul. Life is more than a piece of mechanism fortuitously thrown together by blind forces. Life is not simply protoplasm acted upon by chemical osmosis and electrical reactions. The duration of a living organism is dependent upon something more than a chance accumulation of cells, gotten together by natural selection and held together by the survival of the fittest. Bergson was ashamed that men should be thought of as machines. And Bergson ventures to hope that life may outlive mortal limits. No barriers can be set up before the onward march of life. He declares that the whole army of the living is sweeping on to some mighty achievement, and at last it may "beat down resistance and clear the most formidable obstacles, *perhaps even death itself.*"

Bergson comes closer to the point of this book when he says: "To explore the most sacred depths of the unconscious; that will be the *principal task* of psychology in the century which is opening. I do not doubt that wonderful discoveries await it there." If the psychology of the West would lend an ear to the Eastern Masters, they would not be long in making these discoveries presaged by Bergson.

Thinking men have set up two radically opposed views in biological science. They are *Vitalism* and *Mechanism*. Vitalism presupposes a cause of life entering into matter from a plane of being above matter, as we know it. Professor H. H. Newman of the University of Chicago thinks that the vitalistic view is opposed to that hypothesis which has led to all scientific achievement. But we doubt the truth of this, however much the good professor may believe it so. All that the scientist needs to assume is the orderliness of Nature and the universality of laws operating in the world of matter. This assumption is surely not opposed to the vitalistic hypothesis. The scientist may then proceed with security. But the ultimate cause of biological manifestations is quite another matter. We may assume that electricity works according to a set of fixed laws. No scientist will question this, but the cause or the source of electric energy still remains one of the unsolved problems of physical science. So it is with regard to the source of life itself. Like electricity, we see life's marvelous display of activity, but physical science does not presume to say whence it comes nor whither it goes. The source of both electricity and life remains yet to be discovered by science. Why is this so? Because physical science has not yet the means of following either one of them to its ultimate source. Yet the Masters have such means.

One trouble has been that the advocates of the vitalistic theory have assumed the existence of an 'unknown and unknowable' force to which they attribute the phenomena of life. This has been the one weakness which has deprived them of any chance to establish their own theory in rational thought. If this subtle force is indeed unknown and *unknowable*, then we may not blame the materialistic scientist for his mechanistic assumptions. The one theory is about as good as the other, or as bad. The fact remains that the position of the physical scientists is not proven; neither do they claim that it can be proven. They simply assume it and then believe it unscientific and undignified for them to acknowledge the existence of any force which cannot be demonstrated in their laboratories. And we cannot blame them for this attitude. Until they know something of the science of the Masters, their hypothesis is doubtless the more rational. But the Masters are not so limited as are the physical scientists. Their science is more inclusive. Unlike all others who hold to the vitalistic hypothesis, the Masters do not assume the existence of an 'unknown and unknowable' force giving rise to the phenomena of life. They assume nothing. This is not simply an hypothesis for them. They deal with forces which they *know*. And the Masters *know* that life is due to a force extraneous to matter, and they *know* that biological phenomena cannot manifest as a result of the known laws of matter and energy. On the contrary, these phenomena exist as the direct result of the action of spirit upon matter, through the intermediary action of extremely subtle substances or forces that science has not yet demonstrated. These finer forces are, in fact, the more refined forms of matter, which up to this date have not been demonstrated in the physical laboratory.

That mind and spirit play a vital part in every manifestation of life upon this planet is, of course, not yet known to physical science. But it is well known to the Masters. Physical science is in no position to deny this fact so well known to the Masters. The Masters are able to penetrate into the deeper substrata of Nature. They can see the inner workings of all laws and processes. There is not a blade of grass or an insect or an animal which is absolutely devoid of mind and spirit. Furthermore, mind and spirit are the activating forces of all forms of life. Without them both, no living thing could survive for a single moment. When matter is quickened by the all-pervading, life-generating mind and spirit, working in harmony, it begins to manifest the phenomena of life. When mind and spirit are withdrawn, life ceases at once and disintegration sets in.

All that physical science knows is that life manifests in certain ways. It follows certain well-attested laws. Scientists do not even try to guess the ultimate causes of life. Only the Masters, having access to the higher planes of being where the phenomena of both mind and spirit can be seen by them, *know* that without mind and spirit both, no life can manifest on this physical plane or on any other plane where matter is a factor in such manifestation. As a matter of fact, no physical scientist can possibly prove that this is not so. They are simply obliged to say that they know nothing about it. Then to support their weakening prestige they naively assert that no one else can possibly know anything about it. They are loathe to allow the assumption of mind and spirit animating Nature. But this is no assumption to the Masters. As said before, they *know*. It is just as 'unscientific' to assert that the mechanical laws of matter and energy can produce life as to assert that they cannot. Neither can possibly be proved by the physical scientist working alone. Therefore, one assumption is as good as the other, even from the viewpoint of the theologian who claims that an *unknown and unknowable* force does produce life. But, as said before, the Masters assume nothing. They speak from perfect knowledge and they know that all biological phenomena on the physical plane of life are due to the interplay of both mind and spirit acting upon matter. The Masters know what the oldest and most renowned scientists have always assumed as the fundamental law of biogenesis.

Our masters of the laboratory must not any longer try to 'squeeze all the cosmos into a test tube'. It cannot be done. The spirit is abroad in the daylight and it must be heard. At the same time, we need not worry lest science run away with religion and bury it in the potter's field. We need not join with Rousseau in an effort to curb scientific thinking for fear it may snatch away our pet god. If they can take the god, let them have it. It is only a rag baby. We have no need to push aside the demands of science to enthrone religion and intuition. Science and religion are no longer enemies. Indeed the hour is approaching, and now is, when these two angels of light shall meet in mystic union, and then it will be seen that they are not enemies, not even friends, but *are one and the same being*. And then will dawn the new age, the Golden Age.

That will be the Age of Reason spoken of by Thomas Paine. And it will be the age of the super-science, the period of the super-genius, the arrival of the super-man.

Just as the physiological psychology of James and others can never reduce mind to the materialistic level of brain cells and nerve ganglia, "secreting thought as the liver secretes bile," so the established facts of science can never displace spirit from man or the universe. The most they can say is that they know nothing about it. Science will eventually be obliged to recognize that spirit is the supreme force in Nature, as well as the immortal spark in man himself. When science becomes vitalized by spirit, the age of true science will dawn. But at present science has no way of demonstrating this fundamental fact of Nature, and it is not to be blamed for its limitations. We would only suggest that it avoid dogmatism until the day of its enlightenment. The two currents are now running along side by side, and as men gain in scientific knowledge, a few are beginning to look for the solution of spiritual and religious problems by the scientific method. When the world's thinkers adopt the scientific method in religion, both science and religion will experience a new birth. Then it will be seen that all truth is one, its several aspects being but parts of the same radiant being. And this is exactly what the Eastern Wisdom is now trying to bring about. As Francis Bacon threw into the sky the torch of science, and gathered about its blazing light the whole of thinking Europe, even so the scientific method of the spiritual Masters now offers to the world a system which will enable all men to enter the domain of certified knowledge in religion, just as truly as in chemistry or biology. When the masters of physical science shall, at the same time, qualify as spiritual Masters, the age of pure science will open up. All spiritual Masters are also masters of physical science; but up to the present they have been very few in number, and their own work very pressing. Besides, the teaching of physical science is not their mission. We believe, however, that the time must come when the spiritual department of science will be considered by all odds the most essential part of the curriculum to be undertaken by the student who aspires to be called a real scientist.

Upon this splendid foundation the new social order will be established. Soul culture and mental culture and physical culture, all working hand in hand, will produce the educated man. Without them all, no man can lay any claim to genuine culture. There must be a resetting of cultural foundations. Political and social ideals are changing; even ethical standards are not what they were half a century ago. This has led many good people to shiver with dread, lest the future witness the total wreck of civilization. They need not worry. Out of the dying past, a brighter future will spring, enriched by a spiritualized science.

The days of the political demagogue are numbered, even in America. The ideal of every dreamer, from the days of Plato down to the last high school boy, has been to establish the social utopia upon the basis of natural science. Moore and Plato only reflected that which is in the substratum of every thinking brain; viz., that no ideal social order can ever be established until science is made the foundation of government. And this can be done only when the politician and money-monger are thrown out of office and men eminent in science are given the reins of government. But even that is not altogether safe and sound as a working policy. Men of brains, of scientific training, experts in all branches of science, each a highly skilled specialist in his own department, *must also be morally sound,* that is, they must manifest soul as well as intellect. And this will be an accomplished fact just as soon as religion is placed upon a scientific foundation—not before. That will mean an all-around development of our specialists. When that happy day arrives, such men as aspire to governmental positions will first have to show that they are guided in all essential matters by an enlightened conscience, inspired by an unselfish love. After that, they will qualify in their several departments of science. A government by such experts, call it oligarchy, or what you will, shall constitute the first *civilized* government of history.

5. No Democratic Government Known

Man talk and write much about democracy. I suppose many Americans fondly believe that they live under a democratic form of government. But that is a pet delusion, a tale to be told to children along with other pretty fairy stories. It may be good for Fourth of July orators or men seeking election to office. But it is no more than an illusion. It only appears real because men and women vote to elect their favorites. There is not a real democratic government in the world and there never has been one. There is nothing but *oligarchy*, and that is mostly an oligarchy of wealth. It is not even an oligarchy of culture. That would be infinitely better. Voters are simply manipulated. A few men rule the nation. The masses move like sheep and do as they are told. Can you imagine a hundred million people going to war of their own free choice? They are always led into war or driven into it by a few ambitious or misguided politicians. Of course, when one nation goes to war, the attacked must defend themselves. And that is the only time when a war is fully justified. But what starts the aggression? The five passions, ignorance, misunderstanding, on the part of the leaders. The real people, the hoi polloi, are not governing themselves. "A government of the people, by the people, for the people" has never existed, except in the noble heart of a Lincoln or some such friend of man. What we really have is an oligarchy of 'the men of influence'. And that generally means men of money. We know that is so.

Hence the ideal government, as herein suggested, would mean nothing more than the substiution of a noble oligarchy in the place of an ignoble one. But even that is not the ideal. It may be added here, as a matter of fact, that the *real government* is an absolute monarchy. But the difficulty about that is that in order to secure such an ideal monarchy, it would first be necessary to find an ideal monarch. There is the rub. There is but one class of men on earth who can qualify for that position, and they will not accept it—the great Masters. Their work is of a different sort. The next best plan is a spiritualized, scientific oligarchy. That oligarchy will lay all the emphasis upon the spirit.

Let us make a significant suggestion. Suppose a whole nation is inhabited by the great Masters alone. What would be their form of government? Shall we venture a guess? No government at all. And that is, after all, the ideal social body. But such an ideal can never be established until all men become ideal in character. All that such a body would need would be keepers of records and centers of exchange and directors of channels of communication. The expense of such a nation would be but a millionth part of what the poorest nation now spends for the poorest government. Of course, such a body of men is but a dream in this age of Kal Yuga.

I shall never forget one day at the University of Chicago, when President McKinley was addressing a mass meeting of faculty and students. Professor John Dewey, then head of the department of philosophy, sat by this writer. He was keenly interested in every word spoken by McKinley. It was apparent, even to a tyro like myself, that here was a man alive with the fires of genius. McKinley made some remark about the educated young men of the country carrying the scientific spirit into all channels of social activity. Professor Dewey turned to me and said, *"That will never be done, until spirit shall vitalize the processes of science. Spirit is the soul of the universe."*

I do not know if his later teaching bore out the import of this remark. If in his *Democracy and Education* he fails to lay enough emphasis upon the point which he so eloquently declared that day, perhaps it was due to preoccupation with other and, to him, more immediately urgent matters. He had a profound interest in humanity and it was his wish to contribute somewhat to the building of a better social order. His aim was to do this by means of rational, scientific education. It was natural that he should lay the emphasis upon scientific training in actual work. The culture of the spirit might be left to men whose speciality that was—the Masters. It seems such a pity, however, that Dewey did not know a real Master. He would have made a most illustrious disciple.

So, when the day arrives that the work of the educators, the scientists, the philosophers, all converge and join with spiritual culture in a new and universal science of all sciences, that will herald the dawn of the new age. That will constitute the inauguration of the new social order. If Dewey fails to give much credit to the Bergsonian *élan,* it is perhaps because he does not feel the necessity of talking too much about irrelevant things. He was busy with other matters. If Dewey appears to be wholly Darwinian in his fundamental hypotheses, that does not mean that he has altogether forgotten the spirit. If he thought to establish the naturalist point of view in all fields of endeavor, it does not mean that he believes the universe to be a jumble of blind adjustments to environment. Dewey sums up his conclusions by saying:

> The only way to see the situation steadily, and see it whole, is to keep in mind that the entire problem (of all philosophy and endeavor) is one of the developments of science and its application to life. Moral philosophy returns to its first love: love of the wisdom that is nurse of all good.

It may be added here, although Dewey did not have that in mind, that "the wisdom that is nurse of all good" is the wisdom of the great spiritual Masters. Dewey may have realized, or he may not have realized, that in the realm of the spirit lies that wisdom which is the very mother of all good. When mankind learns to enthrone the spirit and when it seeks enrichment of the spirit by the scientific method, then we shall enter upon the first actual renaissance of all history.

Man is the highest form of creation on this planet and he is only a sojourner here. Once his eyes are opened, he knows that this world is not his home and that he is no more than a feeder of swine among strangers, while far away the light burns in his father's palace. He knows that this world is only a dark outhouse in the magnificent palace grounds of his father's kingdom. The Master tells us that above and beyond the confines of this terrestrial speck of dust, lie innumerable worlds full of light and beauty. To explore those worlds at will and to possess them during this lifetime is only a portion of our heavenly birthright. But to most people that vast universe of finer worlds is locked and impenetrable. To many it is but a fabric of poetical fancy. But it is not so in reality. It is locked indeed, but the Master holds the key and he offers it to all who will qualify. By that key the entire universe of starry worlds may be unlocked and their shining heavens explored. Just how this is to be done constitutes the sublimest secret of the Eastern Wisdom.

Chapter Two

A REVIEW OF WORLD RELIGIONS: THEIR MEANING AND ANALYSIS

1. The Spiritual Plight of Mankind

THERE is no wonder that men take to religion, even if they have to invent one. Voltaire has said that religion is the solace of the weak. Nietzsche has repeated this in substance. Be that as it may, the weak need some support, and I would not take their religion away from them, even if I knew well that it was only an illusionary product. Religion has been a haven of refuge for millions who mourned and suffered. It is undeniable that it has generally been the unhappy who sought surcease of sorrow in any religion which happened to be near them. And who can blame them? A drowning man will grasp at a straw.

The world is full of darkness, pain and grief. That fact could not be kept from the noble prince Siddhartha, secluded as he was in his father's palace. And when he saw it in all its ghastly features staring him in the face, he went forth, filled with compassion to seek a remedy. *Every individual in the world must seek the Path for himself,* and walk upon it for himself.

Spiritual darkness broods over the world and all men are sick from it. Spiritually, and often physically, the whole of mankind is sick, blind, deaf and dumb, and covered with sores. Cancers of moral corruption eat their way slowly into the vitals of the human race. Not a man escapes entirely.

Truly the world is in 'a lost condition'. This is a theological term, but we may use it because it is most applicable to the situation. Every man is not only sick, but he is lost in a dense wood, a tangled forest, without path or compass, no sun and no stars; because he is blind. Moreover, he is suffering from the worst case of amnesia ever known. He has no recollection of his original home or inheritance. In this deplorable condition, he wanders on from year to year. In addition to this mental and spiritual plight, many are suffering from physical ills; they are heartsick, worn and weary.

This is a picture of the great majority of the human race in some degree or other. Are they not lost? They stumble on, generally hopeless, pressing their weary way, they know not whither, and sometimes by the way they stop and pray. But there is no response from the rocks and the trees, and their gods are as silent as the cold, distant stars. Each night drags by, and the day brings on increased weariness. They cry for bread and there is nothing but stones. We are not speaking of the favored few, but of the masses of the poor and ignorant. Are they not lost? Even the majority of the rich and highly placed are not happy. Here and there an isolated individual laughs, while others seek relief in mad passion.

This picture is not too dark. If you know the world as this writer has seen it during the last seventy years, you will agree. But why am I calling attention to the dark side of life? In order that I may point to the remedy. Nearly all men, in addition to their other troubles, are beset on all sides by the five enemies, the passions—driven by them under the lash, sometimes almost to madness. This affects the rich as much as the poor. When they cry for appeasement, for a little comfort, a little moment of respite, the passions mock their victims with a tantalizing drop, a crust, sometimes a moment of deceptive pleasure, and then they drive them on through the long days and the maddening years. The young grow old in the vain search for a little light, an hour of peace. Everywhere there is a constant fever of unrest, a never-ending search for what they never find. Most of them do not even know for what they are searching.

If some dear optimist feels inclined to blame me for telling this truth, for painting a dark picture, let him know that I am diagnosing the case with one hand while I hold the remedy in the other. I am not a pessimist. Neither do I believe it wise to shut one's eyes to plain facts. Where is the man who can say he is happy? If anyone is a little less burdened today, who can say but tomorrow may find him again deep in the shadows? Where is the man or woman who can claim immunity from sin and the passions? Moral strength is practically nil, except in the case of a few superior souls. Of spiritual light there is no more than a feeble glimmering, a flickering candle here and there in the universal darkness. The bulk of humanity has neither morality nor spirituality. The masses are really sick, groping their uneasy way toward an unknown destiny. There is no freedom, not even physical freedom. Who can say he is master of his own body? The entire human race are but driven slaves. Truly the condition of mankind is deplorable. Men struggle up and down the world in a fever of unrest, all the while crying for something, they know not what. And then a few turn to religion for relief. If a man attains a little pre-eminence in some of the virtues, he is seized by one or more of the tormenting passions and is again dragged down to the common level. If not that, he is always trembling on the verge of collapse. There is no rest. From youth to old age, cares and anxieties multiply, while the angel of death always stands in the background awaiting his day and hour. There is no security. Wealth, health, power, momentary pleasures, pass in a flash and are gone. Happiness? Where is it? Who can say that he has not a single heartache or worry? Last of all, a man faces that dark unknown —at which he shudders and wonders. The great reaper mows him down and the night falls upon him, mingled with his kindred dust.

At best, life offers only a few pleasant sensations, a brief delirium of power, a mad moment of passion. Then comes the lonely silence, the long silence, out of which no voice of consolation reaches those who are left behind. Is it any wonder that in such a plight men turn to religion? Is it surprising that many desolate souls, seeking peace of mind and spiritual light, rush away to some convent or to some jungle cave? That is better than suicide. Religion is a very good anesthetic for the dull pains of life. But who can say that it cures the disease?

Pressed by the common ills, the great majority seek one of three points of refuge; they either set up the mournful dirge of the pessimist, or rush into the mad whirl of the bacchanalian revel, or they take to religion. Of the three, the last is surely the best. No good to sit down and cry. No good to complain and indulge in self-pity or find fault with others. Still worse it is to commit suicide. It is always "better to endure the ills we have than fly to others we know not of." It is useless to preach pessimism to people with a healthy liver and good stomach. They simply will not have it. A torpid liver and a constipated bowel have led many people to seek comfort in religion or to hate their neighbors.

If a man plunges into the whirl of passionate sensations, he emerges with bankruptcy staring him in the face. Always he is met with the stern demand: "Please remit." Every kiss has its price. Every pleasure comes with the bill attached, and sooner or later he is pressed to pay, *pay, pay!* We watch the passing show. We chase after the mirage. Finally the disillusioned soul goes out in search of Reality. He is so tired of the sham and the counterfeit. But where shall he find Reality? Frequently he turns, like Noah's dove, homeward again, finding no resting place in the whole world. Nothing but a dreary waste and turbulent waves. At last the seeker comes to realize the aptness of the Master's picture of the man in mid-ocean in a small boat, tossed and drenched by gigantic waves, with imminent death staring him in the face. This explains the situation confronting most of the human race. The more enlightened man feels much as Silenus did when asked by King Midas what was the best fate for man. He replied:

> Pitiful race of a day! Children of accidents and sorrows! Why do you force me to say what were better left unheard? The best of all is unobtainable—not to be born at all. The next best is to die early.

Many brave souls have quivered upon the brink of destiny with such an outlook. Many have gone voluntarily back into the darkness.

2. Does the Remedy Cure the Disease?

As a remedy for all of these ills, men have persistently turned to religion. But has it cured the disease? Is there less pain and sorrow in the world than before? At best, religion is no more than an anodyne, a palliative; in big doses, a sort of anesthetic. But there is no cure in it. Mankind, in pure desperation, has created religions to cool its fevers here, and to escape hell in the next world.

A guilty conscience must, of course, assume a hell of some sort. But did it never occur to you, as you read, that hells are all created for the other fellow? Like laws, they are created to regulate the other fellow. Out of the brooding shadows come the priest and the prophet holding a candle in their hands. Men fall at their feet and bless them for that candle of hope. It is no exaggeration to say that at least three thousand different forms of religion have appeared since history began, and each one has been eagerly grabbed up by hungering souls. The whole world, sick and weary, longs for a remedy for its ills. It seeks rest from its intolerable burdens. But where shall it find relief? That is the ever-recurring question. Thousands and thousands of answers have been given to this question, and still there is no answer—except one.

While many have turned to religion, a few ultra-scientific minds have boldly declared that they find nothing in religion. They find no trace of a god, and nothing at all comes out of the silence beyond the grave. The ashes of the funeral pyre give no whisper of what has become of the life that once animated them. Men must just go on suffering and fighting bravely, and then lie down and die bravely. And that is the end. But such doubtful souls might profit by the words of Socrates of the old Greek dialectic school. In a moment of humble surrender he said:

> Perhaps what is not intelligible to me is not therefore unreasonable. There may be a realm of wisdom from which the logician is banished.

And so the great Masters say. Perhaps there may be worlds

of wisdom from which even the modern scientists are banished. If so, their banishment is self-imposed. At least it is not wise that these scientists should assert dogmatically that such worlds do not exist simply because they have not been able to see them. The Masters have seen them. And the Masters are prepared to point the way so that any scientist may see them if he wishes and has the humility to accept the necessary conditions.

But in the absence of knowledge, the multitudes have generally turned to religion. Out of the common need, many forms of religion have sprung up, each struggling toward the light. But even a candle is better than no light at all. It may be accredited to the infinite mercy of the great Over-Soul that so many religions have been given to the world, each one serving its purpose in its own day and time, when people were not ready for anything better. The greatest trouble with these religions has been that they exhibit a deplorable tendency to live too long after their day of usefulness has passed.

The infant is nourished by a loving mother when it cannot take solid food. A boundless love shelters and supports the human race and gives it, in each day and age, what it can best assimilate. It is only in the day of its majority that it is drawn to the banquet table of the King where the Master presides.

One difficulty has been that the founders of religions, usually men of spiritual insight, who themselves had penetrated to some subtle plane, were obliged to leave the world so soon. Their work was not complete; they left it to immature disciples who generally made a mess of it. Life is so short. So seldom do the disciples become real Masters. The Masters tell their disciples that they have realized God in themselves, but as soon as they depart, the disciples begin to say that they *feel* God in themselves. Therein lies a vast difference. The Masters see God. They do not *feel* him. And that constitutes an essential difference. Feeling is more or less blind and wholly unreliable. The Masters actually enter and explore the kingdom of heaven, but the disciples read about it in books and begin to speculate.

Religions have been fostered through feelings and metaphysical speculations. But in every case, the founders of such religions claim that they got their knowledge by sight and hearing, not by feeling. Thus they speak from *personal knowledge*. Hence the ever-recurring need for living Masters. Let us not assert that we have no need for a living Master. How does anyone know that he has no such need? He is judging a thing about which he knows absolutely nothing. It is idle to plead that we have a book, and that all revelation is closed. You will not find any such statement in any religious book; and who is so wise as to make the assertion? That is the most unwarranted assumption that has ever gone down into history. A sick man may, with as much reason, assert that he has no need for medicine because he has a book which gives him the prescription. The living Master is the great Physician who diagnoses our individual cases and then administers the medicines. That is exactly the difference between all world religions and the scientific system of the living Masters.

Before giving the teachings of the Masters, it appears fitting, even necessary, to sketch briefly the several world religions and try to point out, not their faults or weakness but their best elements, and also the services which they have rendered to mankind. If we indicate incidentally some of their shortcomings when compared with the system of the Masters, that will be done only to enable us to offer constructive suggestions. As said elsewhere, the best way to indicate the deficiencies of anything is to set by it something which is perfect. The difference then becomes apparent.

No religion is to be condemned. No religion is to be denounced as false. It may be said, we believe, that all religions are gifts from the great Superintendent of world history. The world is not running wild without a director. Let us not be so pessimistic. Neither is the devil the captain of this ship. Let us not think so poorly of supreme wisdom. The world has been benefited by all religions in the days of their inception. If some of their adherents have misused their religion, that is perhaps no fault of the religion itself. Neither should we condemn or disparage any of their brave and ardent champions. Much less should they be persecuted because of their beliefs. There is no greater or more heinous crime in history than religious persecution.

Each period in world history has had its own peculiar needs. Generally a religion has sprung up, apparently automatically, to supply that need. But we should never imagine or assume that any religion is the last word. Only the science of the Masters is final, and that is so because it is not a religion. It is a Path by which men in any age of the world may enter the kingdom of heaven. It is a science which may be demonstrated anew any day. Thus it is ever alive and fresh, because it is always in touch with the Ultimate Source. Any system based upon scientific demonstration must be the same in all ages. Its established facts of Nature cannot change. Hydrogen and oxygen have combined to form water ever since the earliest mists began to hover over the pristine rocks. And so it has been that the method of approach to God, which was established by the Creator himself, has always been the same, and will be the same, so long as the human race, or the planet itself, endures.

We ought to remember the words of Vivekananda about churches, and religions in general. We could not say it better, so let us quote him:

The end of all religions is the realization of God.

(And this does not mean that one must 'feel' him; feeling is generally the result of suggestion.) He says:

There may be a thousand radii but they all converge at the one center, and that is the realization of God. Something behind this world of sense, this world of eternal eating and drinking and talking nonsense, this world of false shadows and selfishness. There is that beyond all books, beyond all creeds, beyond the vanities of this world—and that is the realization of God within oneself. A man may believe in all the churches in the world; he may carry in his head all the sacred books ever written; he may baptize himself in all the rivers of the earth—still if he has no perception of God, I would class him with the rankest atheist. And a man may have never entered a church or a mosque, nor performed any ceremony; but if he realizes God within himself, and is thereby lifted above the vanities of the world, that man is a holy man, a saint, call him what you will. . . . I will add that *it is good to be born in a church, but it is bad to die there.*

It is good to be born a child, but bad to remain a child. Churches, ceremonies, symbols, are good for children; but when the child is grown up, he must burst, either the church or himself.

Since the great Swami so strongly emphasizes the *realization* of God, it is fitting that we should try to make plain exactly what that means. In most writings on the subject, there is but little clearness of statement. That is because the writers themselves have never experienced it and they have but a hazy idea of what it means.

First of all, it is not a *feeling*. Secondly, it is not a metaphysical speculation nor a logical syllogism. It is neither a conclusion based upon reasoning nor upon the evidence of books or persons. The basic idea is that God must become real to the individual, not a mental concept but a living reality. And that can never be so *until the individual sees Him*. Personal sight and hearing are necessary before anything or anybody becomes *real* to us. I have never seen Montreal, hence that city is to me only a mental concept. But I have seen London, and so that city is to me a substantial reality. To practically all men, God is simply an abstract idea, a mental concept. How can one worship and love a mental concept? When most people say they love God, it simply means that they have a certain emotion superinduced by suggestion. It has not the least thing to do with God-realization.

Now, the purpose of all religions is, according to the Swami, to convert that mental concept into something that is real to experience. It is only then that the worshipper can sing, *"Cognosco unum Deum Patrem Omnipotentem!"*—"I *know* the one God, omnipotent Father." But the poverty of all religions has been their inability to make God real to their devotees. Can you imagine that men would live as they do, think and act as they do, if God were real to them, if they had actually seen him and loved him? It is unthinkable.

It must be confessed, sad as that confession is, that no one soul in all history has been able to realize God by and through religious doctrines and ceremonies, not even by prayers and mental devotions to an ideal. We know this is so, because such realization can never be achieved by such means. In the very nature of the case it is impossible. The best they can do is to enable one to *feel* a little closer to Reality or to quicken the imagination a little. If by prayer—*smarana,* or *simran,* and concentration, one gets into subtle regions, even to some small degree he will experience a little uplift. And that is good, so far. But that feeling will never carry him to complete God-realization. What then is to lead him to that supreme *desideratum*? The Masters can give you the answer, without equivocation. There is but one method of making God real to the seeker—that is, to make him *see God and hear Him*. If you say that it cannot be done, that is because you are unacquainted with the Path and the method of the Masters. When the disciple of the Master enters the higher planes and there beholds with his own finer vision some majestic embodiment of God clothed in divine power and beauty; and when he hears the enchanting music of the *Nada-Bindu,* the audible vibrations of the Lord himself, he then begins to realize God. But that realization is not complete, even at that point. When he rises by the aid of that Life Stream to the still higher planes, and there in great joy blends his own spiritual being with the Supreme Sat Purush, it is then that he experiences perfect God-realization—not before.

From this fact, it must be manifest that no religious ceremony can accomplish so much. No mental process can do it. It is a personal experience that cannot be had upon this earth plane. It is not an experience possible to physical consciousness. One simply must enter the superphysical planes to get it. Not only so, but he must rise to very exalted regions; and this can be accomplished only on the Path of the Masters.

When the disciple of the Master ascends the inner worlds, one after another, until he enters Daswan Dwar, the third heavenly region on this Path, he there beholds himself as pure spirit, stripped of all materiality. And that is 'self-realization'. After that, if he advances to the fourth and the fifth regions, he there beholds one or more of the most sublime manifestations of the Supreme One, and then, merging himself with these manifestations of God, he comes to know God. And that is genuine God-realization. There is no other. No man can ever *know God* until he consciously becomes *one* with God. Anything short of that is more or less speculative, imaginary, visionary and imperfect.

This is the summing up of the whole matter. Churches, formal religions, belong to the immature periods of human thought and evolution, that is, to the childhood of the race. Each religion serves its own purpose in its own day and time. But each must eventually give way to something more complete as mankind advances. Throughout the whole of human history, the very essence of religion has been an effort to realize God. But how few have succeeded! Only the great spiritual Masters have had the perfect system by means of which it can be done, and the Masters have been very few among men. Efforts toward God-realization have always failed, except and only when they have followed the Path of the Masters; for there is no other way.

If now we pass in review each of the great religions for a few moments, we shall be in a better position to see exactly what good purpose they have served, and wherein and how they have failed in the supreme objective of all religion. If ardent devotees of certain religions insist that many people have succeeded by their own methods, that is because they overestimate a partial success. Something is gained, no doubt, by nearly all forms and ceremonies, by prayers and deeds of charity. But not complete God-realization—not even perfect self-realization.

---

3. The Religions of China

The religions of China which invite attention here are Confucianism and Taoism. Confucius is generally regarded as a great teacher and founder of an ethical system, a scheme upon which he hoped to build his ideal government, his perfect social order. It was not exactly Plato's republic, but it was to be the ideal monarchy with an upright citizenship. Ethics, however, is not religion, and there is but little among all the ethical systems of the world which is unique or individual. To know how to live properly among one's fellowmen is not the same as being able to realize God. The two things are fundamentally different.

In the early periods of Chinese history, a form of religious ceremonies and occult practices came to be known as Taoism. Its inception is shrouded in obscurity. We believe it dates back to extremely remote periods, when some real Master gave it out as an elucidation of the *Santon ki Shiksha* of his time. But when it first appeared in history, it had already undergone the usual degenerative changes. In spite of that fact, it still has some of the earmarks of the fundamentals of the Master's system. All scholars agree that *Tao* means the Way. But this Way has been badly obstructed by the usual rubbish of ceremonies and superstitions. Then came Lao Tse, a great philosopher and reformer, who gave to Taoism somewhat of its original interpretation. He appeared to see in it the deeper and more vital meaning. Lao Tse wrote a famous book called *Tao Teh Ching*. This book is an exposition of 'the Way', according to Laotsean understanding. In it are echoes of many of the precepts of the Eastern Wisdom, chief among which is the meaning of Tao itself, the Nada-Bindu of the Vedas, the divine *Shabd* of the modern Saints.

It will be noted that Lao Tse was not satisfied with the mere ethics of any system. Ethics can never constitute the Way. By ethics no man can escape the eternal *awagawan*, the coming and going in regions of matter. To gain the heavenly kingdoms, to escape forever from material worlds, the student must leave the walks of men and go where ethics have no meaning. He must transcend the field of ethics, for ethics has to do solely with human relationships. In the regions of Light, where God is to be realized, there is no ethics, no right and no wrong—there is nothing but pure love.

Lao Tse had a great disciple who wrote the following beautiful words: "The perfect man employs his mind as a mirror. It grasps nothing: it refuses nothing. It receives, but doesn't keep. Thus he can triumph over matter, without injury to himself."

The idea is that when we become too closely bound up with matter, we descend to its level, much to our own injury. This brings to our attention the great precept of the Indian pundits and masters—*vairagya*, meaning complete detachment from the world, while still living in it. Do not allow it to cling to you. Do not allow yourself to be dragged down into the mire of it. Keep the self above all worldly entanglements, like the lotus flower, which holds its beautiful head above the muddy waters, even though its feet are buried in them. This is the *wu-wei* of the Chinese sages, the doctrine of the non-assertion of the self. There can be no doubt but if we could get down to the pure and original Taoism, we would find a system very closely allied to, if not identical with, that of the Masters.

Taoism emphasizes the doctrine of karma. The Chinese term for karma is *yin quo*. Nothing in all Nature is more certain than the fact that no single thing or event can stand alone. It is attached to all that has gone before it, and it will remain attached to all that is to follow it. It was born of some cause, and it must be followed by some effect in an endless chain. That which is set in motion by any individual, be that individual man, dog, tree, or river, must in effect eventually return to that individual. It is a fixed law of Nature. Attention and love are the means of connecting us with objects external to ourselves. Whatever we desire begins at once to travel toward us unless a stronger desire from a different source attracts it. Everything in the universe is subject to Newton's laws of motion. By desires we are bound to objects of desire. This is why the complete detachment of self from every worldly object is necessary. It avoids bondage to those things. This is why *we should love nothing with a desire to possess it.* The moment we do so, we enter the first stages of slavery. We should not even desire rewards for our actions. *He who looks to rewards will become a slave to such rewards.* So long as a man craves rewards, he is bound to those rewards, and yin quo is his master.

From complete vairagya, perfect mental detachment, one enters *nie-pan*, the blessed *nirvana*. He then becomes one with the Tao, the eternal whole. So Tao means not only the Way but the supreme Goal as well. A man must attain that state of mind which is like the sun, shining upon all alike, yet asking nothing in return. The soul lives forever by giving, not by receiving. And this is the grand paradox, not only of Taoism but of all philosophy—*you get most by giving most.* Conversely, by receiving much you impoverish yourself. By selfish accumulation you become bankrupt. As

Emerson says, "You run in your own debt." For, in the long run, you can never get something for nothing. Every farthing must be paid. The law of balance in the moral and spiritual realms is just as inflexible as the law of gravitation. To give and give only, not once thinking of rewards, is the beginning of immortality. No man becomes a Buddha, a Kakusha, a Tathagata or a Bodhisattva by fleeing from pain or by seeking comforts, or by demanding rewards. Accept alike all that comes to you, and go on giving, giving; be indifferent alike to reward or blame. Only give. And all the while you are giving, make the mind one with the Tao, the Universal One, whose musical vibrations fill the universe. Of course, that Universal One is none other than the Audible Life Stream, the Creator and Preserver of all. It is written:

> When every phase of our minds shall be in harmony with the mind of Kakusha [the Sat Purush] there shall not be one atom of dust [of our dust] that shall not enter into nie-pan.

This is a fathomless precept of wisdom.

That noble sage taught that man shall not glory in his own enlightenment while he looks down upon all others who are struggling in pain and ignorance, holding himself upon a pinnacle of self-righteousness.

> For your true self is the whole of life, and the wrongs of all others are your own guilt. Do not blame men when they err, but purify your own heart. Do not be angry when the whole world forgets the law and ceases to abide by the Tao. Look for the fault in yourself. The root of all evil is in you.

Can anyone set a higher standard? It is an excellent preparation for the higher Path of the Masters. It is in fact their teaching, and that is why we emphasize it here.

---

4. What Is the Meaning of Tao?

The word has been variously translated. It is given as God, Providence, Law, Life, the Infinite One. In Sanskrit, modern scholars have translated it as *Aum* or *Om, Dharma, Atman, Alaya*, etc. It is evident that there is no certain agreement among scholars as to the exact word to be used in translating *Tao*. Perhaps there is no word in any language that will convey the exact meaning. One thing is evident, they have all lost the inner meaning and today only the Saints hold the key to that meaning. That key is the Shabd, the Audible Life Stream. I am aware that all scholars do not see in Taoism the real Shabd; as said before, that is because they have not the key to its understanding. Macauliffe made an exhaustive study of the Sikh religion and translated the Granth Sahib, but he never discovered the most precious content of that book. He closed that work without an inkling of the real value of the Adi Granth. So it has been with most commentators of the great work of Lao Tse. Of course, this was because they had not the Master's key. This has been the fate of nearly all the sacred books.

The Audible Life Stream combines in itself the meanings of nearly all of the interpretations which have been given to Tao. It is Law, it is Life, it is God. It is the real Om. It is the Supreme Atman. It is the moving life of all Dharma, and it is the universal Alaya. It should have been translated into English as 'Word', although that is not an exact translation. It is the divine Word which is back of all creation, which was in the beginning with God, and which was itself God, by means of which all things were created. It is Sound, the vibrating Shabd, whose heavenly music enlivens all worlds. And it is this Shabd which constitutes the central theme of the great Masters of all ages. And this is Tao, as it is understood by this writer.

One of the meanings of Dharma, according to the Mahayana school of esoteric Buddhism, is Ultimate Reality. It comes from *dhar*, 'to uphold'. It refers to the all-creative Current, the Audible Life Stream of the Masters, which not only creates but sustains all things. It is the Fountain of Life, out of which springs all life in any world and all biological phenomena upon this plane. Hence it has come to mean also the form of all things, the sum of all phenomena. Underlying all of these meanings is the central idea of the creative current, the Life Stream.

This translation of the word *Dharma* is exactly equivalent to *Tao*. If we translate *Tao* as '*Atman*', it is also correct. For it is the Supreme Atman, or spirit, which again is the creative Life Stream, the causeless cause of all. If we translate it as '*Om*', we have the same meaning. '*Om*' was, to the ancient Hindus in general, the highest and most sacred sound symbol of the Brahm. And Brahm was to them the Supreme Being. Thus it would appear, however we may approach it, that Tao is no more nor less than the Supreme Word. Of course, it is the Way. It is the Royal Highway of the Saints. Translating the word as 'Way', we have the same meaning, because the Audible Life Stream is preeminently the Way. It is first and foremost the Way of the great Masters. It is the Path by which the Masters and their disciples travel homeward. Without this Life Stream, there is no way back to the feet of the Supreme. All Saints travel by the sacred Sound Current. They ride upon it. It is that which draws them up and which carries them upward on their journey. It is that which they give to their disciples by tuning them in with it. It is that powerful enchantment by means of which they overcome the world and rise to spiritual freedom.

So, if Tao is the Way, it must be the Way of Sound, the Way of the Saints. For there is no other Way. It certainly does not mean a system of ethics. Even if Taoism has been covered over by the rubbish of a hundred centuries, it has, nevertheless, exerted a wholesome influence upon Chinese life. It is doubtless due to the influence of this grand concept, joined with the noble ethics of Confucius, that enabled the Chinese empire to hold together so long. A remnant of it, lingering among the Chinese people, may yet redeem them and enable them to build a new civilization upon the ruins of the old empire. Under the terrible stress of war, they are today showing signs of a renaissance. If so, however, it must be purified and given as a new message by some living Master. That old wisdom gave to the best of the Chinese people a culture and a dignity which they have not entirely lost, even to this day. But no ethical system, no precept of law, not even the knowledge of the Tao itself, can endure against the disintegrating hand of time. No nation or people can permanently withstand the downward drag of the passions unless they have living Masters to make the Way dynamic for them. And China has not had a living Master born among her people for more than a hundred centuries.

Here is an important secret—the real cause of national, racial or individual degeneration is the lack of a living Master. Without a living Master, they simply cannot withstand the downward drag.

China has sat complacently, wrapped in her robes of a rigid formalism, for seventy centuries, at the same time boasting of the most ancient civilization. She had such a civilization, no doubt, when the pure Tao prevailed; but it is no credit to her that she lost it. She gradually sank into a stagnant philosophy of fatalism and ancestral worship, the downward drift of which could not be stopped even by Confucian ethics and the abstract doctrine of the Tao. But why blame China? All nations do the same thing, give them time enough. Only a true Saint can now supply the needs of China. Perhaps, when a war wakes them up, a Master will appear and give them the new message.

5. The Zoroastrian Faith

The Zoroastrian Faith was founded by the great Persian or Iranian sage Zoroaster, more correctly speaking, Zarathustra. He lived six hundred or a thousand years B.C. To him is attributed the religion of the Magi, though doubtless the teachings and practices of the Magi were a much later modification of the real teachings of Zarathustra. Its modern representatives are the Parsees of India. They are sometimes called fire *worshippers*, though incorrectly. This is because they look upon fire and especially the sun as symbolical of the Supreme One. Fire is regarded as an appropriate symbol of God for many reasons, and the symbolism is rich in thought. Fire converts everything into itself. The flames always try to ascend heavenward. Fire is the great purifier, destroying all that is unfit to endure. It also suggests the purity of heart which alone can prepare one to see God. Jesus and all the Masters agree on this point. Fire also cooks the food that nourishes us, just as the Holy Shabd gives us the spiritual nourishment, fitting it to our requirements. As fire warms us when we are cold, so the divine Current gives us life, light and warmth—which means love. Much more is included in this beautiful symbolism if one cares to pursue the subject.

A collection of the sacred writings of Zoroaster and those of his early disciples now comprise the Zend Avesta, the bible of the Zoroastrian faith. After the departure of the great teacher, a group of Zarathustra's followers formed what came to be known as the Magi or 'the wise men of the East'. These Magi were probably the original Sufis. It was from among these men that messengers went to see Jesus at the time of his birth. For all truly Wise Men know when another Mahatma is coming.

Zoroastrianism prevailed over the ancient gods of Babylon and Nineveh from the time of Cyrus, although it gradually drifted into its decline. When sifted down and washed of its accretions, many nuggets of golden truth will be found in the teachings of the noble Iranian. And this fact links it definitely with the work of the great Masters. As to whether Zarathustra himself was a real Master or Saint, the best way to answer that is to invite you to the living Master, who himself will give you the method by which you may know all about it yourself, without even taking the word of the Master. The same may be said regarding Jesus or any of the great religious characters of history. The Master can give you the key by means of which you may win the right to a personal interview with any of those men. You will then know of a certainty their standing, not only at the time of their life on this earth but of their present status. You may meet them personally and converse with them.

One of the central truths of the Zoroastrian faith is its doctrine of the universal brotherhood of man. Zoroastrians believe in one Supreme Being, notwithstanding many assertions to the contrary. The superficial student may readily fall into the error of believing that they taught two gods, one good and the other bad, a statement which may be found in some books. We know that the great Zarathustra never taught such a thing. The idea of two supreme beings is self-contradictory. No great teacher has ever suggested such a thing. Zoroaster taught that the Supreme Lord was Ahura-Mazda, or Ormuzd, and that he was the origin and embodiment of all good. At the same time he mentions the existence of a Negative Power called Ahriman. This dark power ruled over the world and was the focal point of all that we call evil; the sum, the embodiment, of all that affects man adversely; in quality—darkness.

Here is a gem of truth not to be overlooked: It is strongly suggestive of the teachings of the Masters, for they frequently mention the existence of a Negative Power; but he is a subordinate to the Supreme One, and he rules over the regions of mind and matter, representing the darker side of creation. This does not mean that he is altogether bad, but in the very nature of things, what we call evil[1] inheres in negativity. It is simply a lesser good.

There can be no doubt but this religion came to Persia and the surrounding country like the falling of showers upon a dry land. Its restorative action came during that period when modern civilization was but an infant in its Mesopotamian cradle. The foundations of culture were laid by the Sumerians, and then by the Sumerian-Akkadian empires, more Semitic in character, under Sargon I and his successors. The first empire known to history made Erech its capital at the head of the Persian Gulf. That empire was fed by the fertile valleys of the Tigris and the Euphrates. In this valley many tribes contended for supremacy during a period of fifty centuries or more. Into its gathering populations poured streams of Dravidians, Semites, Chaldeans and Aryans, the latter being mostly Medes and Persians. The old Assyrian empire gave way to the new when Nineveh fell into the hands of the more vigorous invaders in 606 B.C.

When the teachings of the Masters become obscured and corrupted, a new Master comes. In Mesopotamia a score of contending tribes, confusing languages, conflicting customs, then found a new and unifying influence in the philosophy of Zarathustra. The one great message of the ages found a new statement. When Cyrus the Great established a broad empire upon the

---

1. The nature of evil itself will be discussed in Chapter Five, Section 7, and Chapter Seven, Section 10.

basis of the new culture, he prepared the way for the impetuous Alexander to spread its influence to the remotest bounds of the known world. Degenerate as Alexander himself was, he had been prepared for that very mission by the tutoring of Plato. Hence the chief service which Alexander rendered to mankind was to break up the old crusts of world thought, or rather of non-thought, and then cultivate the soil of the intellectual world for a new seed-sowing. The seed was to be the wisdom of Zarathustra, Socrates, Aristotle and Plato, each of which bore in its core the germs of the Eastern Wisdom. Say what you like, but the one thing that has given life and perpetuity to the philosophy of the Greek Masters is its central golden thread of the Eastern Wisdom: the wisdom of the great spiritual Masters.

However, before Alexander came, the pure teachings of Zarathustra had already undergone the usual degenerative changes, at least to some extent. When the philosophy of Plato and Aristotle was disseminated throughout the world, the religion of the Magi had already become covered over by a mass of senseless ceremony and corrupt practices. When Alexander was born, his mother was steeped in this poison of Magian superstition. But the great Iranian had done the work for which he had come. His teaching had given a new impetus to philosophy and religion. The dull minds of the masses had been forced to do a little thinking. All future civilization was to profit by its wholesome influence. It is thus that thought, philosophy and religion are reborn from age to age, as stated in the Gita.

But one thing must not be overlooked in this connection. *When any Master leaves his theater of action, the doors of the kingdom of heaven are automatically closed for new seekers so far as he is concerned.* This may at first appear to be a very strange thing, even unjust. But it is not so; because every Master is succeeded by another, and to him all may go who are ready. We may not forget that *this world is never without a Master. To him all will go who are "duly and truly prepared, worthy and well qualified."*

The rest are then like the five foolish virgins who brought no oil in their lamps. Whenever and wherever men run after creeds, priests and organizations, they may find a religion of some sort;

but they will never find the Way to enter the kingdom of God spoken of by all the great Masters. Only a living Master has the key to that kingdom, and he alone can help the student to enter it. In the religion of the noble Iranian, two or three features must be emphasized because they bear a very close relationship to the teachings of the Masters. The most lofty ideal, the highest concept of a perfect life, was expressed in the Avesta by the word *Asa*, which in the Vedic terminology is equivalent to '*Rita*'. It is closely related to the Hindu '*Dharma*', and to the Muslim word '*Islam*'. Its central idea is righteousness, a life in complete harmony with the great Law, meaning, fundamentally in harmony with God. The Supreme Father, Law-Giver, Life-Giver, they called Asura Pita Nah, the same as Ahura-Mazda. The way of approach to him was *Ash*, the way of righteousness. From their sacred scripture comes the unequivocal declaration: "There is none besides the Creator, Ahura-Mazda: everything emanates from Him and merges back into Him at the end."

Thus he taught a definite monotheism. This Supreme One was formless, all-pervading and beyond all attributes known to us, like the Nirguna Ishwara.

According to Zarathustra, there are six different ways the Supreme One can make himself known to men. They are also called rays of light from the Supreme. They are spoken of at times as if they were personalities—*Amesh-Spenta*, 'Holy Immortals'. They are: (1) *Asa-Vahista*, Supreme Will manifested in the world; (2) *Vohu-Mano*, good mind, divine wisdom, pure-mindedness; (3) *Khashathra-Vairya*, the all-creative, all-sustaining power; (4) *Spenta-Armaiti*, perfect piety with single-minded devotion; (5) *Haurvatat*, absolute wholeness, perfection, spirituality; and (6) *Ameretatat*, immortal life, freedom from death or dissolution.

These six represent both the maternal and paternal qualities of God; the first three the fatherly, and the last three the motherly, nature of the Supreme. If we add to these six the great central figure of Ahura-Mazda, we have the sevenfold Lord, as taught by the prophet Zarathustra.

To students of the royal Path of the Santon ki Shiksha, there is one thing more in the system of Zarathustra which is of peculiar interest. In addition to the above-mentioned seven rays of the Divine One, he mentions another ray or power which he calls *Shraosha* or *Sraosha*. The name is derived from the Sanskrit root *Sru*, meaning 'to hear'. This is most significant. It is quite clear to the student of the Masters that this ray of the Divine One is *something that can be heard*. Of course, this refers to the *Shabd Dhun* of Santon ki Shiksha. It can be nothing else. It is the Audible Life Stream of the Saints. And we may well infer that this important fact was not unknown to Zarathustra. Perhaps, if we had his teachings in their purity, it would be found that he made this Sraosha his central theme. He distinctly says that this is the supreme thing for man to seek and to cultivate. He says that when one fully attains to Sraosha, the way of salvation stands open before him, all obstructions being removed. This is in exact accord with the teachings of the Masters.

In a prayer composed by Zarathustra himself (see the Zend Avesta), he says: "Oh, Mazda, may Sraosha go, together with Vohu-Mano, to the person whom thou lovest!" He thus gives emphasis to Sraosha as if it were the one thing of supreme importance. This is again perfectly consonant with the message of the Saints. The person whom the Supreme Lord loves, he always brings into contact with the Holy Shabd, and then his mind is purified, after which he is taken up to his own home. The Saints all agree that the Audible Life Stream is the only Path of mind purification and final approach to God. This is only another instance of how all world religions, when properly understood, support the fundamentals of Santon ki Shiksha.

The way in which the problem of evil is explained in Zoroastrianism has already been referred to. In harmony with the system of the Masters, the Iranian taught the existence of a negative power who ruled over the regions of mind and matter, as subordinate to the supreme Ormuzd. This places evil in the category of pure negation. It has no actual existence. It is a lesser light. When light is abundant, there is no shadow; and in absolute darkness, there is no shadow. So it is with evil. The Masters see in evil only a shadow, a state of incompleteness, a phase of growth, perhaps a necessary concomitant of evolution. But in our ignorance, believing the darkness to be something real, we grope about in the shadows. But it is only a negation. The man who never saw light or heard of it would not suspect that he was in darkness. To him that darkness would be normal. So it is with evil. It is only because we know of a greater good that we feel the pain of the evil.

To sum up the entire philosophy of evil, we must conclude that, as a matter of fact, *there is no such thing as evil*. Evil as a reality is philosophically unthinkable, and there the matter must end so far as metaphysics is concerned. The assumption that evil is a reality has caused much confusion in philosophy and religion. It is of no use to deny the difficulty; we must assume that if evil exists, God is responsible for it. And such an assumption lands us in a maze of philosophical difficulties from which there appears to be no escape. Driven to the wall by this stern fact, many thinkers have declared that there is no God. How can there be a good God in charge of a world full of woe and sin? It is only the illuminating philosophy of the Masters that removes the difficulty. In a universe created by an all-wise God, whose fundamental essence is goodness and love, there is no room for such a thing as evil. It simply does not exist. But there are many degrees of good, of the light. In its final aspect, there is nothing bad in the world, neither is there sin nor fault in anyone. What appears so is due to our limited understanding.

But just what is it that we are all worrying so much about? What is it that we call evil? Whatever it is, it appears quite real to us. The answer is that anything which we do not like is evil to us. This is, of course, the narrow and egoistical viewpoint. And it is just this obtrusive ego that plays all the mischief in our thinking. But it is the common way of looking at things.

A little boy is called in from play to have his face washed. He doesn't like the procedure. To him, that is an evil. He howls his displeasure. He disobeys his mother and has to be punished. To him, that is another evil. He sees nothing in it but evil. To him the whole world is a theater of evil simply because it has so many 'don'ts' in it and so many washbasins. A man allows his passions to get the upper hand over him, and he commits a crime. He has to go to prison. To him that prison is an evil. But society does not regard that prison as an evil. A man gets an appendical abscess. He has to go to a hospital and undergo an operation. It may be difficult for him to decide which is the greater evil, the appendicitis or the operation. To him it is all bad enough. But society regards the hospital as a real blessing. It all depends upon one's viewpoint, and there is the key to the whole question. A man who was cruel to his wife and five small children got accidentally killed. To that wife, his death was a terrible blow, for it left her with an intolerable burden on her hands. To her, his death was an evil, a calamity. But looked at from an impartial, higher viewpoint, his death was probably the best thing that could have happened, not only to society but to the family itself. A thing becomes an evil only from the narrow egoistic viewpoint. But we cannot follow the subject further at this time. The great Masters sum up the whole matter by saying: "Whatever the Lord does is best."

From the exalted viewpoint of the Supreme One, there is no such thing as evil. For He knows what is best for all.

It may prove suggestive to us if we remember that it is only by bitter experience that men can be brought to the path of love and light. The sooner that change is brought about, the better, even if much suffering is required to impress the lesson upon one's mind or upon the minds of the entire human race. And so it often happens that the more keenly men suffer, the better it is for them. Then suffering is a great blessing in disguise. It is safe to assert that everything which men call evil in this world, involving suffering of any sort, has its ultimate objective to bring the sufferer to the path of love. That means the Path of the Masters. When we enter definitely upon that Path, all semblance of evil disappears, even as the night flees before the rising sun. If there were no other reason in the world to account for the presence of suffering, this one reason would appear to be sufficient. It is equally certain that just as soon as all men, the whole human race, come to the path of love, evil will disappear from the world.

Here is at least one rational solution for the problem of evil. This is the thesis: evil, suffering in any form, has as its primary object to impel people to turn toward the path of love. This we are not giving as the word of the Master, but as a suggestion. There may be deeper reasons also. But in any case, we may rest assured that the plan of human life, including what men call evil, is the best possible plan for the human race under present conditions. We may be permitted to make a suggestion: it is our opinion that germs, bacteria, are here to assist in dissolving, eliminating the weak and unfit, and they will not successfully attack the perfectly fit. They may appear to be an evil, but are not so. Many other things appear to be evil because of our ignorance concerning their proper place in the general scheme.

6. Buddhism in India

Gautama Buddha appeared almost simultaneously with Zara-thustra in Persia and Confucius in China. Lao Tse also belonged to the same period. It was a time in world history when the minds of men were just beginning to awaken from the slumber of ages. Always when the time is ripe for the sages to get a hearing, they come. What impression do you think an Emerson could have made upon uncivilized people? Saints always come when there is a fair chance of their getting a hearing, and today there are more Saints manifesting than ever before. When more people are ready for them, more will come. We are sometimes asked why no Saints come to the big European centers or to America. The answer is that when those people are ready for the Saints, they will go there. It is often said that among those people there are surely many good people, even better than some who come to the Masters in India. And that may be so. But moral goodness is not the only qualification for meeting a Master. Certainly, great intellects are not the primary qualification. *The fundamental requirements for meeting a genuine Sat Guru are humility, love, and freedom from the bonds of creeds.* If a soul has nothing else and still has these three, he is close to the Path of the Masters. There is one thing more, however, which he must have in addition to these three. He must have earned that right during his past life or lives. If his past karma is not good enough, if he has not earned that su-preme good fortune, he cannot get it no matter how saintly he or she may be in this life. But if a person is particularly worthy during this life, it means that almost certainly he will meet a Master in his next life.

Today there is a better chance than ever before in this Yuga for the Masters to get a hearing, and more people are coming to them. When still more people are ready for them, more Saints will come in different parts of the world. No enlightenment can possibly take place until the people are sufficiently awakened to listen to the teacher. This is self-evident.

Ages upon ages the higher faculties sleep. Men live the life of animals. You may shout your divine message into their ears, and it will only annoy them. They don't want to be disturbed. They will probably drive you away or kill you. They cannot hear what you say. They are engrossed in sensuality while all of the spiritual instincts are covered under the rubbish. It is only a waste of time to attempt to enlighten them. And that is the chief reason why the great Masters have not been able to give their message to the whole world. They simply could not do it. The people would not have it. When a new teacher comes, he is always obliged to adapt his message to the capacity of the people. He cannot always give his complete message to them. But the people get a little glimpse of the light, a few glimmerings of the truth. The teaching, even if not the highest, gives a new impulse to right living and thinking. One step is gained toward the goal. Gradually the soil is prepared for the coming of a real Saint who is able to give them the highest truths. Then history once more repeats itself. After that Saint is gone, his teachings are, in time, corrupted and forgotten.

At the time Buddha appeared, India was suffering from a stagnant Brahmanism. Life in that country had been fairly secure ever since the great Aryan invasion. This is the blessing of a strong government. Even if it is a foreign government, it gives the country security against foreign invasion and safety from internecine strife. So India, under the early Aryan regime, had peace and security. But when a people have periods of rest that are too long, they grow fat and lazy. The people of India became measurably prosperous, peaceful, happy, dreamy and lazy. The priesthood grew in numbers and powers, speculated and, of course, collected their revenues. Many of them became quite rich. Rajas endowed them with great wealth. Then the rajas turned over to the priests their own sins and worries and went hunting for big game in the jungles. The common people told love stories, ate their sweetmeats, and lay down to sleep. They awoke the next day to spin more fine theories, make love and eat.

Into this sort of life came the noble prince of the Sakya clan, Siddhartha by name. He became known later as Gautama Buddha. He was born about 650 B.C. From his father's gardens he could look up to the snow-covered summits of the Himalayas, while the rest of India, hot and dusty, stretched away toward Ceylon—at that time called the Golden Lanka. As the boy grew up, he was carefully guarded even from the sight of any evil or disagreeable thing. But later, when old age, suffering and death came to his notice, he resolved to seek release from these sorrows, not only for himself but for all mankind. It was an ambitious but noble adventure. He left his father's palace and his beautiful young wife and son. Mounting his white horse in the stillness of the night while all in the palace slept, he rode forth 'in search of the Way'—the Way, the Tao of liberation. After six years of rigid asceticism, painful struggle and deep meditation, light came to his inner sight, and he became the great apostle of the Enlightenment. He had found the Way—the Aryan Path, as he called it. He was overjoyed, fairly singing his triumph. Thus the enlightened prince began to teach. The Deer Park in Banares rang with his inspired voice, revealing to all comers 'the Four Great Truths' and 'the Eightfold Path'.

7. An Unnecessary Sacrifice

There are more people in the world today who follow Buddhism than any other religion, and these millions regard the sacrifices of Buddha as the noblest example of unselfish love ever manifested. It is true that the grandeur of that sacrifice cannot well be overestimated. It was beautiful beyond all words. But in the light of the Master's teaching we know that such a sacrifice was quite unnecessary. It was unnecessary, even for his own enlightenment, because he could have gained full and complete enlightenment at home. Asceticism is not at all necessary for spiritual development, as Buddha himself discovered after much suffering.

It is an individual problem. Every man in this world must find that Path and walk on it for himself. No one else can do it for him, any more than one man can eat for another. All these things the science of the Masters will make clear to the student. And in every age there has lived a real Master who was able to point the Way to the highest attainments. But Buddhism was successfully advertised, and so it became known the world over through the system of itinerant monks sent out by the Master.

The Masters teach that any system or religion which cannot be followed by all mankind is not an essential part or component of real religion. If a spiritual science is to be of use to mankind, it must be a universal science. If it is not suited to all men, under any and all conditions of life, then it is not universal. The role of the ascetic monk, the hermit, the wandering *sadhu,* may be spectacular. But it is not a spiritual role. To put on a distinctive garb and set oneself apart from the rest of mankind may be flattering to the vanity of that class, but it is not spirituality. It is no part of a universal religion. Anything which cannot be made a part of the daily regime of all men cannot be an essential element of any religion, which is to appeal to mankind as a whole.

The Masters teach that austerities are a waste of time and energy and lead to little else than increased vanity. It is true that the Masters often undergo great self-denials, and in the past have suffered persecutions and death; but they do not purposely torture their own bodies, nor do they undergo needless hardships for exhibition purposes. The Masters lay down a definite method by means of which the inner enlightenment may be gained by anyone, just as certainly and just as fully as Buddha gained it. A few hours daily given to the proper exercises as outlined by the Master will lead to the inner enlightenment in due time with unfailing certainty. And the beauty of it is that by this method not one or two isolated, exceptional individuals in history may find the Way, but unlimited hundreds and thousands of men and women may gain it. Under the directions of one of the greatest of the Masters, they are doing so now, as personally witnessed by this writer. The way is open for any number more. If Buddha gained anything at all to justify his sacrifice, it was to recover some knowledge of the Path, knowledge that had been almost entirely lost among his people.

There can be no doubt that in esoteric Buddhism, some knowledge of the Sound Current is shown. But how many Buddhists today know that Path? Today the whole world is just about where it was before Buddha came, so far as spirituality is concerned. What has his heroic sacrifice accomplished except to found another religion? The ethics of Buddhism are good, one of the best systems, but there is nothing unique in it. The same things had been taught before, and they have been taught by many other religions since his day. A new system of ethics was hardly needed. Besides, ethics never yet opened the Way to the inner kingdoms. Ethics may clean the mind and prepare one to knock at the inner door, but it will never open that door. That can be done only by one of the great Masters.

To know that sorrow exists, that the cause of sorrow is desire, is not to rid the world of sorrow or of desire. The same thing had been taught in the Gita, by Krishna, long before the days of Buddha. If all the world knows that sorrow is born of desire, what is the good of that knowledge unless one has a cure for desire itself? But the world has no cure for desire, nor has any religion such a cure. Only the Masters have the remedy. And that remedy must be applied individually and directly to the disciple by the Master himself. To read about it in a book, or to listen to a lecture on the subject, will never remove desire, nor will it alleviate sorrow. The cure is in the Audible Life Stream, and that can be made available to the individual by the Master only.

I may know that my pain is due to the sting of a scorpion, but that knowledge does not lessen the pain. Buddhism can tell you how to live a wholesome life; but few religions, if any, can tell you how to get in touch with the Audible Life Current, and thereby escape from the mad vortex of desires. Only the Masters can do that. The beauty of it is that the Masters not only tell you about it, they themselves administer to you its healing waters. They do not write a prescription or read to you a chapter out of a book as doctors and priests do; they give you the real medicine itself. You drink of it and live. There is the entire thing in a nutshell.

The Life Stream is the only means of escape from the fatal wheel of eternal coming and going, desiring and suffering. And not a soul can find his own way to that Stream, but every soul whom the Master connects with that Stream must find his way to liberation from all desire and suffering. He cannot fail. It is quite useless to tell any man that he must overcome desire. He cannot do it unless you give him the proper means of accomplishing such a stupendous task. Only the Masters can supply the means. And this fact explains why Buddhism ceased to be dynamic soon after the departure of its illustrious founder. The same fate has overtaken all other religions without exception. It must always be so.

The example of such a noble individual, making such a sacrifice as Buddha did, appeals to the imagination and sympathies of mankind. It gained for him much admiration and a great following. But no one ever stopped to inquire if such a sacrifice was really necessary or if by chance it could ever accomplish the purpose for which it was designed. The same may be said of the death of Jesus on the Cross. The pity of it is that the whole world fixes its attention upon the sacrifice itself rather than on the life and teachings of the Master, as if that were the all-important fact of his life. But Jesus knew that his death on the Cross was not the thing for which he had come. He prayed: "O my father, if it be possible, let this cup pass from me."

He didn't want to go through with it. But he had brought upon himself the wrath of the Sanhedrin by doing so many miracles, contrary to the long-established rule of the Masters. Finally, his bleeding hands and feet made a powerful appeal to public sympathy. People did not stop to ask if such a death could possibly do any good. Of course, they thought of the age-old doctrine of human sacrifice. If Jesus himself had remained with his disciples for a period of forty or fifty years, he might have perfected his disciples in his own system of development and finally sent them out into the world to give that method in its original purity, as he had received it from his Indian Masters. How infinitely richer would have been the world with such a treasure carried everywhere by the whole Jewish people! The history of the world itself might have been much brighter.

As to the teachings of Buddhism, both ancient and modern, we do not think it wise to take up space here to give them in detail. Our purpose in this book is not to describe other religions, but to mention some of their salient features so as to afford us an opportunity to introduce the system of the Masters by way of comparison. There are many good books which give excellent elucidations of the Buddhist system.

One thing we may mention is of peculiar interest to the modern student. Buddhism is receiving much attention nowadays by a certain class of students who have been most keenly disappointed in Christianity. Not knowing where else to go, they are turning to Buddhism in the hope of finding that which was lacking in their own and other religions. Some few believe that a revival of old Buddhism is what the world needs now. History may repeat itself in succeeding ages, but history never runs backwards. Buddhism has done its work, and it will pass, as all other religions must pass in time.

Buddhism is now divided into two main branches, the *Mahayana,* or 'great vehicle', and the *Hinayana,* or 'little vehicle'. The former prevails in the north, and the latter in the south—another illustration of the fact that religion is often a matter of geography. The difference of doctrine between these two schools is not vital, though many think it is.

> Buddhist philosophy has been concerned with the nature of the Real, and the relation between the real and the unreal, the phenomenal and noumenal; and speculation on this problem has ranged from the most extreme forms of realism which asserted this phenomenal world to be the only reality, to the most extreme form of idealism which denied all reality to the phenomenal world. The middle path between these two, the monism of the Mahayana school, sees existence as one aspect of reality, phenomenal and noumenal being but two sides or poles of one transcendental, eternal reality, which unified them both.

All of this reminds one of the endless metaphysical speculations of the medieval Christian theologians. In marked contrast to
all of this, behold the simple, direct statements of the Masters,
based not upon speculation but upon what they have seen and
heard, and therefore personally experienced—facts reduced to an
exact science.

---

8. Islam, the Religion of Mohammed

The word *Islam* means 'submission' (to the will of God). Islam's
founders and advocates regard it as an exposition of the Law of
God. Islam, like all other religions, came to fill a gap, to supply a
need. It closed up a gap in history. Arabia had been for more than
fifteen centuries a reservoir of Semitic tribes, born and nurtured
'sons of the desert'. They were nomadic, warlike, vigorous and
restless. They had a splendid physique, but in mind and morals
they were little more than savages. In religion they were idol worshippers. Mecca, even then, was a noted center of pilgrimage, and
the sacred Kaaba was already an object of worship.

While Mecca thrived upon its revenues from pilgrims, the
people derived some religious notions from Judaism and an effete
Christianity, both of which had their devotees in Mecca and
Medina. They were a jolly lot, and merry went their songs, ming-
ling with the tinkling of the camels' bells. Into this medley of
religions, this hodge-podge of beliefs and sensual pastimes,
Mohammed was born in the Christian year of 570. He was a
poor shepherd boy. He was imaginative, enterprising and deeply
religious. He married a rich widow named Kadejah. That marriage gave him prestige, and when his wife became his first disciple, his real work began and rapidly gained in momentum.

At first timidly, and then more boldly, Mohammed began
to preach against the prevailing idol worship. "There is one
God, Allah the Merciful." This was his first public declaration,
and certainly that pronouncement was greatly needed in Arabia.
Of course, this antagonized those who profited from the idol-wor-
shipping pilgrims. That struck at the tender spot among Meccans.

Did they not prosper and drink their wines at the expense of idol worshippers? Such disloyalty to the city was not to be tolerated. Mohammed was finally driven from his home in Mecca. He and his closest friend and best disciple, Abu Bekr, barely escaped with their lives. But they were welcomed in Medina, to which a good number of his followers had already fled. This is called the *Hejira,* or *Hijrah,* and it occurred in the year 622 A.D.

Gaining a considerable following in Medina, the now-ascending prophet returned to Mecca at the head of an army. He had but little difficulty in convincing his former enemies that they had been mistaken—of course, Mohammed was the true prophet. They had not understood him. That was all. And what was more important, Allah was superior to their idols. They must now give them up and follow the one God and his prophet.

Then followed eleven years of vigorous propaganda. The matter was urgent. Strong arguments had to be used. It was no time for hairsplitting metaphysics which the illiterate Arabs would have never understood. Mohammed knew that he was giving them something infinitely better than what they had. He came to Arabia like a great physician with a cleansing purgative. All Arabia came under the sway of the new prophet. The desert stood up as one man and declared for the new order of things.

And then one day at an inopportune moment, Mohammed died. His work was not finished—it had hardly begun. His devoted friend and disciple, Abu Bekr, became his caliph and carried on in his name—Abu Bekr the Faithful. The new caliph was the soul of the movement from that time forward. He was the will and the strength of the campaign. Under him the religio-political conquests were carried forward to an amazing success. When Othman, the third caliph, died twenty-four years after the death of Mohammed, the empire of the prophet extended over all Persia, the valley of the two rivers, almost to the Indus on the east and as far as the western border of Egypt in the other direction. It embraced all Syria, wresting vast territories from the enfeebled hand of Rome, and extending northward as far as the Oxus.

Thus, almost eager to die in the holy cause, the more virile tribes of the desert, fired by a hitherto-unknown zeal, fought for

Allah and his prophet. Islam swept, like a prairie fire, over adja-
cent countries. The weak, unorganized and apathetic governments easily fell before the sturdy, driving hosts of the new faith.
The moribund civilizations of the whole of Asia Minor and a part
of the Mediterranean coasts now fell under Islam and found in it
a new, unifying and invigorating power. Truly, the torch of Islam
set fire to the religious rubbish of extensive regions and restored a
measure of health to an enfeebled civilization. Besides that, it set
people to thinking.

There is one good thing that war does—it awakens the
slumbering mentality and quickens the circulation in the rheuma-
tic limbs of an aging morality. At that time the greater part of
Europe was in a state of mental torpor. It had entered the dark
age of European history. Religion as a formal organization
flourished; but that period marked the low tide of intellectual
activity and spirituality. Torpid Europe was badly in need of some
sort of stimulant. Then Islam came to them like the wine of life.

It took a long time to quicken the enfeebled circulation of a
decadent period but eventually the learning, fostered by Islam in
its chief centers like Alexandria, Cordova and Baghdad, gave the
stimulus to the great Renaissance which was soon to shake all
Europe. Judaism had lost much of its former vitality. The dark age
of Christendom had spread its black wings over the remnants of
the Roman and Byzantine empires. Europe itself was stagnant.
Islam prevailed, not only because it was pushed by armed forces,
but because it deserved to prevail. Again it was simply a case of
the survival of the fittest.

Islam offered more appealing ideas and a better social order
than anything else to be found at that time. Let it be remembered
that Islam was born among a barbarous people in a barbarous age.
The stern and relentless creed of Islam was more or less a by-
product of the times. What else could be expected? If the need is
urgent, the remedy must be heroic. It is well to remember also
that the Supreme One is in charge of world affairs, and whatever
he does we may accept as the best thing that could be done under
the circumstances. Can you imagine the effect upon those wild
desert people if Mohammed had preached to them the sublime

idealism of the Gita, or the Sermon on the Mount? They would not have had the least idea what was being said. Mohammed gave them about the only thing they could comprehend, and no one may doubt that it worked well.

When the Moslem invasions had worn on to a close, when the Islamic organization itself had become enfeebled by too much success abroad and by strife at home, when unparalleled absorption of conquered wealth had given the conquerors moral and intellectual indigestion and auto-intoxication, then Islam began its own inevitable decline. For this is the history of all such movements from the beginning of time.

The empire of the prophet now extended from the Indus on the east, Turkestan and the Caucasus on the north, over all northern Africa, and into Spain on the west. When, in 1422, Constantinople fell to the final rally of the armies of Islam, the old church of Santa Sophia was converted into a mosque, and the last Greek Christian wept bitter tears as he fled from the city of Constantine. Had it not been for the strong hand of Charles Martel at the battle of Poitiers, the victorious hordes of the prophet undoubtedly would have passed the Pyrenees and swept through all Europe. In that case—who shall say?—perhaps our fathers would have bowed to the Arab, and today we ourselves might have been saying five prayers daily with our faces turned toward Mecca. The teachings of the camel driver of the desert, instead of the Syrian carpenter, might have been preached in all the churches of Europe and America. After all, religion is not only a matter of inheritance and habit but also of geography.

And so, what is Islam, that virile religion which even today dominates the minds of 20 percent of the human race? Let us give it a little careful study. Its theology is not complicated. We know of no world religion so simple, direct and unequivocal. Its principles are few and clear-cut:

(1) First of all, a firm adherence to the belief in *One* God, the unity of the Supreme One. *"There is but one God and his name is Allah."*

(2) "Mohammed is his prophet." Other prophets had come and gone but Mohammed was the last and the greatest of them all.

It was, therefore, the duty of all the faithful, aye of the whole world, to give him their undivided allegiance, their utmost devotion and veneration.

(3) The faithful are offered a double reward: riches and honors in this life, and a paradise of delights in the next. That had the approval of the all-merciful Allah.

(4) The Koran, or Quran, is the holy book of Islam. It is made up of a collection of revelations, or messages received direct from Allah himself for the edification and control of the faithful. The Quran is written in beautiful Arabic language. It contains much that is wholesome, stimulating and inspiring. Its substance is a code of ethics and laws, mostly suitable to the peoples of the day. Like any wise physician, Mohammed gave them what was best suited to their needs at that time.

Let us give to the Arabian prophet all the credit due him for an honest effort to pull his people out of the mire of superstition. That he rendered them a very great service cannot be doubted by any unprejudiced student of history.

Today, if a seeker for the light goes to a Moslem and demands to know just how he may enter the kingdom of heaven here and now, he will discover that Islam, just like all other religions, has no answer to that question. In this respect all religions stand in the same category. Islam has not the least clue to the answer. At best it offers a guide to right living among men—that and certain promises of rewards in the future life. It enjoins devotion to one God instead of many. That there have been real Saints among Moslems is a fact of much importance. Saints are not limited to any particular country, or to one people or one religion. The Saints never got their higher knowledge from the Quran or from the Bible or from any other book. They never got it from priests. Masters get their instructions and their initiation from other Masters. Then they demonstrate it for themselves. That is a fixed law.

The *Surat Shabd Yoga* has been known to some great Moslem Saints. Among them were Hafiz, Shams-i-Tabriz, Maulana Rum and Kabir Sahib. But the orthodox Moslems do not credit these men because they were not altogether orthodox in their teachings. The point of greatest importance is that this central truth is not derived from any fixed and organized religion but is given from mouth to ear by Saints who have themselves experienced it. It is quite impossible that this all-important knowledge should be incorporated into a book and given out by a priesthood. It cannot be handed down that way. Hence the vital necessity of an unbroken line of living Masters.

There is one very important principle which we should all learn and hold fast. It should constitute the mariner's compass when he starts out to explore the wide sea of world religions. It is this:

> *Any religion which at present bases its authority upon one man or one book, and fails to indicate the way for any other man to gain the same truth and the same spiritual eminence, fails to meet the most urgent spiritual needs of mankind.*

In the light of this principle, all world religions will be found wanting. Only the science of the Masters can meet the inflexible demands of this principle. The Masters do not tell you how to live among your fellowmen and then inform you that if you so live, you will go to heaven when you die. On the contrary, they tell you that if you live rightly among men, and then devote yourself to the practice of the Surat Shabd Yoga, you will enter the kingdom of heaven *while you are still living in the body*. And that constitutes a world of difference between the spiritual science of the Masters and all religions.

The followers of Islam have had the same difficulty to contend with as the followers of the Bible. But their devotees do not realize that, and they would probably resent the suggestion. This has always been the case with formal religions, where it is laid down in a book just what one is to believe. No one can then go beyond the book. Thought becomes crystallized and progress ceases. How can it be otherwise? As soon as a man joins a formal religion, he ceases to look for anything new or better. He is bound. It has always been so since the earliest days of the Vedas. There has always been a tendency to crystallize religious thought and finally to write it down in a book as the very last word to be said. This means stagnation, ossification.

This tendency has in it another deadly menace. The next logical step is to try to compel all men to accept what is written. Then follow persecution and murder in the name of God. Can history show a more ghastly tragedy? Usually when people accept a book as the authoritative word of God, then they assert that all revelation is closed. The last word has been said. Believe it now or be damned. This has been the supreme tragedy of history. The Vedas, the Shastras, the Puranas, and the Gita, the Mahabharata and the Ramayana in India; the Zend Avesta in Persia; the Bible in Syria; the Quran in Arabia; and other religious scriptures—all these are books to be worshipped and obeyed. They are declared, *ex-cathedra,* to be inspired word of God. Ergo, it is the duty of all men to accept and believe them. And all of them are fetters to intelligence, no matter how good they may be in and of themselves. They become fetters because their followers insist that all revelation is closed. All spiritual instructions are finished. Instead of listening to a living Master in each age, their respective books are considered the infallible word. Crystallization of thought always goes before moral stagnation. Without a living Master spirituality wanes, as a lamp goes out when the oil is exhausted. As soon as a religion becomes fixed, static, crystallized, upon that foundation a corrupt priesthood is established, and at once the whole thing begins to decline into an inspired formalism. This is history. It is no theory.

Only when the living Master comes with a vitalized and dynamic science, only then can he 'speak as one having authority'. After all, what is a holy book at best? It is a statement of the inner experiences of a living Master. Then why not listen to the living Master now? Why not see him and hear him yourself instead of reading about some Masters who lived centuries or thousands of years ago? In every age, if you are prepared in your heart to stand before a Master, you will have no great difficulty in finding one. You must find him, for he will find you. Let me assure you that if you never meet a Master, it is your own fault. You have yourself shut the door against him and barred him out.

Every true Master says, in substance, just as Jesus did, "The works that I do, ye may do also."

There is no monopoly on the Path of the kingdom of heaven. The doors always swing wide open to all who give the right knock. They are closed only to the unworthy. If your religion is true, if it is the word of a living Master, it will show you how to enter the kingdom of heaven here and now. It became very tiresome for me to hear about what I was to get in heaven if I believed so and so, and what I would get in hell if I didn't believe. When the Great Master told me so graciously that I had it in my power to enter that kingdom of light here and now, my heart fairly leaped with gladness. That is what we all want.

The real Master always teaches you that the *kingdom of God is within you,* and also that *whosoever seeks shall find.* He does still more: *he always shows his disciples the exact Way to enter that kingdom.* More than that—he *helps* them to find it. For this very important reason a living Master is always essential. No matter how great your past Master, he cannot now act in that capacity. *The disciple in a human body must have a Master in the human body.* That is a fixed law. At the time of his passing, a Master turns over his work to another Master who is in the body, and he carries on until his time comes to go.

9. The Bhagavad Gita

One of the most meaningful and interesting of all the sacred books of Indian literature is the Bhagavad Gita, meaning 'the Song Celestial'. It is a part of the immortal classic called the Mahabharata. It was supposed to have been given by Lord Krishna to his favorite disciple and friend, Arjuna, on the battlefield. As a matter of fact, the Gita was not originally a part of that great epic, but was written much later by a great *rishi* named Vyas. Hence the teachings of the Gita did not originate with or from Krishna at all, but from the rishi, to whom all honor is due for its exalted teachings.

I am going to give a few quotations from the Gita as a special concession. This 'Song Celestial' is so highly regarded by so many people, both East and West, that it appears fitting to reproduce certain portions of it here. Moreover, it sets forth about the clearest and most explicit statements concerning the mental preparation for the Path of the Masters. No earnest student of the Path can fail to profit by reading these extracts from the Gita. They are of universal interest. They do not mark out the Master's Path, but they indicate the mental preparation for that Path.

Those who regard ethics as the chief thing in religion will find in the Gita about the highest standard of ethics ever written. If the moralist would accept the Gita as his standard, he would never need any other book to guide him on the path of moral rectitude. If the whole of human society would adopt the Gita as its standard textbook of ethics, there would follow the most revolutionary and wholesome reconstruction of society the world has ever known.

The Gita leads the student up to the very gateway of the Path of the Masters. All it lacks is the living Master himself to open the gates and go in with the student. But just here lies all the difference between success and failure. No matter how perfect your preparation may be, no matter if you have memorized the whole of the Gita, the Bible, the Quran, and all the moral precepts of a thousand sages, yet if you have no means of actually making the entry into the kingdom of heaven within you, your preparation is useless, except to give you a little better placement in the next life and a little peace of mind in this life. Remember always that it is not 'right living' here that counts first in importance. It is the actual entry into that kingdom which lies within. Doctrines and theories will not help. The cleansing process alone, which comes through right living, will never open to you the door to those inner worlds. The Master alone holds the key to that door. That upward journey itself can never be made except by the aid of a living Master. If an earthen vessel is cleansed, that is only preliminary to filling it with the elixir. The living Master, and he only, can fill the vessel with the water of life.

The following extracts are a few of the finest portions of the Gita.

10. Quotations From the Gita

The wise grieve neither for the dead, nor for the living.   *(II:11)*

The contacts of matter, O son of Kunti, giving heat and cold, pleasure and pain—they come and go; they are impermanent. Endure them bravely.   *(II:14)*

This dweller in the body of every one is always invulnerable, O Bharata; therefore, thou shouldst not grieve for any creature. *(II:30)*

Since the real man cannot be harmed either in life or in death, there is no reason to worry about what may befall anyone.

Taking as equal both pleasure and pain, gain and loss, victory and defeat, gird thee for the battle.   *(II:38)*

The Vedas deal with the three *gunas* [attributes]. Be thou above these attributes, O Arjuna; beyond the pairs of opposites, ever steadfast in purity [*sattvas,* meaning the attribute of equilibrium, of truth and light]; careless of possessions, full of the Self [the Supreme Self].   *(II:45)*

Thy business is with the action only, never with its fruits. So, let not the fruit of any action be thy motive; nor be thou to inaction attached.   *(II:47)*

Perform actions, O Dhananjaya, dwelling in union with the divine, renouncing attachments, and balanced evenly in success and failure. Equilibrium is called yoga.   *(II:48)*

Far lower than the yoga of discrimination [*viveka*] is that of action, O Dhananjaya. Take thou refuge in the pure reason [*buddhi*]. United to the pure reason, pitiable are they who work for fruits.   *(II:49)*

One abandoneth here both good and evil deeds; therefore cleave thou to yoga. Yoga is skill in action.   *(II:50)*

The sages united with the pure reason. They renounce the fruit which action yieldeth and, liberated from the bonds of birth, they go to the blissful seat.   *(II:51)*

When the mind, bewildered by the scriptures [reading too many books] shall stand immovable, fixed in contemplation [*samadhi*] then thou shalt attain unto yoga [union with the Supreme].   *(II:53)*

When a man abandoneth, O Partha, all the desires of the heart [literally *manas,* 'mind'] and is sustained in the Self [Supreme] by that Self, then he is called stable in mind [*pravna*]. He whose mind is free from anxiety amid pains, indifferent amid pleasures, loosed from passion, fear and anger [the five foes of man] is called a sage [*muni*—one who observes the vow of silence] of stable mind.

(II:55, 56)

He who, on every side, is without attachments, whatever happens fair or foul, who neither likes nor dislikes, of such a one the understanding is well poised.   *(II:57)*

It may be well to remember that this does not imply a callous indifference to all things. It is something vastly higher than that. It means a soul serenely detached from the love of material things or events, from all concern about them. The student attains this attitude because his love is centered upon that which is above the things that perish.

Man, musing on the objects of sense, conceiveth an attachment to these. From attachment ariseth desire; from desire, anger [*krodh*] cometh forth. From anger proceedeth delusion; from delusion, confused memory; from confused memory, the destruction of reason [*buddhi*—discrimination, ability to reason]; from destruction of reason he perisheth.   *(II:62, 63)*

Here is a marvelous analysis of the downward path, step by step.

But the disciplined self, moving among sense objects, with the senses free from attraction and repulsion [interested only as a spectator of the passing show], mastered by the Self [Supreme] he goeth to peace. [That is the path of the real yogi, so beautifully contrasted with the downward path of self-indulgence]. In that peace the extinction of all pain ariseth for him; for of him whose heart is peaceful, the reason soon attaineth equilibrium.   *(II:64, 65)*

Such of the roving senses as the mind yieldeth to, that hurrieth away the understanding, just as the gale hurrieth away a ship upon the waters.   *(II:67)*

He attaineth peace unto whom all desires flow as rivers flow into the ocean, which is filled with water, but itself remaineth unmoved.
(II:70)

It remains unmoved just because it is filled with so much water. Similarly if a man is filled with the Life Stream, he cannot be moved.

This is the eternal state, O son of Pritha, having attained thereto, none is bewildered [meaning that all knowledge is clarified]. Whosoever at the death hour is established therein, he goeth to the Nirvana of the Eternal.   *(II:72)*

This is true only of those who by the aid of the Master have conquered first the lower and then the higher worlds.

In this world there is a twofold path—that of yoga by knowledge, and that of yoga by action.   *(III:3)*

This again directs attention to the *Gyan Marg* of the pundits and the *Dharma Marg,* so persistently emphasized by certain schools of thought, both East and West—the path of good works. But this leaves out the third path, so urgently taught by the Masters. It fails to call attention to the supreme Path, that of the *Surat Shabd Marg.* But the *Bhakti Marg* is referred to elsewhere in the Gita. That is the Path of devotion.

Balanced in pleasure and pain, self-reliant, to whom a lump of earth, a rock or gold are all alike, the same to loved and unloved, firm, the same in censure and in praise, the same in honor and ignominy, the same to friend or foe—he is said to have crossed over the qualities [*gunas*].   *(XIV: 24, 25)*

He from whom comes no disturbance, who cannot be disturbed by others, who is free from joy [free from exhilaration over ordinary pleasure], from anger, fear and anxiety, such a one is my beloved. He who does not depend on anything, who is pure and active, who does not care whether good comes or evil, and who never becomes miserable; who has given up all efforts for himself alone . . . such a one is my beloved *bhakta*. A man winneth not freedom from action [*karma*] by abstaining from action; nor by renunciation doth he rise to perfection. Nor can anyone for an instant remain wholly action-less. For helplessly is everyone driven to action by the attributes [*gunas*], born of Nature [*prakriti,* which means matter out of which all creation is evolved].   *(XII:15–16; III:4–5)*

He who controls the senses by mind, O Arjuna, with the organs of sense uninterested he performeth yoga by action. He is worthy.
(III:7)

It still remains a fact of history that not one man has ever con-trolled his organs of sense just by the power of his own mind, simply by willing it so. By will power one may hold impulses in check, follow or not follow his desires. But if one is to overcome the desires and impulses completely, one must find something which the mind likes better. It can never be accomplished by nega-tion alone. This supreme need is supplied only by the heavenly melody, the *Bani.* That is the Audible Life Stream, and it is found only upon the Path of the Masters.

It is desire, it is wrath, begotten by the guna of motion [*rajas*]—all-consuming, polluting—know this to be our foe here on earth. A flame is enveloped by smoke, as a mirror by dust, as an embryo by the amnion, so this [the whole world] is enveloped by it [the whirlpool of motion, engendering desire]. Enveloped is wisdom by this con-stant enemy of the wise, in the form of desire which is as unstable as a flame.   *(III:37–39)*

Thus understanding Him, as greater than the reason [*buddhi*], re-straining the self by the Self, slay thou, O mighty armed, the enemy in the form of desire, difficult to overcome.   *(III:43)*

This imperishable yoga I declared to Vivasvan; Vivasvan taught it to Manu [a prehistoric sage, or rishi]; Manu to Ikshvaku told it. Thus handed down the line, the king-sages knew. Thus yoga, by great in-flux of time, decayed in the world, O Parantapa.   *(IV:1–2)*

And so it is today. Who but a true Master has any knowledge of the yoga which leads to the heights of spiritual attainment?

This same ancient yoga hath been today declared to thee by me. For thou, O Arjuna, art my devotee and my friend. *It is the supreme secret.* *(IV:3)*

And yet this supreme secret offers no more than a good preparation for the real yoga of the Saints.

Whenever there is decay of righteousness [*dharma*], O Bharata, and there is exaltation of unrighteousness [*adharma*], then I myself come forth. For the protection of the good, for the destruction of the evildoers, for the sake of firmly establishing righteousness, I am born from age to age. *(IV:7–8)*

Nothing could be more definite than Krishna's own words concerning his mission in the world. But Saints come to deliver men from this world-bondage, not to improve the world itself. Thus it will be seen that there is a vast difference in their missions. It is the duty of the Negative Power to keep this world in a livable condition. Although bad enough at best, it must not be allowed to become too bad. The Saints often compare the two missions, the one of the Negative Power and the other of the Positive Power represented by the Saints, by referring to a big prison. The inmates may be in need of all sorts of things to make their lives more tolerable. So a charitably inclined man comes along and offers them better food or better clothing. Another man makes improvements in the sanitary conditions. But the poor devils are still in the prison. Finally comes another man armed with power from the governor, and he opens the prison cells, swings wide the doors and tells them all to go free. Which one do you say was the real friend of the prisoners? The Master is the great liberator, while the agents of the other power seek only to ameliorate the conditions of prison life but do nothing to set free the prisoners themselves.

Note carefully Krishna's own words as to his mission. They are the authority which no man can question. He says he comes not only to establish righteousness but *to destroy the evildoers*. Masters redeem evildoers; they never destroy them. If the student is not exceedingly alert, the real significance of this passage from the Gita will escape his attention. Krishna comes from age to age to establish righteousness and to destroy evildoers. But the great Masters come not to destroy, but to save sinners. Jesus said: "For the son of man is not come to destroy men's lives, but to save them" *(Luke 9:56)*.

Saints pick up the desolate souls, hungry and weary, and by the aid of the Shabd they deliver them from earthly bondage and take them back home. And this constitutes the essential difference between the work of the real Masters and the agents of the Negative Power.

11. The Yoga of the Gita

As to a method of yoga or meditation, Krishna says:

> Let the yogi constantly engage himself in yoga, remaining in a secret place by himself, with thought and self subdued, free from hope and greed. In a clean place, established on a fixed seat of his own, neither very much raised, nor very low, made of cloth, black antelope skin, and *kusha* grass, one over the other; there having made the mind [*manas*] *one-pointed* with thought, and functions of the senses subdued, steady on his seat, he should practise yoga for the purification of the self. Holding the body, the head, and neck erect, immovably steady, looking fixedly at the point of the nose, with unseeing gaze. The self serene, fearless, firm in the vow of brahmacharya [keeping the vow of continence, celibacy], the mind controlled, thinking of *me*, harmonized, let him sit, aspiring after *me*.
>
> *(VI: 10–14)*

Here is the secret method of the Krishna yoga. If we add to his method the ancient custom of repeating the sacred word *Om,* you will have about all that the ancient or modern yogis have ever employed in their meditations. In fact, Krishna himself says:

Aum, the one-syllabled eternal, reciting, thinking upon me, he who goeth forth, abandoning the body, he goeth on the highest path.

(Gita VIII:13)

Besides this method of yoga, there is no yogic system of any great importance except that of Patanjali. Even that is scarcely an improvement upon the Gita method.

Now, if the student undertakes his practice on this basis, he will surely get some results. If he is lucky enough to escape the risks which frequently attend such practices, he will get some light and increase of powers. He will gain some degree of mental poise and he will find increase of joy in living. He will soon feel assured that he is on the right path leading to full realization. He will be stimulated to more love and charity toward all. He will, in other words, become a better and more useful citizen, while a serene hope will fill his heart as he approaches life's sunset. He will at the same time earn a long, quiet sojourn in the astral heavens, but to return at last for a rebirth in regions of matter. In other words, that student will become a real yogi, with a yogi's understanding and powers. And let it be emphasized always that this is no small thing. But we must also remember that a yogi who has not gone beyond the Brahm Lok is not a Master or a Saint. This is a very important distinction to be kept in mind when studying this Path.

There is one more danger which besets the path of the yogi. He may be misled into believing that he has actually attained the highest there is on the spiritual path; that he has reached the regions of immortality, beyond the play of birth and death, beyond the fatal 'wheel of eighty-four'. Many noble souls have so believed, only to discover their mistake when it was too late. Some have not yet discovered their error. It may be after thousands or even millions of years, they will suddenly find out that they must return to the scenes of their former struggles. It is somewhat like a man earning a sum of money and then going to a foreign country to spend it. He may live there for many years, in the enjoyment of all that the country can give him, but when his capital has been spent, he is obliged to return again. Just so the law of karma works

out on the astral and causal planes. There is no real immortality
there.

By the method of the Gita no soul has ever yet escaped from
the regions of mind and matter. It is quite impossible. Such escape
can never be effected by any means within the powers of any man,
except a true Master. Millions of noble souls rise to beautiful
planes of the two lower worlds of light, and there experience pro-
longed periods of rest and enjoyment of earned good karma. It is
all a clever scheme of the Negative Power. Even the Gita itself
says that for such a yogi there is no more rebirth or death. Many
have labored under this delusion. It is a pity. So cunningly arranged is this system, leading to the belief that they have found
the perfect way, while the Negative Power still holds them prisoners within his empire.

The path of the yogi is good and it may be highly recommended so long as there is nothing better in sight. But the Path
of the Masters is infinitely better. It alone leads to complete liberation and absolute immortality. He who wishes to escape for
all time and eternity the wheel of birth and death, this eternal
awagawan, let him seek a living Master and enlist with him on the
Path of Surat Shabd Yoga. No need to quarrel with fate because
there is no other way. Why should you wish any other way? The
Creator has established a Royal Highway to the supreme regions.
Isn't that good enough? It is only on the Path of the Saints that
anyone ever has risen or ever can rise to regions beyond the play
of karma, beyond the downward drag of mind and maya.

The length of life upon the Brahm plane is very long indeed.
It often extends to thousands and millions of years. But the Saints
are familiar with vast regions far beyond and above the highest
regions known to ancient yogis or rishis. Moreover, the Brahm
region itself must sooner or later come to an end, when the periodic dissolutions take place. This is taught by both the Vedas and
the Gita, and it is repeated in the Upanishads. If that region itself is destined to come to an end, how shall its inhabitants enjoy
immortality? There is no assured immortality until the soul has
reached the regions of pure spirit, far beyond all materiality. Only
then is the soul above the complications of mind and beyond the

grasp of karma, beyond all dissolutions and grand dissolutions.

Let us note now the final instructions of Krishna to his disciple, especially to his beloved *bhakta*, Arjuna. This is his great Word, the supreme word of the Gita.

It is called the *Mahavakya*, the crowning note in the grand diapason of the 'Song Celestial'. It is this:

> With the Lord in thy heart, with all thy being, with his grace thou shalt attain to the supreme peace and the eternal status. So have I expounded to thee a knowledge more secret than that which is hidden. Further, hear the *most secret, the supreme word* [*mahavakya*] that I shall speak to thee—*Become my-minded.* [Compare—'Let this mind be in you', which was also in Christ Jesus.] Devoted to me, to me do sacrifice and adoration. Infallibly thou shalt come unto me; for dear thou art to me. Abandoning all laws of conduct, *seek refuge in me alone;* I will release thee from all sin. Do not grieve.
> *(XVIII: 62–66)*

In closing this section on the Gita, we must drop one word of caution. It is referred to in many places in this book but it cannot be overemphasized. Do not imagine that you may become an accepted disciple of Krishna or of Buddha or of Jesus by reading instructions in a book and saying a prayer to him in your imagination. It can never be done. Their messages were spoken to their own disciples.

Truth itself may be universal, but a spiritual Master can function here as a Master only so long as he lives in a physical body. How do we know? Because the Masters all say so; besides, the very reasons that impelled him to take a human body in the first place suggest that such work as he has to do can be done only in a human body. If it were otherwise, then he never had any need of coming in human form. This is not because the Master is limited, but because the disciple is limited. He cannot receive help from a departed Master. To try to make a departed Saint one's own Master now is only to hug a fond delusion. There is no spiritual liberation without conscious contact with the Shabd Dhun, and that you cannot possibly get without a living Sat Guru. As will be seen in another chapter of this book *(Eleven:9),* the three links of the golden chain are absolutely inseparable. They are:

Sat Guru, Shabd Dhun, and *Jivan Mukti*—the Master, the Audible Life Stream, and salvation during this life. If you want salvation, you must first secure the other two. There is no other way.

When Krishna said those lovely words to Arjuna, promising "infallibly thou shalt come to me,".they applied to Arjuna only or any other of his beloved disciples, but not to the public in general nor to any future time when someone just imagines himself to be a disciple of Krishna. And the same applies to all other past Masters, all other sacred books and all other religions. In every case, the living Master is necessary if we are to pass beyond the threshold of the heavenly kingdom, beyond the gates of materiality. Every student who has gone to higher regions knows that the higher one goes, the more difficult it is to go without a Master with him. Soon the stage is reached where it is quite impossible to go another step without the presence and aid of a Master.

12. The Four Vedas of the Hindus

The Vedas are among the most notable of the ancient scriptures, generally conceded to be the oldest literature in existence. However, long centuries before the Vedas were reduced to writing, perhaps before there was a Sanskrit alphabet, the Vedas were repeated from father to son, almost in whispers, so sacred were they considered. The Vedas are venerated because they are old, as well as for their contents. But if one were looking for a book of knowledge, he would not go back to the childhood of the race. Santon ki Shiksha, antedating the Vedas by vast eons of time, is the oldest system of spiritual philosophy in existence. Yet I fear if it depended upon its age for veneration, it would get but scant consideration from modern thinkers. That system is today much appreciated because it is living Truth.

The four Vedas are:
(1) The Rig Veda
(2) The Yajur Veda
(3) The Sama Veda
(4) The Atharva Veda

In the Vedas we are confronted with the same difficulty that puzzles us in regard to all old scriptures. It is very difficult to determine what was originally written and what has been added during the succeeding centuries. All scriptures have suffered such additions and modifications during the centuries.

The Vedas contain one hundred thousand *shlokas*, or couplets, of which eighty-six thousand deal with problems concerning life in this world. Fourteen thousand deal with spiritual problems, God and the gods, and the heavens beyond this earth. There are many lofty precepts in the Vedas, but unfortunately mixed in with much that is not so elevating. But even that is due to the fact that they were written for a people who were low in the scale of spiritual evolution, and human relationships were necessarily used to illustrate spiritual truths. Doubtless, if we had the pure original songs of the great rishis, we would have a very beautiful spiritual literature.

The Vedas exhibit a definite knowledge of the Audible Life Stream. In them it is called *Nad,* or *Nada.* Doubtless their authors had experimental knowledge of certain phases of the Holy Nada. This Life Current manifests on all planes, and it may be heard in Sahasradal Kanwal, the Turiya Pad, and the Brahm Lok.

A revival of interest in the Vedas has come out of the life and work of Ramakrishna and his illustrious disciple, Swami Vivekananda. In fact, it was Vivekananda, more than anyone else, who stimulated interest in the Vedantic philosophy throughout the world. The writings of Max Mueller have been widely read, but chiefly among scholars, even as the lucid expositions of Sri Aurobindo Ghose, who had given to the Gita a new birth in the land of its origin.

The Upanishads are some of the finest portions of the sacred writings of India. Most of the original writings of this class have been lost, according to some authorities. One hundred and eight have been preserved, and of these not more than twenty are of superior value from our viewpoint. Out of that number, thirteen have been translated and discussed by Robert E. Hume. This work ought to be read by all who wish to make a careful study of the Upanishads. Duessen, a great German student of Indian literature, says: "To every Indian Brahmin today the Upanishads are what the New Testament is to the Christian."

Schopenhauer said that the Upanishads had been a lifelong inspiration to him; but his recommendation is not so valuable as that of philosophers who, abandoning the darker aspects of things, exalt their own lives by the nobler precepts of the Indian literature.

Clearly the Upanishads teach that the Path to spiritualization is fundamentally self-abnegation. Added to that, they enjoin viveka and vairagya, quite in harmony with the teachings of the great Masters. By all these means they teach the disciple to know the Supreme Brahman, knowing whom, the disciple becomes Brahman. But we insist that mere knowledge never leads to liberation. The *Jnana Yoga* is not the chief means of enlightenment. But the Upanishads lay down some other aids to spiritual attainment. Among them are *Sama, Dama, Uparati, Titiksha, Samadhana, Shraddha,* and *Mumukshutva*. The latter two, which mean faith and longing, are also enjoined by the Masters as excellent aids on the Path. Especially is the last one regarded by the Masters, as well as the Upanishadic pundits, as 'the driving force' on the spiritual Path. Of course, the object of longing must be so ardently desired that all else becomes of small importance.

In Mundaka *(II. ii. 3–4),* the Upanishads give an apt simile for the devotee:

> Taking the great weapon, the bow, fix the arrow sharpened by meditation. Drawing it with the mind, rapt in the Immutable, pierce that target, that very Immutable. Om is the bow, the soul is the arrow, and Brahman is the target. One must pierce *it* with a concentrated mind and so become like the arrow, one with *it*.

Of course, this applies to such as go no further than Brahm Lok, and to whom *Om* is the most sacred word.

Again we must call attention to the important fact that the Upanishads, however rich in knowledge, lack the living Master and Audible Life Stream, both of which are absolutely necessary to full spiritual realization. Karma Kanda and Jnana Kanda, either singly or together, can never bring to any student Jivan

Mukti, which is the goal sought by all. Surat Shabd Kanda is an absolute necessity. So the Upanishads, like all other sacred books, belong to past ages, and lack the quickening power of a living Master. Even supposing that the Upanishads, like other sacred books, were written by Masters or inspired by them, why not go to a living Master now? We must always beware of the illusion that a mere knowledge of a thing will bring to us its benefits.

In the Nada-Bindu Upanishad of the Rig Veda—some claim that this is not is the original Rig Veda, but of a later date—the Audible Life Stream is plainly referred to and partly described:

> In the beginning of practice, the devotee hears many loud sounds, ten or more. They gradually increase in pitch and are heard more and more subtly. At first sounds are like those coming from the ocean, from the clouds (like thunder) and from cataracts. In the middle stage, such as proceed from the *mardang*, the bell and the horn. At the last stage, those proceeding from tinkling bells, the flute and the bina. Thus he hears many sounds, more and more subtly.

It is thus that the old Hindu scriptures definitely speak of the inner sounds. Then this same Upanishad enjoins:

> The mind, having at first concentrated itself on any one sound, fixes firmly to that and is absorbed in it. The mind, becoming insensible to external impressions, becomes one with the sound, as milk with water. Having abandoned all thoughts and being freed from all actions, he should always concentrate his attention on the sound. Just as the bee drinks the honey and does not care for anything else, so the *chitta* [the mind], which is always absorbed in the sound, does not long for sensual objects.

And so the Masters teach that the Shabd, the Sound, is the only thing that will cure the mind from wandering after sensual objects. "The sound proceeding from Pranava, which is Brahman, is of the Nature of effulgence; the mind becomes absorbed in it."

All this is in full accord with the teachings of the modern Masters. But most of the present-day *sannyasis* have lost all practical knowledge of the Sound Current. This in spite of the fact that they claim to follow the Upanishads as their Bible. Instead of listening to the Sound itself, they read some book that tells about it. And then, because they cannot hear the Sound themselves, having lost all knowledge of the method, they try to explain it away as a mere figure of speech. This is now being done by most of the Sikhs regarding their Granth Sahib, which is full of mention of the Holy Shabd. The same has been done by Tagore, the beloved poet of Bengal, in his translations of Kabir Sahib.

The Samhitas is a collection of Vedic hymns sung in praise of the various gods and devas—Indra, Varuna, Mitra, Parjanya, etc. Hymns sung to the gods while they—both gods and men— drank their soma juice and frolicked. These are perhaps the oldest specimens of Aryan literature ever reduced to writing.

13. An Epitome of Vedic Philosophy

We believe that the entire substance of the Vedic philosophy, which has stood the acid test of rational criticism, may be summed up in one of the classical sentences. It may give us the key to the understanding of all Vedic literature, besides much that is modern. Note it well:

Ekam sat vipra bahudha vadanti.

It means: "That which exists is one; sages call it by various names." This was first written probably ten thousand years ago. It has run through all Indian philosophy like a golden thread. It teaches not only that there is unity in the Supreme One but unity among men and in all life. In fact, all that lives is one life, one in origin, one in essence, and that essence is permeated and vitalized by the one universal spirit. It is in that One that all things live and move and have their being.

If Hindu philosophy had never done anything else than give to the world this one sentence, it would have justified its existence. It has modified all philosophic thought from prehistoric times down to this day. Out of it has grown modern monism, which is so profoundly affecting all recent thinking. Until we see nothing in the world but the Infinite *One*, all of these evils of which men complain will continue to beset our path and harass us. We shall make much of distinctions, and selfishness will take precedence over altruism. It is only in the Lord, in the Spirit, in the Life Stream itself, that we come to know of a certainty that we are all one. When our entire consciousness blends into that Divine Current, then we shall see nothing but that light and hear nothing but that music. We shall become one with it. Until we see the Beloved One and hear the enchanting melodies of 'the all-embracing Sound', we shall wander through the universe like stray comets.

Until we see and hear Him in everything, even in evil, perfect unity will not exist for us. The very heart of this doctrine of oneness is love. Love is the divine cement which unites all living beings into one temple of light. The higher we go into the inner worlds, the more apparent this oneness becomes. Sitting in Sat Desh, the supreme region, one beholds the King of kings and says: "I am He!" Love is the holy bond that holds all worlds together. What a pity that individuals should war ignorantly and blindly against each other.

Side by side with this sublime concept, which teaches the oneness of all that exists, is another Sanskrit expression which sums up in three words the entire philosophy of our kinship with all that lives. It offers a philosophical basis for universal love. It does away with distinctions. It then prepares the mind to enter the Path. It is, "*Tat twam asi.*" It means, "*Thou art that.*" Its underlying concept is identical with the other sentence just quoted. It has a twofold actual meaning. First, it means this individual is that individual—no distinction. Second, it means that each individual is the Supreme Lord.

There is a point in the upward travels of the student of the Masters when he beholds the majestic beauty and grandeur of one of the great Lords of the upper worlds. His name is Sohang. When the student sees him, the consciousness comes to him with an overwhelming joy —"I am that." This is the meaning of the word

Sohang. At that moment of sublime realization, the student *knows* that he is one with the Supreme. That is pure Santon ki Shiksha; but it finds a distant echo in the Vedas.

It was scarcely necessary that Spinoza should enlarge upon this basic Truth. His entire philosophy was no more than a thesis founded upon this ancient text. That text embodies the original idea of all modern dissertation upon the unity of things. It is the legitimate mother of the doctrine of universal brotherhood of man and universal fatherhood of God. If we all sprang from one God and are still one in Him, we must be very close brothers. If all men had remembered that golden ideal, they would never have persecuted or sought to destroy one another. And this is today one of the noble precepts of the Masters. Whatever my brother is, I am, whether good or bad. Into this sublime concept, if we pour the stream of universal love, the world itself will become a paradise. All that ails this old world today is its lack of love. But men forget, and so they suffer. As said in another section, when all men turn to the path of love, suffering will cease.

All Vedantic systems agree on three things: first, a belief in God, or the gods; second, that the Vedas constitute the revealed message of God, or the gods; and third, a belief in the cycles of world history.

The Vedas are divided into two portions, two currents running through all four of them—the Karma Kanda, or work portion, and the Jnana Kanda, the knowledge portion. This is the Gyan Marg, or the yoga of knowledge. The Upanishads belong to the Jnana Kanda portion. They are intended to give enlightenment. They are also called Aranyakas, or the forest books.

The yoga of works and the yoga of knowledge are both taught in the Vedas; but the yoga of devotion, the Bhakti Marg, does not seem to us to be sufficiently emphasized. The Bhakti Marg, when vitalized by the Nada-Bindu, the divine Shabd, is the supreme yoga of the Saints. It is their Path back home.

The Vedas teach another thing of great importance, a vital truth; namely, that all men should seek to know one thing, knowing which, all else is known. What is that one thing? The inner self. Hence the importance of the injunction, "Know thyself."

The Vedas offer a very beautiful simile:

> Multitudes of people are like the million dewdrops in which the one
> sun is reflected. Untold millions of them, but only one sun. So is our
> relation to the eternal One.

The Vedic idea of creation is worth our mention here. In Sanskrit the word which is commonly translated as 'creation' is literally 'projection'. The ancient sages could not conceive of something being created out of nothing. The Supreme One projects himself into form and material substance. Therefore he is still in it, still its life and essence. Everything that exists is then a unit in the universal being. In material things it means that his vibrations are lowered to the material plane in order that he may manifest upon that plane.

This is illustrated by the phenomena of mind. Manas, buddhi, all of the elements of mind, are simply the projections of the cosmic mind, the *mahat*. This mahat then becomes manifested in vibrating thought. Nothing is ever created new except in its form. Its substance is as eternal as the Creator himself, and through everything the creative essence runs.

The Vedas teach that from stone to intellect all is the product of one substance, *Akash*. The difference lies solely in the greater or lesser degree of its manifestation. As there is but one substance at the substratum of all things in the material universe, so there is but one primary force from which all other forces are derived. Its name is *Prana*. Prana, acting upon Akash, produces all forms. To gain control over all forces and materials in Nature, one has only to gain control over Prana, the primal force. And therein lies one of the big secrets of the yogi. Yet that is only half the problem. To gain control over Prana, one must first gain control over his own mind—therein is the secret of secrets. This is the order of Nature.

Mind is superior to all other material forces and substances. Mind controls all else. In fact, mind is the primary motive power throughout Nature. We do not see it as mind because we are not able to observe mind in action. It is like electricity—we can only see its manifestations, not the thing itself. Mind controls all, but mind must act through some agency, some intermediary. There are many of these intermediate substances and forces in a series graded from fine to coarse. At last we arrive at electricity, well down in the scale; yet it is the highest in the series that science has been able to grasp and manipulate for its own uses.

Science has already come near to proving that electricity is the one substance into which all other substances resolve themselves, everything ending at last in protons and electrons. But the practical point for us is, if we wish to control the forces of the material world, we must begin with mind control. Gaining complete mastery over the mind, we then direct the mind toward the Prana. Controlling Prana, we compel it to manipulate the lower substances with which we have to deal. Among those lower substances, the first one to become visible to us, that is, visible in its manifestations, is electricity. Gaining that, we may play with Nature's forces as we desire. And this is the secret of all miracles. There have been thousands of yogis or mahatmas of different degrees, in every age of the world, who have been able to do so-called miracles. Any Master can do them. Many of his disciples can do them. Guru Nanak said: "Conquer the mind and you conquer the world."

And this is a truth known to everyone who has made some advancement upon the Path. The practice of real yoga arouses the latent powers in everyone—powers possessed by everybody, but lying dormant in most people. When fully awakened, such powers enable the individual to transcend the limits of reason and sense perception. This suggests the very great value of true yoga. Hermann Keyserling says: "It is amazing that the enlightened West has not made study of yoga a part of its public school curricula."

Every careful student knows that one of the greatest handicaps to progress is the lack of ability to concentrate upon the task in hand. Yoga teaches people to concentrate. The average mind is like a pool of water violently agitated by windstorms: storms of passion, of desires, of duties to be done, of a hundred demands upon one's time, of restless hurrying to-and-fro, of irritations, anxieties, worries and a thousand other ills of mind. Concentration is the cure. Do not allow yourself to be deceived into imagining that you will concentrate when you have circumstances shaped to suit your convenience. That time will never come. But if you will concentrate first of all, you will soon be able to shape circumstances to suit yourself. There is practically no limit to what may be accomplished by concentration.

14. The Yoga of Patanjali

The following is the system of yoga according to the Patanjali interpretation of the Vedas. It is not part of the Masters' system, but since it is so well known to students of the occult in all Oriental countries, we wish to give it here simply as a study. But we must warn all students not to attempt to use it, except under the directions of a true yogi. It has its dangers. It is given in eight stages, as follows:

(1) *Yama*—Restraint. The non-killing of animals or men; truthfulness, honesty, continence, non-acceptance of gifts, but giving freely to all who need.

(2) *Niyama*—Internal and external purification; study, worship.

(3) *Asana*—Sitting in the proper posture, body erect and the mind in perfect poise.

(4) *Pranayama*—Controlling the Prana, the vital force. This is generally done by the old yogis, mostly by controlling the breath, together with the exercise of the will. The result of the perfect practice of Pranayama is *Udghata*, the awakening of the *Kundalini*. This point has been much emphasized by the yogis. The Masters say only a little about it, except to warn students against dabbling with forces which they have not mastered. Pranayama is not a part of the system of the Saints and is not recommended by them. All of its beneficial results the Masters gain in another way, as will be shown later in this book. *Kumbhaka* is attained by restraining the Prana through concentration on internal and external objects. This is supposed to remove all coverings of the chitta, and give one-pointed sight.

(5) *Dharma*—Perfect concentration of mind by drawing it to one point and then holding it there, keeping the mind one-pointed. This is much emphasized by the Masters.

(6) *Pratyahara*—Withdrawing the attention entirely from all external objects of sense, then going into the inner world. This means, in the language of the Masters, 'closing the nine doors'. It is like going into a room and then shutting all the doors and windows so as to avoid disturbances from without. Mind becomes calm after it is withdrawn from the sense world. It is then ready for the next step.

(7) *Dhyana*—Holding the mind in fixed contemplation upon one object. This may be the Master or any other object; but in the system of the Saints, it is the Master only.

(8) *Samadhi*—Going beyond the sense world and entering the region of inner reality, that is some superphysical plane of consciousness. The body being now senseless, the mind and spirit rise to a state of superconsciousness. *Samyam* is an exalted stage of Samadhi wherein the consciousness is only aware of the inner meanings of things. It is at this point that the student penetrates into the hidden mysteries of the universe. The whole world then is clear as crystal, and all knowledge stands naked before him. This is pure Samyam. But there is a state of consciousness even above that. It is called *Nirvikalpa,* that changeless state of mind when the mind rises above all time changes, and itself changes no more, possessing all. This is as far as yoga can go with the Vedantists.

On the Path of the Masters the student rises above Nirvikalpa into that state where mind itself is dropped as of no further use, and the pure soul—unfettered by any instrument—knows all things by direct perception. But this is a state entered when the soul passes above and beyond all materiality, even beyond the cosmic mind itself.

On the way to the higher attainments, there is one exalted state of mind much emphasized by the Vedantists. That state is gained when the mind is not disturbed by any sort of opposition or any evil thing. If attacked, the mind remains quite undisturbed, calm as the still waters. There is then no sort of resistance, no antagonism, not even in thought; no hatred, no fear, no anger, not a ripple on the calm surface of mind. This very exalted state of mind is called by the pundits *Titiksha*. But in actual practice it is hardly reached before the degree of Master has been won. To the ordinary yogi it is mostly theoretical.

The student is taught by the Vedas, and by the Masters also, to practise *viveka*, 'discrimination'. But there is a very high degree of discrimination which is not attained until the soul illumines the buddhi. When the ordinary faculty of discrimination is quickened by the direct rays of the spirit, we generally speak of that as intuition. But when this process is carried to perfection and the mind is completely illuminated by spirit, then it is called by the pundits *nityanitya viveka*, meaning that it is a degree of discrimination beyond which there is nothing more to see. The ordinary discriminating powers of the mind, the buddhi, are not able to rise to the same height as when lit up by the spirit itself. The Western psychologist may call this 'reason combined with intuition'. But it is simply the buddhi, the intellect, quickened by spirit to an unusual degree. Until they enter the Path, only a few individuals are so endowed.

Perfect nityanitya viveka can hardly be attained until the soul is free from all coverings and is able to operate by direct perception. It may begin this state while yet a film of mind hangs over it. Only when the soul has passed beyond that sphere where matter obscures its vision, does it gain the true *pratyaksham*—direct perception and true knowledge. This leads us somewhat beyond the field of the Vedas. The regions of pure spirit, beyond all matter and mind, are unknown to the Vedas. They are known only to the Masters.

There is a degree of spiritual illumination which comes to the individual as a result of purity alone. The world has seen many such characters. Let us call them natural-born saints, although they are not real Saints in the technical meaning of that term. When a person never thinks an evil thought, never dwells upon things of the sense world, nor desires any pleasant sensation for self-gratification, that person spontaneously attains a degree of spiritual illumination called by the pundits *Pratibha*. This is the light of the supreme genius, the great poet, the great artist, the great philanthropist. But such as these are born, not made so by their own thinking.

The above classes are closely related to those who are said to radiate a light and a knowledge called *Dharma Megha*. The soul appears naturally to be clothed in light and virtue. This is spoken of as 'a cloud of virtue'. Such a great soul, wherever he goes, is clothed in this mantle of glory. It can be seen by all who enjoy astral vision. But such people are very rare.

Ahimsa is that attitude of mind which makes it impossible, for one who possesses it, ever willingly to cause pain of any sort, mental or physical. This is a very noble virtue and it is a decided step forward on the Path. He who has attained it, is close to the Kingdom.

Abhava is that form of yoga in which the yogi sees himself as zero, nothing, having no commendable virtue—void of all vanity. This is good but it is a negative virtue. It only serves to purify the vessel but puts nothing into it.

Then comes a still higher yoga called *Mahayoga*. This means a more exalted state of mind in which the yogi sees himself not simply as nothing, but as one with the Supreme One, free and blissful. This is to be attained while cherishing the most perfect humility. Otherwise it is useless to think about it.

There are three concepts which it would be good to understand: *Desa, Kala, Nimitta*—space, time and causation. This is the composition and order of the universe. Other and higher universes may know no such limitations. It is well known to the Masters that in the highest regions both time and space disappear automatically. This would go to show that they are simply limitations of material worlds. In those higher worlds all events and things, which we see in time and space, stand forever present before the observer. Then two of the fetters which bind us here are gone. There is no absolute reality in time and space. They are simply our method of separating things and events. But when we are free, those limitations naturally disappear. When the soul has all knowledge, all power, and is itself the very essence of love, what is there to limit it? Time and space are limitations. The free soul is unlimited. Therefore, to it there is neither time nor space.

It is one with the Supreme. This conscious oneness is then the basis of the most perfect liberty, as well as perfect joy.

We have given extremely brief sketches of the highlights of Hindu philosophy, and we have given those portions which we believe are of the greatest value to the student on the Path of the Masters. We are not concerned with those speculative portions which have no practical value for us. We have given those sections, those gems of thought, which coincide more closely with the teachings of the Masters. This we have done not to throw light upon the teachings of the Masters but to offer corroborative evidence. The science of the Masters does not contradict or negate any of the good things of the old scriptures. It simply offers additional light. It accepts what has been proved true in the old systems and then uses them as steppingstones to go higher.

15. Jesus Christ and the Christian Religion

Let it be understood at the very beginning of this discussion that there is a very great difference, a fundamental difference, between the Christian religion of history, that is, institutional Christianity, and *the precepts and practices* of Christ himself.

> In the modern Jesus of the Christian church, we find the ideal of the imaginative Ireneus, not the adept of the Essenes—the obscure reformer of Galilee. We see him under the disfigured Plato-Philonean mask, not as the disciples heard him on the Mount.

It is one of the saddest aspects of religious history that the original Jesus had to disappear to give place to an ecclesiastical icon. The historic religion of that name was not founded by Jesus Christ. It was formulated and given to the world by St. Paul, an educated Jew. He was schooled in the Hebrew Law, also in the Neo-Platonism of the Alexandrian school. It was Paul who gave to the world the Christian theology. His central idea was based upon the old Judaic system of sacrifice, and that itself was handed down from time immemorial, a bloody stream that has colored all history. When the new religion was formulated and given out, it was but little more than an allegorical metamorphosis of Judaism. Jesus was now made the sacrificial offering, "the lamb slain from the foundation of the world." It was his blood that was to take away the sins of the world. Thus the real mission of Jesus, which was to lead his disciples to realize the kingdom of heaven within themselves, was turned into a bloody tragedy. The whole system was made into a complicated mixture of spiritual precepts and ma- terial practices nailed to the cross. The lofty ideals of Jesus were dragged down to the grossly material ceremonies of the sacrifi- cial altar. Human blood was mixed with love and spiritual precept. This was a gross insult to the sublime idealism of the Masters.

One of the strangest and most absurd of all systems of the- ology took shape as the dogmatic religion of historic Christianity. The clean, gracious life, teachings and deeds of Jesus offered to the world something very different. Almost from the day of his de- parture, his spiritual mission and teachings began to undergo the usual corruptions and misstatements. The Master was not un- derstood even by his most intimate disciples, and later his very name was seized by a corrupt priesthood to be utilized by them as an instrument of self-aggrandizement—history repeating itself once more.

According to the most authentic sources, Jesus was a Jew, son of Mary and Joseph, who was a member of the Essene Brotherhood. The Biblical story of 'the immaculate conception' may not be taken too seriously. That Jesus had no earthly father, but "was begotten of the Holy Ghost" was doubtless invented to fit in with the theology which was at that time being formulated. Upon this theory the theologian could claim that Jesus was "the only begotten Son of God." The responsibility of his parentage was assumed by Joseph after some explanations were given to him in a dream. That Jesus was born according to natural law cannot be doubted by anyone who is acquainted with the Eastern Wis- dom or with the principles of human genesis. Even the greatest of Saints come into this world just as other people do.

Jesus himself bore the name of Joseph until he was grown up and received his initiation. He did not assume the name of Jesus until his spiritual mission was declared. It was probably given to him by his later disciples. The title of Christ was given to him long after his departure. He himself made no claim to such a title, neither is it anywhere recorded as his own statement that he laid claim to any quality or character not possessed by all men. On the contrary, he definitely asserted that the work which he was doing could be done by his disciples. And it must be kept in mind that miracles are not proof that he who does them is something more than a man. It means only a developed man. Later statements making Jesus a demi-god by birth bear all the earmarks of inter-polations. Jesus was brought up as a carpenter, living with his parents in the humble village of Nazareth, according to the New Testament.

Probably a year following his first reported discussion with the elders of his people at Jerusalem, he was taken to India by one of 'the wise men of the East' who had visited him at the time of his birth. Those men were the Magi of the Mesopotamian school. But there is no doubt that they had communication with India, from where all spiritual teachings had emanated since before the beginning of history. It seems probable that the one who took Jesus to India was an Indian yogi who at the time of the birth of Jesus was visiting in Persia and Mesopotamia.

It is certain that Jesus was deeply imbued with both the spirit and the method of a part, at least, of the Eastern Wisdom. So far as his own words can be separated from the mass of additions and other changes made in the record, his entire life and words were in perfect harmony with the teachings of the Oriental Masters. Only one thing in his life differed radically from the method of the Saints—his doing of so many miracles. That is never done by the Saints although they have plenary powers to do them, and they can do whatever they like; but they do not believe it a wise policy to do them, except in rare instances.

16. Teachings Emphasized by Jesus

There are two things emphasized by Jesus which are also stressed by all the great Masters. They are:

(1) The vital importance of *love*, without which there can be neither wisdom nor religion;

(2) The immanence of the *kingdom of heaven*, which is to be found only within man himself.

These two great precepts are cardinal in the teachings of the Saints. Whether Jesus had ever contacted a real Saint in India or had met only yogis, is another matter. From his own life and words it would appear that he had as his masters only advanced yogis. But he returned to his own country and found people burning with enthusiasm and love. When he returned to Syria, he was more an Indian yogi than a Jewish prophet. He had picked up much of the teachings of the Magi in Mesopotamia and of the Pythagoreans in Egypt. He was not unacquainted with the philosophy of Plato and Aristotle. Being of pure heart and noble purpose, impelled by a very great love, he at once set to work healing the sick and preaching the good news of the immanence of the kingdom of God.

This heavenly kingdom was by no means a far-off thing to be realized after death, but a very present reality to be entered upon here and now. As masters of all countries and ages have taught, so Jesus too insisted that the people should immediately depart from the ways of sin, and look for the kingdom within themselves, not in heaven. But alas! His message was but poorly received and meagerly understood even by his own disciples, much less by the multitudes. They were quite unprepared for such lofty idealism, such refined perceptions. Least of all could they understand the main point in it—that the kingdom of heaven was a present reality to be known and entered upon in this life.

And it has always been so. Even today, among the most enlightened in the world, but few can grasp that sublime idea. They can imagine a heaven to which people may go after death, but when they are told that they can pierce the dark veil and enter upon that kingdom now while in the body, in full possession of their senses, they hesitate. Most of them set the whole thing down to an overwrought imagination. Yet this very thing was the heart and soul of the message of Jesus, as it has always been a cardinal point in the teachings of the Saints.

Here lies, in fact, the great stumbling block of all religions. They simply cannot believe it. They cannot imagine how anyone can possibly enter the kingdom of God while in the body. Only the Masters, differing from all churches and religions, offer a definite method and point to an exact Path by which the kingdom may be entered now. With them it is no theory, but a vital experience.

In the time of Jesus, the Jews specially looked for a temporal kingdom, and they prayed for a Messiah, a great warrior, who would deliver them from the Roman yoke and make them the rulers of the world. But Jesus spoke of a *kingdom inside of themselves,* which to most of them was rank nonsense. They were not interested in his fancies, impractical and subversive of all of their fond expectations. How could they be expected to break away the material crusts that bound their minds and look inside for a kingdom which they deemed only a mirage of an impractical dreamer? Jesus told them that the great kingdom was closer than hands or feet. But they turned away their incredulous ears. Jesus taught the Way, the Tao, the heavenly Bani, the Bhakti Marg, the Surat Shabd Path, but the people could not grasp it. Even his disciples scarcely comprehended. Jesus insisted on the divine Logos, the Word, which was the prime factor in all creation. But it went over their heads. He taught them as one having authority, and it only ruffled their feelings.

Naturally, his teachings brought Jesus into conflict with the authorities, especially the high priest and the Sanhedrin. His early death was a foregone conclusion. After the merest mockery of a trial, he was condemned to death on the cross, the most ignominious method of execution. The death sentence was approved, under a mild protest, by the Roman procurator, Pontius Pilate. At the last dark hour the prophet-yogi expired.

Just why he was forsaken at the last dark moment by God, in whom he had trusted, is still one of the profound mysteries remaining to be solved by the theologian. But to the Eastern science, the explanation is clear. He had assumed the bad karma of too many sinners whom he had healed, a radical departure from the method of all great Masters. It is a well-known law that if we do too much for people who have not themselves earned such favors, the giver must assume a part of the burden of the karma of the recipient. If you give a thousand dollars to anyone who has not earned it and who may misuse it, you yourself must be prepared to suffer the loss, not only of what you have foolishly given away but of a double amount in addition. Possibly you may suffer other penalties as well. Love must be given constructively.

The day dawned sinister and gray over the Judean hills. The streets of Jerusalem were packed with the mob assembled for the annual Passover. The noise and the clamor surged back and forth while a slow procession made its way toward the north gate. The condemned prophet was compelled to carry his own cross, but fell under its excessive weight, his face grimy with perspiration and dust. Lucky was that Cyrenian whom they forced to help bear the cross. Great his good fortune that he was selected for that service. Better for him than if he had ridden out of the city in a chariot escorted by Roman legions. How glad we think we would have been to render that service, to have stood by that wayside, lifting a portion of the heavy cross, perhaps also wiping the sweat and dust from his face—that face which had smiled with compassion upon so many sick and weary. I think it would have been a pleasure almost to have taken the nails in our own hands if we could have saved the noble one a single pain.

Over and over we have asked ourselves, why is it that the best friends of man have so often to suffer most at the hands of the ignorant mob? And then they drove the nails into his hands and feet—those hands which had so graciously dispensed food and health to those multitudes. Yet they crucified him, and they hung a thief on either side of him. Better the good fortune of one of those thieves, dying by the side of Jesus with a prayer on his lips— far better his good fortune than that of the high priest and the Roman Procurator. Dreary are the years to come for them when the Law shall demand payment in toiling up the long and rugged hills of time while bearing their burden of karma. Far better the fate of the thief dying by the side of Jesus with a prayer upon his lips.

Religious bigotry, ignorance and blind prejudice, fired by the five passions, know not the terrible fate of karma they weave for themselves. And so the gentle son of Mary died on the cross, but it would have been better for his murderers if they had not been born.

Jesus perished before his work was fairly begun. He left a bunch of ignorant disciples, poorly trained and bitterly disappointed. From the terrible shock, but few of them ever rallied. It does not appear that any of his disciples, except possibly Matthew and Luke, could have written the books attributed to them. The four Gospels themselves bear the stamp of Alexandrian influence, and one authority makes bold to declare that all four Gospels were written by Alexandrian monks three to four hundred years after the death of Jesus and his first disciples. There appears to be no certain knowledge on the subject. There is positively no contemporaneous history to support the story of the Gospels. To assume that they are true history, just because one wishes to believe them or has been taught that they are sacred scriptures, is to go around in a circle.

17. Paul, the Founder of Christianity

The Epistles of Paul belong in a different category. They were written much earlier than the Gospels. They exhibit an effort to remodel the old Mosaic system into a religion based upon Jesus as the sacrificial lamb. The ancient idea of bloody sacrifice prevailed in both. Paul now made an attempt to resuscitate the Jewish system, unite it with the stories about Jesus, and then combine them into a new religion which might possibly be acceptable to both Jew and Gentile. Of course, Jesus was slain for the sins of the whole world. This was the central theme. Judaism and Christianity could now combine in a reborn and rechristened world religion. The Jewish scriptures would find their fulfillment, and the disappointed followers of Jesus could rally around the new interpretation.

In this manner Paul founded a reconstructed Judaism, which went into history as Christianity. The pure spiritual philosophy of the Eastern Wisdom was submerged in a mass of dogmas which was neither Indian nor Jewish nor even Christian. It was neither

Egyptian nor Magian. Neither was it Platonian nor Pythagorean. It was neither spiritual nor material. It was neither sacrificial nor was it intellectual. It was nothing definite. It was made of a little of everything that had preceded it. Had it not been for the powerful organization of Rome first persecuting and then embracing it, it is doubtful if this strange mixture would have survived the age of mystic speculation in which it was born. That gentle spirit who so loved his people had wasted his pearls at the feet of ungrateful swine, and then died a victim of his own gracious energies. Had he followed the long-tried method of all the great Masters, that tragedy of history would not have happened.

We cannot here trace the history of the Church, nor can we go at length into the dogmatic theology of the creeds. For three hundred years the followers of Jesus met in secret places and quietly spread the doctrine of the redeeming blood of their crucified Master. At first stunned and rebellious at the unexpected death of their Lord, after they had so confidently looked forward to his kingship of the world following the destruction of the Roman power, they then rallied under the new stimulus.

Paul had explained the dark mystery. There was an old saying that it was fitting that one should die for the whole people. And the world has always adhered to that principle. Even so late as in old Mexico, human blood ran freely—they declared—"for the benefit of the whole people." It is the age-old doctrine of sacrifice which was made a part of the teachings of the Vedas. Sacrificial deaths had always been accepted as a matter of necessity: of course, Jesus had died for the sins of his people! Why had they not thought of that before? Now the death of Jesus found its justification and its rational explanation. After all, their faith had not been in vain. They had simply not understood the divine method. But now it was all clear. Although Jesus was their long-expected Messiah, he was, in a more vivid sense, their sacrificial lamb. He had died for the sins not only of the Jews but of the whole people, the whole world. This latter concept, however, was an enlargement upon the original idea. It was a generous expansion of the first idea, and this made the new faith a world religion.

To an uncultured and emotional people, this new appeal was

very powerful. With minds fixed upon the nail prints in his hands and feet, his disciples were ready to die in the name of the crucified. The doctrine spread until no inconsiderable portion of the Roman Empire were Christians. They were found even in the royal family. Many of them died for their faith, and yet their numbers increased until finally the religion was made official by the decree of Constantine in the early part of the fourth century. The climax of that evolution was the crowning of the head priest in Rome as the pope-emperor of all Europe. But by that time the religion of the Church bore but slight resemblance to the simple and pure spiritual philosophy of the prophet-yogi who gave it the initial impulse. Paul only needed Gregory the Great to set up his religion as the sole arbiter of human destiny, backed by the most powerful religious organization ever created. The religion which the empire had so bitterly persecuted now rose phoenix-like from the ashes of a burned and vanishing Rome, to set up for itself a throne of universal empire.

When Jesus came, there was no virile religion in the world. Paganism had already run its course, and most of the world was in a dream of moral and spiritual lethargy. It enjoyed its soothing ceremonialism and drank its wines with untroubled conscience. Spirituality was practically nil. In Greece the people had set up an altar to the unknown god. That was surely the climax of religious liberalism. The devotees of every religion found what suited them in the Pantheon. Only Greek philosophers could have thought of that. And they showed a keen sense of humor. The gods were for the mob and the old women. Let them each have the god he liked best, while the philosopher calmly looked down upon them from his serene heights of self-complacency. What could the mob know about philosophy anyway? Let them have their pet gods. There was no harm in it.

The spirit of the times was reflected in a remark made by Pilate when Jesus was brought before him. When the humble Nazarene spoke of bearing witness to the truth, the Roman asked, "What is truth?" *(John 18:38)*. And then turning away, as if he knew that no man could answer the question, he gave permission to murder the only man in the Roman Empire who could have told him what truth was.

If ever the world needed a spiritual teacher, it was at that time. In that hour of need the gentle son of Mary came, and they crucified him. Filled with wisdom and love, he had just returned from the Orient. He would have embraced the whole world, banished its pains and filled it with joy. It was like the beautiful dream of the Sakya prince. But they would not listen to him. They shut their eyes and cried out: "Away with him! Crucify him!" Love—mocked and crucified! Was there ever a sadder spectacle in all history? The heart that ached for his people was pierced by a Roman spear. Both Jew and Roman conspired to kill the best man in the Roman Empire. Such has always been the nature of religious bigotry and blindness.

18. The Substance of the Teachings of Jesus

What new thing did Jesus offer to the world? What was his special contribution to spiritual world-enlightenment? He gave nothing new to the world, but he did restate some of the old truths with such clearness and beauty that they went directly to the hearts of his people with the force of new truth. We may assume that he spoke from the conviction of personal experience because that is the only way that any man can speak with authority. There is no doubt but Jesus had personal contact with the Audible Life Stream. He had doubtless traveled inward upon it.

As said before, Jesus laid stress upon two points, viz.:

(1) The vital importance of love as the soul of religion,

(2) The immanence of the kingdom of heaven.

In these respects, the message of Jesus was in exact accord with the Eastern Wisdom, from which he had derived his inspiration. The dogmatic assertions of his disciples in later years need not concern us here. The following are a few of his most pertinent sayings, rich in moral and spiritual values:

Blessed are the poor in spirit; for theirs is the kingdom of heaven.

(Matt. 5:3)

Blessed are the pure in heart; for they shall see God. *(Matt. 5:8)*

One of the above sayings strikes the very keynote of the teachings of the Masters:

Blessed are the pure in heart; for they shall see God. *(Matt. 5:8)*

The Western world, as a whole, had never had the remotest idea of the real meaning of this statement. It means that anyone who is pure in heart is able to enter the kingdom of heaven consciously, during this lifetime, and there behold God clothed in light. Indeed, blessed are the eyes that behold such a sight! A clean mind and a pure heart are the prime necessities for such an achievement, and so teach all the great Masters of history. How this is to be done constitutes the main theme of this book.

Ye have heard how that it hath been said, Thou shalt love thy neighbor and hate thine enemy, but I say unto you, love your enemies, bless them that curse you, do good to them that hate you, and pray for them that despitefully use you and persecute you.
(Matt. 5:43,44)

For whosoever shall do the will of my Father which is in heaven, the same is my brother, and sister and mother. *(Matt. 12:50)*

Be ye therefore perfect, even as your Father which is in heaven is perfect. *(Matt. 5:48)*

Verily, I say unto you, Except ye be converted and become as little children, ye shall not enter into the kingdom of heaven.
(Matt. 18:3)

This is another vital precept of the Masters. No one is able to penetrate the evil until he rids himself of all vanity of the big 'I', and becomes as humble and self-forgetful as a little child. Again, a similar expression:

Whosoever therefore shall humble himself as this little child, the same is the greatest in the kingdom of heaven. *(Matt. 18:4)*

How often do the Masters emphasize the sweet humility which makes a strong man like a little child! Humility is one of the first essentials of citizenship in the kingdom of light.

> Then Peter came to him and said: "Lord, how oft shall my brother sin against me, and I forgive him? till seven times?" Jesus saith unto him: "I say not unto thee until seven times, but until seventy times seven."   *(Matt. 18:21–22)*

> "Master, which is the great commandment in the law?" Jesus said unto him: "Thou shalt love the Lord thy God with all thy heart, and with all thy soul, and with all thy mind. This is the first and great commandment. And the second is like unto it: Thou shalt love thy neighbor as thyself. On these two commandments hang all the law and the prophets."   *(Matt. 22:36–40)*

In this one statement of Jesus we have the summing up of his entire teaching. In all philosophy and religion there is nothing of any importance except love. If every book in the world were destroyed, every code of ethics, every sacred scripture—every printed line on earth—except this one quotation from the lips of the humble and loving Galilean, the world would still have all it needs as an ethical code. Its only other need would be a living Master to lead it into the inner kingdoms. There is nothing in the world that anybody needs, *except* love and a little food, clothing and shelter.

> This is my commandment, that ye love one another.   *(John 15:12)*

As if to impress this great law upon his disciples, he embodies it in one direct command. Here is the solution of all social problems—*love to God and man.* He who can measure up to this standard will be the ideal citizen of the ideal commonwealth in any age of the world.

Then Jesus gave to his disciples the supreme test of discipleship. As if he knew that many would live up to the great law, he gave them a definite criterion, a perfect measure, an infallible mark of discipleship, which should hold good in any day and age of the world, and in this regard it may well be accepted that Jesus speaks for all true Masters:

> By this shall all men know that ye are my disciples, if ye have love to one another.   *(John 13:35)*

We believe it safe to say that if the disciples of Jesus had lived up to this test throughout history, three-fourths of the world's population would today be Christians. And it is equally true now that if any other body or group of men and women would emphasize love as the sole law of their lives, living up to its ideals universally and unfailingly, that body—no matter by what name—would sweep the world like a prairie fire. This is the standard so urgently emphasized by all great Masters. It is almost unthinkable, incredible, that a man so filled with lovingkindness, and preaching and living a gospel of love, should himself be cruelly murdered by a blind mob of his own people. We believe there is nothing in the world so hellish as religious bigotry and blind fanaticism.

> Now ye are clean through the word which I have spoken unto you.
>   *(John 15:3)*

Here indeed is a puzzle to most thinkers. How can a word or a teaching make anyone clean? A more correct translation of that sentence is:

> Now ye are clean through the *word* of which I have spoken to you.

What is that Word? It is the supreme cleansing agent of this and all worlds. It is the all-purifying Audible Life Stream, mentioned in the first chapter of St. John as the prime Word out of which everything has emanated. That is what purifies the mind as nothing else known can purify it. This is taught by all the Masters. And all history is full of failures, for men have tried to purify the mind and gain spirituality without knowledge of this Current. When the disciple of any Master enters upon that Stream consciously, he is cleansed of every earthly impurity and made fit for higher worlds.

If ye abide in me, and my words abide in you, ye shall ask what ye will and it shall be done unto you. Herein is my Father glorified, that ye bear much fruit; so shall ye be my disciples. As the Father hath loved me, so have I loved you. Continue ye in my love. If ye keep my commandments, ye shall abide in my love, even as I have kept my Father's commandments and abide in his love. *(John 15:7–10)*

Here is a stumbling block to most Christians:

If ye abide in me, and my words abide in you, ye shall ask what ye will and it shall be done unto you.   *(John 15:7)*

It is only the science of the Masters which makes the meaning of this sentence clear, but very few Christians believe it true or possible of realization. Yet it is true that if any disciple lives up to the instructions of the Guru, the Master, and does the practice as the Master directs, abiding always in the love of the Master, steadfastly thinking of the Master and his words, very soon that disciple reaches the degree of development when his least wish or act of will is automatically fulfilled. Not only will he get whatever he asks for but he has only to will the thing and it is done. But how sadly had the Church lost the real meaning of these words! Words of infinite value, and yet so meaningless to most people. This again shows the familiarity of Jesus with the Eastern Wisdom.

A new commandment I give unto you, That ye love one another. As I have loved you, that ye also love one another.   *(John 13:34)*

This is only reiterating what he said earlier with so much emphasis. Yet again he repeats the divine admonition:

He that hath my commandments and *keepeth them,* he it is that loveth me: and he that loveth me shall be loved of my Father, and I will love him, and will manifest myself to him.   *(John 14:21)*

How clear is this; how identical with what all the Masters teach—that if any disciple loves the Master and practises what the Master teaches him, he will surely enter that kingdom of light where he will see the Master in his Radiant Form. And that is what Jesus meant when he said:

I will manifest myself to him.

The disciple will actually see the Master inside. This is one of the rewards for faithful practice. Anyone who has had that experience will tell you that there is no joy in this world so great as that which the disciple experiences when he first beholds the Radiant Master. It is the culmination of ages of struggle. It is the signal of victory in his long battle with mind and matter. He is then halfway to the end of all his labors for spiritual liberation. I know scores, even hundreds, of disciples of one great Master who daily sit in their own rooms in silent meditation, go into the inner realms, there behold their Radiant Master and converse freely with him. This is the manifestation referred to by Jesus. The Master always manifests himself to those who love him and walk in his light.

I am the resurrection, and the life: he that believeth in me, though he were dead, yet shall he live: And whosoever liveth and believeth in me shall never die.   *(John 11:25–26)*

This is literally true of all disciples of any Saint. To them there is absolutely no death.

The last enemy to be conquered is death.

To every disciple of a living Master, death is an occasion of rejoicing, for the liberated spirit simply steps out of the body as one would put off an old garment. Death utterly vanishes. It is finally conquered during the normal course of his development when the disciple learns to leave his body voluntarily to travel abroad in the higher regions. Thus, by entering the regions of so-called death while in full consciousness, with great joy, the fear of death disappears.

> If ye continue in my Word, then ye are my disciples indeed;
> and ye shall know the truth and the truth shall make you free.
>
> *(John 8:31–32)*

The full meaning of this passage can never be realized until, rising upon the life-giving Stream to the regions of truth, one crosses the threshold of the higher planes. Only then can anyone *know* the truth, and only when one knows the truth can he be free. Knowing the truth and attaining freedom are parts of one and the same process. Rising to higher planes liberates the soul as naturally as mounting to the skies in an airplane relieves one from the drudgery of walking on the ground.

> I am the light of the world: he that followeth me shall not walk in
> darkness, but shall have the light of life.   *(John 8:12)*

Every Master is the light of the world. He brings with him the light of the Eternal One. If anyone centers his attention upon the Master and walks in his light, there can be no more darkness in him. If the disciple opens the gates of light in himself, as the Masters urge him to do, he walks unobstructed into the kingdom of heaven. But he can do this only by the light of the living Master. It was this elementary truth which Jesus was trying to inculcate.

> Verily, verily, I say unto thee, Except a man be born again, he can-
> not see the kingdom of God.   *(John 3:3)*

Here again is an extremely important message which has remained in obscurity among Christians, although men continue to write books on it. It simply means being brought to light from the darkness, from ignorance to enlightenment, from blindness to sight, by the action of the creative Life Stream within. This will be explained more fully in the section which treats specially of the Shabd.

> Suffer the little children to come unto me, and forbid them not: for
> of such is the kingdom of God. Verily I say unto you, Whosoever
> shall not receive the kingdom of God as a little child, shall not enter
> therein.   *(Mark 10:14, 15)*

No one can possibly carry with him a load of vanity through the narrow gates of light.

> If ye had faith as a grain of mustard seed, ye might say unto this sycamine tree, Be thou plucked up by the root and be thou planted in the sea; and it should obey you. *(Luke 17:6)*

How well every yogi in the world knows the truth of this statement. Much more is this true of the great Masters. It can be done by every disciple of a great Master who has made even a little progress on the Path. No need of a series of mental gymnastics to dispose of this statement of Jesus. Accept it as it stands. Don't try to wriggle around it. It is a glorious truth. But the great trouble is that your churchpeople have all lost the method of realizing it. You have to go to a living Master to get that secret.

> There be some standing here, which shall not taste of death, till they see the kingdom of God. *(Luke 9:27)*

This latter quotation is given here for a special purpose. It is to show that Jesus expected his disciples, some of them at any rate, to enter the inner kingdom during their lifetime, just as all Masters expect their disciples to do. This definitely shows that Jesus was acquainted with the Sound Current and had a system of yoga which should enable them to go inside during this life.

The above examples of the teachings of Jesus will, we think, be sufficient to give their general import. His religion was smothered, almost in the hour of its birth, by its overenthusiastic nurses. Had not the life and teachings of Jesus been covered over by dogmas and superstitions, it might have been handed down for all time as an illustrious example of the Eastern Wisdom. Instead of that, a clever substitute was brought forward long after the days of Jesus and christened with much pomp and ceremony.

19. The Church Needs a Living Master

Concluding this discussion of the Christian religion, let us not lament the present-day loss of prestige suffered by the Christian churches. It is a good sign. It presages a day of increasing light. What the Church needs today is to rediscover its own Master, but the key to that rediscovery is in the hands of a living Master only. Will they go to him for it? Theological dogma, elaborate ritual and meticulous ceremony are no longer able to hold the attention of thinking people.

The loving Jesus himself is even today a brighter star in the firmament of thought than he was on the cross of Golgotha. To understand him as a real spiritual Master enables one to appreciate and love him; but to think of him as the theological prodigy of the Church is to make him impossible to comprehend. The light of his life shines with a luster not dimmed by time, if we can see it free from the theological rubbish. But it is a pity that he is not understood by his professed followers. They are quite unable to see him apart from his theological robes with which the Church itself has clothed him. He has now left this theater of action, and because he has left it, he cannot take new disciples. That work is in the hands of his successors.

Students must now turn to the living Master, who alone can initiate them and take them up to regions of light. If you have found solace in contemplating Jesus in your imagination, then place your destiny in the hands of a living Master, whom you can see and whose voice you can hear, and with whom you can walk on the Path of liberation. Come direct to the living Master, and he will show you the way. The gates will swing wide to him who gives the right knock.

Finally, permit me to say that you will never understand the life and teachings of Jesus until you come to a living Master. You may hold diplomas from all the theological schools in Christendom, but you will never understand the life and method of Jesus until you learn them from a living Master. If you wish to gain admission to that inner kingdom of light, so much stressed by that humble preacher of Galilee, you will gain it only by the science of the Masters under the direction of a living Master. But just so long as the Church hugs an ecclesiastical image of Christ, it will be extremely difficult to get it turned loose long enough to discover the real Christ.

Only this week I had a letter from a good missionary. The gist of his letter was that he had experiential knowledge of Jesus as his Lord, and that I could not have had any such experience or I would never have given him up. Therefore, I never was a real Christian. This letter shows two things: first, that the good missionary had been thoroughly saturated with the theological hodge-podge of St. Paul, and that has so colored his vision that he cannot see any other system; second, that he is basing his "experiential knowledge of Jesus as his Lord" upon his *feelings*. He has seen nothing, he has heard nothing, but he has had a lot of feeling. By a long course of suggestion through early and late teaching, he has a superinduced emotional attachment to an imaginary image, and that emotional attachment he calls his 'experiential knowledge'.

I have had the same experience. I am not speaking ignorantly of these things. Neither would I speak lightly of such an attachment. I know how much it means to those who still hold to it. I had all the feeling, all the emotional worship that I ever heard of anybody having. I was as thoroughly 'converted' as anyone. I preached Jesus as my 'crucified Savior' as earnestly and as sincerely as anyone could ever do. But after many years of study and critical analysis, I found that the whole system would not bear analysis, and that my own *feelings* were not sufficient proof of the reality of my faith.

Since then I have conversed with many men of different faiths, and I find that they all have feelings which they allege as proof positive of their religions. A devoted Moslem told me only recently that he "felt in his soul that the Prophet was with him daily and was leading him to the true God, Allah the Merciful." In Honolulu I talked with a very fine Englishman who assured me that "the spirit of the Lord Buddha was all-sufficient to guide him on the path of enlightenment." His inner feelings were to him proof positive that Buddhism was the best of all paths leading to spiritual regeneration.

As said before, it is perfectly certain that feelings are no safe guide. Anybody may have feelings in plenty, in proof of anything which they have imagined to be so. The only safe guide is to look for information which can be corroborated by three of the five senses: sight, hearing and touch. Then add emotional experiences to that, if you like. And this conviction is why I began to look for a Master whom I could see and hear and touch, and then he put me in line with a definite program during which I was taught to see and hear on the inner planes of light, quite independently of any feelings or emotions. It was then that I began to walk by sight and knowledge, not by faith alone. (I hope the reader will pardon this personal reference, but my missionary friend could not account for my change of faith except by challenging the genuineness of my former religion.)

The main point is that anything can be 'proved' by feelings. A dear devotee insists that she has experiential knowledge of her Savior. An equally devoted Moslem or Buddhist has the same 'experiential knowledge' of Mohammed or of Buddha. And what does it all mean? It means that feelings are not a reliable guide in such matters. Every religion has its devotees who are just as sure of their 'experiential knowledge'. On the Path of the Masters, however, the student enters the superphysical worlds of reality in full consciousness, even superconsciousness—more wide awake than he is upon this plane. There he beholds the Radiant Lord, he hears the enchanting music of those higher planes, he converses freely with his own Master upon that plane where deception is impossible, and there he comes to *know,* not believe. If he has been a Christian and is still devoted to Jesus, he has an opportunity, on those exalted planes, to meet Jesus in person and talk with him. And this is no emotional reaction. It is genuine 'experiential knowledge'.

Last of all, let it be kept in mind that no one has to give up his devotion to Jesus because he walks on the Path of the living Masters. By this Path, in fact, he becomes a far better Christian because he comes to understand the real Jesus instead of the man-made one. If a man objects that he cannot have two masters, we may say that no such claim is ever made by one who understands this Path. This writer has lived during the reign of five different British sovereigns. I may still have a feeling of admiration and profound regard for any one of those four who have gone.

I profess loyalty to the one who now occupies the chair so long as I am under the protection of his flag. But that does not imply that I am now devoted to five British kings. My relations, as a loyal subject, are with the one who is now living.

In like manner, we have to do only with a Master who is now living, or at least was living in the body at the time of our initiation. We cannot possibly have any relation with a Master whom we never saw, any more than we can now be a loyal subject to an emperor who has long ago passed from this plane of action. To be a loyal subject to the reigning emperor does not imply any disloyalty or lack of love and devotion toward the one who has gone. Neither does devotion to a living Master imply any lack of love for the departed Master. But in the very nature of the case, we can have no dealings with him, except that of loving memory, while we are on the earth plane and he is on some plane of the heavenly worlds above.

20. Theosophy

Theosophy (*Theos*, 'God', and *Sophos*, 'wisdom') is a system of religio-philosophical teachings, together with a certain degree of personal experience, which purports to be a summing up of a portion of the Eastern Wisdom. But it is based almost entirely upon the Vedas and other scriptures of ancient India. It does not deal at all with the science of the Masters. There can be no doubt that its leaders and founders had some knowledge of the Shabd, as may be seen in *The Voice of the Silence* and other writings of Theosophy, but the all-important fact of the real Santon ki Shiksha has been completely sidetracked by the bulk of Theosophical writings.

The system was founded by Madame Blavatsky and her coadjutors, Colonel Olcott and others, during the latter part of the last century. Theosophy claims to embrace all philosophy and religion, embodying all wisdom concerning God or spiritual matters. But in that regard it may be compared with the more recent movement called Anthroposophy—which claims to be a complete exposition of the sum of wisdom relating to man. Rudolph Steiner, the founder of the latter movement, discovered that all wisdom might not be couched in Theosophy, and he decided that if we could not know all about God, at least we might discover something more about man. This may be a less ambitious undertaking, but certainly a more practical one.

The world must acknowledge that Steiner has done much. It was an unhappy day for Theosophy when Steiner withdrew from it. But perhaps it was better for philosophy itself. Steiner was brought up as a careful student of the natural sciences. He was no impractical dreamer, as many have imagined him. He sought reality, however, through recognition of the spiritual in Nature. He was anxious that the vital connection between our common physical life and the occult should be known and recognized. By this means he hoped to enrich both the physical and the spiritual sides of human life.

Plato looked for truth in spiritual ideas and ideals, while Aristotle placed the emphasis upon truth as revealed in this world. It was the noble ambition of Steiner to combine the two and thus enrich them both. And this, we believe, was a decided step toward the ultimate solution. It appears a pity that the great movement of Theosophy, so auspiciously inaugurated, could not have had the advantage of Steiner's splendid personality and rare gifts to enable it to achieve a nobler destiny. As it was, that organization lost its most brilliant member.

We do not believe that even the Theosophists themselves would claim to have discovered a perfect science of God, any more than Steiner would claim to have developed a perfect knowledge of man. And there is no doubt but both have contributed somewhat to European understanding of many occult truths. If the Theosophists had developed a perfect science of God, then we might all adopt the policy of Omar when he ordered the Alexandrian library to be burned. If they disagreed with the Quran, they were pernicious. If they agreed with the Quran, they were superfluous. Therefore, why encumber the ground with them? Let them be burned.

Theosophy's main precepts are:

(1) The underlying principle that the manifest universe is the only way or means by which the Supreme One can be known; that the Supreme One embraces all, is infinite, eternal and unchangeable.

(2) That divine and universal principle manifests itself as man on this plane; then the individual man attains his evolution by successive reincarnations under the law of karma.

The system is taken mostly from the literature of the East, and may be said to embrace the best there is in the Vedas, the Shastras and the Puranas. In fact, Theosophy is an attempt to formulate the teachings of the Vedas in modern language, adapted to the requirements of the Western civilizations.

(3) The unity of all life-consciousness runs through the Theosophical discourses. Theosophy does not accept metemphychosis. This appears to be a concession to European sensitivity on the subject. But metempsychosis cannot rationally be separated from karma and reincarnation. It is a third leg to the tripod.

Theosophy speaks with apparent authority concerning 'the Great White Brotherhood', who make their headquarters in the depths of the Himalayas. That is said to be the governing body not only of the Theosophists but of the Rosicrucians also. Its functions are said to extend to the spiritual government of the whole world, while keeping a vigilant eye upon the physical aspects of world evolution. Its hierophants, arhats, bodhisattvas, mahatmas, lords, etc., all busy themselves chiefly in world betterment. They are said to control the stream of evolutionary influence among all races and nations. To what extent this claim is justified by the facts, we are not called upon to say. The policy of all great Masters has been from the beginning, as it is now, not to judge others. That this brotherhood and all similar organizations have their mission to perform, beneficial to mankind, may not be doubted. Also, that their mission is identical with that of Krishna, as stated in the Gita, may not be questioned. This fact definitely places them.

The visible headquarters of the Theosophical Society are in Madras. Annie Besant was the guiding genius of the Society for

many years. Bishop Leadbeater and others have written volumi-
nous expositions of its doctrines and methods of operation. There
was a time in the history of this writer's study when he regarded
the teachings of Theosophy as the best summing-up of the Eastern Wisdom. But that was before he knew anything about the
real Masters and their science. Yet there can be no doubt but
that Theosophy is a decided step forward in spiritual knowledge
as it is generally available to Western students. It is a pity it stops
so early in its work of marking out the Path, and it is a greater pity
that it has no readily accessible Masters. It is but little comfort to
a hungry soul crying in the wilderness to be told that in some
distant day, if he works hard enough and lives long enough, he
may be granted a momentary glimpse of some of the great ones.
If a man feels the need of a living Master now, he will cry in vain
to the noble hierarchy in their snow-covered Himalayan retreats.

One word more may be said here concerning the stated purpose of the Great White Brotherhood. They claim that their most
important work is to guide the world in paths of peace and righteousness, in other words, to so regulate the destinies of mankind
as to make always for world betterment. This is certainly a laud-
able aim, and doubtless many great souls believe they are doing
the noblest and most unselfish service when so engaged. But in the
light of the Masters' teachings there is seen to be a very grave misunderstanding concerning world betterment. World betterment
is no doubt a good thing to keep in mind. It is a noble incentive
for work, but as a matter of fact it is but little more than a fond
delusion.

Permanent world betterment can never be accomplished
during the present world cycle. The world will improve slowly
from now on, but this improvement will not come about by any
human effort. The change will come by means of a greater spirituality being diffused through the whole human race, as the new
Golden Age approaches. But there is very little that any of us can
do to speed its coming. And yet, of course, we should continue to
do all in our power, if only for our own sake. Philanthropy is its
own reward. It registers good karma in all who devote themselves
to it. It cleanses the mind and purifies the heart. But we should

never forget for one moment that our chief concern is to seek our own spiritual evolution. This is so for two reasons: first, because we can do but very little for others until we ourselves are qualified; second, self-improvement is what we are in this world for—it is our first duty, our most sacred obligation.

All these facts are well known to the Masters; therefore, they do not waste their time in premature efforts at world betterment. The great Saints work on individuals, rather than masses, aiming to remove them forever from this 'wheel of eighty-four' instead of trying to improve the prison in which they now live. In these material regions, sorrows, pains, disease, death, and what men call evil, are all inevitable. They can never be eliminated entirely from earthly life. In the Golden Ages these evils are reduced to a minimum, but they are inherent in material regions. The great Saints, knowing this, propose to remove souls from this region forever instead of trying to improve their conditions. That exalted world of light to which the Saints take us is infinitely above and beyond Triloki, or the three worlds, known to the Great White Brotherhood. Those superheavens are known only to Saints and their students, who are themselves on the way to becoming Saints.

The mission of the Great White Brotherhood, as declared by themselves, is identical with that of Krishna as stated in the Gita, namely, to destroy wickedness and establish righteousness. There is therefore a perfect fellowship and unanimity of purpose between Krishna and the Brotherhood. But the far higher mission of the Saints is to remove souls forever from the regions of evil. If you find a child stuck in a mud hole, wouldn't it be better to pull him out of the mud hole, clean him up and take him home, rather than engage all of your energies in cleaning up the mud hole itself, while the child is left in the mud?

And so, this constitutes the chief difference between the mission of the Saints and that of mahatmas of other grades.

One of the great difficulties now with Theosophy lies in the fact that if a neophyte goes to one of their representatives to ask for a definite method of yoga by means of which to rend the veil and enter the inner kingdoms, he gets a reply couched in vague allusions and indefinite postponements. Its Masters are too difficult to approach. But any man who comes from the four corners of the earth to see a real Master may walk right up to him, sit down and talk with him face to face. That is a very vital difference to a hungry student. How earnestly did this student knock at the Theosophists' doors, only to be told that if he worked and waited long enough, it was just possible that someday he might be granted a glimpse of one of the great ones. But when he arrived from America and sat down at the feet of one of the greatest of Saints, he was welcomed with love and full instructions.

Of course, this is not intended as a criticism. Theosophy is simply a different method. Let each carry on according to his own plans. But it is the extreme good fortune of any man who finds a Saint, a real spiritual Liberator, instead of a world builder. Constantly referred to in Theosophical literature, the 'masters' sit serenely in their far-off Himalayan retreats and offer but little comfort to beginners. At best, the chances of ever advancing to full fellowship with those august beings are quite remote; they are neither tangible nor visible. When a student is struggling hardest with his own complicated problems, he is told by some outpost subordinate of those exalted ones to just go on struggling. If he wins the battle, he may ultimately be granted the boon of the mahatma's *darshan*.

But how different when the weakest and the poorest may come and sit down at the feet of the Great Master, look into his eyes and receive his fatherly encouragement! Priceless pearls of wisdom fall from his lips, free to all who can receive them—no guesswork, no dark uncertainties, no vague hopes, no long waiting and wondering. The great Father simply takes his children home, wrapped in a mantle of light.

But there is something of still greater importance to the student, even if he succeeds in gaining the darshan of the Theosophical masters. Theosophy has not grasped the full import of the Audible Life Stream. Yet that is the most vital of all considerations. It is alluded to in *The Voice of the Silence* and some other literature. But its great importance is not brought out. This great central fact so vital to the student is covered over by a mass of details, which has but minor value, if any at all. Neither does

Theosophy introduce you to a living Master who is able to 'tune you in' with the great Life Stream. Yet this is the main precept of the Masters. Nowhere in all the Theosophical literature is that central fact of Nature set before the aspirant as the *sine qua non* of spiritual attainment.

Many people talk loudly and write voluminously about mind control. Yet they know absolutely nothing about the most important factor in mind control. The Saints tell us, and many of us know by personal experience, that mind control is never accomplished except by and through the Shabd, the Audible Life Stream. Indian history is full of instances of noble yogis who sat in meditation, even for centuries, striving after mind control, but failed at last when confronted by temptation.

Far back in an early age, one great rishi, Vishvamitra, is said to have sat for several thousands of years, and then, all of a sudden one day, he fell for a pretty girl. He had tried to control his mind by negation. But it cannot be done. The mind must have something which it likes better, or these worldly temptations will invariably sweep one off his feet. Any system which does not make the Surat Shabd Yoga the central portion of its scheme in spiritual exercises can never withstand the downward drag of mind and matter, with its numberless appeals to the senses. And what is still more important, without the Shabd the student cannot go far on the road of spiritual liberation. That is the great oversight of Theosophy, as it is of all other religio-philosophical systems.

Finally, the highest goal of Theosophy falls short of the objective of the Saints. According to their own literature, the greatest of Theosophical 'masters' go no further than the first, or possibly in a few instances the second, station of the Saints. This is only a beginning on the Path of the Masters. It is apparent then that where Theosophists stop, the Saints begin their upward journey. From that point they proceed to the highest planes, and to the highest individual achievements. The mahatmas of Theosophy, great and noble as they are when judged from the viewpoint of ordinary men, are only beginners when compared with the great Masters. This is not a matter for disputation or argument. It may be determined in the most scientific manner by personal sight and hearing.

Attach yourself to one of the great Masters; then go inside and see for yourself. On the inner planes all things are made clear. Masters of the lower order do not even know of the supreme heights attained by the Saints because they themselves have never gone that far. They generally imagine that they have gone to the highest regions when they reach Brahm Lok, the second region on the Path of the Masters. In that respect they are like the followers of the Gita and the Vedas. This is because they are not able to go further than Brahm Lok without a real Master to take them. They believe also that Brahm is the supreme deity of all. For the Theosophical masters themselves the assumption may work out very well, but for their students it is extremely unfortunate.

21. Christian Science as a Religion

Christian Science is one more of the considerable number of offshoots from orthodox Christianity. There are vastly increasing numbers who realize that modern Christianity is not the genuine teaching of Jesus. Loathe to give up the Christian system altogether, yet imbued with the scientific spirit of the age, great numbers of conscientious Christians have sought some sort of reconciliation. Mary Baker Eddy, a brilliant student, began to study, write and lecture on what she regarded as a reconstructed Christianity. She built up her system—perhaps unconsciously—upon the law of suggestion, and gave it the catchy name of 'Christian Science'.

Her idea appeared to be to combine the essential elements of the Christian religion and then infuse the compound with a wholesale decoction of modern science. She recognized, as many religious thinkers realize today, that any religion which appeals to the emotions alone, depending upon them for the renovation of character without satisfying the intellect, cannot long endure. If she could offer a religious system acceptable to modern thought, adapted to modern needs, it would be the greatest boon of the age. It was a noble conception. Her system was a heroic attempt to bridge the old gap between religion and science, to mollify their warring antagonisms.

The new doctrine spread rapidly. Many of the most intelligent and awakened people of America embraced it gladly. It was a distinct advancement and, had it not been for the new system itself falling into philosophical niceties, that system might have led its votaries out into the light, ready to follow a real Master. Alas! It would be difficult now to say which of the two, the dogmatic theology of the Church or the metaphysical postulates of Christian Science, is the more difficult for the intellect to accept.

Of course, one of the most virile and appealing tenets of the new faith was its emphasis upon the healing of bodily ills, at once and without medicines. Its amazing record of cures cannot be doubted by any honest investigator, although a very considerable percentage of them were not permanent. (Neither are the cures of doctors always permanent, any more than those of Christian Science.) But some were permanent.

The system still adheres to Christ as the great healer of disease. Christian Scientists do not agree that their cures are made through mental forces acting under the law of suggestion. Jesus is still the healer. In grappling with the age-old problem of sin and evil versus a good God, Christian Science tried to escape from one horn of the dilemma only to be impaled upon the other. The new doctrine denied the very existence of evil, insisting that evil was no more than a delusion of the carnal mind. *All sin, all pain, sickness, all evil of every sort, are only mental illusions*. But since evil seemed to be tied up with matter in some sort of inseparable connection, it became necessary to do away with matter itself in order to get rid of evil. Evil was only the darker side of matter, and matter itself was only an aberration of mind, a dark phantasmagoria, incidental to this mortal existence.

Thus Mrs. Eddy made a clean sweep of the entire problem, and it was doubtless a master stroke if only it could have found place in rational thought. There is neither evil nor matter. Still people kept on believing that they had bodies, and what was worse, they continued to feel pain in those bodies—even Christian Scientists themselves. How could they get rid of that? Mrs. Eddy replied that since neither matter nor evil existed, pain could not exist, even if you did feel it. What people believed to be pain, the thing they longed so to get rid of, was only another delusion of the mortal mind. If there were no body, it was clear that there could not be any pain in that body. The pain was only a small delusion within a big delusion. That was logical enough.

Logically it should have been clear sailing from that time on. When confronted by bodily sickness, or what people persisted in feeling as such, the calm practitioner simply told her patient that she had nothing at all but a mental illusion. Drop it. Forget it. The prescription was simple enough. Just correct your thinking, and evil automatically disappears. It was a beautiful theory, and it seemed to work in some cases. But people kept on getting sick and dying, Christian Scientists as well as others. Even Mrs. Eddy herself had to pass the same way as all others. She couldn't entirely dispose of the errors of her mind.

There is still a powerful appeal in the system. Suffering humanity will grasp eagerly at anything which offers relief. Incidentally, it offers one of the most serious indictments of medicine. If medical therapy were as efficient as its advocates claim, Christian Science would probably never have come into existence. If religion and physical therapeutics can be combined in one palatable dose, what more can anyone ask? Its religious aspect is but little more than a new attempt to restate orthodox Christianity in practical terms. Christian Scientists have been quite too busy with their healing work to think much about theological problems. Anyway, those problems have only a remote interest for them.

The student of first principles will ask what the key is to that large measure of success which Christian Science has enjoyed. As said before, the answer lies in the well-known laws of suggestion. Mind is the greatest power operating in this physical universe— mind activated by spirit. Of course, all mind is vitalized by spirit, but once activated by spirit it is mind that controls all physical forces through Prana, the primary force.

Mind is the chief instrument of spirit for all contacts with the physical universe. Mind has its methods of operation. In what is called the subconscious reservoir of mind, there lies an almost limitless store of energy. If by any means that reserve power can be made available for our use, there is practically no limit to its scope of action. It has been found that by and through suggestion, the conscious mind may draw upon the subconscious for its reserve power. Christian Science offers a method of applying that power to human needs. If the conscious mind can be made to accept the dictum that there is a power available to remove pain and cure disease, beneficial results must follow.

But the new system added one more factor to the healing process. It taught that this latent power did not reside in all men to be drawn upon at will, but it was given by the Lord on occasion. If we have faith, the power comes when we offer the proper prayers. This appealed to the religious sentiments. Many people to this day have no idea that it is simply a method of suggestion and auto-suggestion. They firmly believe that they are healed by direct intervention of the Lord. And so this is the explanation of that considerable degree of success which has attended the spread of Christian Science. It is also the key to the success of all other healing cults and systems, no matter what their names, including 'New Thought' and the much-lauded 'Oxford Movement'.

Christian Science has been so preoccupied with its own reforms and especially with the healing of the sick, that it has had but little time to devote to the major problems of the soul. Every soul hungers for its release from this region of 'mental illusions'. We all have had enough of them. We are more than 'fed up' with them. It may be accepted as a metaphysical apperception that there is no body, and therefore no pain or disease. It may be conceded that all of these things are only errors of the mind—misled and troublesome mind—yet the great majority of people do not seem to enjoy their illusions. They are still looking about for some means to get rid of them. They would like so much to find some means of escape.

But now, after many decades of trial, Christian Science offers no escape. The world is right where it was before Mrs. Eddy was born. Twenty-six centuries ago the noble Buddha thought he had discovered a method of escape from sorrow by pointing out the cause of sorrow. But nothing happened and sorrow went on, like the flowing of rivers. Now Christian Science tries to get rid of it by denying its existence.

Still the whole world goes around seeking a pill to stop its pain. What is the trouble? I have myself seen many good Christian Scientists crying piteously for an anodyne. What is wrong? The old discrepancy between theory and fact. Cures come and cures go but human ills go on for ever. And they will go on. The new system has done nothing at all to provide for the future happiness of mankind when they pass the gates of death. The new system is an excellent ethical society. It inculcates clean living as well as clean thinking. But it has nothing superior to the old church dogmas to offer to the dying man.

When it comes to a study of that kingdom of heaven spoken of by all the Prophets and Masters, *Science and Health* has not a single new suggestion to offer. In this respect it drops to the common level of all religions. Humanity is left to its eternal awaga-wan, its endless coming and going, desolate and weary, to go on nursing its 'mental illusions', while the ages come and go. It is only the science of the Masters which offers the certain Way of liberation from all woes and all illusions.

22. Modern Spiritualism

This movement can hardly be called a religion. Yet in recent years it has built churches and appointed ministers. Its central theme is the *medium* and some sort of communication between this world and the superphysical planes. If we set aside 90 percent of the findings of modern Spiritualism as unreliable, still there are enough authenticated facts to prove its hypothesis. The International Society for Psychical Research offers data to satisfy the most incredulous. If a single well-authenticated communication between this world and that of disembodied spirits can be established beyond all possibility of doubt, then the fundamental hypothesis of the materialists is forever swept aside. And yet not only one instance, but thousands of them have been given. In this regard modern Spiritualism has justified its existence.

That movement has proved conclusively, incontrovertibly, as fully as any fact of science has ever been proved, that the death of the body does not terminate the existence of the intelligence which occupied that body. From its vast accumulation of data, the Society for Psychical Research has made substantial contributions to knowledge. The movement has thus given to mankind a certain assurance which nothing else has ever given on such a large scale. The public consciousness, while recognizing the service which Spiritualism has rendered, yet hesitates to approve of it because it recognizes that Spiritualism is not free from serious defects. The phenomena may be acknowledged, but Spiritualism's methods are not above criticism.

It is well known to students who have become familiar with the seance performance that many serious evils accompany the practice of mediumship. It is no argument to say that such evils are not the legitimate results of mediumship but are due to the abuse of it. The fact remains that evils of a grave sort do attend the practice of mediumship. And the worst disasters fall upon the medium herself. This alone is sufficient to condemn the practice. The knowledge gained through mediumistic process may be desirable, but that knowledge is gained at too great a sacrifice. Moreover, it can be gained by a better method unattended by any harm to anybody.

Far superior information may be gained by the independent method of the Masters, with no untoward results to anyone. In fact, becoming a medium is not a 'development' in any sense of the word. It is the exact antithesis of development—it is a decided disintegration, a deplorable degeneration, an absolute loss. But the method of the Masters, while proving vastly more than Spiritualism ever can prove concerning the higher worlds, at the same time leads to the most splendid development in all that raises the inferior man to the exalted status of the superman. If anyone wishes to follow this subject, he may profitably read *The Great Psychological Crime* by John E. Richardson, at that time known as T. K. This book certainly shows in the most conclusive manner the destructive nature of hypnosis and mediumship. It should be read by every student of the phenomena of mediumship and hypnotism.

While the Eastern Wisdom universally condemns mediumistic control as a bad thing and a decidedly unreliable method of getting messages from the dead, yet the findings of Spiritualism generally coincide quite accurately with the teachings of the Masters—as far as those findings go—but they are generally extremely limited in their scope. The knowledge gained through mediumship seldom goes beyond the outskirts of the intermediate regions between the earth spheres and the very first region of the Masters, that is to say, the pure astral. Hence, the revelations made through mediums are extremely limited.

Contrary to the teachings of the Masters, Spiritualism persists in the fond belief that mediumship is a 'gift'. But in fact it is a terrible loss. Richardson shows in the most incontrovertible manner that the greatest crime which can be committed against individual intelligence is to deprive that intelligence of the right and power to control itself. It is a distinct humiliation, a decided degradation, to reduce the medium to the level of only an 'instrument' to be played upon at will by some other intelligence.

The real Master is never an instrument. He is never a medium. He enters the spiritual regions on his own right and by his own powers. He is never controlled. He has nothing to do with 'controls'. He controls himself. He sees and hears whatever there is to see and hear, independently and freely. There is not the slightest element of subjection in the process of Mastership. It is the exact opposite. All his faculties and powers are unfolded and strengthened, and they remain always under his own sovereign will. This constitutes the essential difference between the subjective process of the medium and the independent method of the Master.

Someone may raise the objection that the Masters exercise subjective control over their disciples. But this objection is due to a very serious misunderstanding of the facts. It is true, we speak of perfect obedience to the Master. But that does not imply that the

Master exercises arbitrary control over the disciple. The Master never controls his disciple except by love. He very seldom, if ever, gives a command. He generally offers advice, and he does that in the most unassuming manner. It is a fundamental law among all Masters, even among good yogis, that the disciple must be left wholly free to exercise unhindered his own powers. If the Master can ever be said to rule at all, he rules with love, not with authority. The slightest wish of the Master is law to the disciple; but that is because he loves the Master, and also because he knows that the Master is always right. It is a fact, as every advanced disciple of a Saint will attest, that there is no such thing in this world as *perfect freedom* for anyone *unless and until he learns to follow a real Master.*

One other subject should not be overlooked in this connection. While the medium seldom goes beyond the very lowest planes of the subastral regions, yet that is not even the beginning point of the upward penetration of the higher worlds by the Masters. Hence, mediums know absolutely nothing about the pure spiritual regions and, in fact, they very rarely contact even the pure astral zones. Their fields of operation are far below that. Their activity is generally limited to the subastral regions or what may be termed 'the magnetic fields'. These lie just above the physical world, and yet far below the purely astral.

In those lower regions it is generally a lower order of spirits which are contacted by the mediums. We believe, and we have good reason to assert, that no high-level intelligence, such as any of the great and noble characters of history, ever come back to communicate through mediums. Therefore, when some spirit claims to be Socrates, or Abraham Lincoln, it is better to dismiss the matter at once. It is only a pretense of some designing intelligences, floating about the lower magnetic planes connected with the earth and who wish to attach themselves to mediums or sitters, or who wish to have some fun at the expense of people who cannot detect their fraud. It is a most pathetic thing that the medium is not in a position to save herself from such imposition. She can see and hear only what her controls wish her to see and hear—nothing more. She is in no sense independent.

When some fond mother is supposed to come and communicate with her family, gives advice and messages of love, such advice should be taken with extreme skepticism. When a medium is led to believe that a mother or father or some noted historical character is her guide or her 'master', such a claim should be set down as false. *No real Master ever works through a medium.* It is quite unthinkable. Nor does any other highly developed spirit ever use a medium. Such a thing is quite impossible. He knows that such a process is wrong. But when we are told that some American Indian is one of the guides, we may accept that as a possible fact. In truth, this is one of the most common of all such procedures. But just how much is their communication worth? If you were seeking advice on some of the most important concerns of life, would you go to an ignorant person for such advice? Certainly not. And do not imagine that because the person has passed to some of the lower superphysical planes, he has thereby acquired vast stores of knowledge which he is anxious to communicate to you. The only difference between a dead person and a living one is the simple fact that the dead one has laid aside his physical body. He has neither gained in wisdom nor improved in character by the change.

Aside from its contribution to the knowledge of survival after death, Spiritualism has but little to offer. Its findings only confirm to some extent the teachings of the Saints. In fact, Spiritualism is a sort of echo, a distant echo, of the old Tantric teachings, with some additions. But the system lacks the exalted idealism of the Eastern Wisdom. It lays its stress upon phenomena, instead of the unfolding of spiritual powers and increase of wisdom. It wants to develop mediums instead of Masters. In fact, it lacks utterly the method for the development of Masters. If it had such a method, it would never tolerate mediumship. Instead of going inside and witnessing real phenomena, as Masters do, it prefers to bring the phenomena outside where it can sell the show for a dollar per seat. (It is only fair to the better sort of Spiritualists to say that such things are not approved of by them. In case of honest mediums who never sell their services, but who firmly believe that they are serving humanity, we commend their motives but deplore their methods.)

Spiritualism lacks the lofty vision of the yogi. His calm self-abnegation is quite unknown to the average medium. And no medium has any increase of natural powers. He suffers a distinct loss of his powers, just in proportion as he falls a victim to the control of others. In all cases, the medium is quite helpless to distinguish between the true and the false. He sees and hears only what his controls wish him to see or hear. Not infrequently mediumship ends in total moral bankruptcy, and occasionally in the insane asylum.

It will be seen that while both Spiritualism and Mastership arrive at the same conclusions regarding the persistence of the consciousness beyond the death of the body, they have very different methods of arriving at their conclusions. The one class—the Masters—work by a normal, natural method, a constructive method, resulting in genuine development and vast increase of wisdom and powers; yet the other class—the mediums—fall victims to the most destructive psychological process which has ever been invented by the Negative Powers to mislead men. The method of the Masters is independent *and constructive*, while that of the mediums is wholly subjective and decidedly destructive.

23. The Rosicrucians

The Rosicrucians are a society of occult students said to have originated in Germany in the fifteenth century. It is now a worldwide organization with headquarters in San Jose, California. Like Theosophy, it has derived most of its tenets from the Vedas. It has its system of meditation and promises its students inner light. In this regard it goes beyond many other systems. Just how effective this yoga may be, we cannot speak definitely, except to say that after two years of faithful practice of these methods, no noticeable value was discovered by this writer. Perhaps it was my own fault. However, looked at now in the light of my experience upon the Path of the Masters, the Rosicrucian system cannot be exalted very highly.

The Rosicrucian Brotherhood claims allegiance to the same Great White Brotherhood as do the Theosophists. Whether it considers itself a twin sister to Theosophy is not clear; but if so, one of the twins was born a long time after the other. Theosophy is still in its infancy when compared with the mature years of Rosicrucianism. To choose between them presents much the same problem as that which confronted the young man who had to decide which of the twins he would marry. He finally decided he would leave them both alone. Since he could not tell them apart, complications might develop in the future.

These two great organizations are both good. They have both done a noble service. But this writer, after years of courting the two, trying to understand them both, finally decided that he had better look for an outstanding system which had no rivals. But this he never found until he met the Great Master. After that event, all other religions and philosophies took their places in the background. The science of the Masters has no rival. Once it is known, all other systems are seen in their relative importance, just as a candle loses its value at the rising of the sun. Yet in the absence of the sun, the candle may be very useful.

The most serious defect of the Rosicrucian system, like that of its sister Theosophy, is its lack of a real, living Master to whom the student may go. Its literature says much about masters, hierophants, mahatmas, arhats, as a caterer would speak of choice salads; but he doesn't produce them. Most of these 'masters' lead an elusive life far beyond the busy haunts of men, in the silent depths of the Himalayas. But when an anxious student inquires just how he may find one of them, he is told that no ordinary sinner may approach their serene highnesses.

The case is much the same as with a man who is very sick and is told that the great physician is so occupied with important matters that he cannot see an ordinary man. But if he can hold out until he is well and strong, he may eventually be permitted an interview. Of all men in the world who are sick and weary, it is the sinner, the struggling soul down in the depths, who needs the strong hand of the Master. Both Rosicrucians and Theosophists promise the student that someday, if he lives long enough and works hard enough, he may get a glimpse of one of these great ones.

Once I wrote to a man who claimed to have spent years with some of the Indian Masters. I asked him how I could find one. He replied: "When ye have gained perfect self-mastery, ye are then in the presence of the Masters."

There is no doubt about the technical accuracy of this reply. Sending out his 'wireless' vibrations to the whole world, that calm and passionless mahatma, who sits serenely in his Himalayan retreat, may do some good, but what I wanted was a living Master, who would give me some personal attention.

I was not much interested in world vibrations just then. I wanted a living Master whose face I would see with these physical eyes, whose cheering voice I could hear, whose gracious hand I could take in mine. There is no doubt but Rosicrucianism is in touch with some of the remnants of ancient yogism, floating more or less loosely through many lands. But as a teacher of successful yoga it does not appear to offer much. That is so because it lacks the clear markings of a definite path to attainment, and it lacks a living Master to guide one. This writer speaks from personal experience, not hearsay, just as he speaks from personal experience concerning the Path of the Saints.

One fact should make the discerning student pause and think—if he should be able to attain all that the most advanced representatives of Rosicrucianism claim, it is even then but a mere glimpse into the higher realities. It is only a beginning on the Path of the Saints. None of them go beyond the very threshold of the real kingdom of light. All this we are saying not to find fault, nor to disparage these organizations, but because it is much better for mankind if the facts are boldly made known by one who is in a position to know them. If any earnest student feels inclined to challenge these statements, let him come to a real Master for the proofs. He may have them in great abundance.

Let us give credit to these two organizations, as to all others, for the good they have done, and let us love them for it. But at the same time, let us recognize their limitations. Let us then seek a Path which has no limitations, and which leads to the very highest spiritual goal. A student who enters upon the study of a spiritual philosophy and selects a definite path should, if possible, know of a certainty that he is entering upon the main highway of the Masters and not upon some bypath. As a matter of fact, as anyone may prove for himself, if a student should gain all that is promised on any of these lower paths, even becoming one of their greatest mahatmas, he will still be only a beginner on the Path of the great Masters. Let us give them full credit, however, for their help to mankind. It would be a very great blessing indeed, if all men had attained a half of their development, a tenth of their wisdom and powers. Let no one be offended at this statement. It is made in humility and love, but it had to be made because great issues are at stake.

Everywhere men are seeking a Way, and with them all, the great question is to enter upon the main highway to the city of light and not to go astray on some other path, leading to a blind alley. It is doubtful if those great souls themselves know of the higher attainments of the Saints or of their higher Path, leading to regions to which the Masters alone have access. How many of earth's millions actually know of the regions attained by these mahatmas of the White Brotherhood? Likewise, there are millions who are now on the planes of the Brotherhood who know of nothing higher. But in any case, we are not to despise the matriculate because we ourselves have the degree of Master of Arts. We are all brothers and we are all striving as best we know.

One more point of importance may be mentioned here. It may help to explain the method of all occult brotherhoods, which operate differently from the Masters. The occult brotherhoods are not seeking to give their light to mankind. It is not their chief mission. They accept but very few disciples and these they train to become their successors. Their work is world betterment and not especially to liberate individuals from the world and its entanglements. However, the work of the great Masters or Saints is to take people up and out of this world to a better world. The world-uplifters come to destroy evil and establish righteousness. *The Saints come to take people to their eternal home.* Working alone—that is, without a living Master—as they have to do in all churches and occult societies, students can make but very little headway at best. Finally they must all slip back into the fatal rounds of births and deaths. From this ever-rolling wheel, no man can hope to escape without the help of a living Master.

24. The Jewish Religion

The Jews have a unique and peculiar history. Abraham, his son Isaac, and his grandson Jacob, were the founders of the Jewish religion. Abraham was Chaldean by birth, of the city of Ur. Ur was then noted for its philosophical speculations, its astrology and its occult sciences. Judaism was almost wholly borrowed, absorbed from the people among whom they lived. By them it was modified and reconstructed into what is now known as Judaism. The world does not seem to understand, especially the Christian world, that the Jewish religion was taken almost bodily from heathen religions. The Jewish religion is as much heathen as is Brahmanism. It was born out of heathenism. But from our viewpoint that is nothing to its discredit. Truth belongs to no race, class or country. It is universal.

The Jews were at first no more than Bedouin shepherd nomads, ranging the lands between Babylonia and Syria. Abraham had imbibed something of the Eastern Wisdom, we believe, and had combined that with a crude sort of sacrificial worship of his tribal deity, Yahveh, or Adonai. The earliest of the Jews were polygamous. Their religious exercises, like those of practically all of their contemporaries in every country, streamed with animal blood.

There seems to be something deeply rooted in human consciousness which has always led man to make bloody sacrifices. What is it? It is doubtless the subconscious recognition that sin must be atoned for, or in other words, that every debt must be paid. And that is nothing more nor less than the Indian doctrine of karma. Karma is only the practice of sacrifice reduced to a fixed law of Nature. Among the original tribes they could not generalize that much. They only felt that something must be done to pay off the debt. Reduced to its concentrate, the law of karma is nothing more than that.

Sacrifice in some form appears in the Vedas and is a concomitant of all early forms of religion. This amounts to an almost universal recognition of the stern fact that Nature demands full payment for everything. But the great mistake of man has been to imagine vainly that he can escape payment by any such trick or subterfuge as offering a sacrifice as a substitute, a payment by proxy. Early man tried to hoodwink Nature by a clever scheme of substitution. Only in the childhood of the race could such a thought ever have entered the human brain. By such a scheme men only deceived themselves. They certainly could not deceive Nature or the Lord of Justice. Not only did this naive plan fail to accomplish its purpose, but it also added to the guilt of the sinner. Instead of cancelling his debt, it doubled it. It worked backwards. By sacrificing an animal or a human being for the sins of the living, fresh sins were committed and more debt incurred. Instead of getting rid of past obligations, the sacrificer added to his debts. His load of karma grew heavier instead of lighter.

Abraham was a shepherd patriarch among the wandering tribes of Amorites, Chaldean in origin. But we are concerned here only with the Jewish religion. That religion is so mixed in origin that it is difficult to trace it. Before the Babylonian captivity, the religion was not very well defined. About six hundred years B.C., the Jews were taken to Babylon in virtual slavery. During the following seventy years, partaking of the culture and philosophy of their masters, they really became civilized. Before their return home, under the gracious patronage of Cyrus, they had become a very different people. And right here is a point of much historic significance, especially for Christians. Since the Christian religion was, and is, so completely a reconstructed Judaism, it must be of interest to know that Judaism itself was a reconstructed Babylonian cult. We may even go one step further back—the Babylonian cult itself was founded upon the teachings of the noble Persian, with some modifications. Thus by a direct line, the Christian religion, as it found its way into history, is but little more than a perverted Zoroastrianism with the name of Christ added as the sacrificial lamb. Sacrifice, except that of a pure and consecrated life, was no part of the teaching of Zarathustra. If Christian theologians and historians resent this statement, they may do well to examine the history more closely. In further proof of this statement, the pure and original orthodox Judaism will be found to resemble very closely the teaching of Zoroaster, as set forth in the Zend Avesta.

The Jews rebuilt their holy city, Jerusalem, and began a new life, stimulated by the culture, awakened by new ideals. For the first time in history, something like national unity cemented them into a people possessing manly attributes. Henceforth, three moral and political intoxicants stimulated Jewish activity: (1) The promise made to Abraham by Jehovah that he would exalt the Jews above all nations and give them world empire. All other nations should be under their feet. They were to rule the world. (2) Jehovah, whom they at first regarded as the greatest of tribal deities, was now proclaimed God of all gods, and finally he was promoted to be the one and only God. But this sublime apperception took centuries in growing to maturity. This idea then ripened into the conviction that the Jews were the chosen people of the one supreme God. (3) Finally, they conceived the inspiring notion that a great deliverer, a Messiah, would soon appear to lead the chosen people to a full realization of all that Jehovah had promised. This fond dream of world empire for the chosen people could not be realized any other way. But somehow Jehovah had either miscalculated or he had set his time for fulfillment too far away in the future. Even now, after three thousand years of weary waiting, there appears less and less likelihood that those promises will ever be fulfilled. National delusions are often endowed with very great longevity.

There is one thing about the Jewish religion which interests us here—the esoteric teachings of its sacred scriptures. In the Talmud and the Torah, from which the Pentateuch of the Bible was taken, there are traces of the teachings of the Eastern Masters. There is an esoteric meaning, they say, in every chapter (some claim, in every sentence), quite incomprehensible to the ordinary reader. Only the initiates could understand that deeper meaning. It wholly escaped the casual reader. Neither was it ever intended for them. The mob could not understand; yet the treasures must be preserved for the worthy. In that hidden teaching, there are many glimpses of the Shabd of the Indian Masters; also, a more or less clearly outlined method of concentration, by means of which the student could penetrate the inner kingdom of light.

It is a fact of supreme importance, which all men should bear in mind, that no system of ethics, no culture, no spiritual philosophy, no information concerning the inner kingdom, is of any value to the student *unless he is at the same time* provided with the means of entering that kingdom. But that is the great oversight of all religions. Only the science of the great Masters offers the definite means, the precise method. It is also known that there have been many prophets and sages among the Jews besides those mentioned in the Bible. Some of them were doubtless well advanced on the Path. Gradually, however, the Jewish faith, like all others in history, deteriorated into a formal and ceremonial institution dominated by a priesthood. Priestcraft, the great menace of history!

There is another point which we wish to make clear regarding the Jewish faith and its relation to the Path of the Masters. That is the very definite marking of the higher Path running through all of the old Jewish Scriptures. We have neither time nor space to trace that in detail. But we wish simply to call attention to it. Perhaps someone else may give it a more detailed study.

There is no conflict between ancient Judaism and the science of the Masters. The latter science simply carries the student further. For example, the Masters speak of the second region on the higher path, and they name it Trikuti. This is the Brahm Lok of the Vedas and the Gita. It is the highest world or plane known to ancient yogis or rishis. It is the supreme region today to practically all religions. In the old Jewish *Kabbalah* that plane was known as 'the Azilotic world'. The entire Kabbalah is replete with hints and references which cannot be understood, except in the light of the Master's teachings.

In the Kabbalah there are six distinct stages in the body and four above. This corresponds to the Vedic system, where there are six chakras below[1] and four in the superphysical regions—they are the sun worlds, the moon worlds, the lightning worlds, and finally the Brahm Lok, regarded by it as the supreme region. In the Kabbalah they are named from below up, Malcuth, Yesod, Hod, Tiphereth, Netzach, Gevurah, Chesed, Binah, Chocmah, and Kether. They are regarded as the ten manifestations of God, each with a name; in each of these regions, the deity takes certain qualities and is named accordingly. They are, in fact, ten different stages of the manifestation of the deity. These several stages are to be attained by meditation upon the corresponding centers.

Kether is the crown region, the supreme, where the soul unites with Eheyeh, attaining what the Hindus name Nirvana. At each of the stages upward, the soul gains certain virtues and powers, and realizes the deity in an ascending scale of glory from stage to stage. For example, in the highest region the soul realizes union with God. In Chocmah, he gains perfect wisdom, and understanding of the whole universe. In Binah, he gains understanding above ordinary men; in this region the deity is Yahveh Elohim. In Chesed, he is imbued with mercy as a chief virtue; in Gevurah, strength, severity, justice, law; in Tiphereth, beauty, harmony, rhythm; in Netzach, victory—God is known there as Jehovah Tzalaoth, the Lord of Hosts. In Hod he is glory, splendor; in Yesod, the foundation of all things, that out of which life flows. This corresponds to the generative center, the *indri chakra* of the Hindus. Last of all, the lowest, is Malcuth, meaning the inner kingdom, the lowest subtle plane, and it is there that the deity is seen as Adonai-ha-Aretz, the lord of the earth, which corresponds to Ganesh of the Hindus.

The mystical philosophy or theosophy of the Jews is called the Kabbalah.[2] The word is derived from the Hebrew *kabal*, signifying 'to receive', because it is the doctrine received from the

---

1. The six lower chakras are named in another section.
2. The following extracts are from the article "Kabbalah" in Albert G. Mackey, M.D., 33, *An Encyclopedia of Freemasonry* (New York: The Masonic History Company, 1921). Copied by Harvey H. Myers, Orange, California.

elders. The word has sometimes been used, in an enlarged sense, to include all the explanations, maxims and ceremonies which have been traditionally handed down to the Jews. But in that more limited acceptation, in which it is intimately connected with the symbolic science of Freemasonry, the Kabbalah may be defined to be *a system of philosophy which embraces certain mystical interpretations of scripture and metaphysical speculations concerning the deity, man and spiritual beings.* In these interpretations and speculations, according to the Jewish teachers, were developed the most profound truths of religion which, to be comprehended by finite beings, are obliged to be revealed through the medium of symbols and allegories.

"The Kabbalah was first taught by God himself to a select company of angels who formed a theosophic school in Paradise. After the fall, the angels most graciously communicated this most heavenly doctrine to the disobedient child of earth, to furnish the protoplasts with the means of returning to their pristine nobility and felicity.... From Adam, it passed over to Noah, and then to Abraham...Moses...David and Solomon.... No one, however, dared to write it down till Simon ben Jochai who lived at the time of the destruction of the second temple. R. Eliezer... then collated R. Simon ben Jochai's treatises and out of these composed the celebrated work called Zohar which is the grand storehouse of Kabbalism.

"The Kabbalah is divided into two kinds, the Practical and the Theoretical. The Practical Kabbalah is occupied in instructions for the construction of talismans and amulets and has no connection with Masonic science. The Theoretical Kabbalah is again divided into the Dogmatic and the Literal. The Dogmatic Kabbalah is the summary of the rabbinical theosophy and philosophy. The Literal Kabbalah is the science which teaches a mystical mode of explaining sacred things by a peculiar use of the letters of words and a reference to their value. Each of these divisions demands separate attention.

"I. *The Dogmatic Kabbalah.* The origin of the Kabbalah has

been placed by some scholars at a period posterior to the advent of Christianity, but it is evident, from the traces of it which are found in the Book of Daniel, that it arose at a much earlier day. It has been supposed to be derived originally from the system of Zoroaster.

"The Kabbalistic teaching of emanation is best understood by an examination of the doctrine of the Sephiroth.

"The Supreme Being, say the Kabbalists, is an absolute and inscrutable unity having nothing without him, and everything within him. He is called En Soph, 'the Infinite One'. In this infinitude, he cannot be comprehended by the intellect nor described in words intelligible by human minds so as to make his existence perceptible. It was necessary, therefore, that to render himself comprehensible, the En Soph should make himself active and creative. But he could not become the direct creator; because, being infinite, he is without will, intention, thought, desire or action, all of which are qualities of a finite being only. The En Soph, therefore, was compelled to create the world in an indirect manner by ten emanations from the infinite light which he was, and in which he dwelt.

"These ten emanations are the ten Sephiroth, or Splendors of the Infinite One, and the way in which they were produced was thus: At first, the En Soph sent forth into space one spiritual emanation. This first Sephirah is called Kether, 'the Crown', because it occupied the highest position. This first Sephirah contained within it the other nine, which sprang forth in the following order: At first a male, or active potency, proceeded from it, and this, the second Sephirah, is called Chocmah, or 'Wisdom'. This sent forth an opposite, female, or passive potency, named Binah, or 'Intelligence'. These three Sephiroth constitute the first triad, and out of them proceeded the other seven...Chesed, or 'Mercy'... Gevurah, or 'Justice'... Tiphereth, or 'Beauty'... and these constituted the second triad. From the sixth Sephirah came forth the seventh Sephirah, Netzach, or 'Firmness'. This was a male potency and produced the female potency named Hod, or 'Splendor'. From these two proceeded Yesod, or 'Foundation', and these three constituted the third triad of the Sephiroth. Lastly, from the Foundation came the tenth Sephirah, called Malcuth, or 'Kingdom', which was at the foot of all, as the 'Crown' was at the top.

"This division of the ten Sephiroth into three triads was arranged into a form called by the Kabbalists the Kabbalistic Tree or the Tree of Life [as shown in the diagram on the next page].

"In this diagram, the vertical arrangement of the Sephiroth is called 'Pillars'. Thus the four Sephiroth in the center are called the 'Middle Pillar', the three on the right, the 'Pillar of Mercy', and the three on the left, the 'Pillar of Justice'. They allude to these two qualities of God, of which the benignity of the one modifies the rigor of the other, so that the Divine Justice is always tempered by the Divine Mercy. C. W. King, in his *Gnostics* (p.12), refers the right-hand pillar to the Pillar Jachin, and the left-hand pillar to the Pillar Boaz, which stood at the porch of the Temple; and 'these two pillars', he says, 'figure largely amongst all the secret societies of modern times and naturally so; for these *illuminati* have borrowed, without understanding it, the phraseology of the Kabbalists and the Valentinians'. But an inspection of the arrangement of the Sephiroth will show if he is correct in his general inference that he has transposed the pillars. Firmness would more naturally symbolize Boaz, or Strength, as Splendor would Jachin or Establishment.

"These ten Sephiroth are collectively denominated the archetypal man, the Microcosm, as the Greek philosophers called it, and each of them *refers to a particular part of the body*. Thus the Crown is the Head; Wisdom, the Brain; and Intelligence, the Heart, which was deemed the seat of understanding. These three represent the intellectual; and the first triad is therefore called the *Intellectual World*. Mercy is the Right Arm and Justice the Left Arm and Beauty is the Chest. These represent moral qualities; and hence the second triad is called the *Moral World*. Firmness is the Right Leg, Splendor the Left Leg, and Foundation the Privates. These three represent power and stability; and hence the third triad is called the *Material World*. Lastly, Kingdom is the Feet, the basis on which we all stand, and represents the harmony of the whole archetypal man.

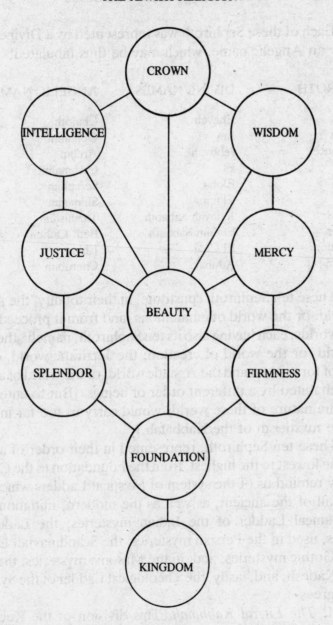

Archetypal Man
according to the Jewish Kabbalah[1]

1. Ibid., Vol.1, p.77.

"Each of these Sephiroth was represented by a Divine name and by an Angelic name, which may be thus tabulated:

SEPHIROTH	DIVINE NAMES	ANGELIC NAMES
Crown	Eheyeh	Chajoth
Wisdom	Jah	Ophanim
Intelligence	Jehovah	Arelim
Mercy	El	Cashmalim
Justice	Eloha	Seraphim
Beauty	Elohim	Shinanim
Firmness	Jehovah Sabaoth	Tarshishim
Splendor	Elohim Sabaoth	Beni Elohim
Foundation	El Chai	Ishim
Kingdom	Adonai	Cherubim

"These ten Sephiroth constitute, in their totality, the Atzilotic world, or the world of emanations, and from it proceed three other worlds, each having also its ten Sephiroth, namely, the Briatic world, or the world of creation; the Jetziratic world, or the world of formation; and the Assiatic world, or the world of action; each inhabited by a different order of beings. [But to enter fully upon the nature of these worlds would carry us too far into the obscure mysticism of the Kabbalah.]

"These ten Sephiroth, represented in their order of ascent, from the lowest to the highest, from the Foundation to the Crown, forcibly remind us of the system of Mystical Ladders which pervaded all of the ancient, as well as the modern, initiations; the Brahmanical Ladder of the Indian mysteries; the Ladder of Mithras, used in the Persian mysteries; the Scandinavian Ladder of the Gothic mysteries, and, in the Masonic mysteries, the Ladder of Kadosh; and, lastly, the Theological Ladder of the Symbolical degrees.

"II. *The Literal Kabbalah*. This division of the Kabbalah being, as has already been said, occupied in the explanation of sacred words by the value of the letters of which they are composed, has been extensively used by the inventors of the high degrees in the symbolism of their significant words. It is divided into three species; Gematria, Notaricon and Temura." Q.E.D.

Much more might be given but it is foreign to our purpose. We have given this much to show that the Jewish Kabbalah, corresponding very closely with the teachings of the old rishis, has some of the esoteric teachings of the East. With some modifications, it resembles the teachings approved by the Masters, but not emphasized by them because they are not of importance on the Path of the Masters.

The Jews, as all know, were finally dispersed and scattered among the nations. Many times they ran the narrow gamut of utter extinction. At the same time, their religious principles underwent changes, now fading out and now reviving; at one time the Jews almost lost their identity and then they gained a new birth. During the Middle Ages, exiled Jewry kept itself alive by various mystical interpretations of its mission and destiny as expressed in a vast Kabbalistic literature, which ultimately found its most unified, most perfect written expression in the *Zohar,* The Book of 'Splendor'. This book did something which even the Bible and the Talmud had ignored. It discovered a new and hitherto unknown kingdom: the kingdom of the soul. Inventing a wholly new terminology, it did this in a specific sense, not then known in mystical Jewry. Says the *Zohar:*

> Believe not that man consists solely of flesh, skin and veins. The real part of man is his soul, and the things just mentioned are only outward coverings. They are only veils, not the real man. When man departs this life, he divests himself of all the veils which cover him.

The author of this was surely close to the Eastern Wisdom. It sounds much like the language of a Master. The *Zohar,* even before its author's death in 1305, had exerted a very great influence not only upon Jewish thought but also upon Christian thinking. How much it may have had to do with the general awakening of that critical time, it may be difficult to determine. But by and by, even the *Zohar* failed to keep alive the vigor of Jewish spiritual ideals. Materialistic world currents were constantly undermining spirituality everywhere among both Jews and Gentiles the world over. It has always been so. It must always be so.

Now the Jewish religion has spent the force of its spiritual ideals, and its inevitable ebb has set in. Jew and Gentile alike must now look for a more dynamic religion which can meet all requirements of an enlightened era. That new religion will be the science of the Masters, which itself is not a religion at all. Religion is like a man or a nation—it has its periods of inception, its infancy, its youth, its manhood and its decline. At last, old age and dissolution claims everything from man to star.

The greatest claim to historic note possessed by the Jewish religion was its gift to the world of Christianity. But strangely enough, the Jews do not seem inclined to take any credit for the gift. They have disinherited their own child and steadfastly refused to give parental recognition to their most illustrious son. Many Jews, however, accept Jesus as one of their prophets. There can be no doubt that if the disciples of Jesus had not tacked on to him miraculous powers and dogmatic assertions, Jesus would have passed down into history as one of the greatest of the prophets, with his Jewish learning enriched, as it was, by a definite knowledge of the Eastern Wisdom.

Today the Jews, like all other religions of history, have practically nothing to offer the hungry seeker after spiritual light except a code of ethics, the best part of which is common to all religions. Having no living Master to keep it alive, the Jewish faith today simply marks time. Almost the whole world, stubbornly pointing its finger at the imperfections of the Jews, forgetting its own muddy face, seems reluctant to acknowledge that some of the world's greatest thinkers and philanthropists have come from that people; for example, Nathan Rothschild, who gave to the government many millions of pounds to purchase and set free the slaves. All the thinking world today acknowledges its indebtedness to Einstein and Freud and many other great Jews.

Above all, it would appear that Christians, instead of hating the Jews, would give them credit for the gift of their own Lord and Master. To hate the Jew just because he is a Jew is not only irrational but quite unchristian. Jews cannot be blamed for what a few bigoted members of that religion did in Jerusalem two thousand years ago. Didn't Christians burn and butcher thousands of other Christians during the reign of the Spanish inquisition? Didn't our own fathers burn witches and persecute to the death all who didn't believe as they did?

Religious prejudice is always blind and full of hate. The capital crime of all history, in the eyes of the people, has been the preaching and the practising of any doctrine subversive of the established institutions. It is safe to say that more people have been murdered for that one offence than for all others put together, including executions for crime. And do you know the psychology of this procedure? Vanity. The 'Holy Inquisitors' imagine themselves to be very godlike, very saintly, because they are defending their own religion. But in fact, they exhibit the most fiendish qualities, the exact antithesis of saintliness. There is nothing more devilish than a thirst for blood, fired by a religious zeal. If any man wonders how human beings can commit such crimes while exhibiting religious zeal, let him be reminded again and again that religion and morality have no relation to each other—none at all. It is only genuine spirituality, as taught by the great Masters, which becomes the very soul of pure ethics.

25. The Sikh Religion of India

The religion of the Sikhs in India is distinctive. It has never gained world reputation. Although now numbering about two and a half million adherents, it is still practically limited to the Punjab in India. A few Sikhs are scattered over the world. Yet this religion is the most universal of all religions in its fundamental principles, and is nearer to the Santon ki Shiksha than all other teachings.

This religion was founded by Guru Nanak, who was born in 1469 A.D., and died in 1539. He was contemporaneous with Kabir Sahib. After Guru Nanak came his nine successors. When the last of the ten, Guru Gobind Singh, died, the rumor became current that no more living Gurus would come, and from that time on, the Adi Granth Sahib, the sacred book of the Sikhs, would be Guru to all Sikhs. Thus the Sikhs bound themselves in exactly the same way as did the Christians—the orthodox body of the Sikhs accepted the Christian dogma of an inspired book and a closed revelation. From that day to this, that dogma has been their chief handicap. Without a living Guru, deterioration must follow as the night succeeds the day. For this is the history of all religions from the beginning of time. It would appear that men will believe almost anything if propounded by some religious authority whom they have accepted. When the Sikhs accepted the Adi Granth Sahib, they assumed that the book contained the entire truth ever needed, and also that it would do the work of a living Guru. This assumption of the Sikhs is no more extravagant than the positions of both Christians and Moslems, who cling so tenaciously to their holy books.

As intimated above, the content of the Sikh religion is so nearly identical with that of the Santon ki Shiksha that there is but little reason to attempt a separate analysis. Guru Nanak, the founder, was a real Saint, a genuine Sat Guru, and consequently his teachings must coincide with those of all other Saints. There never can be any difference between their teachings in any age of the world. A hundred thousand years from now the science of chemistry will certainly teach that hydrogen and oxygen combine to form water in the relation of two to one. So it is with the teachings of the Saints, because their teachings are as much a science as is chemistry. The only problem to be solved now is whether the man is a real Saint or not, and that is usually an easy problem.

There are certain cardinal and distinctive teachings and practices emphasized by all Saints. If a man teaches and practises these things, that is presumptive evidence that he is a Master. He may be accepted provisionally as a Saint, subject to further corroborative evidence. If he does not teach and practise these fundamentals, he cannot be regarded as a real Saint no matter what his other qualifications. He may be a good yogi, a rishi; but he has not gone to the heights attained by all Saints.

Some of the cardinal precepts are:

(1) First of all, the necessity of *a living Guru*, a genuine Saint who has been appointed by the Supreme Sat Purush to act as Guru. By *living*, we mean one who is still in the physical body. It is

a fixed law of Nature that only a humanly embodied soul can act as Guru for those who are still in their physical bodies. After his death, or departure from his body, the Guru will still take care of all whom he has initiated; but he cannot accept new disciples. This is not because the Guru is limited, but because the disciple himself is so limited that he cannot receive the instructions and the initiation from a departed Guru. Only man can teach man, and more especially, only 'man' can initiate man. If a departed Guru could take care of new disciples, then there would be no need of Gurus at all on this earth plane. The Supreme Father could do all that work himself without assistance. But a living, physically embodied Guru is absolutely necessary because a man cannot be taught by any other known agency.

If we stop to think for a single instant, we would know that if God himself could not reach and instruct a man and lead him upon the upward Path, then surely no departed Guru could do it. The fact remains that a humanly embodied Guru is necessary because of our limitations; and that difficulty cannot be surmounted in any possible manner except for the Supreme One himself to come in human form or send someone else. As suggested in many other places in this book, the fatal error of all world religions is their dependence upon a departed Master and the instructions left in a book.

(2) The second fundamental of this system of the Masters, the pure Santon ki Shiksha, is the vital fact of *the Audible Life Stream*. Masters of all ages have emphasized this Stream as the central fact in their system. This Stream is in fact nothing less than the Supreme One, projecting himself on all planes of life in a constant stream of musical vibrations, through which flows the most incomprehensible power, life-giving and creative. These vibrations can be heard, distinctly heard, by all students of the Master after their initiation and a little practice. This Stream is the all-creative power of the entire universe. It is the life of all that lives, and it is the chief means by which the student returns to his original home on the highest planes of existence. It is also the one and only successful means of mind control by which the student overcomes his passions and liberates himself from all

downward drag. This Current is also the central factor in liberation and salvation from the endless rounds of births and deaths. This great fact of Nature is discussed elsewhere in this book more completely (*Chapter Eleven, Section 3*).

(3) The third general truth emphasized by the Saints is complete liberation and spiritual triumph while still living in the physical body. There is no waiting until after death to attain freedom. It is accomplished ____ method of yoga as ta____ ____ f Santon ki Shiksha th____ ____ *the way of spiritual* lib____ ____ *life*. In every case, wh____ ____ ____ng his lifetime, he mu____ ____ ____ or another chance to meet and follow a living Guru. Why? Because that appears to be the plan of the Creator and no man can change it.

[handwritten annotation: Important Quote ? need to profess faith before death]

(4) Unless a man is able to give the initiation and lead his disciple upon the inner planes, he is not a Master and should not be accepted as such. And it must be remembered that *the initiation is of first importance*. No one can travel far on the Path until he gets the initiation and none but a true Saint or Sat Guru can give it. It is therefore the gravest misfortune if a man finds himself wandering after some man or religion without a Master.

Now, all these points are taught by every Saint, by every real Master. There has never been an exception. If they are not taught by any one who claims to be Master, then it is best to look elsewhere. The test is infallible. And all these things are taught with great clarity and force in the Granth Sahib.

26. The Basic Elements of All Religions

It is now in order to sum up the teachings of all religions and try to point out their several positions in the scheme of the Masters. Let us hasten to say in the first place that *the Masters condemn no religion*. None of them are to be set aside as false. If they had not some good, they would not have survived. In fact, they would not have come. If they had not come to fill a real need, they would not have come at all.

There is a decided inclination in these days to insist that all religions are equally good and effective, that they all constitute but different paths leading to the same goal. This is a very charitable and liberal view, and is to be heartily commended. This view is a step forward toward the much desired universal brotherhood, with an end to religious wars and contentions. Many attempts have been made to establish an ecumenical council of all religions. World congresses have been held. This should be encouraged, by all means. It would be a delightful conclusion to the whole matter if we could say here and now that all religions are equally good and that all of them lead to the highest goal. In that case, there would be no more advantage in discussing the subject—no need at all for further books. The Saints themselves would have no further mission. Just turn over the world to a congress of priests and let us all 'go to the movies'. Why worry?

But unfortunately, such is not the case. We may frankly admit that one religion is about as good as another, that they are all equally effective. On that basis all may be admitted into one grand amalgamation. But after that has been done and the compound has been tested, it will be found to have two serious defects. There are two vital points at which all religions fail. One is the lack of a living Master. That is a need which none but the Saints can supply. No religion has it. That requirement, an absolute *sine qua non,* marks the poverty of all world religions. A second lack suffered by all religions is their loss of all conscious contact with the Audible Life Stream; and they do not know how to find it. Yet that is the most vital consideration on the Path of spiritual liberation. We may truly say that without this conscious contact, one's life is unfulfilled; it would have been better not to have been born. If, therefore, you do unite all the churches, all religions, the union itself will still lack the two most essential elements of a universal system of spiritual emancipation or salvation. It will be practically useless, except as a pleasant social fraternity.

There are three great links in the Golden Chain of salvation—*the living Sat Guru, the Audible Life Stream, and Spiritual*

Liberation. These will be discussed more fully in their proper places. They are repeated here for the sake of emphasis.

If we analyze all historical religions, we shall find that they consist of five basic elements. They are: (1) superstitious assumptions, (2) emotional extravaganzas, (3) ritualistic ceremonies, (4) metaphysical speculations, and (5) ethical principles. The proportions of these elements vary from the lowest type of fetichism up to the sublimest ethics of an Emerson. But all religions bear the stamp of these five in differing degrees. Whatever small degree of *bhakti,* 'devotion', or *dharma,* 'good works', may be found in any of them, they all fit into the framework of these five central ingredients. In some of them vague references to the Audible Life Stream are to be found, but for the most part they have lost any adequate knowledge of it. It is quite evident that in these five elements of world religions, there is but little, if any, genuine religion.

What then is genuine religion? *Religion is an individual experience. It is a realization.* No man can say exactly what beauty is. It is an experience based upon a relation between things and individual intelligence. Beauty is a joy springing up out of that relation. Beauty is a step toward Reality. In essence, beauty is a form of love. It is a ray of light from the infinite heart of things. So is religion. It is a light. It is love. It is joy. True religion exists only when the soul finds joy in the Infinite. Religion is not found in creeds or ceremonies. Again, let us emphasize the fact that religion is an individual experience. And just as each individual's experience is different from that of all others, so his religion is different from that of all others. Ergo, there are just as many religions in the world as there are individuals.

Religion is not an outward expression. It cannot be expressed outwardly. It is an inner experience. For this reason religion can never be couched in forms and ceremonies. It can never be bottled up in creeds, like canned beans. It can never be given by one man to another. Neither can it ever be written down in books.

One reason why there is so much confusion in religious understanding is because every man's experience is different from that of every other man. My religion is not the religion of any other person, unless that person has had exactly the same experience as I have had. In some clumsy manner, primitive man began to create a form of propitiation, a ceremony, a sacrifice. He watched with terror the driving storm and he concluded that there must be some sort of malignant power back of it. It is significant, in interpreting human psychology, that man's first conception of God was that of a malignant being. It was eons of time later that Love entered into the idea of God. As man got favors from men and animals by doing something to please them, his next thought was to do something to please those gigantic forces back of natural phenomena. Out of the ceremonies and sacrifices which he then instituted he got some sort of personal experience, and that constituted his religion. But the religion of that primitive man was a different sort of religion from that of a modern Kabir. Yet it was his religion and it should be respected. It was the best he could do.

27. Love, the Essence of Religion

It should not be difficult now for us to bridge the gap of the centuries and arrive at some sort of conclusion as to what genuine religion is. Let it be said with all due emphasis, that *there is no such distinction as true and false religion,* for every man's religion is for him true and genuine. It is his experience. But just what constitutes the differences, which we all know exist? That difference lies in the degree of objective reality which lies back of our individual experiences. If we build a religion upon our own mental images, upon a long period of suggestion and auto-suggestion, our experiences will not be founded upon objective reality. If we build up a form of religion upon assumptions, superstitions, speculations, our system will be like the house built upon sand. When tested, it will not stand. But if our religious thinking and experiences are founded upon reality, our religion will stand every test.

Such a man will experience religion upon the highest possible plane. That religion will yield the finest fruitage because it is nourished in the soil of reality. The logical lesson to be derived from this fact is that everyone should do his utmost to assure himself that his religious theories, his thinking and his personal experiences are founded upon reality, upon facts. And it cannot be too strongly emphasized that no such assurances can be had unless feelings are ruled out, and our convictions are based upon actual sight, hearing and touch. If you think that such a foundation for your religion is not available to you, that is because you have not met a real Master.

And now, what is the content of that religion which will stand all tests? It is the religion experienced by the Masters and their disciples. Its content is *love*. In the infinite heart of things, love and reality will be found to be one and the same thing. The absence of love means the absence of reality. Everything else is illusory. A full realization of this sublime fact is genuine religion. It is a great joy. If there is any one thing that distinguishes a Master from all other men, it is love. The thing passeth all understanding. The Master is the only man in the world who experiences religion in its full and complete sense because he loves most. Hence, if we concentrate the entire discussion into one fundamental thesis, there will remain nothing but love. Love and religion, then, are one and the same thing. Religion, love, reality, are all one.

Having now discovered the precious radium content of religion, it is a simple and logical conclusion that there is no such thing as genuine religion in the creeds and formalities of world religions. Only the living Master can open the doors of light for us. Only he can give us the waters of life. He is the embodiment of infinite love, and he alone can open for us the fountain of love. When he does that, we discover for the first time that there is no other religion nor can there be any other. When we drink of that fountain, we have life eternal. We have a religion which embraces all other religions, a religion of perfect oneness with boundless love.

Some teachers say that we should begin religion by loving mankind. That will lead us to love God, so they insist. That is a very nice theory, and surely anything that leads us to love our fellowmen is a good thing. There is nothing we need more than that. But will this theory work? How many people have you seen who have actually proved this theory in practice? I have never met one. But I have seen many who found their way to God by the shining

Path of a living Master, and after that they became great lovers of mankind. They learned to love even the lowliest of animals, every plant and flower. Their whole lives became flames of creative love. And that is genuine religion. There is no other. But this religion is attained only on the Path of the Masters.

The Masters alone can tune the soul in with the heavenly Bani, the Audible Life Stream. After all, this Life Stream is the source of all love in the world. It is because the Master is one with that Stream that he manifests so much love. It is when we meet a real Master and he unites us with that Stream, that love is born, and with it, its twin—religion. When a man has once gained this inner experience, he has the dynamic life within himself to meet all temptations successfully and live the life called for by the finest code of ethics. Never otherwise. To make morality a means of attaining religion is to work backwards. Ethics is a means of mind cleansing, although not a perfect means at best. But that only prepares one to start on the Path of God-realization. What is still more important, ethics never generated love. Therefore, ethics is neither religion, nor the soil out of which it grows. Genuine ethics is the fruit of love and love is the life-giving fruit of the Great Current. We treat our fellowmen properly because we love them. We do not love them because we treat them right.

Ethics can never form the basis of a universal religion, for ethics cannot create love. This is why we so often witness the strange phenomena of intense religionists manifesting so much hatred. Their theories about God, the heavens and spiritual liberation are not sound because they are not founded on knowledge. Take out of any religion its code of ethics, and it would not survive a single month, except in those forms where its participants value ceremony for its psychological effect. All primitive civilizations love ceremony for its own sake.

We may contemplate a lofty example of loving service to the extent that we feel ready to offer ourselves to it, giving up everything, even life itself. If we do so, it is inspired by the love which wells up in the soul in response to that pull. But that sort of love is not of the highest order. It is mostly sympathy, an appeal to the emotions. So much love is so much religion. We must not deny that many noble souls, with hearts overflowing with loving sympathy and deep interest in a certain cause, have laid down their lives for that cause. But the perfect love, with perfect light, comes only when one melts his soul into the Infinite Soul at the feet of a living Master.

It is true that most religions preach love as the vital factor in religion. Upon love toward God and man, they base their ethics. But with those religions it is mostly a theory. Everybody preaches and desires love, but he wishes his neighbor to begin first. Here again it has been proved times without number in history that institutional religion and fundamental ethics do not always travel together.

The human mind takes many a twist and turn. Some of the worst characters in history have been among the most religious. Nothing is more conspicuous in history than the incessant preaching of love and the incessant practice of hatred. But the preaching of love makes a very strong appeal to intelligence, because we all recognize that love is the saving essence of life. All religions, therefore, make love their foundation, *in theory*. It makes good material for sermons. But few ever build character upon that foundation. The reason for that is they lack the essential dynamics of religion. They have not the all-powerful Stream of Love to give life to their religion. Their love is generally stored away in the library.

Men build beautiful Gothic cathedrals, fill them with music and ceremony and go on preaching ethics and love. But after the ceremony is over, a throng of well-dressed men and women hurry away to their big dinners, their banks, their farms and their secret passions. Where is the love? Where is the religion? And yet Jesus said that love should be the due guard and sign of discipleship. This is the central point of emphasis in the system of the Masters. But unlike all the rest, the great Masters *practise* love.

In the end, all know that the core of religion is the experience of the individual when he has found the great love. It can be nothing else. Religious corporate bodies come and go, but ethics abides. It will abide. But genuine religion is quite another matter. It is not to be confused with any system of ceremonies. It is a thing to be realized only in the deep chambers of the soul when the mystic contact has been made with the divine Bani and the soul learns of a certainty that there is nothing in the world but love.

But in all the prevailing religions, this one essential content is conspicuous by its absence. If an isolated individual here and there is filled with love, unselfish service being the rule of his life, that does not imply that his religion should have the credit. On the contrary, his love has enriched his religion. If it were not for the loving souls who have all brought to their several religions the contributions of their own individual love, those religions would have made a very poor showing. When some noble individual shines out in history, then the priests turn and say: "See what our religion has done!" As a matter of fact, they performed their noble service actuated by a love that sprang up in spite of their religion. Ceremonial religion has never done anything to enrich anyone's life, except for the ethical and esthetic culture of refined ceremony and music. But why offer that in the name of religion? Real culture is far above all religions.

Most religions are like a combination salad—they are made up of a number of evergreen virtues, a choice set of handsome dogmas, a little oil of beauty, a few slices of wholesome philosophy, seasoned with the salt and pepper of good works, flavored with the dressing of prayer, garnished with an attractive ritual, and served by a polished waiter called a priest. This may have some value as a cleansing diet, but the bread of life is not in it. When the hungry soul contacts the Audible Life Stream, then and then only does he enter upon life everlasting. And only then does he experience perfect love, vibrating through every fiber of his being.

When all institutional religions are abandoned, true civilization will dawn. They have always been the most serious handicaps to progress. They have always acted as brakes to the wheels. What then will take the place of those religions? Nothing. The house will be clean. What will men put into the house then? Love will fill every room in it. Love will furnish it and light it. Love will spread its tables. Love will sing its songs. Love will play its games. From its happy doors, love will go forth to subdue the world—nay, to embrace the world. And then all men will know what religion is because they will know what love is.

If you ask again just how the coming civilization is to attain this *summum bonum* of philosophy and religion, I will say, as is said so often in these pages, by and through *the scientific method of the great Masters*. For theirs is the Path of Love, the Prem Marg, the Bhakti Marg, the shining Path of the ages!

28. Key to the Analysis of Religions

To the student of history, especially the history of religions, it must often occur that there ought to be some explanation of the multiplicity of religions and of their many conflicting elements. Where and how did they originate? What is the soil out of which they have grown? If they are so many paths to God, as they all claim, why do they wage such incessant wars against one another? Is there any substratum of truth common to them all? If so, how shall we discover their fundamentals? These and many other similar questions fairly thrust themselves upon the impartial student. We believe there must be an answer to these questions. When all religions are analyzed, there will be a residuum showing a common origin, and exhibiting common properties.

To avoid going into the matter at any great length, let us go straight to the heart of the question. *Religion, any religion, is the inner experience of the individual.* That we have already discussed at some length. To get that experience, he must leave the outer world, in thought at least, and go *inside*. How does one go inside? By detaching himself from the outer or sense world and withdrawing his attention from all sense objects, then concentrating the attention upon something inside. This appears simple enough, and it is the method of acquiring all religious experiences—leaving the outer world and entering the inner world of consciousness. To this rule there can be no exceptions. No matter what the religion is, one must go inside to get it.

To state the matter more explicitly, concentrating the attention upon something inside of oneself is the way to all religious experiences. This is true of the system of the Masters and it is true of all other systems which yield any sort of religious experience whatsoever. But here is the crucial point—as the methods differ, so will the experiences differ. The method of the Masters is scientific and exact. All other methods are more or less haphazard, empirical and uncertain. This very fact explains why the results of the Masters' method are uniform, no matter how many thousands of times the experiments may be performed and no matter how many millions of years apart they are performed. It also explains why there is such endless variety and confusion in the results obtained by all other methods.

There is a vast difference also in the degree and extent to which one penetrates the inner worlds, and so there must be a corresponding difference in the results obtained. This fact further accounts for a great variety of inner experiences and a variety of religions based upon those experiences. One may leave the outer world and enter very slightly into the regions of thought. If he concentrates at that point, thought-forms will build up about him, and his problems will be solved so far as his own thought can solve them. These thought-forms can be seen by anyone who has astral vision. This is the region where mind plays its greatest dramas. It is on this plane that mind goes on creating and molding and shaping as it desires. All the while there is a constant stream of suggestion pouring in upon the individual. This helps to mold his thought-forms. Finally, many of such souls who are more sensitive are actually able to see their own thought-forms and they imagine they have seen some great characters outside of themselves. Those thought-images will often talk to them out of the depths of the subconscious self.

There has never been a religion founded, never a good book written, never a good picture painted, never a good poem composed, never a good invention developed, except *by going inside* to some extent, and there concentrating on the task in hand. Even if one is not conscious of the exact thing he is to accomplish, he gets results by concentration. That is the great thing in the process—perfect concentration, becoming oblivious to the outer world of sense and centering attention upon that which is to be found inside of man. This is the way of attainment, no matter in what line of endeavor. No matter what one is to achieve, this is the one and only method leading to success. Concentrated attention is the key that unlocks all stores of wisdom, of truth and of spirituality.

But there is one difficulty in this process. It is when the student comes face to face with his own mental creations. It is then that he is almost helpless unless he has the guiding direction of a living Master. It has been the unfortunate experience of thousands of good men and women who have entered to some degree into the inner consciousness, that they got the impression that God or some angel or relative was leading them. They hear 'the voice of God', they say. Or they get the impression that God himself is giving them some command or instruction. But such visions or voices or impressions are, as a rule, their own mental creations.

This process is plainly visible to anyone who has independent astral vision, but the individual himself is rarely able to make the distinction because he has not such independent vision. He fondly believes God is speaking to him directly when he is actually hearing nothing but the faint whisperings of his own mind, coming up out of his subconscious self. He is deceived, self-deceived. And so often he announces that he has received a message from God or that God is leading him to do certain things.

Many people say that God has ordered them to commit murder or do all sorts of atrocities, but it is their own disordered mind. I recall a man and a woman who were my fellow passengers on the steamer crossing the seas to Hong Kong. They were going to Tibet as missionaries. They were going to that almost inaccessible region, solely on the strength of a personal 'command from God'. To the student of psychological phenomena, it was quite apparent that their 'command from God' was nothing more than the creation of their own minds, superinduced by a long course of suggestion.

So it has happened many times in history. New cults are started, movements inaugurated, sacrifices made and books written solely on the strength of such 'commands from God'. These individuals themselves are not to be blamed for their mistakes. They are to be pitied. Most of them are very sincere devotees of their religions. The trouble is that they have no safeguard; they have no reliable guidance. They cannot see inside so as to detect the fraud that is being perpetrated upon them by their own minds. As soon as a person enters only a little distance inside, he is always confronted, and fairly assaulted, by multitudes of his own thought-forms. Aided by the suggestions of others, they have nearly all taken shape out of his own past training and the ideas he has held for long periods of time. They spring up out of his own long-cherished desires. In the end, they mislead him into all sorts of bypaths.

This psychological process, we believe, is the real source of most of that endless variety of experiences which people call religious, and which accounts for the great variety of religions. No one is safe from such misfortune until he is directed by a living Master, who himself is able to watch, with clear vision, all internal experiences of both himself and his disciples. Moreover, at the time of initiation, every student of a living Master is given ample safeguards which make such unhappy experiences quite impossible.

29. Guarding One's Own Mental Process

Every student of the Masters is obliged to keep a vigilant eye upon his own mental processes. When he begins to enter the inner planes, even to the slightest degree, he must beware of his own misleading mental creations. In all of his waking consciousness he is to remember that this mind is his worst enemy, as well as his most useful instrument. But the main point is that he must keep it under control every moment. *The mind is a useful servant, but a very bad master.*

It is only the student of a real Master who is given every safeguard against being deceived by his own mind. It is only the follower of a real Master who can differentiate between the true and the false, as he begins to enter those subtle regions of the mind.

He cannot dispense with the leadership of the Master in such dangerous zones. Without the Master, he is almost sure to go astray. The mind plays a thousand tricks. It is most unreliable and it is habitually beset by its own thought-creations, harassed by its own desires and dominated by its own passions.

In the light of all of these facts, is it any wonder that the world is filled with conflicting notions on religions, as well as on other subjects? But as said above, the method of the Masters offers a perfect safeguard against such disasters. That method indicates exactly what your attention is to be concentrated upon and where it is to be centered. It also gives you the most precise and effective means of testing every experience inside. And lastly, it takes you into the inner regions with eyes wide open, with the consciousness more intensely awake than at any other time; and most important of all, the Radiant Form of the living Master is right there with the student to instruct and guide him.

Under such conditions, the student cannot go wrong or make mistakes, neither can he be imposed upon by his own mind or that of anyone else. On the inner Path, the student must understand, he will be met and tempted by a thousand and one different sorts of spirits and conditions. He will be attracted in a hundred ways. Every emotion will be played upon to mislead him. Only with the Master is he perfectly safe.

Again let it be emphasized that everything good comes from the light within. Nothing of value can possibly come out of terrestrial matter or material forms. All these are perishable and of temporary value. The deeper one penetrates into those finer regions of truth and reality, the more perfect is his light. If he has the help of the Master who has himself penetrated those regions and knows every step of the way, he cannot go astray. He never gets a false impression and he never organizes a misleading cult out of his own disordered impressions. He never imagines himself led by God. God never talks directly to people in that way. The sooner we learn that fact the better for the world and our own individual souls. God has his way of leading men to the Light.

There are just two methods used by the Supreme One: First is the method of the whole world, led by Natural Law, personal experience, and experimentation—trial and discard. The whole world is going on this way. They have no Master. They have to look out for themselves. They go on treading the wheel through successive lives and from age to age. They accumulate knowledge by experience. If they live up to the best that experience has taught them—their own experience and that of others—they will rise in the scale of evolution.

The second method is that of following a Master. The Supreme One has so designed it that the Master is to lead all men to the perfect light. It simply cannot be done any other way. We cannot find our way alone. The Master, and he alone, can lead the soul to the perfect light and to the original home of the soul in the supreme region. The plan seems to be that common experience shall lead the people up to where they meet the Guru, and after that the Guru takes them home to the eternal regions.

Outside of these two methods of dealing with the human race, God never interferes in the affairs of men. He never speaks to anyone, he is never seen by anyone, nor does he impress anyone's mind. If one gets impressions or hears voices or sees visions, he must understand that the Supreme One has nothing to do with it. An individual may be impressed by or spoken to by someone—some inferior deity, some angel or some ordinary disembodied soul—but never the Supreme God. If you imagine that he is doing so, believe it not. To get to where you see or hear the Supreme One is an exalted attainment, far above that ever experienced by any mortal, except a real Saint or Master. And real Masters are extremely few in this world.

One further word of warning must be given here. Even if you see visions inside, beware of them. If you meet individuals—men, angels, even someone appearing as God or claiming to be God or any Saint—beware that you are not deceived. If you were a disciple of a real Master, you could not be deceived. You would have a definite and infallible method of testing each vision or appearance to prove if they are genuine as claimed. But if you have not this armament, you are almost sure to be misled.

The mind is most treacherous; and besides that, the lower subtle worlds are filled with millions of other minds who are just as treacherous as your own. Believe them not. The Great Master says we should not even salute them or speak to them unless the Master introduces them to us. If you imagine you see the Lord himself, any Lord whom you regard highly, do not allow that vision to carry you off your feet. If you have not the Master's test, you are more than likely to be imposed upon. The vision may be a creation of your own mind or it may be the creation of some other intelligence or an impersonation. Beware of it.

Once when I was passing through a severe storm in the Mediterranean Sea, we expected the ship to sink any minute. Of course we prayed, as we believed in prayer. I was amused to hear one man actually swearing at his bad luck. Our thoughts naturally turned to that world beyond this world of storms. Being a Christian, my mind naturally turned to Jesus. Long hours I meditated upon Jesus, and prayed occasionally. My poor wife sat by me and prayed, while tears ran down her face. Finally, tired out by long waiting and suspense, I leaned back against the wall of the dining saloon and tried to relax the tension. A lovely vision presented itself to me. The heavens opened and I saw Jesus descending toward me with great light and a host of angels about him. His arms were extended to me in welcome. I was wild with delight. Then the scene was suddenly shut out, and I was brought back to the physical plane by a great plunge of the ship and a hard bump on the back of my head. There is not the slightest doubt in my mind now that I did not see Jesus at all, but only an image of him created by my own mind.

I remember that several months ago, a woman got up in *satsang* here and related that she had seen Lord Krishna many times. She said she had been a follower of Lord Krishna for forty years. Asked if he had ever talked to her, she said, "Many times"; but she was puzzled because he did not always tell the truth. He often told her things which did not come true. The fact is quite apparent that the lady had never actually seen Lord Krishna at all, but had seen only her own mental creations of him. Of course, such creations are not reliable communicants. And so it is with thousands of visions, numberless messages, and host of guides and controls —most of them are nothing more than the mental creations of the people themselves, who have no means of protecting themselves from such impositions.

On the other hand, it may well occur that some visions are based upon fact and are genuine. Take the well-known instance of the founder of Mormonism. Joseph Smith, a religious youth, trying to determine after long prayer and deep meditation which of the many conflicting religions was the true one for him to follow, had a clear vision. He saw an angel and was told by that angel that there were some plates hidden in a rock in the mountainside, the exact place being shown to him. He went there and found the plates and translated them into the Book of Mormon. He might have had a genuine vision of such an angel. Those plates could have been placed there centuries before by wandering tribes who were early Christians, descendants of some of the lost tribes of Israel. The angel might have wished that they be restored to the knowledge of man, and so directed the boy. The boy was a good subject for such a contact. He was of pure mind, singleness of purpose, and he concentrated deeply. Under the circumstances, it was not difficult for him to enter the subtle regions sufficiently to gain a clear vision of the angel.

The main point is that without the clear vision of the Master or the infallible test given by him, no one can ever be sure of what he sees or hears. Until one has the assistance of the Master, it is wiser to avoid all inner experiences. Above all, one should discount all voices that he hears. Even in the case of disciples of a real Master, it is not wise for them to assume that the Master is leading them unless they have something better than impressions to go by. Nine chances to one they will be impressions of their own minds. It is only when the disciple actually sees the Master inside, and even then only after applying the test which the Master gives, may he follow. After the test, if it is the Master in fact, he will remain and manifest himself. If he is a fraud, he will disappear. For there is not a single deceiver in all the subtle worlds who can stand the Master's test.

Take no chances on being deceived, either by your own mind or by anyone else—for it is certain that many will try to mislead you. Not only 'earth-bound' spirits, but many agents of the

Negative Power lurk about the physical plane with the sole purpose of preying upon the ignorance and credulity of the inexperienced. Trust them not. Until such time as you can really see the
inner Master and give him the official challenge, and he responds
to it properly, you should never follow an uncertain lead. Get
your instructions from a Master, either personally or by proxy. It
is much safer. I have known so many good people misled by some
such imposter, and when asked why they do not go to a real Master, they are sometimes offended, saying they have a Master inside. In all such cases, they are deceived, for no real Master ever
works that way.

It is only after you have conquered all barriers and stood before your Radiant Master on the inner planes at a place known
as Ashtadal Kanwal—only then you may safely follow his leadership inside. From that point on you cannot be deceived. Then
you can talk to him, face to face, as freely as you can talk to anyone in the body. Again we say, follow no impressions or voices.
Never. Go by sight and military challenge. Remember, you are
passing through a very strange country, about which you know
nothing, and no language could ever describe to you the multiplicity of ways and means that are employed to lead visitors astray in
order to keep them from going higher. Prove all things; hold fast
to that which is good.

30. Analyzing Religious Movements

Keeping in mind these principles, one may study critically all
ancient and modern religious movements insofar as the data can
be obtained. You have been given the key that will unlock the
mysteries of them all. The perfect science of the Masters will be
your criterion. Apply that yardstick to all religions. Apply the test
to all such movements as modern evangelism, proselytism of
every form and variety, missionary enterprises, the revivalism
of Moody and the Wesleys. Analyze the work of such men as
George Jeffrys and the Oxford movement of Buchman. Study
the work of the Doweys, the Glen Volivas, the Salvation Army,

the New Thoughtists, Unity, and all of the little denominations springing up among the churches as well as in all other religions.

Every world religion is full of differing sects. All these have their psychological interpretations. They are expressions of some phase of religious experience. How many of them may be due to the mental aberrations of their founders, we are not in a position to say. But in each and every case, they have arisen out of some sort of inner experiences, even though it is altogether possible that some of these inner experiences may be attributed to paranoia. (But even then, they may have certain psychological and religious value.) A careful analysis should be made in all cases and the phenomena should be studied impartially as one would study a new disease.

There is another important class of religio-philosophical movements of modern times which demands special attention. Those religious movements referred to as evangelism make their appeal almost entirely to the emotions. They generally misinterpret their own emotional outbursts as the work of the Divine Spirit. They believe and pray and exhort, and read the Bible and sing. They seldom think. They have faith. But there is another class which makes its appeal more directly to the intellect and seeks substantiation from science. In this group may be mentioned Max Heindel, Rudolph Steiner, Ouspensky, Krishnamurti, Vivekananda and Hermann Keyserling.

Seeking reality in the spiritual nature of man and the universe, these men all endeavor to inculcate some aspect of truth, while at the same time they regard the physical world as more or less illusory. The ultimate appeal of such movements is to spirit instead of matter, to an enlightened understanding rather than to religious emotions. We may well concede that each of these men has had personal experience of a higher reality, at least glimpses of something more substantial than the passing material show. Each of them may be given a seat of honor in the great Brotherhood of Light. They have each had their own inner experiences, and each has written down his findings, as best he could, in the hope of contributing somewhat to the general enlightenment. As soon as anybody goes inside, even to the slightest extent, and brings out a new truth or a new interpretation of an old truth, he will get a following. People hunger for truth and reality even though but few of them know what it is that they want.

This process of re-examination and shifting of emphasis must go on just so long as the world lacks the scientific system of the Masters by which to travel on the path of certitude. The Masters, unlike all the rest, guess at nothing—neither do they speculate nor follow impressions. They follow no 'guides'. They hear no voices calling to them out of the darkness. They walk on no untried paths. The Masters speak from personal experiences, based upon a knowledge which was first handed down to them by their own Masters and then proved by themselves. Each fact, experience, or hypothesis is tested by them and proved. After that it becomes their own knowledge and then they can speak as one having authority. They then teach their students to follow the same path of scientific experimentation.

Challenging every phenomenon presented for their consideration, they work also with an awakened consciousness and in broad daylight. When they have tabulated and tested all the facts, they go forward on the basis of certified knowledge. They take nothing on belief. They accept nothing simply because it is written in a book. The book only records the experiences of other men. They seek their own experiences and write their own books. Whatever is not definitely known to them is set aside for further investigation. With the Masters, only positive knowledge has final value. As a matter of fact, in the process of becoming Masters, all knowledge is mastered by them. The net result of their method is that all the Masters are in perfect accord with one another; and that is because they all have found the truth in its completeness, and the body of Truth is one no matter in what age or by whom it is discovered.

Chapter Three

THE MASTERS AND THEIR DUTIES

1. Who and What Are the Masters?

THE terms used to designate Masters and other highly developed men are many. *Master,* as the term is used in this book, is equivalent to *Saint* (*Sant,* in Sanskrit). It is also the same in meaning as *Sat Guru,* although there is an additional meaning to *Sat Guru.* All Sat Gurus are Saints, but all Saints are not Sat Gurus. A Sat Guru is a Saint who has been appointed by the Supreme Guru, Sat Nam, to act as Guru on his behalf. The Guru is a sort of viceroy, or executive officer, who does his work on this plane.

Sat Guru (*Sat,* meaning 'true', and *Guru,* 'light-giver') is the chief instrument of the Supreme Ruler to contact this world of humanity. It is also the same as *Mahatma,* if we refer to the highest order of mahatmas. (This word is often used rather loosely in India, generally meaning anyone who has attained some degree of eminence in spiritual or religious matters—*Mahatma,* from *maha,* 'great', and *atma,* 'spirit'.) A yogi is a mahatma of a lower order than a true Saint. The original meaning of *yogi* was 'one who had attained union with God'. The system of practices by means of which he attained that union is called yoga. But the great majority of yogis, both ancient and modern, are men who have reached only the first degree, or less, on the Path of the Masters.

The Masters themselves divide all mahatmas into four classes:

(1) A *sikh* (*shishya*), meaning 'disciple', one who has gained the first region.

(2) A *sadhu,* one who has attained the third region. By courtesy, one who has gained the second station may be called sadhu.

(3) A *Sant,* one who has definitely gained the fifth region, there being eight regions in all.

(4) A *Param Sant,* meaning 'Supreme Saint', or one who has reached the highest possible attainment in the Supreme Region.

It will be noted that these degrees are based upon personal and individual attainments. They are not conferred degrees. They are degrees which one has to grow into by hard work.

A *rishi* is one who has attained considerable development, similar to that of the yogi.[1] There is a general understanding in India that a true rishi ranks higher than a yogi. This may be so in theory, but in actual practice we doubt if there is any difference. But in both theory and practice the Masters or Saints rank far superior to either yogis or rishis because their attainments are far higher. The Vedas were given out by great rishis. *Maha rishi* is simply a 'great rishi'.

Muni means somewhat the same as *rishi.* The Hebrew word for rishi or muni or yogi is *ro-eh.* The Greek equivalent is *episco-pos,* meaning a superintendent of spiritual ceremonies or practices. It also has an esoteric meaning, indicating one who looks down with clearer vision upon all things and has a higher viewpoint than others. The ancient rishi was half priest and half prophet. He was the *prohita* of the Vedic age, the high priest—counselor of kings. Noted examples of such were Vishvamitra and Vasishtha, high priests to kings. All of these were mahatmas but not Masters.

Among Muslims and Sufis, a Master is spoken of as *Murshid, Murshid-i-Kamil, Faquir, Shaikh-ul-Mashaikh,* or *Pir-o-Murshid.* These terms are intended to be equivalent to *Saint,* although they have been much misused in these later days. They are now often applied to men who are neither Saints nor Masters,

---

1. *Rishi,* Sanskrit for 'enlightened one'.

but may be on their way to mastership and have accomplished something.

As said earlier, in the technical terminology of this science a Saint, or a Master, is one who has reached the fifth region, called Sach Khand, there being eight principal planes in all.

A Sat Guru is a Saint who has been appointed by the Supreme Lord to perform the duties of giving *Nam,* or initiation, and of leading the disciples back to their home in Sach Khand. He is the executive officer of the Supreme Guru.

A Param Sant, or Supreme Saint, is one who has advanced to the highest possible degree, the supreme region of pure spirit. These several degrees can be obtained only by hard work and individual development.

In this book the terms *Master, Sat Guru* and *Saint* will be used synonymously, but meaning in all cases one who has gained the exalted status of Saint, rising to the fifth region by his own efforts with the aid of his Guru. If the student is to gain any proper understanding of this teaching, he must keep this fact always in mind. A *Saint,* as the word is used in this book, has absolutely no reference to a canonical saint of the Church. Such saints are made saints by decree of the Pope, while the real Saints develop into Saints by their own hard work, under the directions of their Gurus and by their help. There is no other way to become real Saints.

2. What Is a Genuine Master?

The Master is the most highly developed man known to history, and consequently by virtue of his development, he has become the most splendid specimen of manhood, the noblest of the noble. Not so much emphasis is ordinarily laid upon physical perfection, but his body must be a good one. A skilled workman must have good tools if he is to do his finest work. It is generally understood that no man with a defective body, any serious deformity, can ever become a real Sat Guru. His mind also must be of a very high type—keen, penetrating, quick of wit, and sound of judgment. He may not have been educated in the schools, but his mind must have undergone the severest training and discipline. A Master attains all knowledge which could possibly be given in the schools, and vastly more. In all respects, the Master is the highest type of man, when judged as *man*. In him all of the excellences of the civilized man reach their highest expression. He must be the super-man in all respects, not in one aspect alone. In him all the virtues recognized by the world are carried to the highest degree of perfection.

If I were looking for a Master, I would first of all make the most critical inspection of the man's life to determine if he had any of the ordinary imperfections of character usually manifested by the average man. If I found him to be *a perfect man,* when studied as man, I would then begin my study of him as a Guru. But if he failed to pass inspection as a man, I would at once give up the search in him for Guru, or Master.

The Master is the only man manifesting in history in whom individualism and universalism are combined in their full expression, in spite of the assertion of some philosophers that such a combination is impossible. That is, the Master stands alone, is a law unto himself, does what he pleases, has what he wants, comes and goes absolutely at his own will, and asks favors of no man. Neither can any man hinder him in the execution of his will. He is the only man who has no need to ask favors of others. He has all things at his own command. If he suffers hardships or inconveniences, that is because he chooses to do so for some purpose. He is the supreme giver, not a receiver; that is, he always pays for what he gets. He is slave to no one, is no time server, is bound by no rule or custom outside of himself and is a citizen of the whole world. At the same time, he is an ideal citizen of the commonwealth in which he lives. He merges himself into the social order and serves all without becoming subservient to any.

The Master is the teacher of all, the light and inspiration of all, whether they know it or not. Everyone who meets him is fortunate, whether he realizes it or not. His own great love alone binds him to all men and animals, to every living creature. He is both the Master of men and their servant, yet he is never fettered by human bonds. All of these he has severed before becoming a Master, yet he never shirks an obligation or fails to perform a duty. He loves, but with serene detachment. Loving in his manner, he can give greater love than any other man without becoming a slave to the objects of his affection.

There is but One to whom the Master bows in humble submission—the Supreme Lord, Sat Purush. His sovereign Will is the only law the Master recognizes, that and the universal law of all laws—*love*. Yet the Master breaks no law of man, but supports all good governments. His life and teachings are universal. He belongs to no race or time, but to all nations and all times. He is a citizen of the world—more correctly speaking, having come down here to bring light, he is a friendly visitor in this world. He is the ambassador plenipotentiary of the King of kings. It is the Master, any Master, together with the Life Stream manifesting through the Master, that was referred to in the statement:

> That was the true Light, which lighteth every man coming into the world. *(John 1:9)*

The Master is the best example for all men, king or peasant. He is generally a man of family, though not always. He is no ascetic and does not encourage austerities. He does not consider it a sin to keep the body comfortable, well fed and healthy; in fact, he says that it is a duty.

The Master lives in the world though he is not of it. He enters the stream of human life to help others, yet he himself stands aloof from the waves of human passion. He has attained all virtues, yet he does not partake of the weakness attributed to virtue by such philosophers as Nietzsche. He believes in developing the highest possible degree of strength, yet that strength must never be separated from the moral qualities. Strength minus love and humility produces a brute. The Master has become strong, stronger than any giant of body or intellect—for he has unlimited power; yet he combines with that strength the noblest virtues of the humble and the gentle. The tenderest sympathies of the mother are not excelled by the all-embracing love of the Master. He thus becomes the ideal of both Plato and Nietzsche. All people find in him inspiration for the building of noble character. At the same time he is equally the ideal for the warrior going forth to defend his country. He is the ideal of poetical song, the genuine romantic character of all idealists.

Lastly, the Master is the ideal in religion. In the innermost recesses of the soul, in every aspect of life, he is everywhere and always king. In short, he is the strong man with no weaknesses, the good man with no faults. In the realm of religion, the Master is a paradox. He has no theology, teaches none, yet he is the most religious man on earth. His system is not a religion, yet it leads to the most complete religious experience, and the most happy. He is absolutely universal in all his teachings. He has no creed, yet he never antagonizes any creed, sect or institution. He never condemns any man or any system. He finds no fault with anybody or anything, yet he draws the sharpest lines between the good and the bad. To the Saint, there is really nothing bad in the world, neither is there real fault in any man. What we generally point out as faults, the Master considers weaknesses, illness. For them he has only pity, not blame. He never criticizes, nor scolds, nor abuses, nor lectures—not even the vilest of sinners. The Master teaches that the habit of criticizing others, or faultfinding, is one of the most serious weaknesses. Besides, it advertises both the vanity and the ill temper of the faultfinder.

The Master lives and teaches positive truth. He overcomes evil with good. To correct faults in his disciples, he simply points out the opposite virtues. He teaches that to point out a fault is only to advertise and strengthen that fault; it never removes the fault. It only accentuates it and at the same time awakens other evil passions in both the faultfinder and his victim. Nor does the Master ever hold ill will, not even against his enemies. He literally obeys the injunction of Jesus to love one's enemies. For he loves everyone, regardless of character. Are not all men sons of the common Father? He gives love to all and seeks to serve all. He is always master of the situation, no matter where he is placed. He is never disturbed by the whirlwinds of passion surging about him. Serenely he watches the mad show and seeks to guide others in the ways of sanity.

Nietzsche warns us that the super-man has not yet arrived, and so we have said in the first few paragraphs of this book, but we were referring to the masses of mankind, and Nietzsche had never seen a Master. The Master has arrived; in fact, he has always been here, since the very beginning of human life on this planet. If modern philosophy must make war against tenderness, let such philosophers behold in the Master the best refutation of their arguments. All men must concede that if strength can be combined with tenderness, wisdom with love, the ideal is attained. Even Nietzsche, in his more lucid moments, acknowledged that Parsifal's gentleness was as necessary as Siegfried's strength. Strength, standing alone, is only half a man at best. It takes the two to make a real man. So the mastership of our super-man consists in combining strength with all of the finer virtues, plus something which is above strength and above virtue. Nietzsche did not know how to combine the two in one man. He had never seen a Master, and perhaps would not have believed that such a being could exist on earth today. If any of our materialistic critics, in a fit of rebellion against what they consider the weakness of the purely 'feminine virtues', disparage religion and discourage love, let them look to the real Master. If they are inclined to look upon Christ as an impractical dreamer, let them make the acquaintance of a real Master.

There is no doubt in the mind of this writer that European philosophy has waited long enough for some definite knowledge of a genuine Master in order that it may perfect its idealism. If materialistic scholars, exaggerating Darwinism, hold that the future welfare of the race demands that all emphasis shall be placed upon strength—strength of body and of mind—without reference to the spiritual man, then let them take note that in the Master we have the super-genius of their dreams, without losing the moral and spiritual values. If they feel inclined to kill off the weak and degenerate specimens of the human race, in the interests of the race itself, then let them watch the Master solve that problem. Let them observe how the Master, with superhuman love, wisdom and power, beyond the ken of the scholar, takes hold of the moral degenerate and makes a strong man of him.

He who advocates such barbarities in the name of social refinement is much like a man with a defective arm having it amputated at once, when with a little rational treatment it could have been restored to normal usefulness. How shall society answer, on the day of karmic reckoning, for the murder of the poor degenerate who is called upon to die in order that the human race may be strong? How shall he be compensated for the loss of his life in order that others may not partake of his weaknesses? A civilized social order must think not only of itself but of the least of its members. The old platitude, "The greatest good to the greatest numbers," is one of the greatest insults to real civilization that has ever been advocated. It has been made an excuse for the cruel murder of untold thousands of helpless victims of a shortsighted policy.

If, like the Roman, the modern philosopher must make bravery, courage and manhood synonymous with virtue, then let him behold the living Master, in whom humility is combined with majesty and strength in such perfect chemistry that, like atoms of carbon in the diamond, they form the purest gem of human character. Finally, if men insist that the goal of evolution is the development of brute strength rather than morality, why not look for an ideal super-man who combines unlimited power with a flawless morality? Either that, or take the opposite extreme, set to work under government regulations to breed giants of mind and body by scientific methods. If that were done, what do you think would happen? At the first provocation they would start a war to destroy one another.

If you have so far believed that a combination of gentleness and love with great strength is impossible, that is because you have not seen a living Master. We know he is a reality. We have lived and worked by his side for many years. Like St. Paul, we can now say:

We testify to that which we have seen, and bear witness to that which we *know*.

This book is not a compilation of theories. It is a statement of facts.

3. The Master More Than Super-Man

Of course, the Master is a super-man. But he is more than a super-man; that is, he transcends all of the limitations of mere man. His field of activity reaches out beyond that which the eye can see or the ear can hear. This, of course, takes us out of the physical laboratory. We must go where the microscope cannot follow, where the scalpel cannot dissect. Just as the astronomer could not find God with his telescope, so you will not find our Master with your x-ray. That there is an inner and finer world, numberless worlds which physical science cannot bring down into its test tubes, may be disputed by our materialist. But that is because he has not seen them, and he does not know how to get at them. At the same time, his egotism is loth to acknowledge the possibility of anything beyond the grasp of his forceps. This may be called the mental habit of the age. Always there is the danger that science, like theology, may become too dogmatic. The individual scientist himself may not be blamed for this tendency. Yet, not only do these inner worlds exist and are well known to the Masters, but any student who follows the formula of the Masters may prove the same thing for himself.

The Master is the super-scientist. The best of our physical scientists, when compared with a real Master, is no more than a child trying vainly to fit together his blocks to build a toy house. Real knowledge is gained only when a man surpasses the achievements of the super-man and enters the regions of Reality. But those regions lie far above and beyond the outermost confines of the physical universe. The mass of phenomena making up the spectacle of this world are but feeble reflections of the sublime Reality.

The physical scientist will at once object that it is impossible for any man to leave the theater of this physical plane and enter that of the superphysical regions. He insists that the physical universe is the limit of the legitimate field of science. Hence he concludes that beyond this field, there is nothing; if there is anything there, it is 'unknowable'. This word *unknowable* is not a word that sounds well in the mouth of a modern scientific student.

It is high time that this word be declared obsolete.

The physicist declares that everything relating to such higher worlds, being quite beyond the legitimate sphere of science, must be set down as mere speculation. Why? Simply because he has not been able to include such experiments in the routine of his laboratory work. But let us ask, is this the scientific attitude? Is it 'scientific' to assert that anything cannot be done, just because it has not been done? Or because he himself has not seen it done? When, a hundred years ago, men boldly asserted that flying through the air without the wings of a bird was contrary to the laws of Nature, and so could never be done—was that the scientific attitude? Today men are making headway by using one law of Nature to overcome the action of another law. The same thing is being done in the work of the great Masters. They are super-scientists. The business of the true scientist is to make due investigation first, then give his judgment afterwards or withhold judgment for further light. The greatest of modern scientists are as yet only in the kindergarten classes of the school of science which is now being built up.

This world is the theater of intellect—at least this is one of its fields of operation. It is the play of the mind. In this field, science has made many a conquest and will doubtless make many more. But there is a vast field far above and beyond the play of the mind, where the developed spirit alone may enter. It is into this higher region of the spirit where the Master goes, and it is there where his real achievements are made. Entering there by methods well known to him, he finds that this earthly world is nothing more than the mud-silt of Nature's vast and complicated structure. Above and beyond this world of shadow and pain lie innumerable worlds of intense light. They are real worlds, full of beauty, color, rhythm and joy.

Escaping for the time being the limitations of the body, the Master travels in those higher worlds, in full consciousness, and then he returns to report what he has seen and heard and otherwise experienced. He knows, among other things, that death is only an appearance, an illusion. When a man leaves his physical body at the time of what we call 'death', he simply steps out into other and higher worlds. He takes with him a finer body, which he now uses unconsciously, and on that higher plane he uses the finer one just as he uses the physical body here. Going about wherever he pleases, clothed in a godlike vesture of light, wisdom, power and beauty, the Master explores the higher regions, wholly unknown to the common earthman. This is but a glimpse of the real Master. To understand a real Master fully, one must oneself become a Master. Can the insect comprehend the man?

So many people find it difficult to believe in Masters. One of the strangest freaks of the human mind is its tendency to discredit all modern things, especially those relating to religion, and to give the emphasis and glory to that which is ancient. It cannot accept that which is right before its own eyes, but it will swallow instantly what was written in a book two or three thousand years ago. It cannot believe in a living Master, but it finds no difficulty at all in accepting the story of some Master who lived in the dim and distant past.

That men should ever have developed the strange notion that all mastership and all revelation of Truth should belong to past ages is one of the anomalies of history. And it is one of the most unfortunate. Isn't it more reasonable to look for the best to come out of modern experience, rather than to look for it among a people belonging to a crude civilization of long past ages? Surely, if we were looking for expert technique in plant culture, we would not go back to primitive man wandering along the shores of some primeval sea. We would think of Burbank, the first thing. But if a man wants expert information on religion, he refers to some prophet or yogi who wandered about the world before man ever dreamed that the earth was round and traveled around the sun. If past ages could produce a Master, a Christ, a Buddha, why may we not look for one now?

Let us be sincere and practical about the matter. It is idle to say that Masters are not needed now because we have a book that tells us about a past Master—as much reason to assert that man does not need food today because he has a printed menu that tells him about the food that was served a year ago. Besides, we know it is a fact that Masters are here today. We have seen them, conversed with them and lived by them for years. The fact that great spiritual Masters live on earth today is the most important, the most cheerful and the most hopeful announcement that has ever been made. And the light of the modern Master is in no way dimmed by comparison with any of the past Masters. Whatever wisdom, love, compassion, or power of miracles, which were possessed by any of the old Masters, these same qualities will be found in the modern Master in no respect diminished.

This book may be regarded as a challenge and an invitation to modern intelligence to come to the living Master and see for itself whether these things be true or not. You will not find the Master hidden away in some Himalayan retreat. You will see his address in this book. He will meet you as a man among men. You may sit down before him and talk to him in any language you may happen to speak. There will be no difficulty. There will probably be someone present to translate for you. And you may remain and study with him so long as you are searching sincerely for the Truth.

4. The Master and the Supreme One

There is one quality of the great Masters which I hesitate to write down here because it is so difficult to avoid misunderstanding on this subject; yet it must be written. It is a fact that there is no difference between the real Saint, or Master, and the Supreme Being himself; that is, there is no difference, except that a Saint is humanly embodied and is to some extent limited by that embodiment. And when we say that the Supreme One is embodied in this man whom we call a Saint, let no one be troubled. We do not mean to say that the whole of the Supreme One is so embodied. We could not be accused of suggesting that the Infinite One has abandoned the presidency of the universe and enclosed his entire godhood in this one poor human body! The Supreme One is the infinite, limitless whole of spiritual existence. It would be absurd to suggest that the universal soul of all souls, of all worlds, could be wholly centered in and limited to this one physical body. But it is nevertheless true that the Supreme Soul has taken form in this body.

Only a few days ago I had a letter from a good missionary in India, accusing me of idolatry and "blasting my monotheism" by worshipping a Guru. I replied that I am not worshipping the Guru in the sense that he meant. I love him; and love is akin to worship. It is about the only kind of worship I know anything about. If he means by 'worship' any sort of fear, then I must confess I do not 'fear' either the Guru or God. I love them. I revere them and love them. The old saying quoted from the Bible that "the fear of God is the beginning of wisdom," I regard as one of those terrible misapprehensions which have crept into literature unawares. Love is not only the beginning of wisdom, but it is Wisdom of the highest order.

Suppose we agree that the Supreme Being is all love, wisdom and power, that he is omnipresent, all-pervading. The Master is exactly the same, except as to his physical limitations. Spiritually he has no limitations. But the body is not the Master. It is only a covering, one of his ready instruments. He may, at will, leave the body and work upon any of the higher planes; each plane that he ascends to gives him greater freedom and scope of action. He himself, being one with the Infinite, has no limitations. Only the materials through which he works limit his actions; in like manner they limit the actions of the Supreme Being himself. Can God himself converse with you, as man with man, without first becoming man? The omniscience of the Lord may not be able to express itself through the physical brain of the Master. But the Master may, in a single minute, rise to regions above the sphere of brain activity, where his consciousness automatically expands even to the limitless. When he returns to this plane he will remember just as much of it as can be brought within the compass of brain action.

The real Master is as ubiquitous as the Infinite himself. And this is no illusion. For example, if a Master has a hundred or a thousand disciples, each disciple will see the Master in the inner chambers of his being, no matter where he may go. Of course, to do this, he must have attained a little development of his higher faculties. The disciple knows his Master as the giver of all life, the Lord of the universe. That is so because on the inner planes the Master is identical with the Supreme One.

If one must ask, "How can these things be?" the answer is, "Because the Master is one with the Supreme, and the Supreme One is expressing himself through the Master's form." The Master's form is the Lord's form. Whatever the Universal Spirit is, the individual Master is, identical in substance and attributes. There is a beautiful and inspiring concept associated with this idea of the Master being one with the Supreme. Each man is a potential Saint, and is therefore potentially identical with the Supreme. He only needs development and realization. Sainthood is therefore the supreme goal of all human evolution.

The Christian theologian may not be so far wrong when he assumes that Jesus, in his very essence, was the one God. Jesus himself said: "I and the Father are one." So all the Masters teach. But the Christian falls short of the grandeur of his own philosophy when he limits that divinity to just one Master in all history. This narrow view robs the noble concept of all its value. But that principle, in order that it may fertilize the entire field of philosophy, must be extended to include not only numerous Masters, but it must include all men as a potentiality.

That scripture which speaks of Jesus as "the only begotten son of God" need not be taken too seriously. It has all the earmarks of an interpolation slipped into the original record to support the contentions of some later disputant. Besides, if this passage is to be taken literally, it proves entirely too much. If Jesus was begotten of God in a manner different from that of any other man, then God himself must have descended to the human level to perform such a function. Certainly the part played by his mother was not different from that of any other normal mother, according to the record itself. Will any theologian go that far? The more comforting fact remains that there have been many sons of God, and there surely will be many more. But when they come into human life, they come according to the method prescribed by the Creator himself. Do you think the Creator would himself disdain to use his own method? If it is unworthy of a 'God-man' to have a mere man for a father, it must be equally inappropriate for him to have a woman for a mother. One is just as human and as sinful as the other.

In the process of their development, all Masters simply expand the godlike qualities with which they, in common with all other men, were born. Any true Master is a divine man, a real son of God. Moreover, every man has in him the latent possibilities of such expansions, to become a son of God. He only requires a living Master to help him develop it. He needs but the flames of mastership in another man to light the fires in himself.

When any Master attains sainthood, he gains conscious oneness with the Supreme. It is true that all men have that oneness to a degree, but few of them are conscious of their noble inheritance. The real Master is conscious of it. That is one of the distinguishing qualities of a Master. He *knows* his relationship with the Supreme Oversoul and is consciously able to exercise his powers and prerogatives as a son of God. He is then more truly and accurately named a son of God than is any earthly man as son of his father. Partaking of his qualities, *ipso facto,* one and the same in essence and endowed with the same attributes, he is literally part of the all-embracing Father. That means that henceforth, while the Master may speak and act through his body much the same as others do, yet in reality he is the Supreme One who is acting and speaking. He is no longer a mere man with clouded and limited understanding, but a man who has become God, and a God who has become man. And then, out of a boundless love, the Master says:

This is for any man who will walk on the Path of the Saints.

5. Time Limit of the Master's Work

There is one very important consideration regarding the work of all Masters, which appears never to have been understood by Western people. This is the fact that their work is time-limited. This means that each Master has a definite period in which to do his work. When that time has expired, his work on earth is finished. That limited period is during the life of their physical bodies. That being the case, logically they cannot work among men without their body. When that body passes or they pass out of it, their work on earth is finished.

Let us assume now that your master of ancient days was a real Saint, a Master, a Prophet, or whatever title you may wish to give him, and that he had all the powers ascribed to him by your religion. What then is the difference, whether you follow him or a living Master? There is a vital difference—you simply cannot follow the departed Master—not at all. Neither can he initiate you on the spiritual Path. If you think you can follow him, you only deceive yourself. It cannot be done. You only imagine you follow him. You may read his precepts and try to obey them, but in that you are not following the real Master. He has nothing at all to do with the matter. He himself does not know you. You may try to put into practice the precepts taught by him. To some extent you may do that. But the teachings of that Master were not his alone. He didn't originate them. They belong to universal Truth. He did not need to come into the world to give out those teachings. They were here long before his time.

Ages before the time of Jesus or of Buddha, every single precept taught by either one of them was well known in the world and formed a part of the fundamental code. If you live up to those teachings, you are not thereby following that particular Master or any one Master. If a given precept has been taught by seven Masters during different ages of the world, are you thereby a disciple of all seven of them? You are simply walking in the light of universal ethical principles, regardless of individual Masters. You will doubtless say that your Master is taking care of you today, but that is no more than an assumption unsupported by a single shred of proof. Your feeling is no proof. Anything can be proved by feelings. The devotees of ten different religions, each claiming to follow a different Master, will all declare with equal emphasis that they all *feel* their Lord inside of themselves.

Where then is the real crux of the problem? Something besides feeling, something besides the authority of a book, is needed. And that need is *a living Master*. No man living today can possibly follow a departed Master any more than a Hannibal or Alexander or a George Washington can lead troops to battle today. The period of their activity on earth has passed. It is the same with spiritual Masters. A child cannot get nourishment or learn vital lessons from a dead mother. A sick man cannot obtain medicine from a dead doctor; neither can a dead jurist try a case at law. The Master of past ages has gone from this field of action, and thus he has finished his work here. Why did he ever come here? To do work which he could not possibly do unless he came as a man. He had to have a physical body to do his work. When his work was finished, he left his body and turned over his work to his successor. And this is the method of the Supreme Father. We need not quarrel with it. We did not order it so, nor did the Masters themselves create it. It is an arrangement ordained by the Supreme Lord himself. God's method of working among men is by and through living men. How could it possibly be otherwise? An animal could not teach us, and we cannot see any being higher than man.

Now, suppose we look to a book. Wasn't that book written by some man, and wasn't it simply a record of that man's experiences? What then is the harm if some man living today has a similar experience and then tells us about it firsthand? Books long ago handed down always suffer changes and appear at last having but little resemblance to the original record. How can we believe them or depend upon them? And even if those records were absolutely true and perfect, it is not the precept we need, half so much as the living Master to take us by the hand and help us where we cannot walk alone. No matter if all the wisdom of all the ages were written down in a book, it still remains a fact that the student can make no headway without a living Master to help him put that teaching into practical effect. It simply cannot be done any other way, as many of us know by experience.

Even if the ancient Master, present in spirit as claimed by so many, were ready to assist us, it is impossible for us to receive his help. If we must depend upon feelings and impressions, we are mixed up with so many feelings and impressions that it is quite impossible for us to distinguish between them so as to know which are from God or the old Master and which from our own subconscious minds. There is, therefore, no safe method, except to walk by sight in the full light, when and where we can see our Master and listen to his well-known voice. This requirement is for today just the same as it has been for all ages. It can never be otherwise, so long as men do not have clear vision on a higher plane.

If it were possible for a departed Master to reach us now, then there never would have been the need for a Master at all. The Creator himself could have come to us and done all that was needed. The very fact that a Master was ever needed is sufficient proof that one is needed today, because the conditions are the same in all ages. Leaving out of consideration the question of the book, the daily and constant guidance and help of the Master is as much needed now as ever. Assuredly, if a departed Master can help now, the Creator could do as much without the help of anyone.

We may concede that neither the Creator nor the departed Master is limited, but we are limited. We cannot with safety or certainty receive help from one we cannot see. Hence, it still remains a fact of Nature that not even God himself can instruct us or give us the needed help on the upward Path without a Master in human form to act as his agent and spokesman. Our ears are too dull, our eyes too dim, to hear and see his manifestations. This is the greatest stumbling block of all religions. Trying vainly to follow him in their imagination, their adherents cling desperately to the dead Master while they reject the living Master.

If you insist that your dead Master is not dead, then I will cheerfully agree with you. He is not dead, but he has left this theater of action. He is no longer in touch with humanity. His present work is elsewhere. There is no doubt but some departed Masters have certain work to do in connection with world affairs, but we are speaking here of discipleship, not other matters.

If you insist that your departed Master is here with you because you can feel him in your soul, then I must insist again that your feelings are a very unreliable guide. Most of such feelings are but the play of one's own mind, a deceptive play of a fond imagination, probably worked up by centuries of theological suggestion.

Let us illustrate this point, for it is of extreme importance. Once the famous Billy Sunday, an American evangelist, told a seeker for spiritual light that he could feel Jesus in his soul. This he offered as final proof that Jesus was actually present in him. He thus assumed that there was nothing more to be said on the subject. But the seeker replied: "In like manner the devotees of all religions can prove the truth of their several claims. They all feel their Masters inside. No religion has a monopoly on feelings." The reverend gentleman had no answer.

All men will recognize, if they think of the matter at all, that feelings are no proof in religious matters. Still your devoted believer goes on never doubting that his feelings are conclusive proof that his religious assumptions are true to fact. The wise man will learn to discount feelings as proof of religious dogmas. What then is left? Upon what shall a man rely as proof? There is but one wise course, but one way to know what you are doing—go to a living Master whom you can see and hear, whose hand you can take in your own, and then use your common sense. The Master does not ask you to take anything for granted or to believe what he says just on his statement alone. He offers you a definite method by which you can prove things for yourself, *not by feeling* but by sight and hearing. Fortunately there is a scientific spiritual Path wherein men may walk by sight with firm and certain step.

6. How Shall We Recognize a Master?

Having said so much about the Master, it is now quite appropriate to ask: How shall we recognize a true Master if we find one? How shall one distinguish between the genuine and the counterfeit? Or by what means shall we find a Master? Whither shall we go to look for one? These and many other similar questions present themselves and demand rational answers.

In reply, the first point of importance is what we may call

cumulative evidence. I have never seen the city of Paris and so I do not positively know that Paris exists, but judging from the cumulative evidence, I believe it does. Accordingly, examine all the evidence supplied by others. Give it careful analysis. Note also the credibility of the witnesses. That is important. Consider their intelligence and general character and take special note of their motives. If many people of high standing and good intelligence believe in a certain man as a Master, then at least you may proceed to look into the matter further.

When you see him, give him the most critical study. For one whole year, I lived and worked and traveled right by the side of my Master and took note of everything he said and did, even watching the expression on his face during crises, such as when he was attacked by opponents with fierce arguments and abuse. I watched his reactions when people came before him confessing their sins. I watched him when he went into the hovels of the poor to see the sick, and I studied him carefully when he entered the homes of the rich. I observed him carefully when dealing with two rajas who tried to bow at his feet. I took careful note when streams of people came along offering money for some public building, like the satsang hall—also when people tried to give him money or other things for himself. Under all conditions, I found him *a perfect man,* as a Master is supposed to be, as perfect character—as a man—is the foundation of spiritual mastership. If a man has not that to begin with, one had better let him alone.

See if a man appears to be all that has been suggested in the preceding pages about Masters. Compare notes. Take plenty of time to find out the facts. Be always on your guard against hasty conclusions, either for or against. Hold an open mind, even long after you think yourself convinced—a little more convincing will do no harm. The matter is extremely important. You cannot afford to make a mistake. It is unfortunate to go to a counterfeit master. But it is far more unfortunate to allow yourself to be turned away from a real Master by some hasty judgment. That is in fact a real disaster. Finally, never mind if you are convinced against your will or predilections. Let facts direct your conclusions.

Secondly, *listen to the voice of intuition*. If you are not sufficiently convinced by the previous considerations, let your own intuition give its testimony. That, like impressions and feelings, is not conclusive, but it helps. If you are at all ready for the Path of the Masters, your intuitive faculties will be well developed. Use them. How does he appear to you? How does he impress you? What effect does he have upon you while in his presence? When you leave him, do you appear to yourself a better man than before or do you feel depressed? Of course, feelings are not at all conclusive. This we have already emphasized at some length. But they may be considered for what they are worth in the sum of evidence to be weighed. How does he impress you the next day? The next month? Does it appear to you that you might possibly love and honor him and be exalted in character by such devotion, or do you feel depressed after leaving him? Do you have to reason yourself into liking him or do you like him in spite of your predilections? These you may weigh well.

And yet all of these things are not conclusive proofs. There is but one way to *know* beyond all peradventure that a man is a Master—that is to see him on some higher plane, where deception is impossible. See him where spiritual qualities are manifest to all. If you *see the Master* there *in his Radiant Form,* you have nothing more to worry about. You have found your Master and you know it just as certainly as you know that you exist. If you go to that higher plane, however, and fail to meet your Master there, then you must look further.

There is one more very encouraging truth that must not be overlooked in this connection. If you are seeking the Master, he is approaching you, and *you must meet him*. It is only a question of getting ready for that great event. One of the oldest sayings of the Eastern Wisdom is:

When the chela is ready, the Guru appears!

In these latter days the writer has had sufficient proof of this ancient maxim. We know it is true, just as we know of the truth of other points in this teaching. Let no hungry soul be discouraged.

You simply must meet the Master if you are ready for him, and to be extremely anxious to meet him is fairly good evidence that you are ready for him. There is nothing within or beyond the seven seas that can keep you away from him. But look well to your preparation. Remember, the vessel must first be cleaned before the water of life can be poured into it by the Master.

Having now found the Master, what next? Follow him with unwavering faith and determination. In other words, after you have once accepted a man as a Master, accept his formula also and work it out with absolute fidelity. If you run up against many problems which cause your boat to rock, hold a steady hand upon the oars of self-mastery and wait while you work. At first there will be puzzling questions. At times you may be inclined to say outright, "I cannot believe it." But just hold such things in reserve and wait. Do not jump at conclusions. Let them come to you. Wait and work. By and by, your questions will answer themselves; you will be surprised how very easily. *When the light becomes strong, the darkness vanishes.*

Remember that your entire life's thinking has now to be reorganized. Do not make the mistake of trying to fit the Master's teaching into your old thinking. It will not work. Neither can you bring your old notions into the new system. Drop them all and start on anew. Later on you can pick them up again, if you do not like the new. Suspend judgment until all evidence is in. Work upon the principle that *Truth cannot be damaged by the light.* Make the scientific method your own, and then go on gathering evidence, all the while holding an open mind. Guard well against vanity of opinion; that only obstructs the Path of knowledge. Opinion is of no great value. Only facts count on this Path. Do not allow an old opinion to block your way to the facts. Remember, this is the Path of scientific demonstration, not a system of beliefs.

7. Objective Indices of Mastership

We mean by objective indices that sort of evidence which other people, anybody, may see and understand. In addition to all that has been said about the Masters, there are a few infallible indices which serve to distinguish real Masters from all others who may pose as Masters. Some of them are:

(1) First and most noticeable is the important fact that real *Masters never charge* for their services, nor do they accept payment in any form, or any sort of material benefits, for their instructions. This is a universal law among Masters, and yet it is an amazing fact that thousands of eager seekers in America and elsewhere go on paying large sums of money for 'spiritual instruction'. *Masters are always self-sustaining. They are never supported by their students or by public charity.*

(2) *Masters never boast* of their mastership or of their spiritual powers or attainments. If any man claims to have attained the highest in spiritual development, that claim of itself may be taken as conclusive proof that he has not attained so much. Masters always show the utmost humility, but they never make their humility obtrusive. They never do anything to advertise their humility or to exhibit it to public gaze.

(3) *Masters never complain* of their treatment at the hands of others. Even if you abuse one, he will not reply angrily nor will he speak of it afterward. They never speak of their hard luck or of the ingratitude of their beneficiaries.

(4) *Masters never find fault or blame others* either to their faces or behind their backs, no matter what the provocation. They speak no ill and they never lecture others concerning their shortcomings. They exalt the positive virtues, keeping silent about the evil, except to answer questions or give necessary warnings.

(5) *Masters never punish anybody,* even their worst enemies or those who have mistreated them. They leave the punishment of evildoers to the Negative Power, whose business it is to administer justice. Their lives are governed entirely by *the law of love.* They give of their light and love, even as the sun gives its light and heat, and ask nothing in return.

(6) *Masters are never given to ascetic practices* or unreasonable austerities. This is one quality which differentiates them from certain types of yogis. Masters insist that everyone should give attention to his health of body as well as of mind and soul. They

always teach that it is a duty to keep the body clean, healthy and well nourished. Of course, they teach that it is wrong to eat too much. And nothing should ever be taken into the body that is not a wholesome food or drink. They teach also that the body must never be made an instrument of passionate enjoyment just for the sake of pleasurable sensations. When you see anyone given to self-torture or to self-indulgence, you may know at once that he is not a Master. Some yogis seek to control the mind by torturing the body, but that is a vain effort. Mind can never be subdued that way.

(7) *Masters never go about begging their living.* They are always self-supporting. The Master is always the giver, but never a beggar. Neither does he permit his disciples to beg their living while sitting around in idleness. So when you see anyone begging his living or charging for his spiritual instruction, you may know that he is neither a Master nor even a disciple of a Master. Guru Nanak says: "He who earns an honest living and gives away something out of it in charity, knows the Way."

(8) *A real Master never performs miracles for public exhibition.* He may do miracles on special occasions and for particular reasons, but in every case it is kept a secret from the public. It is a fixed law with real Saints that they will never do miracles to win disciples. Yogis often do miracles, healing the sick and other things, but real Masters never do them, except on very special occasions and for urgent reasons.

(9) *All genuine Masters teach and practise the Audible Life Stream,* or Sound Current, called in Hindi the *Shabd*. That is the central theme of all their discourses, the very core of their meditations. As this Current is the life of the world itself, so it is the life of every Master throughout all his daily practices. It is the paramount theme of which he talks at all times. If a man preaches and practises the Life Current, it is presumptive evidence that he is a Master although it is not conclusive. But if a man does not preach and practise it, does not mention it in his discourses, that alone is the most conclusive evidence that he is not a Master. This is the universal teaching of all Masters, most conspicuous in their teachings and practices. Let this, then, be your chief test of all men

posing as Masters and of all systems offering to guide you to higher worlds. If they have not the Life Stream as the very essence of their system, they have nothing.

(10) If any yogi or other man claiming to be a Master teaches that Brahm Lok, or the region of Brahm, is the highest of all heavens and that Brahm is the Supreme God, then you may know of a certainty that he is not a Master. For Brahm Lok is only the second of the higher regions, or planes, while above that are six other planes, in an ascending scale, each higher and greater than the one below it. In the Grand Hierarchy of the universe, Brahm, the ruler of Trikuti and the three worlds, is but a humble subordinate under the Supreme One.

The above are only a few of the outstanding indices of mastership. There are many others. But a careful study of these will act as sufficient safeguard against deceit by pretenders. The counterfeit master will always show his cloven foot if he is carefully watched for a short time.

8. Very Difficult to Find a Master

We have already said that if one is ready for a Master, he cannot fail to find one. And yet we must say that it is extremely difficult to find a Master. How are we to reconcile these two statements? It is, in fact, the most difficult of all undertakings for the man who is unprepared, and yet it is the easiest thing in the world for one who is prepared. As a matter of fact, if one is ready for the Master, he cannot fail to find him. To some of us here at the Master's little retreat, it appears simple enough. Anybody from the four quarters of the globe may come to him. There is no secrecy, no mystery about him. He is quite tangible and visible. He lives an open life before the world. He travels in motorcars and trains, as others do. He sits before his disciples and talks to them in groups, large or small. And yet how very few are they that find him! How very difficult to discover him! I think it may be said, in all truth, that *unless the Master himself wishes to be found, no one will ever find him.* And he wishes only those to find him who are ready for him.

It is true, people may hear his name. They may even be told that he is a Master. But they will never discover him as a Master. There are tens of thousands who come and go the whole year around, even listening to his discourses, but many of them never make the great discovery. Villagers living within two miles of him, who have met him scores of times, have never discovered his mastership. We write about him to friends in distant lands, but even though we write pages about him it never dawns upon them that here is a living Master. They simply cannot see it. Educated, thinking men and women come here, attend the satsangs, listen to the Master's words, ask searching questions, and then go away without discovering the Master. They simply cannot see him unless they are ready for that critical point in their long course of evolution.

I remember a man from Europe who came here a few years ago and remained a month. He had no fault to find, even asked for the initiation. But, as later events proved, he had never a glimpse of consciousness that here was a real Master. To this man the Master was just an interesting teacher of spiritual philosophy, one among many whom he had seen. The fellow wrote me long letters afterward, telling in rapturous hyperbole how God was speaking to him in the flowers and singing to him through the birds. But he had no inkling of the divine music which was dynamic in the living Master. He had never discovered the Master. Why? Because he was too full of himself. He believed himself a reincarnation of the poet Wordsworth. He could hear God calling to him in Nature, he said, but his ears were deaf to the voice of the Supreme One speaking to him through the living Master. He was obsessed by certain ideas, all revolving around himself, and that obsession blinded his eyes.

A man once built his cabin in the gold fields of California. He lived there and raised a family. He prospected over and through the hills all about his cabin and at last died in poverty. But his son, digging down to lay the foundation of a new house, struck a rich lead and became a millionaire. Plenty of gold was right under the veranda of his old house, but he died in poverty. Such is often the case in spiritual matters. Those who cannot see the Master because they are self-blinded die in spiritual poverty, while vast spiritual riches are closer than the house they live in.

Many will read this book, of which the main theme is the living Master, yet they will put the book down without catching a glimpse of the Reality. They will never discover the Master. Why? Filled with their own ideas, blinded by their own preconceptions, they will pick up the book and will not be able to see anything in the book. *No one can discover the Master until certain inner preparations have been made.* This is the secret of the whole mystery. You must be prepared 'in your heart'. Whenever and wherever a man is so prepared, is 'of lawful age and well recommended', is willing to disrobe himself of his own rags of self-righteousness and then come humbly before the Master as 'a poor blind candidate', knowing his own blindness and knocking for admittance to the chambers of Light, then and then only will the Master order the door opened to him. Then and then only will he discover the Master coming 'out of the East' to give him Light.

9. Positive Knowledge Versus Beliefs

Before concluding our discussion about the Masters, it is in order to say that the Masters, being what they are and knowing what they know, never guess or speculate concerning the great truths entrusted to their care. Their science is based upon positive knowledge, not theory. They care nothing for mere beliefs or opinions. Their system is a definite and exact science. They therefore speak with the authority of incontrovertible experiential knowledge. Consequently, if a body of great truths—facts—are boldly set down in this book with an apparent dogmatic assumption of finality, let it not be attributed to the egotism of a sophomore. If a man goes to Alaska and later writes to his friends that he has discovered a gold mine and already has in his possession one hundred thousand dollars worth of nuggets, he would not be accused of egotism because he made the announcement. He would just be considered lucky. If this American writer has discovered, and now writes down in a book, certain revolutionary truths worth more than millions of gold nuggets, he need not be accused of unreasonable assumptions. Let the reader take time to investigate these claims; prove them for himself. Apply the acid test.

Some of these facts in the science of the Great Master, never before made known to Western people by a Western man, are indeed so extraordinary that they may at first provoke incredulity. They are amazing and they are extremely significant, more than they may at first appear. The unqualified statements herein made are due to the simple fact that the writer is only serving in the humble capacity of an *amanuensis* to write down exactly what the Great Master teaches in the language of his own people. And he has done the most critical study of the Master and his teaching after more than six years of sojourn right with the Master, and was aided in these studies by a number of Indian gentlemen who were both scholars and long-time disciples of the Master.

The most painstaking effort has been made to correctly formulate a statement of these teachings and present them in a way to be easily comprehended. Therefore, let it be kept in mind that what is written here is neither a set of opinions nor a metaphysical scheme spun out of the web of fancy. It is exactly what the Masters themselves have seen, experienced and therefore known. No more, no less. This account is based neither on hearsay nor derived from books. But very few quotations are given in this work because this book is not intended as a compendium of book learning. The substance of this work was given direct to the writer by a very great living Master, which is at the same time identical with that which has been taught by all true Saints in all ages. This latter fact has been tested by comparison of the living Master's word with the writings of all Saints, so far as they are available in Sanskrit, Arabic, Persian, Hindi, Urdu and Punjabi.

The writing and publishing of this book has been done after the approval and according to the expressed wish of the Great Master, whose life and teachings have inspired these pages. The writer makes no claims for himself and takes no credit whatsoever. He has simply done his best to prepare these materials for publication. In doing so, he wishes to record at this place his gratitude to the Master and his everlasting obligation for the privilege of living in daily association with him for all these precious years. During all that time, the Master never tired of giving instruction, patiently listened to the many questions—endless numbers of them—and carefully elucidated all problems with limitless patience and untiring endurance. Hours upon hours, day in and day out, a small group of us have sat around the Great Master, asking questions and listening to his words of wisdom.

Men and women of keen minds and unflagging zeal have come here from all quarters of the earth, plying the Master with every conceivable question, covering every problem in philosophy and religion. To all these discussions we have listened and made notes of the Master's replies. We have never seen the Master fail to have ready a logical and convincing answer; his science is clear and rational. He speaks with equal clearness and convincing force, no matter whether he is talking to an ignorant peasant or a Sanskrit pundit. We have often been amazed to see them all go away convinced and perfectly satisfied, many returning later to ask for the initiation. Not infrequently, we have seen the keenest critics come purposely to find fault, but remain to worship.

Last of all, the Great Master himself lays down the challenge to the whole world to come into the laboratory of individual experience and experiment, and prove for itself the truth of the teachings of the Saints. That must constitute the final test, and the Master welcomes such a test.

We must not fail to publish here one more word concerning the substance of this book and the Great Master who has been its inspiration. That is, the Master himself must not be held responsible for any inaccuracies or other imperfections in this book. The writer alone is responsible for these.

10. The Duties of the Masters

A word may be said regarding the duties of the Masters, although much is to be said elsewhere concerning their functions. The

Masters have many duties in this world, but we shall mention only four of them at this time. They are:

(1) The first and foremost and the primary duty of the great Masters is *to connect souls with the Audible Life Stream* and then take them up and out of this world to their own original home. This is done by a process of 'tuning in'.

By many ages of self-indulgence in these regions of gross matter, everyone has gotten himself out of tune with the infinite Stream of Life. This Stream, wave, or current is comparable to the electro-magnetic wave of the radio. It fills all space around us and within us, but we do not know it and cannot hear it until we are tuned into harmony with it. Being so out of tune, man wanders on for ages in 'the prisonhouse of maya'. And no man can ever get himself into tune again, unaided. It is in this regard that the Saint, the Master, becomes a real Savior, Redeemer and Deliverer. It is a work which cannot be done by anyone except a living Master; and without it being done, no one can ever escape the painful cycle of birth and death in material regions. This is the great work of the Master.

(2) The next work of the Master is *to teach the Way* to his disciples. So the Master is the Great Teacher as well as the great physician and deliverer. He alone has the key to the kingdom of heaven within. He alone can guide the wandering soul to the open door. Without a Master, no soul can ever find his way out of the circle of births and deaths. It simply cannot be done. He may rise a little distance. He may gain the first, possibly the second, region on the upward path, but there he is automatically stopped. Further than that he can never go alone, and none but Masters know the way beyond that. The wisdom and personal help of the Master are both absolutely essential if one is to advance any further than a mere start on the Path.

The secondary function of the Master is that of a teacher. But we should always remember that the great work of the Master is that of a Rescuer, a Redeemer—to liberate us from 'the eternal Wheel'. While his secondary function is that of a teacher, yet the former is by all odds the more important. If the student were given every precept of this science and had the most detailed instructions that could be given of all the secrets of initiation, they would avail him nothing without the help of the Master. And this is the main reason why no book can ever take the place of a living Master.

(3) *The Master is a perfect exemplar* for all mankind as to character, nobility and spirituality. He is the ideal man, and to him all may look for the one perfect example of character and conduct. All may imitate him, follow him implicitly, and then they may rest assured that no mistake will be made. The Master is not only a great spiritual light, he is also a perfect man.

(4) The fourth function of the Master is *to bring light and love into the world,* so that all men, not simply his disciples alone but the whole world, may profit thereby. This is a part of his secret work. No one may follow him into the secret chambers of his retreat and there see all features of the great work that he is doing. His special work is for individual disciples, but he works also for all mankind. Let us state this point in the most concise language, so that it will be understood. *There is not a living being in all the world who does not receive benefit from the Master.* This statement may not be easy to understand at first, but it is literally true. The Masters are sometimes criticized for "not coming out and doing something for the world." But how little do such critics know about what the Masters are doing! The Master is "the light of the world." The Master increases the sum total of the light and the love of the whole world, and every sentient individual gets some benefit. We need not worry over the method. The fact of greatest importance to us all is that the Supreme Father illumines and blesses the whole world through and by the agency of the Master. And he liberates every individual soul by the same instrumentality. This is his method. If the critic insists on knowing why he has adopted this method, he may be referred to the Creator himself for the answer. It is out of the sphere of my knowledge. I am content to know that it is so, and that knowledge is a source of great joy to me.

11. Why Surrender to a Master?

I am sure many of our critics will say: Why surrender your individual will or personality to a Master? Isn't that going back into voluntary slavery? Isn't that another way of crushing individual initiative and strength of character?

The answer is that *complete surrender to the Master is the only avenue or path to complete liberation*. This may sound rather paradoxical, but it isn't if you understand what complete surrender to the Master actually means. First let us say that the word *surrender* is not a suitable term for what is meant in this connection, but it is about the best term we have. It would be better to say that one fully trusts the Master. That is equivalent to saying that a person trusts his higher interests in the hands of an expert. It is as if a sick man goes to a skilled surgeon. An operation is needed. He has thought over the entire matter. He has decided on the competency of the surgeon and then places his life in that surgeon's hands.

Another illustration may help. Suppose you are lost in a dense forest. You haven't the least idea of the way out. You might wander around in there for days or weeks and finally die of starvation and thirst. But along comes an expert woodsman fully acquainted with the woods. He offers to show you the way out. Now, will you quibble about surrendering your own will to his? You gladly accept his offer. But suppose, in addition to being lost, you have become very ill and weak, quite unable to walk out. Now our strong woodsman kindly offers to carry you out. Will you quibble about surrendering your individual will to the woodsman? That were the height of folly, certainly. Yet this is an exact parallel to the plight of the soul, which is lost in the mazes of this world of mind and matter and does not know how to make its way to spiritual liberty.

Even if while you were lost in the forest you had all the necessary maps and charts and knew which way to go, you could not get out because of your illness; and for that reason you need the help offered. So it is with the Master. He not only shows us the way out, but he offers to help us where we could not possibly make our way alone. This is why no book is of any use to us and nothing else is of any value, unless we can get the actual help needed. The greatest friend we could possibly have is one who not only tells us how to escape from our difficulties, but who offers us the needed help. This is the real Master.

Again, another illustration may help to clarify the matter. A man is to make a journey to a foreign country. He considers the means of travel. He studies the different ship lines, the railroads and the airlines. After careful discrimination, he chooses his means of travel. He enters, let us say, the particular airliner and sits down. The plane takes off. Now his period of individual judgment and discrimination is finished. He surrenders himself to that ship and its pilot. He cannot dictate. His duty is to sit down and trust all to the pilot. The skill of the pilot and the trustworthiness of the ship are now depended upon to take him safely to his journey's end. He can no longer dictate. His period of independent choice is over and the time of absolute trust has come. So he makes his journey. The same situation confronts everyone who wishes to make the journey to higher regions and escape this world of darkness and pain. He may use all the reasoning powers, all the keen intellectual discrimination he possesses, *in selecting the Master;* but after he has done that, he must trust the rest to the Master. The reason is that the Master is expert about those things of which he himself is totally ignorant. And if he is ever to make the journey, he simply must trust the Master.

The surrendering of the individual will is only a bugaboo. It is a cry of the ego, a vain alarm. It has no value at all. You really surrender nothing to the Master which you ought to keep. It is merely a case of entrusting your higher interests to the hands of an expert. You accept his aid and guidance over a Path quite unknown to yourself. How could you ever get out of the wilderness if you objected to the proposition of your friend who wishes to save you? How could the man make his trip in the airliner if he persisted in his right to pilot that airplane himself when he knew nothing about it? A man is sick, and an expert physician offers him medical aid. If the sick man says: "No, I will not allow anyone else to give me medicine; I will be my own doctor or surgeon"—

such assertion of the ego is not only foolish but suicidal.

It is a well-known fact that no true Master ever imposes his own will upon any student. It is a cardinal principle with all true Masters never to cramp the freedom of their disciples. Of this they are extremely careful. The Master is the last man living to dominate any intelligence. He seldom ever gives a command. He simply advises.

What is really meant by complete surrender to a Master is this: Out of perfect confidence and great love, the disciple gladly follows where the Master leads. That is the sum of it all. No need of quibbling over something that has no value and no meaning. Let it pass. Use common sense. By perfect surrender to a Master, in this sense, one gains everything, ending in the most perfect liberty. This is well expressed by one great Sufi, who said: "Give us all you have and we will give you all we possess!" By surrendering all to the Master, you gain everything.

12. The Masters' Change of Policy

One very important change in the policy of the great Masters has recently taken place and many may wonder at it. This change of policy relates to their method of accepting disciples. In ancient times, even down to the last few centuries, the great Masters were very exclusive in their choice of disciples. Hence novitiates were few. Disciples were accepted only after the most severe tests, the most trying ordeals. The select few who passed these tests received the initiation. But now that policy has been modified. The Masters, during the last hundred years or so, have accepted practically all who applied, unless their karmas were too bad. Soami Ji and Baba Jaimal Singh each initiated about four thousand during their lifetimes. (The number initiated by Guru Nanak is not definitely known.) But the living Master, Baba Sawan Singh Maharaj, has already initiated approximately eighty thousand. This is a marvelous record, far beyond anything in history. In one single month, April 1933, he initiated forty-nine hundred, a number exceeding that of any other Master in history during the whole of his lifetime.

What is the meaning of this change of policy? First, because so many more have applied for initiation in late years; and that is undoubtedly because so many more are ready for the Path. Second, the Masters have now abandoned the rigid tests formerly imposed upon applicants and are now willing to accept disciples of lesser qualifications. Why? The Masters themselves know best. But we may offer a suggestion or two here which will explain the matter, in part at least.

In this Kal Yuga, the Dark or 'Iron' Age, the ills of life upon this planet have greatly multiplied. Hence, the mercy and loving sympathy of Sat Purush, the Great Father, has led him to meet the willing-minded more than halfway. Now practically every person who feels inclined toward the Sat Guru and wishes to follow his Path is accepted by him. To reach that momentous decision is the one thing of paramount importance in all one's life. What is the result? Many initiates, entering the Path half-heartedly and but ill-prepared, naturally fall by the wayside when assailed by severe temptation. But what is the harm? Some good has been done. The precious seed has been lodged in their minds and souls. Sooner or later they all must return to the Path. That return, according to the Master's teachings, cannot be later than three or four subsequent incarnations. In the meantime, they have been greatly helped in their upward struggles. This is done out of great mercy and lovingkindness of the Sat Guru himself and the Supreme One.

The main point is that each individual who gets the initiation, after ages of pain and struggle, has at last come to the decision to place his destiny in the hands of the Guru, and of his own free will and accord has asked for the initiation. He then meets the Sat Guru, the executive officer of the Supreme, and the Sat Guru takes over the charge. The final liberation of that soul is then absolutely assured. Nothing in the universe can possibly defeat that end. It is only a question of a little time. What does it matter if that soul does stumble frequently before he learns to run alone.

One more significant point must not be overlooked. The

critic has no right to demand perfection in the character and conduct of every initiate. Beginners on this Path are all struggling in the clutches of mind, pursued and harassed by the five passions. It must be expected that these passions will get the better of them occasionally. The only important point is that if they do stumble and fall, they fall with their faces toward the light. No man who is once initiated into this Path can possibly get the consent of his own mind to turn the whole of his life into channels of evil. If initiates fall, they have only to get up again and go on, that is, if the critics will let them alone, or better still, give them a little love and sympathy. If they fall, the Master himself never condemns. The sinner is just as sure of the love and help of the Master as is the most saintly disciple. The only difference is that the sinner loses what he has gained and slips back on the Path.

The attitude of the Master toward the offender ought to be an example to us. We must always scrupulously avoid laying the blame either upon the disciple or upon the system itself. No matter what anyone does, initiation itself carries no instant and radical change of character. It alone confers no perfection of character. Perfection, requiring possibly years of hard work and close application to the task, is a matter of slow growth.

Still another point, if properly understood, may help us to be more charitable toward our erring brothers. It is a fact of common experience, well known to the Masters and other careful students, that among thousands of people who appear for the initiation, many otherwise very noble souls will have a one-sided mind. That is, one side will be highly developed, trained, of a noble quality, while the other side may still be under the sway of the vilest of the passions. This fact has often proved a great stumbling block to observers.

Remember, the mind is a part or an agent of the Negative Power. The Negative Power is the Universal Mind. But the soul is a spark from the Supreme One. Every mind is what it is from ages of past experiences. It is rare that any person has an all-round development. Nearly all are one-sided to some extent, and not a few are terribly warped. These are to be pitied, not blamed. Negative traits will appear so long as there is not an all-round and well-advanced disciplinary training.

In the meantime, the divine spark in each one, always struggling for freedom, striving hard against adverse currents, reaches out a feeble hand toward the Master. In great kindness the Master takes that hand, unclean though it may be. After that, it may require years of patient study and hard work to build up the character, to strengthen the will and throw off the evil passions. To such as these, let us give cordial sympathy and ready assistance, not forgetting the time when we ourselves were passing through the fires. Happy the day when everyone shall learn never to find fault with any other person until he himself is faultless.

13. The Function of the Spiritual Master

Far back in the Vedic age, the great rishis said: "Three things which are rare indeed are due to the grace of God, namely, a human birth, the longing for spiritual liberation and the protecting care of the perfect Sat Guru."

The question is so often and persistently asked: "Why the need of a Master?" It comes to us from all parts of the world and it will not be denied an answer. The egotism of the average man, the Western student in particular, is always ready to assert that he needs no help. He says proudly: "I am the architect of my own fortune. I shall direct my own destiny. I demand the right of direct approach to God. No one else has any right to stand in my way."

This is a proud and bold declaration, worthy of the bravest Castilian. It reminds me of a little kitten which I once met on a mountain path. He was feasting on the remains of a lizard. When I came near him, he bowed up his back and began to growl at me in a very threatening manner. Out of respect for his rights, I walked around him at some distance. So, if the bravest of men see fit to announce their independence—even of the Master—I must not quarrel with them. I respect their position, but I am very doubtful of their security when the deep waters overwhelm them. In the day of his opportunity, such a man shuts the doors of the kingdom in his own face.

I believe this proud attitude is partly a reaction of modern intelligence against the useless intervention of the priest. As such, it is a wholesome reaction. But the position of the Master, relative to his disciple, is as different from that of the priest as day is different from night. At best, the priest is only an imitation master with a commission to act as a teacher. He teaches not what he himself knows but what he has read in a book. The Master occupies a unique position, even as a teacher. He teaches not what he has read in a book or learned in a school, but *what he knows from personal experience*. Besides, the Master is more than a teacher —much more. Teaching, while extremely important, is the least important of the Masters' work. The entire field of the activity of the Masters is vitally important and we must spare no effort to understand it. In this book we must make it clear to the reader, if possible.

Perhaps the matter may be further elucidated by the use of an illustration, a comparison. Let us suppose that a man living on the plains of the Punjab wishes to make an airplane trip to Lhasa, the capital of that almost inaccessible region of Tibet. We will assume also that everyone who makes that trip must fly his own plane. A modern airplane, equipped for flight, now stands on the field ready to take off. But our man knows nothing at all about flying. He was never in an airplane in his life. What can he do? Get into that plane all by himself, pull the throttle and take off? The chances are nine-to-one that he will wreck the plane and break his own neck. So he hesitates in spite of his own egotistical impulses.

Now comes an experienced pilot. He has been over that route many times and he has a license to enter that region, also for stopping at intermediate stations. He offers his services. But the man proudly replies: "No, thank you; I shall fly my own plane. I need the help of no one else." He doesn't even know how to get into the plane, nor how to start it if he were in it. Its doors are locked and he has no key. The pilot has wisely left the plane locked, for if an inexperienced man should undertake to start it before he knew what he was doing, he would surely bring disaster upon himself. And that is exactly the situation regarding those people who imagine they can ascend to spiritual heights without knowing anything about how to even start. In any case, even if he were to get started, the man never could make the journey. A hundred difficulties stand in the way, absolutely insurmountable difficulties for the inexperienced man. But finally coming to his senses, he humbly says to the pilot: "Take me as your pupil and teach me to fly." It is a momentous occasion when a man or woman comes to this attitude in spiritual matters.

The two of them now enter the plane. The experienced hand of the pilot now guides the plane as it leaves the ground, while the beginner, getting the touch gradually, also holds the controls. They make a short journey into the sky and return. The student has had his initiation. He has begun a new life; but he is not much of a flyer yet. The lessons are repeated daily. The flying sense of the student grows little by little. He becomes 'air-minded', as they say. Gradually he becomes more independent. Now he can take off by himself and guide her through the air for long distances. But he does not dare to go alone yet. Flying is no child's play. One has to grow into it. By and by, he is able to fly independently and alone.

Anyone who has ever learned to fly an airplane will never forget the day and hour when he first ascends the sky all by himself. Then he gets his license. He divests himself of every impediment and is prepared to go higher than ever before to make the journey which he had in mind from the beginning. He is keen to start on that long and perilous journey, although he cannot make this trip alone. He has never been over that way and he has not the remotest idea of the course he is to take. Neither can it be told to him in advance. There is no map, and the directions cannot even be reduced to writing. So here again he is helpless without the pilot. And even if he knew how to go, there is still another difficulty. He is unknown to the watchmen along the way, and he has no license to enter those regions. He will not be recognized and will surely be turned back at the first landing.

The very nature of this trip is such that he must first make the journey and meet the authorities of the various regions before he can get his license to enter alone. This he must do in company with an experienced and licensed pilot, who will introduce him and recommend him. There is still another difficulty. If he were to undertake the journey alone, the chances are ninety-nine-to-one he would be led astray into some dangerous region far off the way. The *way* he can learn only by traveling over it in company with the experienced pilot.

Still another difficulty confronts our traveler. He has to land at four intermediate stations, at each of which his entry will be challenged; and when admitted, he will require special information concerning the journey, which no one will give him except the pilot who travels with him. Without that he will certainly be obliged to turn back. At each of these intermediate stations, he is obliged to rest for a time and accustom himself to the rarer atmosphere of those higher regions. It is now manifest for many reasons that he cannot make the trip at all without the experienced pilot, even though he is able to fly his own plane. The experienced pilot therefore sits in the plane with him; together they cross mountains, valleys and many regions never before traversed by him, rising higher and higher.

At length he approaches his first landing, and he looks down upon a wonderful sight: a great city, more beautiful than any he has ever seen before. He is enchanted; a thousand varicolored lights, gleaming brilliantly in one grand cluster. So he lands and looks around the city. His pilot-companion meets all challenges and opens the way for him. He is so delighted that he would like to remain there forever, but his pilot urges him to advance. They must go higher without too much delay. The journey has only fairly begun. So they enter the plane once more and climb the luminous sky, the air filled with millions of diamond-like particles resembling stardust. They come to a second landing, more beautiful than the first, with new colors affecting them like strains of beautiful music. But again the pilot orders an advance after a short rest. The third and the fourth landings are made, each growing more beautiful than the preceding. Now they are in extremely rare and pure atmosphere, the snow-covered peaks of the Himalayas gleaming in the sunlight.

Finally, they look down upon the old city of Lhasa itself, the end of their journey. They come to rest and the watchmen challenge the newcomer. How did he manage to find this region, and for what purpose has he come? By whose authority has he entered these sacred precincts? Then the pilot himself steps forward and vouches for the visitor. The watchmen recognize the pilot and bow low before him. They know him as the executive officer of their Supreme Lord. His power and authority to enter that and all other regions are universally recognized. They proceed then to the court of the King himself, where our visitor is made welcome, and the pilot is affectionately embraced by the King. It is then for the first time that the newcomer knows that the pilot was no ordinary man.

This is but an imperfect yet apt illustration of what actually takes place when a disciple is taken up to Sach Khand by his Master. The airplane is the life-giving Shabd, and upon that both Master and disciple ride upward to their home in the supreme region, crossing all of the intervening regions. By this journey the traveler is emancipated from the slavery of crawling upon the earth. Of course, the pilot is the Master. So the Master performs the double function of first teaching his disciple and then of actually taking him upon the upward journey. After all contacts have been made on behalf of the pupil, and he stands before the King of kings, he receives his power and authority to travel in the future on his own responsibility and by his own right. But the first journey simply must be made in company with the Master. It can never be made any other way, for reasons suggested in the narrative.

Our illustration falls short in one respect—while the trip to Lhasa may possibly be made on foot, even though it is laborious and difficult, yet the trip to the higher regions, more subtle worlds, cannot be made by any other means than the Life Current, symbolized by the airplane; and the student must have the company of the Master on his first journey up. Those subtle regions lie far above and beyond the remotest bounds of the physical universe, as we measure distances. And the Way no man knows, nor can he ever know by intellectual activity alone. He simply must travel over that Path in person and he must have the company of a living Master to take him where he could not possibly go alone. That Path of Light to the city of Light, no man has ever traveled except in company with the Master-Pilot.

There is one more point to which it may be well to call attention. It is known to all Masters that many good yogis, rishis, etc., have made the journey to the first region, corresponding to the first landing in our illustration. By the slow and laborious, sometimes perilous, methods of Pranayam, of Patanjali, and other systems, they have made their way to the first region, known as the astral. They have made the trip on foot, so to speak. And this is no small achievement. They deserve much credit. But the one sad feature about their achievement is that there they are automatically stopped. They can never go beyond that region by their own unaided efforts. Many of them, being quite satisfied there, do not even wish to go further, while many others do not know that there is anything further on. Some great religious and spiritual leaders, well known to history, are to be seen there today doing their meditations, and they are quite happy. But as a matter of fact, they have made no more than a fair start on the upward journey. Eventually they all must return to earthly life for a new birth in order to meet a genuine Sat Guru. Without such a Master they can never enter those many higher regions of incomprehensible light and beauty.

From our illustration it will be clearly seen that both the Master-Pilot and the airplane, the Sat Guru and the Shabd, are absolutely necessary if one is to make the complete journey to those bright worlds of immortality. It can never be made in any other way. It is a logical conclusion, therefore, that the chief concern of human life is to seek a true Master and place one's destiny in his hands. If one fails to do this, his life remains unfulfilled, no matter what else he may accomplish.

Chapter Four

THE CREATION AND ORDER
OF THE UNIVERSE

---

1. The Cosmogony of the Masters

T HE science of the Masters, in dealing with man and his destiny, must also deal with the universe of which man is a part, a unit. No one can gain even an intellectual understanding of his own interests until he has some comprehension of the universe of which he is an integral part, and with every part of which he is in some manner related. By the word *universe,* as it is used in this book, we mean vastly more than a few galaxies of stars, suns and planets pointed out by astronomers. We must include an almost endless series of higher and finer worlds above and beyond the sweep of the telescope, or of any telescope that can ever be made. These worlds are utterly beyond the borders of the physical universe.

Any science which ignores those higher and more subtle worlds cannot claim to be an all-inclusive science. In fact, the real scientist has no more than learned the alphabet of his science until he passes beyond the last star that glimmers in space, and he enters those regions where the physical eye cannot function. Happily, every man is endowed with a finer vision, which may be awakened and used on those higher planes.

The cosmogony of the Masters will be found quite different from that of all other systems. This is so because the Masters have a far greater range of knowledge than any other men. Their fields of operation lie far out and away from all physical suns and moons. They know about the creation and order of this universe of so many parts from personal study and exploration. Beginning from the lowest stratum of earth and ranging upward to the highest heavens, the Masters know every foot of the ground. The nonmaterial and the supersensuous are just as familiar to them as are the rivers and the mountains of this terrestrial sphere. Besides their ability to see the entire past history of the universe, the universe as it is today is an open book to them.

The great Masters do not concern themselves too much with how or when this universe came into existence. They know this also, but they do not hold this knowledge of any great value to a student beginning on the Path. They do not care whether the entire universe came into existence by a word of command out of nothing, or whether it all came into existence as a 'projection' from the Creator. (The latter view was held by the old rishis and other Indian philosophers. It may be that worlds appear and disappear like bubbles on the waters of an infinite ocean; or it may be that universes appear and disappear like a tortoise extending his feet and then drawing them into his shell again. The old Sanskrit scholars could not conceive of something coming out of nothing, hence their word for creation is accurately translated by our word *projection*.) The Masters do not attach any great importance to the problem of whether there ever was a time when the universe did not exist or if a time may come when it shall cease to exist. Although they do know these things, they attach but little practical importance to them. They set themselves the far more important task of liberating human souls from this world bondage. They seldom discuss the ultimate problems of the Infinite.

Let us accept things as we find them and try to make the best use of them here and now. This appears to be the working principle of the Masters. When we have had the good fortune to ascend the supreme heights, when all knowledge is ours by and through the orderly expansion of our capacity to understand, all of these questions will doubtless be answered to our entire satisfaction. They are already matters of common knowledge to the

Saints themselves, but they find it almost impossible to convey that information to the ordinary human intelligence. Fortunately, we are able to grasp something of the creation and order of this universe, including all universes of a higher order, and we are able to correlate them all into one grand system. This is due to the grace of those great Masters who have broken the bonds of time and space.

2. The Four Grand Divisions of Nature

The entire universe of universes is divided into four grand divisions, each marked out and differentiated from the rest by certain characteristics of the substances composing them, and the nature of the phenomena to be seen there.

(1) Beginning with our own world as the point of departure, the first grand division is the physical universe, called in the language of the Masters 'Pinda'. It is composed chiefly of matter of varying density, coarse in quality, but mixed with a small percentage of mental and spiritual substance—just enough to give it life and motion. Spirit is the only self-acting substance in existence. Without spirit, matter is dead, inert. In fact, there is nothing in all creation wholly devoid of spirit, for without spirit, matter itself would cease to exist. Matter is not therefore a thing apart from spirit, but it may itself be considered as spirit in a much depleted form. So it may be said of mind.

A comparison may be made with the oxygen in our atmosphere. Fifty miles above the earth's surface there is insufficient oxygen in the air to sustain human life; its percentage in the compound is so small. This is somewhat similar to the percentage of spirit in compounds of the physical universe. The lower end of creation, of which the physical universe is a part, may be called the negative pole of all creation, in which spirit—although it inheres as the essential element of its existence—is in a highly expanded, unconcentrated form. To enable us to get a mental grasp of the situation, suppose we imagine the pre-creation substance to have existed somewhat in the form of an egg. The large end may be thought of as the positive pole, in which the original substance existed and still exists in a highly concentrated form. So it is polarized. The small end is the negative pole, in which the same substance exists in a less concentrated form.

In the process of creation, the smaller end, or negative pole, becomes not separated but differentiated from the original mass, and then subdivided into three distinct portions. The uppermost of these subdivisions is Brahmanda, the middle portion is Anda, and the nethermost one is Pinda, the physical universe. All this end of creation, this lower section, is composed of coarse matter, while the higher sections are much finer in substance, as one is advancing to higher regions. This lower section has a much lower rate of vibration than any section above it.

(2) As said earlier, the grand division just above the physical universe is Anda. The word means 'egg', referring to its shape. If we must place it in space, let us assume that Anda lies just above and beyond the physical universe. But here the terms *above* and *beyond* have but little meaning. The fact is that these higher worlds are separated from this world more by their ethereal qualities than by their location in space. It is just as accurate to say that those worlds lie in the same space limitations, separated by their qualities only; but when a person passes from one to another of them, it appears that he traverses immense space.

We may say that he ascends from one set of three dimensions to a higher set, from a lower plane of consciousness to a higher one. But all that is not so easy to comprehend. Those expressions convey but little idea of what actually takes place. For convenience of expression, we may as well speak of these regions as planes, one above the other. They are certainly above in the quality of their substance, in vibration, and in their light and beauty.

The substance of Anda is much finer in the structure of its atoms, in its vibratory activity and its degree of density. The concentration of substance increases in degree as one ascends to higher worlds, and it becomes more positive.

Anda is also much more vast in extent than the physical universe. The central portion of that universe makes up what is com-

monly spoken of as the astral plane. Its capital or governing center
is named Sahasradal Kanwal by the Saints. In that grand division
lie many subplanes, so-called heavens and purgatories, or reformatories, all abounding in an endless variety of life—numberless
continents, rivers, mountains, oceans, cities and peoples. All of
them are of a higher order than anything known on earth, more
luminous and more beautiful—except the reformatory portions,
which have been specially designed and set apart for that purpose.
They are both schools and purgatories, intended in every case to
rebuild character. To these schools many of earth's people pass at
the time of their death.

Of course, all these are invisible to the physical eye because
of their higher vibrations. They do not, for that reason, come
within the range of our vision. In terms of the solar spectrum, they
lie above and beyond the ultraviolet of science. But the students
of the Master develop a higher instrument of vision, by means of
which they see those regions as plainly as they see this world with
the physical eyes.

(3) Next above Anda lies Brahmanda, the third grand division. This term means 'the egg of Brahm'. It is egg-shaped, like
Anda, but is much vaster in extent. It is also more refined and full
of light, markedly more than the physical universe. This third
grand division is composed mostly of spirit substance, but is mixed
with a refined sort of matter. As Anda contains more of spirit substance than Pinda, in like manner, Brahmanda is richer in spirit
than Anda. In fact, spirit predominates in Brahmanda just as matter predominates in Pinda, while Anda is rather on the dividing
line between the two.

(4) Last of all, we arrive at the highest grand division in all
creation, the finest and purest, composed entirely of pure spirit.
This region is definitely beyond the sphere of matter; nor is there
any mind in this region. The plane of Universal Mind is the lower
end of Brahmanda. Just as mind is the highest order of matter in
existence, it is left below the pure spiritual regions. It is excluded
from the supreme grand division. The lower end of Brahmanda is
made up almost entirely of mind substance. It is so conveniently
situated that when a soul descends into material regions, it may

take on its necessary mental equipment, required for all contacts with material worlds.

In this last and highest grand division we discover the region of Universal Spirit. Its name is Sat Desh, which means in our language the 'abiding country' or 'real country'. It is the region of Truth, of Ultimate Reality. Of course, this grand division is much vaster in extent than any region below it, also far more beautiful and full of light. The light of that world is so intense that no man on earth can form any sort of estimate of it. If we say that one single soul living there radiates a light equal to that of sixteen times the total light capacity of our sun, it is true, but utterly beyond all comprehension. The Lord of the lowest section of that exalted region, whose name is Sat Purush, radiates a light from his body equal to many millions of our sun. But who can form any sort of mental picture of it?

Whatever may be said of that region, the Masters, who have themselves seen it, tell us that no words can convey an adequate idea of what is there. It is inhabited by countless multitudes of pure souls who know no stain of imperfection, no sorrow and no death. The happiness of its inhabitants is perfect. What more can one say? Perfection means there cannot be anything better. Sat Desh is itself divided into four distinct planes, the highest and last of which is the supreme seat of the Infinite, the Absolute, the Source and Creator of all that is.

As said before, the creation and division of the whole of existence into four separate sections may be due to the polarization of the pre-creation substance, the primordial element of all worlds. This primordial substance may be called God, if the monists insist, or whatever term the reader may prefer. The upper portion was the positive pole, and the lower was the negative, while the middle portions were neutral zones, partaking of the properties of both, but growing more positive from below upward. When the creative impulse was given, the positive pole became more concentrated, while the nether pole became correspondingly depleted. Then out of the negative pole—its extreme end—were fashioned all material worlds, these constituting the suns and planets with which we are familiar.

The two intermediate grand divisions are subdivided into almost numberless worlds or zones, each having its own forms of life. Among these lower subdivisions, especially in Anda, are to be found nearly all the heavens and paradises of the various religions. It will be remembered that the top, or zenith, of the positive pole is charged with spirit substance to an extreme degree, while as we descend toward the nadir, the extreme negative end, spirit substance undergoes a gradual diminution. As a result of that thinning-out process, those zones experience a corresponding darkness, until finally they take on more and more of those qualities which we associate with evil.

All that human consciousness classifies as evil, or bad, is made so by a diminution or a depletion of spirit. This means darkness, of course, lesser life, lesser light. Man cannot live happily without spirit, and the more he departs from spirit, the more he experiences what to him is evil. As with an individual man, so it is with worlds themselves. The less spirit substance in them, the darker they are and the more troubles are experienced by their inhabitants.

We have now given but a mere outline sketch of the four grand divisions of creation. We will now take them up in greater detail. A knowledge of these worlds is of great value to us in many respects; besides, the subject is extremely fascinating. A Master could write a book or many books on each of these great worlds.

Again, let us remind the reader that what is written here is not a web of fancy, but is literal fact based upon the experience of the Masters and their disciples. They have traversed those regions times without number and are as familiar with them as we are with portions of this world over which we have traveled.

3. Sat Desh, the Highest Region

Beginning from above and going downward, we come first to Sat Desh (*Sat*, 'true', and *Desh*, 'country'). Many other names have been applied to it, such as Nij-Dham, Sat Lok, Mukam Haq and

Sach Khand. These names are usually applied to the lowest section of Sat Desh, but occasionally to the entire grand division. This is the region, or plane, of pure spirit. All enjoying the greatest conceivable happiness, its inhabitants are pure spirits in such countless numbers as no man can estimate. It is the supreme heaven of all heavens, but it is quite unknown to any of the world religions because their founders had never reached that exalted region. It is known to Saints only, who alone can enter it. It cannot be described. In substance and arrangement it is wholly unlike anything known in this world. Neither can the human mind imagine it. This section is so vast in extent that no sort of understanding of it can be conveyed to human intelligence. No mind can grasp it.

All that the Saints can say of Sat Desh is that it is limitless. It is the only region which the great Saints insist is practically limitless. We may say, although no mind can grasp the thought, that it embraces all else, and is both the beginning and the end of all else. It is the great center about which all other worlds revolve. Anything which we might say about it would be incomplete and only partially true, so declare the Saints. If the entire physical universe with its countless millions of suns and their planets were all gathered together in a single cluster, each sun being a million light-years distant from any other sun, yet this entire ensemble would appear no more than a few dark specks floating in the clear and luminous sky of Sat Desh. In that happy country, a sun such as ours, but a thousand times larger, would appear as a tiny dark spot, so very great is the light of that world.

This region is the grand capital of all creation, the center of all universes, and the residence of the Supreme Creator—Lord of all.

From this center of all light, life and power, the great Creative Current flows outward and downward to create, govern and sustain all regions. It passes out from this region somewhat like the radio emanations going forth from a great broadcasting station. It is the Audible Life Stream, the most important factor in the system of the Masters. This Stream permeates the entire system of universes. A thing of great importance to us is that the music of this ever-flowing Current, the stream of life, can be heard by a real Master and also by his students who have advanced even a little on the Path. And let us reiterate that unless a Master teaches his students how this Current is to be heard, he is not a Master of the highest order.

This grand headquarters of all creation is the region of immortality. It is unchangeable, perfect, deathless. It is forever untouched by dissolution or grand dissolution. So are its inhabitants. This region will be referred to many times in this book. It is subdivided into four distinct planes, each having its own characteristics and its own Lord, or Governor. But the difference between these subdivisions is very slight. From above downward they are named: Radha Soami Dham (meaning 'home of the spiritual Lord'); it is also called Anami Lok (meaning 'nameless region'). The next plane below the highest is Agam Lok (*Agam,* 'inaccessible', and *Lok,* 'place'). The third plane is Alakh Lok. (*Alakh,* 'invisible', and *Lok,* 'place'). The last of these higher planes is Sach Khand (*Sach,* 'truth', and *Khand,* 'home'). The last one is also called Sat Lok, 'the true place'. By the Mohammedan Saints it has been called Mukam Haq, meaning the same as above, 'the home of truth'.

The light of all four of these regions is so very intense that it is impossible for any mortal to get an understanding of it. It cannot be described. The great Soami Ji sums up his statements regarding this region by saying simply that it is "*all Love.*"

4. Brahmanda, the Second Grand Division

The second grand division from above downward is Brahmanda (meaning 'the egg of Brahm', as said before). This refers to its shape and also to the Governor or Lord who is its ruler. This Brahm is supposed by most of the old rishis to be the Supreme Being of all creation, because they knew of no one higher. But the Saints know that there is not only one Brahm, but countless numbers of Brahms, who are governors over so many Brahmandas.

For it must be understood that there are countless Andas and Brahmandas, each circling about the supreme region in its own orbit, and each of them has its own governor or ruler. Brahm was the highest God known to the ancient rishi or yogi, and so the name of Brahm is retained by the Saints to designate the ruler of the Three Worlds, which include the physical universe, Anda, and the lower portion of Brahmanda, named Trikuti. The upper portion of Brahmanda is called Par Brahm.

As said before, this grand division is mostly spirit in substance, but is mixed with a certain amount of pure, spiritualized matter; it is the finest order of matter and includes mind. This is called the spiritual-material region because spirit dominates the region. The substance of that division gradually becomes less and less concentrated as we descend toward the negative pole of creation. The lower portions become coarser in particle, and more and more mixed with matter. In the lower end of Brahmanda, mind is supreme. It is practically all mind, for mind itself is matter of the finest order. Of course, even mind is mixed with spirit substance to some slight extent, otherwise it could not exist. All worlds become a shade darker as we descend, because there is less and less spirit substance in the composition. Trikuti, the lowest section of Brahmanda, is the home of Universal Mind. It is from that region that all individual minds are derived, and to that region all minds must return when they are discarded during the upward flight of the spirit.

Brahmanda is extremely vast in area when compared with the physical universe, but small when compared with the first grand division. It is itself subdivided into many distinct regions or planes. Some mention six subdivisions; but as a matter of fact, there are scores of subdivisions in that one grand division, almost numberless subdivisions, each constituting a separate and distinct world. Divisions and subdivisions shade into one another so imperceptibly that it is not easy to say just where one ends and another begins. This accounts in part for the many different descriptions of those regions and the great variety of names assigned to them.

5. Anda, the Lowest of the Heavens

Anda lies nearest to the physical universe. Its capital is called Sahasradal Kanwal, meaning 'a thousand-petaled lotus'. Its name is taken from the great cluster of lights which constitute the most attractive sight when one is approaching that world. This great group of lights is the actual 'powerhouse' of the physical universe. Out of that powerhouse flows the power that has created and now sustains all worlds in our group. Each of those lights has a different shade or tint; they constitute the most gorgeous spectacle as one enters that magnificent city of light. In that city of splendors may be seen also many other interesting and beautiful things. Also, here may be seen millions of the earth's most renowned people of all ages of our history—many of them are residents of this great city and country. Naturally they are quite happy. It is far superior to anything ever seen on this earth. Yet this is but the first station on the upward Path of the Masters.

This region constitutes the negative part of all the superphysical zones. That is, it lies most distant from the positive pole of creation. This region is sometimes classified as a part of Brahmanda, but the Saints prefer to consider it as a separate grand division of creation. It has many distinctive features of its own. Lying nearest to the physical universe, it forms the port of entry for all the higher regions. All souls who are passing to still higher regions must pass through it. The great majority of human souls at the time of death pass to some subplane of this region. But very few, comparatively, go direct to this central portion of the Sahasradal Kanwal region. It is through all of these regions that the Masters and their disciples must travel on their way to higher worlds.

This section of creation is not immortal or imperishable—neither are its inhabitants. Many of its inhabitants believe that they have attained immortality because their lives there go on for extremely long periods of time, but there is no assured immortality until one reaches Sat Desh. All below that is subject to death and dissolution.

There are two kinds of dissolutions. The one, *simple dissolution,* which reaches up to the lowest section in Brahmanda, a region called Trikuti; this occurs after many millions of years. The other is *the grand dissolution,* which occurs after immeasurably long periods of time and extends up to the top of Brahmanda. Of course, both of these dissolutions include the entire physical universe—every sun, moon and planet in it. At that time every star and its satellites are wiped out, and then follows a period of darkness equal in duration to the life of the universe. When the period of darkness has expired, a new creation is projected, and the heavens are once more alive with sparkling stars. With each new creation begins a new Golden Age for each planet and its inhabitants. But between minor dissolutions there are also periods of renewal for the life of each planet, when Golden Ages succeed dark ages.

There is a general idea, finding its way into most religions, that this world is to come to an end. And so the Masters teach. But the end is a very different proposition to what it is generally supposed to be. It will come at a time when all worlds of the physical universe will be dissolved, and after periods of darkness and silence new worlds will take their places. The inhabitants of all of those worlds to be dissolved are drawn up to higher regions in a sort of comatose state to be re-placed upon those worlds when they are ready for human habitation. They will then begin a new life here under more favorable conditions. These periodic dissolutions come to the physical universe after many, many hundreds of millions of years. No man need worry now, lest that time is near at hand. It is many moons away yet.

6. The Grand Division of Pinda

The fourth grand division, beginning from above, is called Pinda. It is the gross material or physical universe. Here coarse matter predominates, there being but a small percentage of mind and a still smaller amount of spirit. Our earth is a small and insignificant member of Pinda. It embraces all the suns and their planets known or unknown to astronomy. It extends out into space far beyond the reach of any telescope. Astronomers have never been able to count these worlds—although as their instruments become n.ore perfect, the range of their observations is extended. Who shall set limits or indicate bounds to those starry depths? Who can number the numberless? Who can circumscribe the boundless? To the farthest extent of space, wherever there is a material sun or a speck of dust, they are all included in this fourth grand division which the Masters call Pinda.

In this division, coarse matter predominates. Permeating this coarse matter are many finer substances, including mind, and last of all there is a modicum of spirit to give life to all the rest. In this lowest of all divisions of creation there is but little light and a very low grade of life when compared with Brahmanda. But if compared with Sat Desh, this world is pitch darkness, and the life here, in comparison to that, is scarcely knowable at all. Its substance is coarse, clumsy, inert and full of all manner of imperfections. These imperfections, as said before, are due to the paucity of spirit at this pole. This condition of negativity is the soil out of which all evil grows.

However real it may seem to us, negativity is the absence of reality, and the absence of reality is the absence of spirit. Food is a reality to us, but hunger is also a real condition to our consciousness. Hunger is due to the absence of food. In its last analysis, all pain, all longing, all desire, is only a cry of the mind and soul for more light, more spirit. In like manner, evil is due to the absence of spirit. And the reason we have so small a percentage of spirit substance at this end of creation is because this is the negative pole of all creation. Pinda is the extreme negative pole. It is consequently so far depleted of spirit that it lies in a state of semi-death, a condition of heavy inertia over which broods deep shadow.

Out of this condition rise all the manifold difficulties experienced by mortals on this plane of life. As one leaves this lowest plane and begins to ascend toward the positive pole of creation, the light increases, and hence more life, more beauty and more happiness. This is all entirely due to the increase in the percentage of spirit on the respective planes. Love, power, wisdom, rhythm, perfection of every sort, take the place of negative conditions which prevail in the lower sections of the universe.

It should be said here, with all possible emphasis, that just in proportion to the degree of spirit substance prevailing in any region, world, person or thing, will its perfections be manifest. And vice versa: In proportion to the lack of spirit, imperfections will show themselves. In proportion as matter predominates, those states which we call evil will become manifest. A depletion of spirit is, therefore, the one fatal disease of the physical universe. Out of that state all other diseases spring up. In the last analysis, we believe there is but one disease in the world—spiritual anemia.

Chapter Five

GOD AND THE GRAND HIERARCHY
OF THE UNIVERSE

1. The Perplexing Question of God

THE biggest and oldest question ever propounded to human intelligence is: "Is there a God? If so, who or what is he? Where and how may he be contacted, and has he any word of himself for mankind?" Although trainloads and mountains of books have been written in attempts to answer these and similar questions, there has never been but one answer given, and there never can be but one. That is the answer given by the Masters. Why? Because only the Masters *know* the answer to any of these questions. All others only guess and speculate.

You hear much about meeting God, as if he were merely a sort of king-emperor, and all you required was a priest to give you an introduction. Men philosophize about 'God-realization'. Men of all schools of philosophy agree that the *summum bonum* of all existence is 'to realize God'. But they have no idea how to go about it. So they read and talk, and many set themselves up to teach the Way. But nobody on earth has ever met God or realized God except by the method of the Masters or the Path of the Masters. It cannot be done any other way. The Masters are the only men in the world, therefore, who are qualified to discuss the subject of 'meeting God'.

Groping after the truth in all ages, men have attempted to find their way to God, or to catch at least some glimpses of understanding on the subject. But their success has been problematical. They have carried on their search by many and devious paths, and over far-reaching fields. Yet the search itself has led mankind slowly toward the light. From the rishis of old, from Zarathustra and the Magi, from Hermes and Plato, down to Kant and Edwards and Northrup, these questions have been repeated in plaintive wails, and a lonesome echo has been the only answer. Who can really know God but one who has himself ascended to the spiritual heights, where God is openly manifest to sight?

At the same time, throughout history men have gone along creating gods in their own image. To the material scientist, God is a mere abstraction, silent as the sphinx. Many sincere students take refuge in agnosticism. They say, with Ingersoll, that man stands between two great mountain peaks, the eternal past and the eternal future; and no man can see beyond either of those peaks. Only hope may give a little encouragement. Theologians, in a frantic effort to prove the existence of God, point to the construction and order of Nature, the rhythm of the universe, its fixed laws and its onward flow, which they say suggest an all-wise and all-powerful Creator. But after all, any argument based upon logical premises is just as likely to lead us astray as the dogmatic assertions of the theologians.

Just as one cynic has said, "There is no lie like history"; so it may be said that there is nothing more misleading than logic. God can never be made a reality to any man by mere logic, by books or by feelings. And I sincerely believe that anything which has to be proved by long processes of logic is not worth proving. In other words, if the thing is not self-evident, it is of little use. If any theory or teaching has to be established by laborious processes of reasoning, I think that very fact shows that we are on the wrong track and should seek new methods of establishing the hypothesis. The only method of proving the existence of God which is worth our time is the experiential method of the great Masters, because no other method has ever succeeded and none of them can ever succeed.

Did it never occur to you as a very strange thing that God has not given to mankind any definite and easy method of knowing about him? Yet as a matter of fact, he has given out such a method and it is accessible to all, but men have blinded themselves to that Path through ages of self-indulgence, and now they stumble along in the darkness which they themselves have created. And yet the method is here and it is well known to the Masters; all others may have it if they will accept it. Men blame God for their own blindness, when they will not enter the doors of light which stand open right before them.

Hearing no voice of the Supreme One in all the dark caverns or starry galaxies of Nature, some of our best scientists and philosophers have come to the conclusion that there is no answer to our original question. They declare that this universe is built upon the laws of physics and chemistry, and that all life, including man, is the product of a vast mechanism, guided solely by fixed laws and predetermined processes. It is only a broad ocean throwing up the multiform phenomena of this world, as whitecaps on the sea are thrown up by the winds and the waves. Even human thought, they claim, is nothing more than evanescent and useless flames emitted by the heat of cerebral commotion. God, they say, is an invention of the fearful, a refuge of the coward. Men create him in order to propitiate him in the hour of trouble. Man himself is only a physical accident tossed into the vortex of existence so that he may eat, sleep, breed, and then die. Because men can find no God with their telescopes or their microscopes, because they cannot locate him in the nervous system of the cadaver, they decide with a grand flourish that there is no God! *C'est fini, un point, c'est tout!* The discussion is at an end.

Only a few weeks ago, I read in the papers a statement by Professor Julian Huxley, a scientist of a distinguished family. He said that he could find no proof of God, and moreover he felt no need of the God hypothesis. It is a pity that such men have no knowledge of the Masters. It is our notion that Professor Huxley does not know the fullness of his own inheritance. He is like a man who has drunk deeply of fresh water, and for that reason he feels no thirst. What new worlds of thinking and rejoicing would open up to him if only he had definite knowledge of the Path of the Masters!

I must note here an extremely interesting coincidence. At the very time that the English papers were announcing that this grandson of the distinguished scientist, Thomas H. Huxley, felt no need of the God hypothesis, a great granddaughter of another immortal scientist, Alexander Agassiz, was actually here in India to seek definite knowledge of God through the science of the Masters. Thus the various currents of history run along their several courses. In spite of all doubts and blind alleys, the world will never give up its search for God. As Saint Augustine said:

> Thou, O God, hast made us unto Thyself, and the heart of man is ever restless, until it rests in Thee.

A year or so ago, there was a noted Indian Arya Samajist who had spent the greater portion of his life in public lectures, devoted to God, religion and human service. He had a fine character. But just before his death he made the astonishing announcement that he had spent his life teaching something of which he had no proof at all, and that he was approaching his end, gazing into blank darkness. This is pathetic indeed. If only for a single moment he had placed his hand in that of a living Master! There is no other means or proof which can stand the final test. He who walks upon the Path of the Masters knows about God, and he knows about the Home of the soul, to which he is traveling. He walks in the light all the way, in increasing light!

Mechanical and materialistic concepts are perhaps no better and no worse than the doctrines of God derived from religion. The one set believe in God without rational proof, and the other set deny the existence of God without rational proof. I imagine that a gracious, infinite Father would look with equal pity upon both classes; for they are like children stumbling along in the darkness, too proud to place their hands in the hands of their father that he may guide and support them.

The many doctrines of God, both for and against his existence, are only the inevitable by-products in the manufacture of the super-man, in that age-long struggle for the truth that shall strike the last shackle from the super-man and set him free. It is good that men so struggle and speculate, even write books when they have nothing else to do. It is better than playing in the mud. Never mind if they do not contain a shred of truth. Out of all these labor pains, the super-man will be born crying pitifully for the milk of life which only the Masters can give. That cup of bounty the Masters hold in their hands, inviting the thirsty world to drink. Already the reaction had set in, even before the materialistic wave had half spent itself. Before the flowers of sweet charity had covered the graves of Darwin, Hegel and Spencer, comes Bergson to tell the philosophers:

> The rapid adolescence of Spencer's philosophy is due largely to the replacement of the physical (fixed and mechanical) by the biological standpoint in recent thought; by the growing disposition to see the essence and secret of the world in the movement of life, rather than in the inertia of things. And indeed, matter itself has in our day almost taken on life [a truth taught by the Masters during all the ages]. The study of electricity, magnetism, and the electron has given a vitalistic tinge to physics—so that instead of a reduction of psychology to physics—which was the more or less conscious ambition of English thought—we now approach a vitalized physics, and an almost spiritualized matter.

This is a heroic struggle toward the position of the Masters. When physical science has had its labor pains and enjoyed them, it will perhaps sit still long enough to see that it was only suffering from pseudocyesis. Possibly it may then listen to the voice of the Masters, who alone can tell them with certain knowledge that the moving force in all Nature is Spirit, and that the fountain source of all spirit is the Supreme One whom men have named God.

2. A Word of Caution to Scientists

Some modern scientists boldly assert that they do not believe in God, and they give as reasons the two following assertions (they cannot be called more than assertions): First, they say that there is no evidence to support the contention; and second, they say they do not need the theistic hypothesis to explain the existence of the universe. Of course, they leave out of all consideration the more gentle voices of faith and intuition. These, they say, have no place in real science. Thus the whole subject is relegated to the attic of metaphysical junk.

But surely this is an unfair, as well as an 'unscientific' disposition of the matter. Back of this attitude of the scientists is, of course, the gratuitous assumption that the existence of God is both unknown and unknowable. It is therefore, so they assume, at best no more than an hypothesis invented by an unscientific age to try to account for the universe. This school of scientists declares that no one can *know* anything about God. But I suggest that this assumption itself is no more than another hypothesis based upon their own lack of knowledge. Why should any scientist assume that because he knows nothing about God, nothing is known or can be known? This is surely not the scientific attitude. Secondly, standing securely, as they believe, upon the mechanistic theory of the physical universe, they serenely declare that they no longer need the theistic hypothesis. And because they do not need it, therefore it is useless. Ergo, they do not believe in God; that belief is an old woman's superstition.

If God's existence were no more than an hypothesis, and nothing definite or certain could be known on the subject, then we may as well concede that the position of the mechanistic school is unassailable. But fortunately the knowledge of the Masters is not founded upon hypotheses. They have certain knowledge on the subject, as definite and as scientific as anything in mathematics or physics. Of course, there are many hypotheses which await demonstration on the part of the beginner. I remember well when my professor in mathematics gave me the old problem in Euclid: "The square formed on the hypotenuse of a right angle triangle is equal to the sum of the squares formed on the other two sides." I had to demonstrate it, prove it, before it was real knowledge to me. And that is exactly the method of the Masters. They know of God because they have made the experiment and have the proof.

The Masters know that there is a supreme and all-sustaining One, whose chief attributes are *wisdom, love and power*.

It must also be understood that the knowledge of the Masters is not a slow product of evolution, an accumulation of learning gathered up during long ages of study. It is not the sum of knowledge accumulated in libraries to be memorized by students. It is not a record of acquired information. The method of the Masters is unique. Every Master gains the entire sum of knowledge during his development. That knowledge is gained by a definite line of individual endeavor and personal experience. It is not something gathered up by him from many sources, but it is gained from within himself by the expansion of his own consciousness. Any man may gain this development and this knowledge, provided he has the scientific method of the Masters. In the light of this illuminating fact, one of the assumptions of physical science disappears. A definite, certain knowledge of God can be acquired.

May we now venture a word of caution? Is it not possible that the mechanistic hypothesis of the scientists is no better than the theistic? May it not also turn out to be true that even if the physical scientists know nothing about God, nor even recognize the need of one, yet in spite of all that, others may know something about him? Remember that the great Masters do not speculate. The God of the Masters is not a God invented by metaphysics, nor is he a creation of theological dogma. If some man or class of men, like the Masters, should eventually be found who declare that they have certain knowledge of God, knowledge that has been obtained by and through a method just as scientific as any known to the physicists, may we not give them credit for their great achievement? Will the scientific world be fair enough to give them a hearing? Shouldn't the physical scientists tread a little more cautiously upon ground with which they are not familiar?

Besides, what is the harm if scientific men should give a little more kindly consideration to the voice of hope, of intuition, of faith? If love whispers to them in the secret chambers of the soul, shouldn't their intellect be willing to listen? It ought not to be considered beneath their dignity. But over and above all other considerations come the great Masters who give us the most positive assurance that some certain knowledge of God has been gained by them. Shall we not at least listen to them? If some obscure astronomer should announce that he has discovered a new nebula far out in space, the whole scientific world would sit up and take notice. Why this painful lethargy in matters of the greatest importance? A listening ear is one of the first qualifications of a real scientist.

3. Who or What Is God?

The most common concept of God is that of a Creator. We can only think of a Creator as doing something, and so we picture him as creating and managing the universe. We are obliged by the urge of our own minds to account for things as we find them, or at least to try; and so the most natural conclusion is that some power has created them. For the present we may leave out of consideration the curious query as to whether God created man or man created God. History proves the latter contention; logic assumes the former. But we have already said that *both logic and history are unreliable.*

If we steal back into the shadow of dim prehistoric ages and there watch our ancestors puzzle over the multiform phenomena of Nature, we may readily conclude that God or the gods sprang out of the imaginative faculty of man. Most of the gods, even in the Vedas, are so like men in character that their parentage is quite unmistakable. To the careful student of history there is nothing more clear than the fact that mankind has been busy constructing gods after its own image. Yet when we read, even in a book so modern as the Bible, that God created man in his own image and likeness, we find ourselves not so highly flattered after all. If the God who made us is not greatly superior to our image and likeness, we need not feel so proud of our lineage. The job, so far as we can judge it at present, is not so complimentary to the Creator if we are supposed to be like him. Of course, this may be due to the fact that we are still in our sprawling infancy. We may yet grow up more in the image of our Father. Let us hope.

So the world is full of gods. In India alone there are said to be many millions of them. The rest of the world is not so rich in gods as India. A man can always have plenty of gods when he hasn't much else. The Western world is more interested in pounds and dollars than it is in gods. After all, perhaps the Western viewpoint is more practical. Pragmatism is the watchword of Western civilization. Too many gods, anyway, like cooks, spoil the broth. And this writer is doubtful if any mere man can use in his philosophy more than a few dozen higher-level gods. Perhaps one is enough.

But so much depends upon what one means by the word *God*. Here, in fact, is the very heart of the question. The big discussion about God and the gods is mostly a display of words and *ahankar*, 'vanity'. Seldom does the writer on such subjects know even the alphabet of what he is trying to discuss. How can he know? He has never listened to the message of the only one who really *knows*—the living Master. What is the practical value of going around in a circle talking about God? If you were going to study any other important fact of Nature, you would go to an expert who himself has reduced that subject to an exact science, if such person and such science could be found. If there is no science of it or even reliable knowledge, then why take up time and energy discussing it? The Masters are the only men on earth who possess accurate knowledge of mind, of spirit, and of the Way of approach to God. And their science, like all other real sciences, is based upon actual individual experience.

4. Names of the Supreme Being

In the literature of the Saints, God is expressed by many words, such as *Soami, Ekankar, Nirankar, Radha Soami, Akal, Nirala, Anami, Agam, Alakh, Sat Purush, Prabhu, Prabhswami, Hari Rai, Akshar, Parameshwar, Akshar Purush*, etc. All of these words have been coined in an effort to convey to human intelligence some idea of what the Saints think of God, or Lord God, the highest power. *Ekankar* means the 'One oneness', the body of oneness. *Nirankar* means 'without body or form'. *Soami* or *Swami* means the 'all-pervading Lord'. *Radha Soami—radha,* 'soul', and *Soami,* 'Lord'—'the Lord of the soul'. *Radha,* when reversed, becomes *dhara,* or 'current'. As soul has to revert to its source, so its dhara, when reversed—when its current is turned toward God—becomes radha.

Akal means 'timeless'. *Nirala* means 'peerless', having none like him. *Anami* means 'without name'. *Agam* means 'inaccessible'. *Sat Purush,* 'true Lord', is the really existing Lord as distinguished from all hypothetical gods. That which is not *sat* does not really exist. *Sat* means 'truth', 'reality', 'existence'. Hence the fundamental idea of *truth* is existence. The untrue does not exist; the true does. Hence *truth* and *existence* are synonymous terms. *Purush* implies 'being', and 'being' implies 'creative energy', predominating and presiding Lord, the source of creative energy. *Prabhu* means 'Lord, having power and control'. *Prabhswami* means 'all-pervading Lord, having power'. *Hari Rai* means the 'Lord who has real power', the actual king of all, like Sat Purush. This is used in contradistinction to *Dharam Rai,* the Negative Power, who controls the Three Worlds. It implies law and order. *Dharam* is 'law', 'order', 'system', and it is used also to designate religion or any religious system. Hari Rai is Sat Purush, or Akal Purush, while Dharam Rai is Kal Purush, Kal, or Brahm.

The whole universe is considered as *one,* the true Ekankar. There is perfect oneness in the universe, which is also coexistent with God, infinite, unlimited. Hence the Soami is Nirankar, that is, formless. As such, he is without personality, hence without name. He cannot be said to be 'anywhere' as he is everywhere. Since he is everywhere, all and everything, he must be impersonal. Of course, he may assume any number of forms, but none of these forms embrace his entire being any more than one sun embraces the sum total of physical matter.

When Soami limits himself to some extent, however slightly, he becomes Agam Purush. If a little more limited, he is Alakh Purush, and when he takes a definite form for the purpose of administering the affairs of the universe, he then becomes Sat Purush, or Sat Nam. Sat Nam then becomes the first definitely limited manifestation of the Supreme One. But he is not limited, except as to form. *Sat Nam,* 'true name', is that which defines his individuality, and points definitely to the first *personal* manifestation of the Infinite One.

The names of the Supreme Being in other languages besides the Sanskrit and Hindi are as many as are the ideas of Him. *God* is an Anglo-Saxon adaptation of 'good'. He is the chief good or the sum total of good. *Deus* is the Latin name, signifying something like 'supreme emperor'. *Theos* is the Greek appellation, meaning the chief of those august powers who sat upon Mount Olympus and ruled the world. *Adonai Elohim* or *Yahveh* are some of the Hebrew names assigned to the god who was first a tribal deity of the Jews, but was later proclaimed lord over all gods and worlds. He was the supreme lawgiver, the commander of all the armies of Israel. He was the majestic warrior whose wrath was so much to be feared. This is the God to whom Sir Richard Burton refers when he writes in his *Kasidah of Abdul el Yezdi:* "Yahveh, Adon, or Elohim, the God that smites, the man of war!" Fancy the psychological reaction of tender childhood under the teaching which daily held up such a god to them! No wonder Kingsley, in *Alton Locke,* says: "Our God, or rather, our gods, until we were twelve years old were *hell,* the *rod,* the ten *commandments,* and public opinion."

How true it is, as most of us know by experience, that these are the four shapes assumed by the God who presided over our childhood! I was brought up in a very strict orthodox Christian home, but not once do I recall ever being told that God was a being of love. Of course, I read in the New Testament:

> God so loved the world, that he gave his only begotten Son.
> *(John 3:16)*

God loved the world, of course, but he hated me, and it was always a toss-up whether I was to land in hell or heaven. According to most of my relatives, the betting was about ten-to-one it would be hell for me. It was always a mystery to me how God could love the world, nasty and wicked as it was, so much better than he loved his own son whom he allowed to be killed. And if God was all-powerful, why did he allow his own son, whose innocent blood flowed down his side where the spear had pierced it, to be nailed on the cross, to pay for the sins of the world? If he had more power than the devil, he could easily have told the devil to stay in his own hell and leave the world alone.

I would have been ashamed to acknowledge, with Kipling, that such a God was the God of our fathers. How accurately he portrays this same God in his "Recessional" when he says:

> *God of our fathers, known of old—*
> *Lord of our far-flung battle line—*
> *Beneath whose awful hand we hold*
> *Dominion over palm and pine—*
> *Lord God of hosts, be with us yet*
> *Lest we forget—Lest we forget!*

The Saints are not sticklers for names. They frankly concede that the Supreme One is *Anami*, 'nameless', and so they say, in substance, "Take your choice as to names."

Allah the Merciful, of Islam, sent his last and greatest prophet, Mohammed, to gather into one army the desert tribes and break up all their idols. Varuna, the greatest and the best of all ancient Hindu gods, shines out in great majesty among the hosts of gods mentioned in Vedic literature—Brahm, Rama, Brahma, Vishnu, and Shiva, and a host of others, all gods of the sacred books. Modern Indian students are fond of the terms *Akshar, Parameshwar, Purush* and *Purushottam*. The last name particularly refers to the supreme creative and governing power. Zarathustra spoke of *Ormuzd*, and the Norseman had his *Thor*.

Om is the Sanskrit sound symbol for the Supreme One. The North American Indians speak of their *Manitou*, the father of them all, who ruled over all the tribes. (It is a significant fact, worthy of more detailed study, that among all of the North American Indians the prevailing idea of God was that of a Father.)

The Saints have given many names to the Supreme Being, according to the country in which they lived and the language used by them. But all Saints recognize that no name is adequate. No name can ever describe God or convey any fair conception of his attributes. It is not good to contend for a name. What is the difference whether we say *Radha Soami* or *Rama* or *Allah?* It is quite immaterial whether we say *pani* (Urdu), *eau* (French), *amma* (Cherokee Indian), *hudor* (Greek), *aqua* (Latin) or *water*. They all mean exactly the same.

So we see that among all peoples and in all languages, not only is the name itself different but the fundamental ideas of the deity are different. In almost every land, the people, in total ignorance of God, have gone on creating anthropomorphic gods to their heart's content. These gods, their recording secretaries at their right hands, are all given high seats in the heavens from which they keep a vigilant eye upon erring mortals. Nothing escapes 'the recording angels'. How I disliked those prying mischiefs when I was a boy. Of course, the idea must be right, as by the law of karma we must pay for each offence is due course. A knowledge of the karmic law is certainly the source of all such ideas as recording angels or punishments for sin.

In spite of all the confusion regarding names and characteristics among the gods, there runs like a golden thread through all the accounts the central idea of a great overruling power which is greater and better than man. That much has been universally conceded, ever since the race emerged from prehistoric savagery. The gods are mightier and better than man. Therefore, we should look up to them with fear and trembling—in some instances with reverence. A few great teachers like Jesus taught that God was to be loved. All the Masters throughout history have taught that love of God was the central virtue of all virtues, and at the same time they have all taught that God was love itself. The old idea that he was a being of wrath to be feared was nothing better than a survival of primitive savagery.

That the Supreme Father, now in this age of semicivilization, should demand that his innocent Son, pure-minded and loving, pour out his blood upon the tree to wash away our sins, appears to me so utterly inconsistent with any idea of a spiritual God whose chief quality is love, that I am amazed that civilized man could think of it for a single moment. And yet I used to believe and preach it with great zeal. I wanted to snatch a few souls from the impending fires of divine wrath! I hope my loving Father has forgiven me for such crude notions of him. It was all due to ignorance and wrong teaching.

But no one has ever given any description or analysis of the divine attributes. Nor has anyone ever imagined himself capable of doing so. We must give the theologians credit for such modesty. God bless them. Nothing more than shrewd guesses have been offered. About the best we have been able to do is to attribute to the Creator human virtues in infinite degree. And this is not illogical. Since man was created by an Infinite Good, he must have derived his good qualities from that Infinite Good. We may concede, as a matter of fact, that man himself has created most of the gods or devils known to history; yet in spite of this, the Supreme Reality stands out far above all sham gods. He is truly the sum of all good.

No sooner, however, are we comfortably settled in these wholesome convictions when the knotty problem arises as to whence we got our evil propensities. These are so painfully manifest that they must be explained. Shall we attribute them to that same Infinite Good? The one conclusion is just as logical as the other. If we didn't get our evil qualities from the Creator and author of all good, where did we get them? Again we must be careful that our logic doesn't prove too much. Right here lies one of the most difficult problems of all religion and philosophy. Frantic efforts have been made to reach some sort of a satisfactory conclusion, but so far in vain. It is only the knowledge of the Masters which offers the key to this knotty problem: What is the origin of both good and evil, and what are good and evil, *per se?*

The old-timers could think of no way to solve this problem of evil, except to call on the devil to account for it. So the burden was laid upon him without the slightest proof that he was the guilty party. So far, they have never been able to produce him in court to answer to the charge, for the simple reason that they have not been able to find him. They only assume that he *is;* secondly, they assume his guilt.

We all find ourselves in possession of two opposite sets of qualities, the one we call bad and the other we call good. These two sets work in opposition to each other. They tend in exactly opposite directions, and they end in totally antagonistic results. Hence, life is largely made up of wars waged incessantly between these two opposite sets of qualities and tendencies. This much is generally conceded by all schools of thought. But where did we get these antagonistic qualities? What appears to be still more important since we all know we have them is—how are we to get rid of them? These are big questions. It is neither logic nor common sense to assume that such opposite qualities can be derived from the same source. Can men gather both figs and thistles from the same tree? The answer to these two enigmas will be given in another section of this book *(Chapter Five, Section 7)*. We repeat here that only the wisdom of the Masters holds the perfect solution to these problems.

But the Masters do not attempt any sort of analysis of the Supreme Being. In that they are wiser than many others. Men have written voluminously, laboriously, about God. They have talked about him as if he were their next door neighbor. These fellows remind one of the little princess who was asked by the archbishop to go for a walk with him. She replied: "All right, I will go, but if you are going to talk about God, you needn't bother. I know all about him already!" As a matter of fact, the less men know about God, the more familiarly they talk of him. The great Masters, who *know most,* are content to sit in silent reverence, even at the thought of the Supreme Father.

No description of God can ever be given to mortal man. That is because no man could understand such a description if it were given, and secondly, because no language in the world contains the thought-forms necessary. Man on this plane is too limited in comprehension. The reason the Masters know so much more about God than anyone else is because they have fewer limitations than anyone else. Their capacity to know has been vastly increased during the process of becoming Masters.

Let us be satisfied to say that there is a Supreme Creator and that he is the source of all that exists. This much the Masters *know,* and this much may be told to us. But for anyone to assert that he has full knowledge of God is equivalent to saying that he is equal to God. The Masters know a great deal concerning the manifestations of God, but I have never heard one of the Masters claim to know all about the Supreme. The great Masters have explored the entire universe from the physical plane to the pure spiritual, and they have reported many of their observations. Besides, we know that their knowledge is practically unlimited, yet they find it impossible to describe in words all that they see and know of the higher regions. Nor could they find words to express it if they could bring it down to this level.

What then is the answer of the Masters to our original question, Who or what is God? All the Saints agree, and the inhabitants of the higher worlds say, that there is one supreme, infinite Essence; that he or it is composed of pure spirit substance; that he resides in and *permeates* the supreme region, as his headquarters or capital, from where he projects himself into and permeates all regions throughout creation. He is in no way limited. Even if he takes form—which he often does—that form does not limit him because he is not limited to that form. That form is only an infinitely small fragment of himself. He is universal spirit, moving forth in a living stream, vibrating through all space, entering in and vitalizing all that exists. He is the dynamic life of everything that lives. Thus he is impersonal, universal, all-permeating, omnipresent, and all-sustaining. He is the life, the very existence of all. He is existence absolute.

But to this all-embracing, all-sustaining Force no name can be applied which is at all descriptive or expressive. There is, however, universal agreement among the world's best students that the supreme, central power is benevolent; that in it or him, *love, wisdom and power* are combined in their highest conceivable expression. And this is the highest ideal of God ever conceived or formulated in the minds of men. And this is the teaching of all great Masters.

5. Monotheism, Polytheism, Monism and Pantheism

We are now in a position to call attention to one of the most unique features of the Santon ki Shiksha, the teaching of the Masters. This information at the same time solves once for all the much debated question of monotheism versus polytheism. We have spoken of the Supreme Creator as the one all-embracing Essence. We have said that from him proceeds the creative Life Current which not only creates but preserves the entire universe. Now, this should constitute a sufficiently virile and definite monotheism to satisfy the most scrupulous champion of orthodoxy. Let us agree then that monotheism is an established and concrete fact. Anything that we may say hereafter cannot modify or alter this fact. There is, and can be, only one supreme, infinite Essence, creating and intermingling with all that exists, with its life and the foundation of its perpetuity. We need not be disturbed by that class of theists who insist that God is not immanent in his creation but sits apart on his imperial throne separate and distinct from his universe. In any case, the monotheism of the system remains undisturbed.

Many students are alarmed over the words *monism* and *pantheism*, but these words are not so threatening as they may sound. After all is said, these systems of philosophy only mean to suggest a way or a method by which the Creator keeps in touch with his creation. In all cases the Creator is the Supreme One, the same universal Essence. No man can say that pantheism is not a fact, because he cannot prove that God is not present everywhere, and that all things which exist are not parts of him. If a few students follow the Supreme One down into his creation and there lose sight of him, that need not discourage us.

No man can say that monism is not a fact, because no one can separate God from his visible universe. Who shall say that there is anything in existence but God? It would be a bold assertion. The moment we introduce anything into the world which is not a part of God, we introduce a bewildering duality into the scheme of things, landing ourselves in a maze of philosophical difficulties. In any case, there remains the supreme Essence who brought this entire system into existence and is still its Lord. What does it matter whether he has made the universe his body or whether he stands outside of it and, like a master musician, controls his orchestra. In any case, the music is his product. We need not worry too much about technicalities or methods.

If the monotheism of the great Masters smacks of the pantheism of Spinoza, let it be acknowledged that Spinoza was not far from the truth. "God-intoxicated man," as he was called, he was groping near to the great Reality. We may go even a step further—if the teaching of the Masters is not pure monism, then it leads us very close to that position and reveals the element of truth that lies concealed in the theory. After all, who can assume a second creative principle in the universe? Is there any force outside the Supreme One? If so, what is that force and whence its origin? How can there be anything in Nature which is not a product of the monogenetic process of the Supreme One? If so, then there is no all-inclusive Supreme One. Any other conception appears unthinkable and only carries the student around in a whirl of empty words.

After all is said, the cosmos is one, and the creative power operating it is one. It may manifest itself in diverse ways and forms. Who can separate the cosmos itself from the force which brought it into existence and now sustains it? But that form of monism which goes so far as to identify spirit and matter, and make all of these identical with God, is not accepted by the Masters. If that sort of monism insists that the physical universe is itself God, then the Masters will not agree. They will not agree even if they include all higher universes in the grand cosmos and make it identical with the Supreme One. While the Infinite cannot be separated from his creation, even in the innermost recesses of thought, yet the infinite Spirit is not the universe. That Essence is something vastly more.

In a very true sense the universe may be said to be the body of God, but the body of a man is not the man. It is only his physical covering. Such an assumption is a very clumsy hypothesis. The body is not the man, yet the body, down to its last cell, is permeated and governed by the spirit which is the real man. If the spirit is withdrawn from the body, that body dies at once. In like manner, if the infinite Essence were withdrawn from the universe, the whole thing would disintegrate. Just as human bodies die and suffer dissolution, so certain portions of the material universe grow old and dissolve, only to reappear charged with new life and vigor. This is in every instance due to spirit substance being withdrawn from that portion of creation. But spirit itself is not subject to any such change. The soul, like its Creator, is eternal, deathless.

The sum of this discussion is that there is absolute unity in this universe, organic unity and oneness throughout, and there is but one universal Force, creative and all-sustaining, which is never separated from it, nor can it be separated. It is an organic whole. If you wish to call this universal Force 'God', then you have your monotheism in perfection, absolute and unassailable. And you have at the same time a monism which recognizes but one substance in the universe, manifesting itself in an endless variety of forms.

There remains but one philosophical difficulty, and that is due to the inability of our minds to see ultimate Reality. The difficulty lies in our inability to reconcile the doctrine of one *substance* with the manifest differences which we see to exist between substances. At the extreme poles of existence, it is not easy to see how wood or stone can be one with spirit, how a tree can be one with an angel, and still be different from each other. But physical science has given us an illustration which may help us to grasp the idea. It has already proved that substances which show very different properties are composed of identical electronic particles, the difference being due to a different arrangement of those particles. This at least may suggest that what is pure spirit at the extreme positive pole of creation may at the negative pole appear to be something quite different—this difference being due to a thinning out of particles and a different arrangement of what is left.

But this leads us beyond our depth. An analogy may be drawn from another fact of Nature known to the Masters. Looked at from this end of creation, each individual man appears to be a separate doer, acting on his own impulses and being responsible for his own actions. But the same man, looked at from the top of creation, the supreme region, disappears as an individual actor, and in his place the Supreme One appears to be the only doer. Our difficulty lies in being unable to get a comprehensive view of the entire problem from a single standpoint.

As the pundits say that Akash is the primary substance out of which all worlds are formed, and Prana is the primary force which moves all creation on material planes, so now we may have already demonstrated that all matter is resolved into electricity. And the grouping of the electrons with their nuclei is simply the method which Nature has adopted to present us with all the many varieties of matter and material things as we see them. This is only one step nearer to an understanding of the all-inclusive unity of Nature. Working backward in the reverse order from the way in which the present universe has come down to us, we must at last arrive at the one primordial substance out of which the entire universe has been evolved. And when we find that one universal Essence, it will be seen that it is identical with the Supreme Essence which men have named God. In no case can it ever be conceived that any one part of this world can be wholly separated from the rest of it. It is an organic whole. It is one.

6. The Grand Hierarchy of the Universe

In the above discussion, we imagine we have disposed of the question of monotheism versus polytheism. But what we have now to say may at first appear to disturb our monotheism. Yet the disturbance is only superficial. Up to this point this chapter has been a preparation for what remains to be said.

What is the Grand Hierarchy? It is that grand galaxy of lords, rulers, creators, governors, all of the heavenly spheres. We have spoken of the four grand divisions of creation, and brief mention has been made of the many subdivisions. Now, in every subdivision, sphere or plane, from the highest down to the lowest, there is a lord or ruler or governor. These lords, rulers and governors are great souls who have been appointed by the Supreme One to discharge the duties assigned to them in their respective regions. They are each endowed with certain godlike powers and prerogatives, among which is the power of creation.

To obtain a better understanding of the whole scheme, let us sketch very briefly the creative process as it is taught by the Masters. When the Supreme One wished to bring the universe into being, his move was to create the first focus of action, which may be regarded as one step downward toward the nether pole. This was done, of course, after the initial concentration of all precreation materials at the positive pole and the resultant lesser degree of concentration at the negative pole. This first focus of action was called Agam Lok; and its Lord, Agam Purush, who was brought into existence at the same time, was the first individual manifestation of the Supreme One. All subsequent creation was now to be carried on through this first individual manifestation. The supreme creative energy, now working through him, brought into existence the next region below him, which the Saints have named Alakh Lok, and its Lord, named Alakh Purush. Then, working through him, the fourth subdivision and its Lord are created. This region the Saints call Sach Khand, and its Governor they call Sat Purush or Sat Nam.

Sat Purush is now to carry on all creative activity below him. In precisely the same manner every region comes into existence, and at the same time the Lord of each region is created and assumes charge of his station. This process goes on until the last substation is reached, just above the physical universe. This is Anda, as we have already seen. The Lord of that region, Kal Niranjan, now exercising the powers assigned to him, brings into existence the entire physical universe, and the whole creative process is complete.

But the program of creation was not so simple as it may appear from the above statement. It was extremely complicated. Not only a few grand divisions were created, but numberless subdivisions, zones and subzones, region after region, plane after plane, each differing from the rest, and each one ruled over by a lord or governor appointed by the Creator, each with powers in proportion to the duties assigned to him. For example, there is not only one Brahm Lok, the region so prominently spoken of in the Hindu scriptures and believed by them to be the highest plane of spiritual existence, but there are numberless Brahm Loks, each with its Brahm ruling over it. There are great numbers of subordinate worlds, each one revolving about a higher plane or world much as planets revolve about the sun. Each sphere has its ruler. There is not only one physical universe but countless physical universes, and each one of them has its own governor. There is not only one world like this but, as you may suspect, numberless such worlds revolving about their respective suns, and each one has its own spiritual ruler. The number of planets thus inhabited is so great that no mathematician could count them in a thousand lifetimes, even if he could see them.

Thus it will be seen that from the highest subdivision of all creation down to the last and smallest planet or planetoid that may be inhabitable, floating about among the countless stars, there are lords and rulers appointed by the Supreme One through his hierarchy of subordinates. The duty of each of these is to carry out the will and purposes of the Supreme. They are all his executives, his viceroys, his duly appointed governors. As said before, each of these rulers is subordinate to the one next above him, deriving all of his powers from that one.

It is thus that the entire universe of universes was created and organized, and is now governed by the Grand Hierarchy. The lowest member of this governing body is the governor of a single planet and the highest one is Agam Purush, who was the first individual manifestation of the Universal Power. Each individual member of this Grand Hierarchy is Lord God over all below him, and through each one of them all powers flow to the one next below him. Upon each planet there are also many subordinates working under the orders of the planetary ruler. At the foot of this Grand Hierarchy stands man himself. He has his own individual sphere of action, each member of the entire human race; and among all the men of the world are vast numbers of individuals who are selected by the planetary ruler to perform certain functions and duties. As a rule, they are not aware that they have been so selected and empowered. Nevertheless, they are working under orders, whether they know it or not, and they must serve the Supreme Power whether they will it or not. This world is not jogging along in a haphazard, chaotic manner. It is moving on according to the will of the Supreme. It must attain the final destiny willed by the Supreme, and no one can defeat his purposes.

In this Grand Hierarchy, the great Masters occupy a unique position. They are the greatest among men. Not only so, but they work not under orders of the planetary ruler or any subordinate of the Grand Hierarchy but under the orders of the Supreme Sat Purush himself. They are his chief executives on earth and they have a special duty different from that of all others of the Hierarchy, that is, to rescue souls from the maelstrom of material worlds and take them up to Sach Khand, from the bondage of the *chaurasi ka chakar* to spiritual liberty in the supreme region. That is their chief duty and that they are doing, as said before, under the direct supervision of the Supreme himself, quite independently of any of the subordinates, rulers or governors of subordinate regions. They have this unique service assigned to them because there is no other way that human souls can escape from this bondage, this prisonhouse of maya.

Without the Masters, every soul would be doomed to circulate through these regions of matter, worlds of pain and shadow, for endless ages. It is thus that the lovingkindness of the Supreme has provided the means of escape for all who will avail themselves of it, and at the same time the Supreme has converted this material region into a training school for us. If we meet these conditions bravely and do the work as assigned by the Master, we become God-realized ourselves and rise above all material bondage to worlds of light and joy.

Into this general scheme, according to the earnings of his own karma, every individual man and woman takes his place, does the work which he must do, and creates new karma according to the individual liberty of choice which he possesses at the moment. When his work is finished, he departs to some other scene of action according to his karmic earnings. And so the entire scheme carries on from age to age, from yuga to yuga.

An interesting question now arises. Are we to call all of these members of the Grand Hierarchy 'gods'? If not gods, how shall we designate them? For we must not offend our rigid monotheists. If man is a part of the Supreme One, issued from his very being, a projection of his very self, then the individual man is no less than a god, even if a very humble specimen. The son of an animal is an animal; the son of a man is a man, and so the son of a god must be a god. What then shall we call all those great lords and rulers? If we call them gods, then our jealous monotheist will call us bad names for introducing another sort of polytheism. After all, what danger is there in a mere name? Why should it worry us so? We cannot just call them men. They are much above men, as we know ourselves.

Just what is a god, anyway? Let us define the word if only to clarify our discussion. *A god is a great being endowed with super-human powers and prerogatives, among which are the creation and governance of worlds.* We acknowledge that this definition is somewhat original. You will not find it in the dictionary. But it suits the purposes of this book and it accords with the teachings of the Masters. It will help us to keep our meaning clear when we use the term *god*. There are, therefore, many gods with varying powers and degrees of authority; and still there is, presiding over them all, but one God in supreme authority. More accurately speaking, all gods in existence are so many individual manifestations of the Supreme One. This should be acceptable to our monotheists.

One other point requires a word of explanation. We are not accustomed to think of any but the Supreme Being as endowed with creative powers. This was because we were not acquainted with the teachings of the great Masters. They know that many of the Grand Hierarchy have creative powers, practically all of them to some extent. For example, it has been stated above that Kal Niranjan is the creator of the physical universe. For this very reason he has been often mistaken for the Supreme God of all creation. Many devotees who go no higher than his region firmly believe him to be the Supreme God. But as a matter of fact, he occupies a comparatively humble seat in the Grand Hierarchy. In spite of this, he is the creator of this entire physical universe and he remains its governor. He carries on here according to the will and the orders of the Supreme One, as handed down to him by his superiors. He is generally referred to as the Negative Power because he is stationed at the negative pole of creation. Yet his powers are very great when compared with man's.

It may be mentioned in passing that every real Master has creative powers. He has the powers of life and death. Creations and dissolutions are in his hands. The powers of any real Master far excel those of Kal Niranjan, who actually created this world. But the function of a Master is not creation. His work lies in another direction. He can do whatever he likes but his work is definitely outlined. It is no part of his duties to create or govern worlds. He lives in this world as a friendly visitor, and while here he does not interfere with the routine management of affairs. This is one reason why he seldom does a miracle; he does not wish to contravene the law.

7. The Negative Power

In the Santon ki Shiksha, frequent mention is made of the Negative Power. We are now in a position to explain exactly what is meant by that term. It refers to that individual in the Grand Hierarchy who occupies the position of Creator and Governor nearest to the negative pole of creation. He is not the lowest in the Hierarchy. Under him are many subordinates. But of all the negative powers, he is supreme. The rest may be called his agents and subordinates. They carry on under his orders, just as he carries on under the orders of his superiors. His name is Kal Niranjan, and his headquarters lie at the summit of Triloki, commonly called the Three Worlds, that is, the physical universe, Anda, and the lower end of Brahmanda (designated as Trikuti or Brahm Lok).

These three great subdivisions of creation, in the minds of the ancient rishis, constituted the entire sum of creation. Beyond that they knew of nothing. Kal Niranjan was then regarded as the Supreme God over all creation. But to the Saints, he is the Negative Power so named because he is at the negative pole of creation with many regions above him. The Saints alone know that he occupies a subordinate position in the Grand Hierarchy. They know also of his imperfections when compared with members of the Grand Hierarchy who occupy higher positions.

Contrasted with this Negative Power, the Saints speak of Sat Purush as the Positive Power. He rules the whole of creation from the positive end of all the universe of universes. While he himself is not the very highest of all the manifestations of the Supreme One, yet he is generally regarded by the Saints as our Supreme Father and Creator. He is, in fact, Father and Creator to us. It is a significant fact that below him no member of the Grand Hierarchy has power to create souls. They have creative powers over everything else, but no power to create a soul and no power to destroy a soul. In Sat Purush, the supreme creative energy comes to perfect manifestation for the first time in all Sat Desh. Agam Purush and Alakh Purush are so close to the Universal, so slightly differentiated, that Sat Purush is generally regarded as the first actual or complete personification of the Supreme One. He then becomes manifest as the supreme executive power of the whole creation. His region, Sach Khand, may then be known as the governing center of the entire system of universes.

Sat Purush is in reality the Supreme One taking form and establishing his throne as the King of kings at the very gates of the Supreme Region. He is the Sovereign Lord with whom Saints have to deal most in carrying out their sacred mission of returning souls to their final home. To him all subordinates pay homage and from him they all take orders. He is the great Father, the Supreme Guru, the Light Giver of all Saints. To him we must all return if we are ever to reenter our original home. He is our true Heavenly Father. He is our God. All gods, lords or rulers below him, we may love and honor, but our supreme devotion belongs to Sat Purush for he is the real Lord God of all worlds in existence. Alakh Purush and Agam Purush, the Nameless One and the Universal, are so utterly incomprehensible, so fathomless and impersonal, that we cannot approach them even in thought. But Sat Purush stands midway between the Infinite Light and the created universe; and so in time, when we have been purged of every imperfection, we may approach him as our Father, see him with our glorified eyes, and receive his gracious welcome back home.

In the meantime, while we sojourn in this dark region of matter, we have to deal with the Negative Power. With him we must contend in our struggles for spiritual freedom. It is his duty to try to hold us here, while it is our duty to try to escape. The resulting struggle purges us and makes us strong, and fits us for our homeward journey. This everlasting fight, this struggle in a welter of pain and blood and heart cries, is designed by the Supreme Father to purge us and make us clean, ready for our homeward ascent. Let us never become discouraged. All of this is designed by the Father for our benefit. It is much as if one enters a gymnasium to take exercise. If we meet these difficulties in the right spirit, we shall greatly profit by them. The idea of pain and struggle is to purge us and inspire in us a longing to rise above the regions of pain and shadow.

At the present time we are sojourners in the country of the Negative Power and our first duty is to find our way back to our own home. While here, we are subject to the laws of this country. It is to these laws of the Negative Power that we refer when we speak of the laws of Nature. He is the author of all natural laws as we know them. For he is the creator and lord of the physical universe. He is the Lord God of the Bible, the Jehovah of the Jews and Christians, the Allah of the Mohammedans. He is the Brahm of the Vedantists, the god of practically all religions. None but the Saints and their students know of any other god; yet this Negative Power, so exalted and so universally worshipped as the supreme Lord God, is in fact only a subordinate power in the Grand Hierarchy of the universe. He is the Negative Power, and as such he must have some negative qualities. Of course, when compared with man, he is very exalted, full of light, goodness, wisdom and power. It is only when compared with the Positive Power that his lesser light becomes manifest. To this very fact we may trace the origin of what we call evil; for evil is but a lesser good. This problem will be discussed more fully in Chapter Seven, Section 10.

Subordinate to the great Negative Power, there are three others whose names must be mentioned here. They are the famous Hindu trinity—Brahma, Vishnu and Shiva. These are called sons of Kal Niranjan. The Orientals are fond of reducing all things to human relationships in order to explain them. It is about the only way the majority can understand them. So these three are said to be sons of Brahm, whose other name is Kal Niranjan. The female counterpart of Kal Niranjan is Shakti, who in fact represents another creative current. Out of the union of these two great currents, three subordinate currents flow into the lower worlds, and to these are attributed the creation of all lower worlds. These three became creators, lords and governors of the lower worlds under their father, Niranjan, and their mother, Shakti. They are said to be more directly under the supervision of their mother.

In fact, these three represent creative currents; they carry the creative impulses from the greater powers above. But they have been given these individual names as persons. It is well to remember that all creative currents may become personal, that is, take individual form and assume individual duties. Now these three have generally been accepted as the Hindu trinity of gods, most commonly known in their pantheon. Millions worship them in spite of their subordinate position. They each perform a certain function in carrying on the work of the world, in producing human bodies, and in keeping those bodies going. They are agents of the Supreme Power in serving mankind. They are not gods to be worshipped. Who will worship his servants? They are subordinates in the Grand Hierarchy. But each of them has certain powers and prerogatives, and within his own sphere he is all-powerful. He carries on according to definite laws and rules laid down for his government. These again are laws of Nature. Brahma, Vishnu and Shiva may be regarded as servants of the Negative Power or his working committee. In all respects, they do his bidding, each in his own department.

Still lower than these three, there is another current or god or power who is also one of the working forces, helping to carry on the administration of the physical universe. His name is Ganesh. He stands practically at the foot of the list of subordinates whose business it is to serve mankind and help to carry on the work of this world. In the subtle regions close to the earth, there is a great host of beings called *devas, devtas,* spirits, etc. These are generally called 'angels' in English. They are beings something above ordinary men and help to serve man in many ways. They have great powers and are quite willing to serve people who live in harmony with them.

Last of all is humanity itself, at the very foot of the Grand Hierarchy. If man works in harmony with all those powers above him, he will surely receive their help and will eventually rise to the position where he will find a Master and then accomplish his final return home.

It may be said with emphasis that between man and all those exalted beings who compose the Grand Hierarchy there is no difference at all in quality, that is, in the essential character of the soul. There is a difference in degree only, a difference in the fullness of endowment. The fundamental qualities of spirit are wisdom, power and love. The larger the measure of these three a soul possesses, the higher does it rank in the Grand Hierarchy. Man, however, has the privilege, when initiated by a perfect Master, to rise above all these planes and reach Home. Hence, he is rightly regarded as the top of creation.

Chapter Six

ANALYSIS OF MAN:
THE PSYCHOLOGY OF THE MASTERS

1. The New-Old Psychology

IN order to discuss intelligibly some of the most important teachings of the Masters, it is necessary to offer at least a brief outline of their psychology. And let us say at the outset that what we mean by psychology is not what that term has come to signify in the modern schools. As the word is used in this discussion, it includes the science of mind and soul—what they both are in fundamental structure and function, and the relation between the two, as well as their reactions under test conditions.

This psychology of the Masters is at once both the oldest and the newest psychology known. It is the oldest because its main points have been known and taught by the Masters ever since they began to instruct students on this planet. That was so long ago that no historian can even attempt to trace it. It was old ages before the Vedas were ever heard of, and it was only when the pure teachings of the Saints began to be obscured and corrupted that the Vedas came. It was old long before the Chinese sages began to speculate upon the abstruse and the unknown, the occult and the mystical. It was old long before the great cataclysm changed the face of the continents and raised the Himalaya mountains to their present height. It was old when the first known empire, stretching back into Sat Yuga, the Golden Age, built its civilization upon the great plateau which is now Tibet and the Gobi desert. It was old before the Sanskrit language was spoken in that central empire of prehistoric civilization; for the Masters' system has watched the decline of the Sanskrit and the simultaneous decline of all known civilizations.

It must be remembered that mastership is not a product of modern civilization. It has been the chief factor in producing all civilizations, including the modern. Masters have existed in this world for millions of years, and the system now outlined in this book has been taught by the Masters to their disciples for millions of years. Always during prehistoric eras, while the majority of the race were on the decline, descending toward what we now call primitive savagery, the Masters have held aloft the torch of spiritual Truth, pointing the Way for all who had eyes to see it. To those as would listen to them, in every age the Masters have taught this age-old psychology and at the same time given exact knowledge of the Yoga of the Audible Life Stream.

The psychology of the Masters is also new, because today scarcely a single scholar in Europe or America has ever heard of it. It has never found its way into any of the modern schools or into any accredited book. Up to the present, few representatives of the English-speaking peoples had ever lived with a great Master long enough to learn his science and to write it down in a book. This book is the first attempt in history to give this science to the West by a Western man. The teachings of the Masters have scarcely been heard of in the West.

It must, however, be kept in mind that this is not another statement of the Vedantic philosophy. It is no more Vedantism than it is Islam or Christianity. The real science of the Masters, as presented in this book, must never be confused with the various Hindu systems, philosophies or religions. It is none of them. This writer was once accused of "going crazy over some Hindu religion." But this is no Hindu religion. It is not a religion at all. Hindu philosophies have many features in common with Santon ki Shiksha; but the most essential elements of this science are quite unique and not widely known even in India among the vast majority of Indian scholars. This is because the Hindu pundits have been so preoccupied with their own systems of learning that they have never taken the trouble to investigate the real science of the Masters. Learning often stands in its own light.

What then, is the psychology of the Masters? This is almost equivalent to asking what is man himself. Because in order to answer the question we must first analyze man. In spite of the oft-quoted statement of Pope, that the greatest study of mankind is man, how amazingly little does man know about himself! The great body of modern psychological dissertations is based upon the phenomena of human consciousness as they are manifested in daily life or in the laboratory. Man himself they scarcely attempt to analyze. They are not to be blamed for this because they are not equipped to do the work; besides, they do not believe that complete knowledge of the constitution of man is available to science. They know nothing of the Masters or of their science. Indeed it is doubtful if the great psychologists have the facilities to make such analysis. They have neither the facilities nor the method.

Of late years, much emphasis has been placed upon psycho-analysis—far too much, we think. What means have the psychologists for a genuine analysis of the psyche? They have written many books on psychoanalysis, which sound so very profound, all attempting to explain mental phenomena in terms of physics and physiology—hence the physiological psychology of MacDougall and others. Great and painstaking efforts have been made to catalogue mental reactions to given stimuli and to establish the relations of each reaction to all others. Out of this more or less fruitful soil grew the far-reaching postulates of Dr. Sigmund Freud, upon which was founded the so-called science of psychoanalysis, a system once so popular but which appears even now to have entered upon its decline.

And so the psychologist continues to study these phenomena, but he has not even touched the more important facts of the constitution of man himself. He is not to be blamed for this, as said before, because he has not the facilities for such a study and analysis. At this writing, we believe that there is not a single noted Western psychologist living who can speak with assurance of actual knowledge as to whether man has either mind or soul apart from his body.

While a man lives, we can examine, record and study his phenomena. When he dies, the scientist puts him on the table, dissecting instruments in hand—and what does he find? Neither mind nor soul, nor any consciousness. No response to his instruments. He finds only an inert thing, a bundle of muscles and bones, of brain and nerve tissues, which gives no response to his technical apparatus. The scientist walks out of his laboratory puzzled and dejected. What has become of his man, that being, who only yesterday thought, hoped, loved, and then died? Certainly it isn't that thing which lies there on the table, that thing which you can cut with your knife, the thing which you can slice off and place under your microscope. Man surely isn't that helpless thing which you wrap in a shroud and lower into the grave to become food for worms? Surely not that!

2. What Is the Real Man?

What are the component parts of the real man? This question will never be answered in your laboratories. Neither will you ever find in your hypothetical psychoplasm the real basis or the genesis of consciousness. The sad fact is that modern psychology knows nothing at all about the real man, nor does it even claim to know so much. Let us give it credit for that. Psychology is not to be blamed for its limitations. We do not blame a baby because it cannot walk. The science has struggled heroically to gain what little knowledge it has, and we cannot deny that it has accomplished much that is of value. It is a pity, however, that its present knowledge is not converted into values. Let us thank its tireless workers. Neither can we blame psychology for its failure to solve the most important problems of its own science. It could not do so. It never can do so. It is working under too great a handicap. It can never solve these problems by the method of the schools. It must eventually turn to the Masters for help.

Who can solve the mystery? Who can tell us with certainty just what is man or his inmost constitution and component parts? When shall the world be startled by the announcement in the morning papers that a man's mind and soul have been isolated and demonstrated as fundamental realities which science must henceforth recognize? We fear that announcement is yet some distance in the future.

But there are men today who can tell exactly what man is in every aspect of his being. There is only one class of men in the world who are equipped to give us this information, and they are not known to the body of scientists. They are the great Masters. They are the superscientists. How does it come that they know so much more than the schools—the great schools of the modern age? It is because they alone are equipped and able to separate themselves from the physical body, look upon themselves apart from that body, and last of all, separate themselves from the mind, and look upon themselves as pure spirit. They are then able to look down from their lofty viewpoint and study the entire phenomena of their own lives as well as the lives of others. Thus they are able to observe the behavior of bodies, of minds, and then of pure spirit detached from all coverings.

The Masters are able to do all this in full consciousness and can report their findings and record them. The Masters can actually see their own minds and the minds of others, and observe their behavior. This process, strictly scientific, may be done under the most rigid test conditions, and may be repeated as often as may be desired and by as many different people as may be qualified for the experiment. Their findings are in all cases exactly the same when done under the same conditions. Certainly the Masters are the only qualified scientists or psychologists. They alone compass the entire field of science, and nothing ever escapes their scrutiny.

The very word *psychology*, taken from the Greek *psyche*, means 'the science of the soul'. That assuredly was the meaning attached to it by the old Greek Masters. But modern scientists have made it almost exclusively a study of the mind, and even at that they are practically limited to psychophysiological phenomena. They never know whether they are dealing with chemicophysiological reactions of brain and nerve tissues or with something which is independent of brain and nerves. No psychologist can tell you with assurance what thought is. But the Masters can tell you because they are able to *see thoughts* and watch them form and disappear. Mental reactions, under all sorts of stimuli, are just as visible to the Masters as physical reactions are visible to other scientists. Finally, the Masters are able to detach themselves even from the mind itself and observe themselves and others as *pure spirit.* It is only then that the Master obtains perfect knowledge as to what man is. When he actually observes himself as spirit only, free from all coverings and mind, then he knows that he is essentially spirit; and that mind and all bodies are but instruments, coverings needed only for contacts with matter in material regions.

Let us now set down a few of the observations of the Masters concerning the actual constitution of man. In doing so, we invite the psychologists of the schools to enter the laboratory of the Masters and make the experiment for themselves. It would be best for them if they came in the spirit of the great scientist, Alexander Agassiz, who said:

> Let the scientific student sit down before the facts, as a little child,
> and enquire of them.

It is useless to come to the great Masters, unless one comes in that spirit.

3. The Several Parts of Man

Beginning with the lower stratum, we may say that, first of all, man is an animal. He is a *physical body,* called by the Orientals *Asthul Sharir.* This much will not be disputed, except perhaps by those who deny the existence of all matter. At any rate, we all

know that we have something which we call body, which sometimes gets hurt or sick, and which finally dies and returns to the
soil.

There is then another man inside of this physical man, a
much finer body called by the Masters the *Sukhsham Sharir,* or
'subtle body', *Nuri Sarup,* or 'light body'. It is commonly called
astral body by Western students who have a little knowledge on
the subject. It is so called because when seen, it appears to sparkle
with millions of little particles resembling stardust. It is much
lighter and finer than the physical body. This body every person
possesses and uses here and now, although he may be unconscious
of it; and it is through and by means of this finer body that the
mind and soul are able to make contacts with the physical body
and the outside world. This finer body takes shape in harmony
with the character of the individual. On the plane where the astral
body functions, no deception is possible. Everyone is seen just
as he is. This astral body has its five senses just the same as
the physical body. When the physical body dies, this finer body
remains as the instrument of expression upon that higher plane
of life.

Inside the astral body, and quite distinct from it, there is still
another body much finer and more subtle than the astral. It is
called by the Masters the *Karan Sharir.* That means 'the causal
body', so named because in it is the real cause or seed of all that
is ever to take place in that individual's life. It is also called *Bij
Sharir,* meaning 'seed body'. This body is as much finer than the
astral as the astral is finer than the physical. It may be divided into two or more strata, each of which is given a different name. It
is sometimes called *the mental body.* It may be regarded as a
portion of the mind itself, acting as a sort of sheath around the
soul, very sensitive to impressions from the soul. Its function
is to receive and transmit impressions between mind and soul,
on one side, and between the mind and the astral body on the
other side.

In this body a perfect record is left of every experience of the
individual, running through all of the countless ages of its existence. Out of all of these experiences character is formed, and

from that character all actions flow. If one is able to read those records, as the Master and many others can do, he can see exactly what that man has done or had done to him during his entire past—also what he is going to do in the future. It is all there, the future in seed form, the past in visible record.

The Karan Sharir is man's highest and finest instrument of action, except mind itself, and it is not easy to differentiate between this body and the mind, as they are both parts of the same thing. It is through this body that the soul contacts all the lower levels of life, working through the still lower bodies, as mentioned above. Both belong to and are taken from Universal Mind and both must eventually be returned to Universal Mind. Both are of extremely high vibrations, and both are full of light and endowed with great power. That endowment comes, however, from soul.

The mind is the fourth unit in the construction of man. We have already said that it is so closely related to the Karan Sharir that it is not easy to distinguish between them. For clearness of thought, let us assume that mind is something finer than Karan Sharir, more subtle and in closer proximity to the soul itself. It is also endowed with much greater powers, because it is in closer relation with the soul.

So long as we are in material regions, we must retain the mind and the Karan Sharir. If we are to manifest on the astral planes we must also have both the Karan Sharir and the Sukhsham Sharir, the causal and the astral. And if we are to manifest on the physical plane, we must have all three of the above instruments. Finally, when an individual rises from the physical to the astral, then the causal, and finally leaves the causal on his upward journey, he discards all three instruments. This is because he no longer needs them. When he reaches the region next above the causal plane, he finds himself clear of all instruments and beholds himself as pure spirit. He then knows all things, rejoices in all things, by direct perception—without instruments of communication or mediation. That region is known to Masters as Daswan Dwar.

It may be difficult for us to understand how a person can discard his mind and still know anything. This is because we have been so accustomed to regard mind as the instrument of knowing, but as a matter of fact, it is not mind that knows. Mind alone is as powerless to know as is an automobile. But it is a good instrument used by the soul to contact objects of knowledge on material planes. But the soul alone does the actual knowing. For this reason, when the soul rises to Daswan Dwar and above, it has no need of the mind or any of the material bodies. It knows, as said before, by direct perception. All knowledge is open to it without any sort of instrument.

The mind itself is sometimes divided into different sections according to the plane upon which one is operating. The *nijma-nas,* 'inner mind', carries the seeds of all actions within itself. It carries the *sanskaras,* i.e., impressions of all former lives. Sometimes we speak of the causal mind, the Sukhsham mind, and the physical mind, according to the region or plane upon which the mind is operating; but it is only a distinction for convenience. A more detailed discussion of the mind is given in the next section.

Last of all, we come to the real man—the soul, or the spirit. These two terms we use synonymously. This is the very core of his being, and it is the fifth unit in the structure of the being we call man, as we see him in this life. Remember, he has all five of these elements while living here now. But all the lower units, which are only instruments, he discards one by one as he advances upward. This is because he has no use for them on the higher planes, each instrument being suited for expression only upon a particular plane of life.

The soul is the real man, the Atman, or as some prefer to call it, *the Purush.* The individual soul is a spark from the Infinite Light, a drop from the ocean of being. As such it is one with him— one in substance, one in qualities. It is in the soul that all consciousness and all power resides. All below the soul, even the mind itself, is unconscious, automatic, and mechanical in action. In fact, everything in existence is entirely dependent upon spirit for its life and activity. Even the humblest plant or the smallest insect lives and carries on its activities by virtue of spirit, the tiny spark of spirit that gives it being. All else in man passes away or is discarded by him on his upward flight toward perfect freedom.

Were it not for the soul's temporary sojourn in these material regions, there would be no need for any of these instruments—these bodies and the mind. Owing to the extreme fineness of spirit, it cannot contact the coarser worlds without an intermediate instrument. Hence it is obliged to clothe itself in some sort of medium of contact. For this very reason the Supreme Being himself cannot manifest on these material planes, or appear to men and give them instructions. A material body is necessary in all cases. This again is one reason why a living, embodied Guru is necessary. It is the only way the Supreme One can manifest himself to man on this plane.

A soul is a soul, no matter how high or low may be its status. Its status is generally measured by its instruments, especially its mind. In any case, the soul is a derivative of the Supreme and identical in substance. The Masters tell us that the entire universe is filled with souls. There is no vacant space where souls are not. Some of them have better minds and better bodies than others. In other respects there is no difference between amoeba and man, between an insect and a savant. This fact makes clear the significance of the teaching of the Masters concerning transmigration. Metempsychosis is not so easy for the Western mind. But when carefully studied, it becomes not only a rational explanation of many mysteries but it offers a most beautiful spectacle.

I look out upon my garden vegetables, fruits and flowers. In that garden are thousands of precious souls kindred to myself, my little brothers, struggling by means of their tiny sparks of intelligence, striving always toward the light, each one slowly rising to something a little higher than itself. They are all ascending the scale of evolution, as our physical scientists would describe the situation. It emphasizes the common brotherhood, the fundamental kinship, between all living beings, including animals. It offers a sublime picture, this grand procession of all living forms, slowly moving toward that "far off divine event" spoken of by Tennyson. It is the best consummation of all evolution when the last grain of dust shall enter the light of immortality.

4. The Analysis of Mind

We are now in a position to go to the very center of our psychological problem. We are ready to analyze mind itself, to discover its several parts and its functions. If modern psychology were prepared to tell us exactly what mind is, it would be in a position to give the world a real scientific psychology. But as said before, the Masters alone are able to tell us exactly what mind is. In the region of Trikuti, the causal world, the mind is acquired. The soul in its descent through that region picks up the mind as its equipment for use on the lower planes. That region is the seat of Universal Mind. It is the region from which all mind is derived. Just as the soul originates in the region of Universal Soul, so now the mind is acquired in the region of Universal Mind. Mind is joined to the soul, not in a permanent union but in a time union. Let us say, after a fashion, it is wrapped about him, covering the soul, and at the same time obscuring much of its light and hampering its activity.

I remember once I put on a diving suit while I was connected with the United States Navy during the Great War. I had to see just what it was like to walk on the bottom of the sea. I know not how much that suit weighed. The boots alone were so heavy that I had to have help to walk to the edge of the boat from which I was to slide down into the sea, sixty feet below. But when I was walking on the bottom of the sea, I felt no particular weight in those boots. But it was equipment I had to have. In like manner, the numerous bodies which the soul acquires on its way down constitute an enormous handicap if one wishes to go up again. But if he wishes to go down or remain down he is obliged to have them.

Now the soul, equipped with this necessary handicap, begins his career in regions of mind and matter. At that moment he begins to accumulate karma. Before that he had no karma, except that which the Eastern Wisdom calls *adi karma*. This is the primal karma, and it consists of the action of the creative force, the real Shabd, whose function it is to bring souls to the material planes in order that they may begin to accumulate experience. Now the soul begins to acquire experience upon his own initiative. His era of *swabhava,* or *swadharma,* 'self-regulation', now begins. This means that he begins to establish an individual law of his own life, his own regime, and to create his own destiny. He begins to enjoy, to suffer, to reap rewards and to pay penalties. And this is the beginning of his own karma. Thus he inaugurates his long, long series of earth lives. By each and every act from that time on, he stores up karma. Even when he is least active, still he is making karma. And in all of this activity, his mind is his chief instrument. It is the mind working always under the law of cause and effect that creates karma.

The mind is not self-conscious nor self-acting, It has no power of automotion or of initiative. It is simply a machine, though highly sensitive and extremely powerful when motivated by spirit. As a machine, it can be made to do what it was intended to do, and that only just like any other machine. It will never do anything different from what it was fashioned and trained to do. Of course, all machines are automatic in action, but we speak of the mind as an automatic machine for the sake of emphasizing that point. This is an important fact which must be made as clear and as definite as possible. It is a new thought to the Western world.

We are not accustomed to think of mind as a machine. We have always been taught that if there was anything that had powers of origination and initiative, it was mind. But that was because we had been taught a wrong psychology. Mind and spirit have been greatly confused in Western psychology. Mind works only when activated by the soul. But in Western psychology mind and spirit are generally confused. But few, if any, know the difference between them. 'Divine mind' is a common expression among certain students. But there is no divine mind. The supreme divinity is far above all mind. Only the Negative Power and his subordinates have minds just like human beings. The fundamental difference between mind and spirit, between the soul and the instrument, must be understood if we are to comprehend the psychology of the Masters or to understand ourselves. Much depends upon this point in our understanding of the fundamental problems of this science.

We have now seen that mind is only an instrument which encumbers the soul, obscures its light and impedes its progress, but it is absolutely necessary while we are operating on these material planes. In the second place, as we have said so many times, the mind is only a machine. Mind alone cannot think, cannot will, cannot love. It cannot remember nor suffer nor enjoy. To do all of these things it must, in every instance, be activated by spirit.

Spirit alone is the motive power to mind, just as the electric current is the power that moves the machinery. Just as we cannot see the current moving the machine, so we cannot see the spirit moving the man. We think only of the machine which we can see. We see the human body and we have become accustomed to think of the mind as the chief power moving it. But every activity in the universe is carried on by spirit, and spirit only. Spirit works through many intermediate substances on these planes. Without spirit, mind is as inert as steel. Mind is matter, just as truly as steel but infinitely more refined. Thus it stands next to spirit in all of its essential qualities. The chief function of mind is to serve as an instrument of spirit for all contacts with the material worlds.

Of course, mind is a most useful instrument, provided it is kept under the control of the spirit. Mind is an excellent servant but a very bad master. Your automobile or your airplane is a fine instrument for travel. But you must keep it under control and guide it. It has no will but your will. So it is with your mind, exactly so. If your car is permitted to run wild, under full power, it is sure to come to grief. It knows no better than to run on as it has been trained to run. It cannot see and it cannot reason. So it is with mind, in every particular. It is your servant, but if it becomes your master it may speedily bring disaster upon you. We have always been taught that mind reasons, but it does not reason. It acts with automatic precision exactly as it is stimulated to act.

Mind is able to carry on deductive processes, but it has no power of induction. How often this is demonstrated in the case of hypnosis. Give the subject certain premises, no matter how absurd they may be, he will act upon such premises with automatic deduction. But such a mind has no power of synthesis and rational induction. Spirit alone has light in it, and spirit alone can work independently and rationally. We have only to observe a little the actions of people the whole world over. Everywhere and all the time, people act more like machines than they do like rational beings. And that is because they are moved by mind in grooves, just as they have been taught to act. It is the rare individual who does independent thinking, and when one does that it is because his spirit has to some extent become emancipated from the domineering control of mind.

5. The Four Antashkarans

This subject is so very important that we must devote a little more time to it. We must make ourselves fully acquainted with the mind in all of its faculties, and its several modes of action. Mind is divided into four parts, called by the Masters *antashkarans*. *This means 'inner modes of action'*. We may say it has four primary attributes, faculties or qualities. These four divisions of mind are named *manas, chitta, buddhi*, and *ahankar*.

(1) *Manas* is mind-stuff, *per se*. It is that which receives and registers impressions through the senses of smell, taste, hearing and feeling. Its chief function is *taste*. It tastes, relishes, enjoys or rejects what it doesn't like. Feelings and taste are practically the same thing. All of its reactions are automatic. The manas enjoys what it has been trained to like, and its reactions are instantaneous. It either likes a taste or rejects it automatically. It then passes on its findings to the buddhi for final judgment.

(2) *Chitta* is that faculty which takes cognizance of form, beauty, color, rhythm, harmony and perspective. It enjoys those things, and what it doesn't like it rejects. It receives its impressions mostly through the *eyes* as its instruments of perception. It then passes on its findings to the buddhi. In all of these reactions, its processes are as regular and automatic as are the reactions of chemistry.

(3) *Buddhi* is the *intellect* proper, that power the soul uses as its chief instrument of thought. It discriminates and decides. It

then passes judgment upon all the findings of the other two faculties. Its decisions are then passed on to the final court of execution, ahankar.

(4) *Ahankar* accepts the decisions of the other faculties handed on to it by buddhi and executes its mandates. It is the executive faculty of mind. It is also the *I-ness* of the individual. It is the faculty by which the individual differentiates self from all else, and it is the faculty which enables the individual to distinguish between his own interests and that of others. It is the faculty which, when exaggerated, becomes vanity or egotism. To sum up the above:

> Manas—receives and tastes
> Chitta—takes notices of form and beauty
> Buddhi—discriminates and decides
> Ahankar—executes orders

This leads us to one of the most important and most practical of all the facts and operations of the mind. The mind has not only four fundamental faculties or attributes but it has five destructive modes of action which manifest themselves when the above-mentioned faculties become disarranged, abnormal or perverted. These five destructive modes are perversions of the normal faculties due to the downward impulses of maya, the world of matter and senses. That is to say, those very faculties which were designed by the Creator for man's use, may become so perverted by misuse that they become destructive instead of constructive, bad instead of good. We call them the five destructive passions. It is extremely important that we understand them. We may think of them as diseased conditions of the mind.

When the mind is working normally in its legitimate spheres of action, it is carrying on the work it was intended to do. But when the least perversion of its normal faculties takes place, these five destructive modes take possession of one or more or all of them, and control the mind. So long as spirit controls the mind, the four faculties perform their proper function and these passions cannot manifest themselves. But when the mind runs wild, out of control, under the impulse of one or more of the five passions, it generally heads for destruction.

These five destructive passions are *kam, krodh, lobh, moh, ahankar*. In English they are 'sex passion' (which has become lust), 'anger', 'greed', 'attachment' to material things, and 'vanity'. These five passions really include all other evil moods of mind which can be thought of. These passions take possession when mind is allowed to run wild, out of the control of the spirit.

Fire is a good servant. But the moment it is out of control, it may become very destructive. It is the same with the mind. Generally the more useful and powerful an instrument is when properly controlled, the more destructive it may become when out of control. It is so with mind. It is the most powerful instrument available to spirit, but it must be controlled.

Let us not condemn Nature, but try to understand and obey her. She is our best friend if we first learn to obey. Understanding her, we may work in close cooperation with her to our very great advantage. It may be assumed that all pain and all suffering, mental or physical, which men are ever called upon to endure, have as their chief function to drive us toward a more perfect cooperation with Nature. If only we could learn that lesson, it would save us many a ruined life, many a heartache, and many a wrecked body. But so long as we do not obey Nature, we must go on suffering endless ills.

We marvel at the powers of electricity. We stand in awe before the gigantic energy let loose at the explosion of a ton of T.N.T. We find ourselves helpless before the onward sweep of a mighty cyclone or avalanche. But all these forces are feeble when compared with the fully awakened powers of mind. The chief difficulty is that but few people know how to awaken or invoke the powers of mind. And it is a good thing that more don't, in their present state of moral and spiritual evolution. But when men become morally responsible, their powers will automatically increase.

There is practically no limit to what mind can do when properly awakened and trained, and vitalized by spirit. A trained yogi, knowing how to awaken and control the powers of his own mind, can stop a train at any place he may wish it to stop. He can start a downrush of rain in five minutes out of a clear sky, or he can dry up a flood of water. He can do almost anything he likes. But this is

only playing with natural forces. All miracles are but the play of
mind. They are not the operations of any divine power, as most
people believe. But to do these things he must learn two things—
he must become morally responsible and then he must learn how
to control his own mind. After that he can do what he wishes. Of
course, he will not wish to break any moral law. If he were to do
so, he would lose his powers at once.

It stands to reason, and it is substantiated by our daily experiences, that if such gigantic powers were let loose, out of control, or
if they could be invoked by an evil mind, it might bring disaster of
the most terrible sort. It is, therefore, a most gracious provision of
the Creator that no man is able to invoke such powers until he has
first learned to control his own passions, check all evil tendencies
and all selfish impulses. Otherwise such a man might wreck the
whole world. But the Masters can do these things—not only the
Master but many of his advanced disciples.

The essential point here is that the mind is a very great power
and it must be kept in control. Rightly used, it may be made to
work marvels, but if allowed to assert itself in a lawless manner, it
may bring unspeakable disaster to its owner, and sometimes to
others as well. Whenever any of the five evil passions is allowed
to run wild, it means in each and every case that a mighty force
which was meant for our good has been turned into an instrument
of destruction. No faculty of mind ever works of itself. It is motivated by spirit, and it is as automatic in its action as is the explosion
of a stick of dynamite. It is only when spirit takes control that mind
is directed in safe and sane channels. It may then be compared to
a fine car with a good driver at the wheel.

Every agitation, stimulation, or excitation of mind in any
of its functions creates thought-forms which may be seen on
the subtle planes. Thoughts are things, just as much as clouds or
houses. The four faculties mentioned before, when set in motion
by any sort of stimulus, begin automatically to create thought-
forms and set waves in motion. And the mind will do these things
with the accuracy of chemistry or machinery. It cannot do otherwise. It has no power to originate independent thought, nor can it
reason upon any proposed course of action.

We are well aware that this is all contrary to our Western psychology. But Western psychology does not understand the mechanism of mind. Mind can never will to depart from its beaten path, any more than a locomotive can will to leave the track upon which it has been set. Habit is the chief method of mental action. Habits are likened to grooves in which actions run. The first thing which mind does, after it is agitated and brought into action, is to establish a groove, which we call habit. After that, it is much easier for it to go on. After many repetitions, the mind runs on very smoothly in its grooves and enjoys it. And it much resents being disturbed and compelled to get out of its grooves. Each time mind is agitated by the same thing, it will react just as it did earlier.

We often hear people blaming others, insisting that they could do differently, if they would. Yes, but they cannot will to do differently. They can choose only what their minds have been predisposed to choose, unless a new impulse comes in from the spirit. And that is not frequent in the average life. People are usually driven slaves of habit and custom.

Mind will never select a new course of action unless a new force enters into it from without itself. Otherwise, it will go on indefinitely doing exactly what it has been trained to do. Mind does not want to do differently from what it has become accustomed to doing. It resents innovation. It dislikes change. It likes variety of action, yes, but it wants that sort of variety which it has already learned to like. Mind accepts without question what it has been taught to believe as truth or right. It will never accept anything else, unless the new thing is forced upon it. Note the unreasoning action of mind under hypnosis. Hypnosis deadens the action of the buddhi, and then the mind cannot act, even on the basis of its own individual experiences. It readily accepts and fully believes whatever it is told, no matter how absurd.

Mind may be trained to a very high degree of skill in any line of activity. And this marks one very great advantage of its automatic quality. Its habits may be turned into great achievements as, for example, in music. But at first, the mind must be compelled to do as desired, and it must be forced to continue in that way until it has become accustomed to it. Then it likes to go on doing it.

The mind, when activated by spirit, forms thoughts, and each thought takes a definite shape on the astral plane. They may be seen there by anyone who enjoys astral vision. Often this occurs on subtle planes much lower than the pure astral, for there are many such. After the mind has become accustomed to create a certain routine of thought, it likes to go on creating thoughts in exactly the same way. It always loves its own way, and it can never believe that any other way is quite as good as its own until that other way has been forced upon it by personal experience.

Mind adores routine. Can you teach a machine to believe that it is not good to run into a tree? Can you convince it that the highway is better? You may argue with it half a day, and then turn it loose on full power and it will go straight into a tree if that tree happens to be in its path. So it is with most people. They will usually go on doing as they did before in spite of all rational persuasion. If a little light filters in from the spirit, a person may change his course of thinking or acting, but never otherwise. If the mind enjoys a certain sensation, it wishes to repeat that sensation as often as possible, quite regardless of whether that sensation is good for the person or not. And this is why we have so many drunkards, libertines and dope fiends. It is also why people indulge in anger, vanity, etc. Mind will usually do what it likes, regardless of consequences, unless checked by fear or some higher impulse from the spirit.

It is only when buddhi interferes that mind will forego an indulgence offered to it. Of course, if it feels pain from a certain performance, it instantly rejects that mode of action regardless of its own ultimate good. It is not easy for a man to stick a lance into his own abscess or allow someone else to do it, even though he knows it is best for him. It is only when the reasoning spirit asserts itself that one will do such a thing for his own ultimate good. Unreasoning children will never consent to be hurt, even when they know it is best for them. Perhaps in such cases the buddhi has not reached sufficient development for the spirit to make use of it.

Mind alone is neither moral nor immoral, any more than your automobile is. It is a machine as truly as your car. Cannibals can see no more sin in killing and eating a man than you do in killing and eating a chicken. To some other people both are sinful. Morality, sin and righteousness are largely matters of custom and geography. Social customs, ceremonies, rites, religions and politics are all based upon mental habits and are usually handed down from one generation to another.

Customs make it wrong in one country to enter a temple with shoes on, while in another country it is wrong to keep your hat on. Custom makes it wrong in one section to have more than one wife, while in another it is a sign of poverty or inferiority to be so limited. Mental habits have all the inflexibility of an iron machine. In fact, iron may be bent; but you try to change a long-established custom and your neighbors will seek your immediate destruction.

The whole human race is a slave to custom. Every single individual in the country may condemn that custom, but at the same time everyone will do his best to perpetuate it. All of this is because mind, both individual and social, is machinelike in its action. It cannot reason. Can you imagine vast armies going out with deliberate aim to destroy each other if they had the power to reason? Crime and moral rectitude are both mental habits. International strife is only blind personal passion run wild, en masse.

There are some advantages in this machinelike action of mind, but there is one very grave menace in it. If the mind, through a gradual process of suggestion and experience, becomes accustomed to certain grooves of action, it often leads to the wreck and ruin of the individual in spite of himself. That is a pathetic aspect of the matter. How many are the cases of this sort within every man's observation! People become entangled in the net of habits and customs, while deep in their hearts they ardently wish to get out of them but have not the power of will or strength of character to extricate themselves. They go deliberately and knowingly to destruction in spite of themselves.

The more a habit is indulged in, the more easily and certainly the mind will run in that groove. Even indulgence to the point of utter exhaustion never conquers the mental bond of a passion. That rather establishes it all the more firmly. At the same time, the soul itself becomes less and less able to impress itself and its wishes upon the mind or even to get a hearing at all. Finally the habit becomes so strong, so overpowering and dominant, that it simply runs wild when fired by some passion, sweeping all before it to ruin.

I recall once I was walking along the streets of St. Louis with another man. He was a pitiable drunkard. He had been entrusted to my care by the hospital management where he was being treated. We passed by saloons, and in every such instance he hesitated, gazed longingly into the saloon, while his whole body stiffened and trembled. An awful struggle was going on in his mind. The old mind wanted to take him into the saloon. But for my mind and my strong right arm acting in an opposite direction, he would have gone into the saloon in spite of his own better judgment. But his power of judgment had become weak. Reason no longer sat upon its throne. It lay paralyzed in the wreck of his manhood. Passion for drink had usurped the throne.

It must be known that the soul is an exceedingly fine and delicate thing. It has tremendous power in its own sphere of action. But on the fields of coarse material, it has but little power of self-expression. On the other hand, if the soul has a trained and responsive mind, it may do almost anything it decides to do. That is why mind control, through spirit, is so important and is so insisted upon by all the Masters.

Mind may again be divided in another way, besides the four faculties. It may be spoken of as the higher and the lower minds. This is a common classification. But it is not a scientific classification. There is only one mind acting on different planes. It may also be divided into three parts: the Pindi mind or the lower-world mind, that mind which manifests itself in the common affairs of this world; second, the Sukhsham mind, that mind which works on the astral plane; and lastly, the Karan mind or the nijmanas, the true inner mind, or the causal mind.

These three correspond to the three bodies of man, and the three worlds in which the three bodies operate, each in its own sphere. But with equal logic we may say there are six minds, because each of the above-mentioned three may be divided into two, a higher and a lower. In this world, for example, we may speak of a higher mind which engages itself in the highest forms of thought activity, such as philosophy, literature, music and art. The lower mind engages itself in grossly material things, money-making, eating, drinking, and the indulgence in any of the passions. But in any case, there is only one mind functioning on different planes and upon higher or lower things on each plane.

At the top of all, the mind which lies next to spirit is the real nijmanas, the purest and best. Below that, each substratum of the mind becomes more and more adulterated with coarser and lower substances. Last of all, at the very lowest stratum, there is a sort of mind which is but little more than electromagnetism. When the attention is on this lower plane, it is the lower mind which works. It is here engrossed in its own desires, its passions and its plays. When the attention is on the astral plane, it is the Sukhsham mind which is used, and when the attention is on the causal plane, it is that mind which is working. But in every case, it is the same mind playing upon different planes of existence.

The higher mind, the nijmanas, is a sort of pilot or gyroscope, whose function it is to receive the impressions of the soul and pass them on to the subordinate minds for their regulation. But the important point is that all aspects of the mind are automatic. None of them ever calculate results or assign a moral content. Each of them accepts what is given to it and reacts upon it without question or consideration. Neither does any aspect of the mind ever consider what is best for the individual, except just what it has been taught by experience to like or dislike. In other words, mind is not a rational entity. It reacts *automatically* and always upon the basis of what it likes or dislikes; it never considers what is best. If any element of calculation enters into the process, you may be sure that a little of the light of spirit is entering into the affair. The mind, if given a stimulus, or as we say, a temptation, will always act in accord with the sum total of its own past experiences. It cannot act in any other way. It cannot even will to act any other way.

6. A New Force Enters the Mind

The reader may now ask, very appropriately—if the mind always acts automatically, and in exact line with its own previous training, how do we account for any new or radical departure from the beaten path of its habits and desires? The answer is—on the basis of a new driving force entering the machine from without. How can a child quit its play, wash its face and go to school? Only because a driving force from outside of itself enters the machine. How does a man check himself from something he wishes to do, turn around and do the exact opposite? Because a different driving force enters the machine, and he obeys—has to obey—the stronger of the two impelling forces.

A friend of mine was in mortal combat with the enemy on the battlefield. One of the enemy had drawn his bayonet to pierce a comrade of my friend. My friend shouted to him to halt, at the same time leveling his gun on the man. That man was bent upon destruction. His whole impulse was to kill. He supposed it was his duty to kill. Then why did he stop and drop his bayonet? Simply because a new force had entered the combat—the fear of losing his own life. The stronger of the two forces prevailed, compelling him to drop his weapon and hold up his hands in a token of surrender. It is always so.

Physics is the best groundwork for the study of mental phenomena. There is not a single action of mind which cannot be reduced to Newton's Laws of Motion and the reactions of chemistry. It is no wonder that modern physicists are inclined to bring all mental reactions under their mechanistic theory of the universe. In the absence of complete knowledge, they are fully justified in their conclusions. If we had to deal always with mind alone, and spirit never entered into the problem, the mechanistic theory would apply with perfect accuracy. It would fit every fact of experience. But when intelligent spirit begins to enter the play, there is no foretelling what may happen. Spirit operates by its own light. And mind must follow whether it likes or not.

If now we can fully recognize the astonishing fact that mind is only an automatic thing, insentient and nonintelligent, subject to the laws of physics and chemistry, we are prepared for the next great truth in the psychology of the Masters. It is the illuminating fact that *all intelligence, light and power come from the soul.* This statement is without qualification. It is literally and universally true. All light, all intelligence, harmony, rhythm, beauty, wisdom, love, morality and power come from the soul. They are all derived from the spirit and are all imparted to the mind by the spirit, just as the electric current gives power to the bulb to make it incandescent.

The soul, however, often works under a serious handicap, as previously suggested. This world is not its native habitat. Here it is obliged to work under and through a series of coverings, analogous to my cumbersome diving suit—coverings of mind and matter. Though mind is a refined sort of matter, we are accustomed to speak of it as apart from matter. Under all of its coverings, the soul finds it exceedingly difficult to express itself and have its own way. It often finds itself quite unable to control its own mental instrument. Its ability to express itself at all depends upon the responsiveness of its chief instrument. If that instrument becomes unruly, defective or diseased, the soul is powerless.

All the coverings worn by the soul serve to burden it and to weaken its powers of expression. Mind may be called the cerebrum of the soul. If that instrument has become perverted, misshapen, distorted, diseased, then the soul cannot work normally through it, any more than the mind can work through a diseased brain. The finer forces of mind and spirit simply must have fit instruments of expression, or they cannot function on the material planes. The mind can become diseased just as much as the brain. Then the soul is helpless. It can only sit back and watch the wreck, and suffer in silence.

The balance of adjustment between mind and soul is exceedingly fine. It can easily become disturbed by throwing into their delicate structure a foreign body. These foreign bodies are the vile passions.

The Master sometimes compares the uncontrolled mind to a camel without a guiding string. It is likely at any moment to stampede and run away. It may then run on madly to its own destruction. Remember that the soul sits in the innermost chambers of being like the captain in his ship. He sits there in the cabin and controls his ship. But his control depends upon his ability to keep open the lines of communication with all parts of his ship, and then upon the instant response of all subordinates to his every word of command. But if mutiny breaks out due to a keg of whisky being brought on board among the crew; if the pilot is imprisoned and replaced by an enemy, and the captain locked in his cabin, then that captain is helpless even though he be the king himself. He is only a prisoner in his own ship. This is precisely the situation of the soul when the five mutinous passions run wild and take possession of the ship—the mind and body.

Remember that the soul is in the enemy's country, and is always surrounded by those five faithful servants of the Negative Power, the passions; and besides, these five are much addicted to intoxication. These five are commissioned to mislead the soul and mind and make trouble for them. It is their business. The worst feature of this is that the mind itself rather enjoys being swayed by them. It has a close fellowship with them and it lends a ready ear to their whisperings. They seek constantly to stir up mutiny, all the more so when one of them or all of them together become intoxicated with some new temptation. It is then that they all cooperate to set all of the faculties of the mind in a whirlwind of rebellion against the spirit, the real captain of the ship. Of these five foes we shall speak more particularly in another section of this book (*Chapter Six, Section 7*). It is sufficient to say here that both mind and spirit must be forever on guard against them.

The soul and the mind may be likened to the captain and his mate, the chief executive officer. If they relax discipline for a single moment, the enemy may gain the upper hand. One must be always keenly alert. A little bird lands in my garden to seek food. While doing so, I notice that it never relaxes attention for a single instant, but is keenly watchful lest a cat or other enemy might approach. It is always ready to take flight. So it should be with us. We must be ready any moment to retreat into our haven of refuge where the five enemies cannot come, the sacred chambers of the soul and the holy Shabd.

There is one thing in particular which the soul should guard against, that is, the insidious creeping-up, serpentlike, of bad habit. All habits tend to grow stronger with repetition, as we know. All indulgence fastens the chains of habit. At the beginning they may be easily checked and broken by a determined will. But by and by they become so strong, the outward and downward movement so impelling, that the soul is quite helpless. It then rushes on to disaster. Every one of the five enemy passions uses the method of habit to fasten its claws in the heart of its victims.

A man in a small boat was drifting down the Niagara River just above the falls. People on shore shouted a warning to him, but he paid no attention to their warning. When, a little later, he felt his craft impelled forward with increasing speed, he awoke to his peril, but it was too late. He was then quite powerless to escape the current. So it is with all bad habits. There is a point, a fatal moment, a deadly crisis, when the soul is no longer able to handle the situation. It cannot reach the mind, and the mind itself is in the grasp of a relentless fate created by its own conduct.

7. The Five Perversions of Mind

Any outline of the psychology of the Masters would not be complete without particular mention of the five modes of destructive mental action called *the passions*. We have said that these are perversions of the normal faculties. They are so. If a mind doing its duty only is kept strictly within its legitimate field of action, it will never become subjected to these five destructive processes. They are really mental diseases superinduced by the misuse of normal faculties. They are a species of psychological morbidity. But they play such a tremendous part in the average human life that we must study them as we would study a cancer in the hope of finding a cure.

The Masters have found by ages of careful observation that there are five different modes of destructive mental activity. They are modes of obsession. They are deadly diseases, each giving rise to a distinct pathology in the character of the individual. They destroy by insidious infection and dissolution. Their end is darkness and despair. But we must insist that Nature, or the Negative Power, shall not be blamed for these mental carcinomata. These evil passions cannot take root in man unless they are invited. This fact must not be forgotten. Unless, through self-indulgence, man invites them to become his guests and friends, they can never enter the premises. Unless he willingly plays with them they can get no hold upon him.

Self-indulgence, the worst of all sins, is a flaunting invitation to these five to come in and take up their abode. And where they enter they at once begin to forge the chains of evil karma. When once a man has turned over his conduct to these passions, they place every sort of temptation before him, assuming all possible forms attractive to the senses. They make false pretenses and hold out alluring promises. To gain a firmer hold upon their victims, they give a modicum of pleasurable sensations. They try to make victims believe that these pleasures will go on forever. When disappointment comes, as it must always come, they promise that just around the corner, after a few more struggles, all difficulties will vanish. An endless round of delights will then carry them to a serene old age.

Always the ultimate good is just ahead; yet you never overtake it. They hold up the mirage of wealth, of love and pleasures, of power and position, only to draw us on into the valley of death. The end of all of this is an endless circle of births and deaths, stretching on through the countless yugas, treading the eternal wheel. The end finds us just as securely bound as the beginning. If a man by heroic struggle gains a little higher ground, these five soon drag him down again, driving him under the fatal wheel— the wheel of awagawan, the wheel of eighty-four. And thus the weary ages come and go.

These five deadly passions are: *kam, krodh, lobh, moh and ahankar.*

They are: sex passion allowed to run into lust, anger, greed, undue attachment to material things, and vanity or egotism. We must now examine them in some detail.

(1) *Kam,* or 'lust', is a normal function, but when allowed to run into an abnormal demand, it becomes destructive, degrading. In its broader meaning kam includes all desires. It may include drugs, alcoholic drinks, tobacco or even tasty foods which are eaten simply for the sake of enjoying their tastes—any sort of appetite which seeks indulgence for the sake of enjoying a pleasant sensation. In some respects this is the strongest of the five and so the most deadly. It is dominant over the vast majority of mankind. It holds them as if by iron chains. It drags them along all through life. Day and night it haunts and taunts them. At every turn it displays its attractions. It appears in the most alluring garb and it steps out in unadorned seductive abandon. It blinds the mind. It makes a man forget every moral obligation.

Diverse are its methods of intrigue. Various are its blandishments. Alluring and false are its promises. Last of all, when you have wasted your vitality in its indulgences, it tosses you upon the rubbish heap. It coarsens its victim to the level of the animal. It clouds his perceptions and dulls his wits. In return for all of this terrible loss, what has it to offer? A pleasant sensation, a mad moment of delirium, which men call "having a good time." A passing frenzy, and an hour later its victim finds himself sitting alone in the gathering darkness, with new chains forged about his neck, wondering why he was ever such a fool.

Kam pulls men and women down to the common animal level and keeps them there. It obliges them to fix their attention upon that which is common to both man and brute. It is a principle of psychology verified by the experience of everyone that whatever the mind dwells upon, that thing becomes a part of the individual. We grow like that which we contemplate. The more vividly the thought dwells upon anything, the more that individual becomes like the thing he thinks about.

As a man thinketh, so is he.

But this law of mind can be utilized for good as well as bad. If our attention is absorbed in the good, we partake of that good. If we daily contemplate the Master, we become like him. If we think long and earnestly upon the Supreme Father, our love for him increases and we become more and more like him. But if our thought dwells upon the bad, the same thing takes place—we partake of it, become saturated with it and grow more and more like it. Then we are attracted toward it and crave it.

> Vice is a monster of so frightful mien,
> As to be hated, needs but to be seen;
> Yet seen too oft, familiar with her face,
> We first endure, then pity, then embrace.
>
> —POPE

This is a warning against the fatal creeping-up of habits which fix themselves in our inmost being. It is like the habit-forming drugs. The hidden object of all this is to blind the mind and bind the soul, reducing them to the animal plane. The net result is that man is thereby reduced to the animal level.

If sex were used for its legitimate purpose, it need not become an instrument of degradation. But when we fall into the trap of self-indulgence, we begin to descend toward the animal plane. Nature has given us something which is necessary for the perpetuation of life upon this planet. It is within our control or should be. But if we reduce it to an instrument of self-indulgence, we simply waste our energy and cloud our minds, ending at last in blank stupidity, like any ordinary animal. When sex controls the individual instead of him controlling it, the degeneration of that individual is already an accomplished fact. He is then simply a biped. How can he call himself *homo sapiens?*

There are many minor phases of this passion. A few are:

(a) the craving for alcoholic drinks,
(b) the drug habit,
(c) the tobacco habit,
(d) gluttony,
(e) the abnormal talk habit, especially telling dirty stories,
(f) sex books and obscene cinemas, morbid sex fantasies, dwelling upon sex pictures,

(g) useless games, cards and billiards, which have no value except to defeat an opponent, a morbid sort of self-gratification, feeding one's vanity; the habit of laziness, or killing time by just lying around in idleness.

All of these are phases of kam, whose central core is self-indulgence, which is the principle of evil in all these things. That in any form is an evil. Every single act of self-indulgence lowers one's moral status and binds him to the world of sense. This is the worst poison for the spirit. These phases of kam pull one down toward the animal plane when one should be rising toward the spiritual plane. Sensuality is an unmitigated evil, no matter what form it may take. It is all kam, and kam is one of the five deadly enemies of the soul.

(2) *Krodh,* 'anger', is the second of the deadly five. Its action is to stir up strife, cause confusion and scatter the mind. Then it cannot concentrate. It is a fact of experience that no person can possibly concentrate his mind at the center of concentration as given by the Master so long as he indulges in fits of anger. It is an utter impossibility. The two cannot go together. Anger destroys peace, neutralizes love, engenders hatred and turns individuals and groups into enemies. And all for what purpose—to satisfy a fiendish impulse toward destruction.

Anger is the extreme opposite of love. As love is the sum of all good, so anger must be the sum of all evil. It is certainly the most destructive of the vile passions. It tears down, destroys, weakens, and annihilates every finer quality of mind and soul. It burns up all that is noble. It is a consuming fire, born of the fires of destruction. At the end, it leaves the victim nothing but a wreck of his better self, burned-out, blackened and dead, like forest trees over which a great fire has swept.

Such is anger, the destroying, consuming passion. Of course, its ultimate object is to destroy the individual who indulges it. Its destructive action is aimed at others, but its most destructive action falls upon the one who indulges it. It creates for him bad karma and binds him more securely to the fatal wheel. If it leads to crime, as it often does, then the shackles of slavery are made that much stronger, the burden that much heavier.

Krodh is a very useful servant of the Negative Power. So long as it dominates the mind, it is impossible for that individual to make any headway on the spiritual Path. Its end is darkness, and death and rebirth under the wheel.

Some of the minor phases of krodh are: slander, evil gossip, backbiting, profanity, fault-finding, peevishness, irritability, quarrelsomeness, surliness, grouchiness, jealousy, malice, impatience, resentment, combat, malicious mockery, destructive criticism, argument for the sake of defeating the other party, haughtiness with ill will, etc. All of these and more are the bastard brood of their mother krodh, a filthy litter of snarling pups.

The law of the Masters, being the law of Nature, is absolute. It cannot be evaded. It must be obeyed or one must reap pain and anguish. That law is:

> Never criticize, never find fault, never abuse;
> Never even blame anyone, either to his face
>   or behind his back;
> Never hurt the feelings of anyone, man or animal;
> Never let a harsh or unkind word escape your lips,
> But speak always words of love, truth and kindness.

A rule laid down by the noble Buddha is a most excellent one for all men to follow. He said that if you propose to speak, always ask yourself: *Is it true, is it necessary, is it kind?*

This is one of the most inflexible of all laws for such as seek spiritual advancement. Let no one imagine that he can ignore this law and still make headway on the Path. It cannot be done. The Path of love leads to enlightenment and liberty and the highest heavens; but the way of anger and an evil tongue leads to the darkest hell.

We believe that anger may aptly be compared to cancer. It is, in fact, *mental carcinoma*. In its effects it is more deadly to the mind than cancer is to the body. It is an ailment which afflicts one the whole of a lifetime. Then when physical death comes, the mind has become so poisoned that there is no moral value left in it. Strangely enough, this terrible affliction has received but slight attention in the literature of mental therapeutics. It has had but little consideration even in ethics. Yet it is one of the deadliest of human ills, and leads to some of the most horrible disasters. We believe it brings more pain and grief into the world than any other disease or perhaps all other diseases.

It must not be forgotten that this mental disease is also a factor in producing many of the common physical ills. Its flood of suffering is worse than any imagination can picture. It is simply appalling. This mental cancer eats its way into and through the inmost mental fiber. The great pity is that it doesn't kill outright. It would be better for mankind if its deadly action were instantaneous, like the fumes of a lethal gas. There is a record of one woman, who immediately after a fit of anger nursed her infant, and the child died from the poison in less than an hour. The pity is that the woman herself was immune and the poor infant had to be the victim.

This disease of anger, leaving everywhere a trail of suffering, of nausea and of terrible heartaches, generally drags on for years. This disease manifests itself by the following set of symptoms:

(a) thinking ill of others,
(b) taking offense easily,
(c) criticizing the actions of others,
(d) lecturing or discoursing on the mistakes of others either to the person himself or to others about him,
(e) chronic fault-finding or pointing out the defects of character or conduct of others, making them out to be really bad,
(f) scolding, nagging or haranguing others,
(g) habitually blaming others for all that goes wrong,
(h) vile abuse and cursing others,
(i) actual fighting, quarrelling or trying to inflict injury upon others.

And the student should always remember that mental injury or wound is often more painful than physical wound, and sometimes slower to heal. These nine symptoms are some of the most common manifestations of this deadly disease. It is generally designated "the evil tongue." Compared with this evil tongue, the plague is a mild affliction. Of all bad habits, of all defects of character, there is nothing that smells of corruption and death so badly. Unlike most physical disorders, which make their victims suffer the brunt of the disease, this affliction reacts upon others even more painfully than upon the patient himself. It is like a poison gas, spreading deadly fumes in the whole neighborhood.

One unique feature of this foul disease is the fact that its victims are generally unwilling to concede that they suffer from the disease but generally insist that it is others who have the disease and they themselves are the innocent victims of the malevolence of others. This is an almost universal manifestation of the disease. To even suggest that the patient is suffering from the disease is usually sufficient to throw him into a violent spasm. You never can tell when this foul abscess is going to explode in your face. It erupts at the smallest provocation, and its malodorous fumes fill the whole neighborhood. It is not infrequent that those who suffer from advanced stages of this disease become sick of life and commit suicide, even if they do not kill someone else. Many times the victim commits suicide, rather than endure the tortures of living near such a person.

One of the most pathetic features of this terrible disease is that death does not end it. In that respect it is so much worse than any mere physical ailment. It is in the mind, and the sufferer takes his mind with him at death, so that even in the next world the disease continues its ravages. It will continue to afflict him, until through suffering and self-control, he learns to remove the ailment himself. This is one disease that no doctor can cure. It must be cured by the patient himself. Suicide only aggravates the trouble. But let us close this discussion. It is unfitting that our minds should dwell longer upon it. This much has been said only to place the terrible thing open to the gaze of all men, in order that they may understand its nature and so learn to avoid it. Every person should shun it as he would the most deadly, the most savage, jungle beast.

(3) *Lobh*, 'greed', is the third member of this unholy group. It

is one of the most poisonous of them all. The function of greed is to bind us to material things, and so cloud our minds to all higher values. It ties us to the baser things of earth. As kam binds us to the animal plane, so lobh binds us to the mineral plane, one step lower. Hence greed is even baser lust. It makes for us a god of gold and silver and jewels. It identifies us with them by fixing our attention and affections upon them. The end is slavery to them. Wealth then becomes master, instead of servant. Like all the other passions, it slowly forges its chains about one.

Man automatically drops down to the plane of the thing he loves. A miser soon becomes but little more than an incarnated heap of gold and silver, of bonds and securities, of lands and houses. He who thinks of nothing else but money and making money gradually becomes hard of heart, and even his face takes on an expression of relentless driving force. He is pitiless. Nothing counts with him but money. He drives other men, even women and children, in his factories, grinding wealth out of them. He goes on grinding more gold out of them. Pity, love and kindness, have long ago departed from his mental processes. He can see nothing but profits. What matters it if human flesh is fed to his mills? The blood of those men and women is to be turned into streams of revenue.

Happily, we believe this picture does not apply to a very large percentage of men engaged in commerce. But it does apply to some. As kam degrades and krodh consumes, so lobh hardens. This passion is probably the most relentless slave driver of them all. A mind under the sway of lobh is but little less than petrified intelligence. Lobh has many minor phases, such as:

(a) miserliness,
(b) falsehood,
(c) hypocrisy,
(d) perjury,
(e) misrepresentation,
(f) robbery,
(g) bribery,
(h) trickery of all sorts.

These are all the usual ways and means of picking up easy money. The poorest man in the world is he who spends his time trying to get something for nothing. It can never be done. His time is wholly wasted. No man has ever gained permanent benefit without paying the price. John D. Rockefeller said just before his death: "The poorest man in the world is he who has nothing but money!"

If the time ever comes when men give thought only for what they actually need, this passion will die of attrition. Civilization will take a tremendous stride forward. If men will think more of *giving,* and less of *receiving,* the human race will stand close to mastership. The Master is the supreme giver.

(4) *Moh,* 'attachment', which means delusive attachment, infatuation, is the fourth of the destructive passions. This is perhaps the most insidious, the most deceitful of them all. It creeps up slowly upon its victims, like the others, or it comes with flares of trumpets like the *tamasha* that goes before the approach of a nobleman. It generally comes with the appearance of well-dressed respectability. It has a noble bearing. It comes as a gentleman, with good credentials. It announces itself as your friend and ally. Its ideas are plausible. So it readily gains a place in the family as a close friend.

It does seem so very reasonable and proper that one should have and enjoy wife, children, positions of honor and of public service, money, houses, lands and securities. Indeed, we may concede that such things are necessary and proper. The individual knows that, and then our gentle friend, moh, steps in with such benevolent airs and says: "Yes, surely you must give diligent attention to these things; it is your duty."

Right there and then moh begins its deadly work under the guise of a most respectable friend. Its method is to blind you to the relative values of your surroundings and associations so that you may begin to set a false valuation upon them. After you have become quite absorbed in them, *then you will have no time for anything else.* That is exactly its purpose. There is the crucial point of the whole matter. No time for self-improvement. No time for spiritual devotions. No time for altruistic service. You are kept forever 'on the go' most of the time between your home and office, busy with your family and affairs. You hardly have time for eating and sleeping, not to speak of self-culture or loving service.

Remember that the liberation of your own soul is the one thing for which you are in this world. Nothing else counts. But it is the sole purpose of this moh to keep you from doing that one thing—if it can keep you from even thinking about the matter, it is well pleased. If, however, you do think about it, it at once steps up and tells you that just now you have no time for that sort of thing. By and by when circumstances are more favorable, you may attend to it.

It is for the very purpose of keeping men blinded to their own higher interests that the Negative Power has employed all of these five passions to dog our paths all the days of our lives. For this reason moh will tell you that you must not neglect your routine duties. They simply have to be attended to. At the same time, to pacify you, it promises that the time will soon come when your burden of duties will grow less, when circumstances will grow more favorable. Then you may attend to your spiritual interests.

Moh is the king of procrastination. You must wait for a more convenient season. But at the same time, it keeps you busy with trifles. Why worry about spiritual matters now? They will take care of themselves when the time comes. No need to worry about them until you are dead. Then they will automatically solve themselves! All the while this smart friend is slyly adding to your burdens and complicating your life. It sees to it that the promised leisure never comes.

Worries, anxieties, and business complications follow every man to his grave. He seldom ever gets away from them. Almost the whole of your life is spent in trying to perpetuate the physical existence, the animal self. The real object for which you came into the world has been forgotten. Perhaps you never even knew why you came. Indeed, but very few people know why they are here. Most of them seem not at all interested to know anything about it.

You are a slave even to your cows, dogs, horses, and cars— ninety-eight percent of your precious time spent in penal servitude to the animal body. And for what purpose? Just to keep it going. And why keep it going? In order that you may continue being a slave to it. When they come back from the cemetery where they have left you in a pretty velvet-covered casket over which they have shoveled the dirt, they settle down to divide up what you have left, and forthwith forget you in that same mad scramble which monopolized all of your attention, until the final darkness overtook you.

And this is exactly what your smooth friend, moh, does for you. It skillfully holds your nose to the grindstone until the very moment when the doctor says it is all over and pulls up the sheet over your face. You have been so very busy all your life, and yet you have not had a moment's time to do the one thing that was really worth doing. You have, in fact, been very busy all your life doing nothing. You have worked like the battle of Gettysburg, but what has it brought you? Only increasing worry, pain, and then the final darkness. You return to the wheel that grinds away through all the yugas. Naked and empty-handed you came here; empty-handed and naked you depart. Results? Nothing, simply treading the wheel. You return to the eternal cycle perhaps even more securely bound than before. Moh has scored heavily for his master.

The only thing worth doing in this life, but few people ever do that, is to find the Path of spiritual freedom and walk on it.

(5) *Ahankar*, 'vanity', is the last of the deadly five. The word *ahankar* has two meanings. First, it is the faculty of the mind which gives us the power of awareness of the self, self-differentiation, the I-ness. It is that faculty which executes the mandates of the buddhi in the interests of self. But the abnormal exaggeration of this faculty becomes ahankar, which is vanity or egotism. It is the enlargement of the ego which becomes a cancer by cell-proliferation.

You know a cancer is a condition in which normal body epithelial cells become much enlarged. So it is here. The normal ego is all right, but when it begins to swell up out of all proportion, then it takes on the nature of a disease. So vanity is an overgrown ego. Ahankar is a malignant enlargement of the 'I'. That faculty, which is quite necessary for the preservation of the individual in this life and for the proper placement of that person in relation to all others, becomes so overgrown that the normal self becomes for him the center of the universe. This is malignant selfishness. This passion is the worst of all in some respects, although it is difficult to say just which is the worst one. Once the Master was asked which of the five was the worst, and he laughingly replied, "Each of them is worse."

Ahankar has a thousand claws by which to dig into the minds of its victims. Its deadly poison infiltrates the entire being. Beginning generally in infancy, it seldom ceases to operate until death. It feeds upon its own refuse, and it waxes strong upon materials furnished by the other four. In fact, it often feeds upon the decaying carcasses of the others. How often vanity is nourished by the death of the others! How vain men become over a partial subjugation of the other passions. Not infrequently do men become vain over their own humility. One of the commonest manifestations of vanity is a pretended humility. This may be conscious or quite unconscious.

Ahankar is the most sturdy and masterful of the lot and it has the greatest longevity. How often we hear old men and women talking garrulously, recounting their former exploits. Nothing can check them. Vanity holds the field and continues to operate long after all the rest are dead. As a matter of fact, it often kills the rest in order to have something to boast about. How many times men are swelled up over some trifling victory or virtue, and women grow vain over their own virtues! Ascetics, posing as the humblest of men, grow vain over their apparent saintliness. Self-righteousness is one of the most prevalent and most malignant of these mental diseases.

It is well known to those who are on the Path that egotism is the last of the hateful five to surrender. Its method is to distort the viewpoint, to present everything out of proportion, making itself the center of the world. It destroys all sense of humor. You never see a vain person with any sense of real humor. If he had, he couldn't be vain. Vanity will set a crown upon its own head and wonder why all men do not rush to acknowledge it king. It will bray like an ass and imagine itself singing in a grand opera. It cannot see itself because it sees nothing but self. It will strut like a peacock with only cabbage leaves for tailfeathers. But it can never see its own imperfections. It sees all of its own short-comings reflected in others, while it imagines itself perfect.

The chief function of ahankar is to block the path of Truth. It is the bosom friend of error. It completely deceives its own vic-tims, making them self-satisfied, when they ought to be seeking their own improvement. It will prevent people from seeking new things. It is the main friend and supporter of ancient superstitions. It establishes creeds, appoints a priesthood and builds up orga-nizations to propagate its own dogmas. It then assumes that out of its own superior wisdom it has selected the only perfect system of truth. It will not then acknowledge that it could be mistaken and goes on hugging its assumptions. It defies the whole world, demanding unqualified support for its declared dictums. And worst of all, it often seeks the instant destruction of all who op-pose it. Its one big assumption is: *I am right; he who opposes me is wrong; to sustain the right, I must destroy my opponent.*

This assumption has soaked the pages of history with inno-cent blood. Today it is busy fermenting strife among nations. Blind egotism and its bastard son, selfishness, are today sowing the seeds of international dissatisfaction and germinating wars. God knows what the harvest shall be.

Ahankar bitterly resents all effort to enlighten it. How can it admit that it is wrong, or that it needs enlightenment? It will go to war at the drop of a hat to defend its own self-asserted rights. It never thinks of the other man's rights. It takes offence easily, like krodh. It is extremely touchy—sensitive, they call it. It sees no weaknesses in itself, but it never ceases to point out the faults of others. It is the boon companion to krodh. Thus, blowing its own horn, it struts across the stage of life. And it blows so loudly that it cannot hear anyone else. The minor phases of ahankar are:

   (a) bigotry;
   (b) self-assertion; in season and out of season, it thrusts itself
     forward;

(c) it makes obtrusive show of wealth or power, it is gaudy in dress, exhibits a domineering attitude, is bossy, scolding and fault-finding. In this phase it joins hands with krodh. Its fundamental assumption is its own infallibility. The man under the influence of ahankar imagines he is advertising his own virtues by pointing out the faults of others; while as a matter of universal experience, he is only advertising his own shortcomings. So it is with all fault-finding. He assumes superior airs, demands his own wishes which he calls rights, and tries to punish others if he is opposed. He tries to attract the attention of others by noise or other show of self, loud and constant talking, or tries to impose his own opinions upon others. He loves office and power over others;

(d) he frequently interrupts others when they are talking;

(e) he likes to make public speeches, is eager to see his own name in print, makes a show of his own piety, loves to make long prayers in public, and he makes it a point to let the world know about it if he gives a penny to charity;

(f) he dearly loves titles, honors, college degrees, and enjoys seeing the mob bow down to him;

(g) in many other ways he exhibits the constantly recurring 'I', ad nauseam.

8. Antidotes to the Deadly Five

To sum up the discussion of the five mental diseases, let us place them and their antidotes side by side. The Masters classify all mankind into two main divisions—*Manmukhs* and *Gurumukhs*. This means those who follow the dictates of their own minds and those who follow the Guru. The Manmukh is the one who follows the mind, obeys its every whim, and does just what it likes. He is a slave to the mind and its passions. But the man whose face is always toward the Guru is the free man and the one who is developing his own powers to the greatest extent possible. He is not under the ever-grinding wheel of birth and death, the grinding wheel of desire and karma.

But this sublime achievement is accomplished only by the help of the Master (the Guru) and the Shabd—the regenerating Dhun, *the Audible Life Stream*. No one can ever do it alone. There is positively no other cure for the passions—none but the voice of God ringing through the soul. When that holy symphony is heard, these miserable five lose their power and drop away. Positively, the only sure cure for these five deadly diseases is the Life Stream, opened up to the disciple by his Master. Some help may be had from contemplating the opposite virtues. But one must never depend on such contemplation for the final reconstruction of character. The soul must become absorbed in that luminous Reality, and it must forget all else. That Reality gives strength and will until the man becomes something more than man. He becomes a living power, reborn and exalted. Then these five evils slink away like beaten dogs. This is real liberty.

Just as the five passions may be regarded as the five black agents of desolation, so the five virtues may be looked upon as five angels. They hover over us always, ready to extend their aid, if we look to them for help or comfort. They will greatly assist in the upward struggle. Weave them into the fiber of your character. They will help much. As those five evil passions include in themselves all other evils, so these five virtues include in themselves all other virtues. They should be contemplated long and deeply. Here they are set opposite to one another, the virtues and the vices:

Passions and Their Remedies

VICES	VIRTUES	
KAM	*Shil*	—— Chastity, continence
KRODH	*Kshama*	—— Forgiveness, tolerance
LOBH	*Santosha*	—— Contentment
MOH	*Viveka*	—— Discrimination
	Vairagya	—— Detachment
AHANKAR	*Dinta*	—— Humility

Chapter Seven

KARMA AND REINCARNATION

---

1. What Is Karma?

THE two doctrines of karma and reincarnation are important considerations in the science of the Masters. They are accepted as facts of Nature not only by the Masters but by practically all schools of Oriental thought. More than half of the human race today accepts karma and reincarnation as established facts of Nature. Since reincarnation depends on karma, let us discuss that first. Karma (from *kr,* in Sanskrit) means that law of Nature which requires that *every doer shall receive the exact result, or reward, of his actions.* In its last analysis, it is nothing more nor less than the well-known law of cause and effect. It is known in physics as the law of compensation or balance or equilibrium. In jurisprudence it is the law of justice. All the courts of the civilized world give official recognition to the law of karma every time they mete out rewards and punishments. In ethics, as in civil and criminal law, it is the basis of rewards and punishments, the decisive principle of right and wrong conduct.

Right actions are those which create good karma. Bad actions create bad karma. This is the simplest possible solution of the many questions of right and wrong. In the ethics of Jesus, karma is reduced to the simple question of receiving what one has earned, reaping what one has sown. In the law of Moses, it was reduced to the rule of an eye for an eye and a tooth for a tooth. This is an exact, even if crude, conception of the law of balance. In employment of labor, it is the principle of fair wages. In barter and exchange, it is the basis of 'the square deal'. In spiritual science it is called karma, but it is the same law.

The underlying principle is that every act performed by anybody must be followed by its natural and legitimate results. This is a law so universal that it is amazing why all men have not grasped its general significance and applied it in ethics, the same as in mechanics. It is recognized in physical science. Without it there could be no science. It is recognized also in social life. All the world over, everybody recognizes that he must pay for what he gets. It is only the fool who tries to get something for nothing. Even the man who imagines that he has succeeded has only run in his own debt, as Emerson says.

It is only the Western people who have not yet awakened to the application of this law to ethics, psychology and spirituality. The Eastern Wisdom, however, recognizes the universality of the law and instead of calling it 'the law of compensation', they call it karma. Anyway, why should the Western world be frightened at the word *karma?* If the student will pick up any book on physics, he will discover the working of this same law in every problem confronting him. For example, a car is moving along the road at a speed which bears a definite ratio to its weight and the amount of power applied. If you wish to increase the speed, you must either reduce the weight or increase the power. In every case, the law of compensation is the chief factor to be dealt with; one must pay for what he gets. From that fixed law of the universe, there can be no deviation, no exception.

Go back to Emerson again. Read his essay on 'the law of compensation'. He shows how the same law operates in every field of human thought and endeavor, the moral and the spiritual as well as the physical. Emerson was not ignorant of the Eastern Wisdom. The Light of his genius came out of the East. And this is the law of karma according to the Masters. It is upon the universality of the action of this law that the Masters construct their ethics, just as definitely as the engineer is guided by that law in building his bridge. Directly applied, the law of karma demands that every living being, every creature, from primordial protoplasm to human brain, from amoeba to archangel, from mind and soul to the Creator of the Three Worlds—every one must receive the exact balance of accounts, the precise compensation for each and every act. And so, this is karma.

Let it be kept in mind that no act whatsoever, no matter how apparently trivial or unimportant, can be performed without its correlated karma. Let fall a billiard ball upon the earth, and the entire globe is affected by it. The world is never again exactly the same as it was before the falling of that ball. It is karma. Let a single word escape from one's mouth, and not only is the hearer affected by it, but by the law of action and reaction a portion of the effects will return upon the speaker. Then as these two are affected, all mankind will be affected to some extent, no matter how slight these effects may be. The law is there. The whole of humanity is never again quite the same as it was before that word was spoken. This ought to make us all stop and think before we speak idle or ill words. Remember the whole of mankind are linked in one mental, spiritual and karmic bond. What affects one, whether for good or bad, affects all, to some extent. Hence our karmic responsibility. The law of karma is the underlying principle of personal responsibility.

It is a well-known law of physics that action and reaction are equal, but opposite in directions. This is the law that brings back upon the doer, in spite of himself, the legitimate results of his conduct. He must gather the fruit of his own actions. That reaction he cannot possibly escape. Hence, every action performed has its double karma based upon this law of action and reaction—it affects the recipient and it returns upon the doer. The doer is always a recipient of the same act. So action and reaction are the dual forms of karma. This extends to the smallest motion of a leaf quivering in the breeze to the sway of a planet in its orbit. It binds the lizard that devours its insect and it binds the philosopher giving his lecture. Karma is a universal law, embracing every unit of the living, throughout the numberless worlds of the universe.

No need to go into lengthy details. The central fact is not difficult of apprehension. It is sufficient to remember that every act of every individual must register its correlated effects. And this applies to every individual in existence, from amoeba to man, from cavern rock to milky way. This law holds sway just as relentlessly and definitely in the vegetable and animal kingdoms as in the human. Nothing that exists is exempt from this law. We may mention, however, that the law of karma extends only up to the region where mind and matter cease. In the empire of mind and matter, karma is universal; but there is a higher universe of worlds where pure spirit governs all, and there is no karma there. How is that? Because in that world there is a higher law which supersedes all other laws—that is the law of love.

2. Karma Binds the World Together

The universality of the law of karma is one of the chief factors which binds all of life together, not only human life but also the animal with the human. Animals and humans compose one big family with a complicated but inseparable history and an inseparable karma. Hidden away in this great law is the main reason why men should not kill and eat animals—also why men should not mistreat animals.

The great fact of importance to us all is that according to this law we are all constantly creating karma, incurring debts, and all of these debts must be paid off. That is the whole problem in a few words. It is a pity that all mankind cannot grasp the full significance of this law. If they could, the whole social structure would be remodeled. Every debt must be paid. To put it otherwise, no man can possibly get something for nothing. He may go in debt; but if he does, that debt must be paid by him sooner or later. The exact day and hour of payment is not always noted by us. It may not be known when we are to pay; but the one fact of importance, which stands absolutely unalterable, is that *everyone must pay*. That is the essence of the matter.

Not only does Nature frequently allow much time for the payment, but it may be extended over long periods, in installments. After all, Nature is generous. She very graciously allows the sinner plenty of time for repentance and compensation. If men were wise, they would never run into her debt. And if they did run into her debt, they would seize the first possible moment to pay off the debt. In any case, men should always bear in mind that they cannot possibly 'beat the game'. It can never be done. Sooner or later full payment must be made, often with heavy compound interest. This very fact of Nature's generosity with time for payments sometimes leads to terrible misunderstandings. The wrongdoer himself is often led to believe that he has actually beaten the game. He imagines that he has contravened the law. But he only deceives himself.

The observer too often complains that there is no justice in the world. He notices the sinner going apparently unpunished, while the righteous are unrewarded. Justice apparently miscarries daily right before our eyes, and there seems to be no hand to right the wrongs. It is just there that the scheme of karma and reincarnation comes to the rescue and offers a rational explanation.

It may happen, and it certainly does frequently occur, that a man's life accounts are not balanced at the time of his death. Is the law then of no avail in his life? Has he really defeated the law and mocked the administrator of the law? By no means. That law itself is inviolable. It can never be set aside. No one can defeat it. But, as said before, Nature is generous and gives us plenty of time for payment. The death of any individual is not the end of his career. It is only the end of one chapter in his long history. But so long as he owes one farthing to the law, he must return to make payment. Also, if there is any karmic relation between two individuals, that relationship can never be terminated until all accounts are settled between them. And this brings us to the associated law of reincarnation.

In *Yoga and Western Psychology* by Geraldine Coster, we read:

> It is our custom to regard this philosophy of karma as one of indolent, easy-going fatalism, and to attribute to it many of the evils of Eastern social life. But it is in reality the complete negation of fatalism, in that it deletes chance, "destiny," in the colloquial acceptation of the word, and the idea of an "overruling Providence," all three fairly common conceptions in the West. It represents man as

the sole and absolute master of his own fate forever. What he has sown in the times of his ignorance, he must inevitably reap; but when he attains enlightenment, it is for him to sow what he chooses and reap accordingly.

This is a point that deserves the special attention of the student. This great doctrine, instead of leading to a dull fatalism, is in fact the only teaching in the world that shows exactly how man is the architect of his own fortune, the creator of his own fate. In this system there is not room for the arbitrary decrees of a capricious deity.

In the law of karma there is the perfect solution of our social and economic difficulties. How? Note well the underlying principle. The whole world, the Western world in particular, is profit-mad. All their energies are devoted to heaping up profits. But the worst feature of this is that they do not care how they get profits or whether they have to give value received. Now suppose this law of karma became deeply rooted in the public consciousness, what would result? Suppose every man knew in his inmost consciousness that *he simply must pay for all he gets,* what would happen? No man would even attempt the irrational and impossible task of trying to accumulate a fortune for which he has given no equivalent. What then would become the *modus operandi* in all business transactions? *Every man would seek first to render a service for what he expects to get.* He would know that he has to pay. His first consideration would then be—*how can I make adequate payment?* Now he thinks first of all—how much can I take from others? How much can I make this business yield? He does not consider whether he is to earn money but only how he can get hold of it.

It may be said now with the utmost assurance of truth, that just so long as this system prevails, the whole world will present a gigantic scramble of robbers, each trying his best to take from all the rest, but the robber does not stop to think of the day of payment. Neither does the average businessman. But if he were familiar with this great law of karma, of the basic law of justice which is automatic in its administration, he would not engage in this moral scramble, but would first of all qualify himself or establish some enterprise whose sole object was to render a service. Then in return he would expect only a just compensation for that service.

This is the fundamental law of a rational economics, of a world interchange of commodities, and of a social equilibrium that will stand all tests. Modern business methods are nothing more nor less than a belated survival of the days of lawless plunder, pillage and the destruction of the weak. And most of this due to a lack of understanding of the law of karma—that is, they do not realize that they simply must pay for what they get. They go on blindly trying to take from others what they want, regardless of moral principle.

3. What Is Reincarnation?

When death overtakes a man, he is simply transferred or transported to another field of action. That is the sum of it. *And his accounts go with him.* That is a point generally not known, or at least it is ignored. To most men death is like a plunge into total darkness. They have no idea where they are going or what is to happen to them. But the Masters know exactly what is to happen to each one after death. And among other things, they know that everybody takes his accounts with him. Settlement has to be made sometime. And so, if their accounts are not settled before death, they simply must return to this world for the settlement. No soul can ever detach itself from its accounts until they are settled. Stored up in each Karan Sharir, the causal body, is the seed of all his karma, an infallible record, in which the recorder never makes a mistake. He can neither leave this record behind him nor can he conceal it. Wherever he goes his record goes with him, just as truly as a dog's tail always follows him! It is a part of him. Wherever he goes he must face this record and pay it. This is a fixed law of Nature, as unfailing as the revolutions of a star in its orbit.

When a soul arrives in the subtle region, he must there appear before a judge whose justice never wavers, who cannot be bribed, and before whom the records cannot be falsified. There he must answer to every item and there he must pay in full. If he finds himself bankrupt in that court, if debts hang heavily upon him, he is assigned to another life under conditions which permit him to make payment. This, however, is the divine justice which is flavored with mercy. If his past has been very dark, he may be obliged to undergo a remedial punishment to impress upon his inmost consciousness that 'crime does not pay'. Then he has another chance. In the subsequent life or lives, even if he does not remember his punishment, its effects remain deeply embedded in his subconscious mind, and so in that subsequent life, instead of liking the thing which brought him so much grief, he will have an innate aversion toward it. He will avoid it. This accounts for many of those deep-seated aversions, likes and dislikes, with which people are born.

If a person's life has been full of good deeds, kindness and love, he is assigned to a heaven or a paradise or some sort of delightful environment—by whatever name one wishes to know it—where he enjoys the full reward of all he has earned. In every case, his karma is met and fully satisfied. He gets exactly what he has earned and nothing else. Remember that karma includes the good as well as the bad. If one earns the good, he must get the good. Nothing can possibly defeat that law. When one's karma has been worked out on any of the subtle planes, and the time is ripe, he returns to earth in a new birth, that new birth and its entire setting being also determined by his good or bad karma. So again he gets exactly what he has earned, but now he has another chance to improve his karma.

There is an old saying that though the mills of the gods grind slowly, yet they grind exceedingly fine. That is only another way of saying that one can never escape his own karma. It suggests that although Nature may be generous as to time, in the end full payment must be made.

Why is another life on earth necessary? Why cannot all accounts be settled on the subtle planes to which one goes after death? The answer is that everyone must return to earthly life in order that he may reap what he has sown, and make all payments under identical conditions of life which ensure perfect justice;

also, to permit the individual to improve his karma to the point where he may eventually escape from the karmic wheel of birth and death. This escape can never be accomplished until his accumulated good karma outweighs his bad and brings him to a living Master. For this is the supreme reward of good karma— meeting the Sat Guru who will eventually take him out of the arena of struggle, out of the reign of karmic law. This latter achievement is always the remote object held in view by the Supreme Father. That is, in fact, "the one far off divine event toward which the whole creation moves"—final liberation of the soul from the wheel of birth and death and a triumphal entry into the Home of the soul beyond the reach of karma.

Now the great Masters, who view this drama of human life from the higher planes, know that the individual *must* return to this life, and that he *does* return again and again in order that he may answer the demands of this universal law. And this constitutes the round of births and deaths which we call reincarnation or 'the wheel of birth and death'. When the hour of destiny strikes, everyone must leave this theater of action. In the same manner and by the same law, every soul who resides temporarily in any of those upper regions must close his eyes upon that scene and come down again to a new birth called for by his karma. The time, the location and the parents for his new life are all arranged by the same law—the law of his own karma. He is then to get what he has earned here, in addition to what he has experienced over there. He is not getting a double karma, as was suggested by one student. Part of his karma is paid over there, and the unpaid portion he is to get here in his new life. He is born into a new body and slowly awakens to the consciousness of a new life on earth. He lives this new life and accumulates a new set of karmas besides paying off the old scores.

There is one other very interesting point to be remembered here. In the new life of a reborn child, the parents are meeting their own karma, just as the child is. So perfect is that system of karmic law, that all individuals concerned meet at exactly the right time and in exactly the right relationship so as to meet and pay off their karmic debts. Suppose that a married couple are under a karmic debt to someone with whom they were connected in some way in a previous life. Now they pay off that debt by their services as parents and the years of care and labor they must give. So the parents are working under the law of karma, as truly as is the child, in returning to this life. Both are meeting its stern demands, which no man can ever escape.

This constitutes the eternal awagawan, so often spoken of by the Oriental students. *Awagawan* means 'coming and going'. So long as the individual lives and operates under the law of karma, he cannot escape this coming and going. This is called by the Masters the *chaurasi ka chakra*. It means 'the wheel of eighty-four'. And this is a marvelous phenomenon. The idea is that the individual, accompanied by the mind and its load of karma, moves on through almost endless ages from birth to birth, passing through the eighty-four lakhs[1] of different kinds of living beings. It means that in this world there are approximately eighty-four lakh species of living beings, made up as under:

> Three million species of *plant* life;
> Two million, seven hundred thousand of *insect* species;
> One million, four hundred thousand kinds of *birds;*
> Nine hundred thousand kinds of *water animals,* and
> Four hundred thousand kinds of *land animals,* men and other beings just above men, but closely related to them, such as devas, etc. These are generally known as angels and demons by Western people. They are sometimes seen by us when conditions are favorable.

This makes 8,400,000, each with its uncounted millions of individuals. A wandering soul, making its way from birth to birth, may be required to pass a long and tiresome course through all of them, provided his karma calls for that. He may pass through only some of them, then return to the human status, but in all cases just as his earnings may allow. The round of all of these forms of life, as said before, constitutes 'the wheel of eighty-four'. It depends

---

1. A lakh is equivalent to one hundred thousand, eighty-four lakh amounting to eight million and four hundred thousand.

upon the individual entirely as to how many of these he may have to pass through. The Masters tell us that there is no escape from this wheel until one meets his Guru and learns to contact the Audible Life Stream. This is more fully explained in Chapter Eleven, Section 3.

Let us now return to the subject of karma. The two subjects, karma and reincarnation, are so interrelated that they cannot be separated. In discussing either one, we must refer to the other.

There are three kinds of karma recognized by the Masters.

(1) The first is called *pralabdh* or *prarabdh* karma, which means 'fate karma'. It is that which has been earned in one or more previous lives, and upon which this present life is based. This sort of karma the individual must pay off during this life. He must live it out to the full extent. There is no escape from it, as a rule, not even if one has a Master. The Master can destroy it but generally does not. That is because this type of karma must be met and paid by the individual. It is compared to an arrow shot from the bow—when once shot into the air, it must go where the force of the bow has determined that it shall go. There is no changing that after it is once shot forth.

(2) The second kind is called *sinchit* karma. This means 're-serve karma'. It may be compared to money deposited in a bank, in a savings account. But in this case it is drawn upon not at the will of the individual but at the will of the Lord of karma. He may draw upon that and assign it to be lived out at such times and places as he may determine. The individual has nothing to say about it.

(3) The third kind of karma is *kriyaman,* the 'daily karma', which we are making from day to day during this life. Now, this sort of karma may be disposed of in any one of three different ways: We may suffer or reap its payment at once or at some other time during this life. Secondly, we may have it stored up as sinchit karma to be drawn upon at some future time according to the will of the Lord of karma. In that case, it may become fate karma for a future life.

It may be said here in passing that when a Sat Guru takes over anyone as his disciple, that fact materially alters his karmic status. His whole destiny undergoes a complete change. That all depends upon the will of the Master, for then the Master is his karmic Lord. The Sat Guru is superior to all other lords of destiny. He may do whatever he pleases with the karma of his disciple; but as a rule he does not interfere with the prarabdh karma of anyone. That is generally considered fixed and final. It must be endured or gathered as what one has sown. With all of the rest, the Master may do as he likes according to whatever he thinks is best for the disciple. He may require the disciple to live out all his sinchit karma which has been stored up against him, as well as that which he is creating from day to day. In this case one may be disposing of all three sorts of karma at the same time.

If a disciple finds himself obliged to endure much, he may console himself that the Master is doing all he can to clean the vessel as soon as possible. When life ends, his record will be clean, and he will be free forever. If the Master does this, it is out of great love, knowing that when the disciple is at last free, he will be thankful that the Master put him through it all at once and finished it. But the Master will never allow the burdens to become too heavy. Often he even bears a portion of them himself, out of great love and sympathy. In any case, the Master always does what he knows is best for his disciple, for he is himself the embodiment of lovingkindness.

4. Metempsychosis, a Bitter Pill

Transmigration is apparently a nasty pill for the Western student. For this reason, in order to please our theosophical friends and those whom Theosophy is trying to please, we would be glad to leave this out, even though it is a part of the Eastern Wisdom. But since it is a part of the teachings of all great Masters, it cannot be left out to please anyone. The Creator has not left it out of his scheme; how can we leave it out? The Masters say it is a part of life itself and it must be reckoned within any scheme of philosophy that tells the whole truth. It is not a question of what we like, but a question of the facts of Nature. It is like death itself. None of us appear to like that any too well, but we all know that we must accept it as a part of the routine of life on this planet.

Our egotism ought not mislead us. The concept is not so bad as it may at first appear. We know we are related to the animals in many ways. We know that our conduct is often like that of animals, sometimes pitiably lower than that of animals. Isn't it a disgrace for your beautiful body to have to return to the dirt, to crumble into a filthy mass of decaying carbon, calcium and H_2O? Yet, that is exactly what happens. It is because that is the way of Nature, and none of us can change it. That beautiful child, innocent and joyous, pure as the lily, sweeter than the rose, must return to earth and become food for worms. Is there anything more appalling? Yet that is Nature. Shall we dare accuse Nature of cruelty? Nature is always generous and kind, even though we may not always like her ways.

If the mind leads an animal life, thinks like an animal and acts like an animal, isn't it quite natural that it should return to the animal form whose character it most resembled during life? The disgrace lies not in descending to the animal form, but in so conducting oneself that it becomes necessary to take the animal form. There again is the operation of the eternal law. You must in every instance get just what you have earned. If you have not lived like an animal, it is certain that you will never return to the status of an animal. We know that degeneration is as much a law of Nature as is growth and evolution. And if a man does go down, is that a more deplorable thing than the descent into the grave of a fair and beloved form to decay into a shapeless mass of corruption? They are both Nature's processes. They are not within our control, but by obeying the laws of Nature we can avoid descending to any lower status. That much is certain. *But no man can violate Nature's laws and escape her penalties.*

You know it is a fact that a man's conduct may be much worse than anything of which an animal would be guilty. Where then is the incongruity if that man returns to the lower level, as the fruit of his own actions? At the same time, isn't it an inspiring thought that an animal which you have loved may gain human

birth and rise to nobility? Doesn't that seem to be more in accord
with the love of the Supreme One? You will concede that there is
no objection to the lower orders of life rising to something higher. Your theory of evolution has prepared you for that. But you
worry much over the idea of a man going down. Isn't there an
incessant rise and fall, as concomitants of evolution? Isn't there
ebb and flow, procession and retrogression, advance and retreat?
Degeneration and dissolution is just as much a part of Nature's
processes as is evolution. Of course, it is not fitting that a man
should descend to assume the animal form. But the real misfit lies
in his conduct which obliges him to go down.

    You do not object to the doctrine of evolution. If you could
look back into some prehistoric jungle and there see yourself as
a wild animal, later rising to the human status after satisfying
the law of karma by suffering and enjoying as an animal does,
wouldn't you feel inclined to bow in reverence to the majesty of
that law which is slowly but surely bringing all forms of life to the
higher levels? If we admit the ascent of living forms, we are obliged to admit the descent of forms. That is so even if we think
of the forms of species themselves, the mere physical forms. We
know they are capable of very great improvement. No one objects
to the idea that this human form has evolved from the more
human animal forms of lower species. Why should we object to
the rise or fall of the minds and souls of individuals? They are subject to the same general laws of improvement and degeneration.
Building up and crumbling down are but the two sides of one
process. We see the two processes going on side by side in all
Nature.

    Catch but a glimpse of the sublime spectacle? Eight million
and four hundred thousand of living species, untold billions of
individuals, in each of whom is a spark of the Divine Essence—
their tiny lights glowing in the darkness, but slowly awakening
to a higher consciousness! Can there be anything more inspiring?
Each one is working on, tirelessly awaiting the day of final liberation from the wheel. If you are a lover of animal life, can you
conceive of a more inspiring truth?

    You insist that you do not object if the lower forms rise to the higher because your theory of evolution has prepared your mind for that. But you do not fancy the retrograde movement. Again let me urge that a man does not need to go down, and he will not do so, if his conduct has been worthy of his status as a man. But if being a man so richly endowed, he deliberately chooses to act like an animal, he forfeits his dignity and invites degradation and humiliation. Even then, all is not lost. If he descends to the animal level by force of his animal-like conduct, he may rise to the human level again when he has expiated his sins and purified his mind—in other words, when he has paid his karmic debt.

The mercy of the Supreme is never-ending. He is long-suffering and patient. No matter how long it may take the prodigal son to come to senses and return, always the Light is kept burning in his father's palace, waiting for him. He must come home when the full measure of his karma has been paid. If a man sinks down by unworthy conduct, he may come up again by suffering and good deeds. If my dog or my horse serves me faithfully and with love, that is sure to stand to his credit. Life is full of giving and taking. If the giving is more than the taking, then by just that much the individual rises toward a higher life. This is the unfailing law of karma, the principle of eternal balance.

In studying the law of karma and its operation, one thing more must not be overlooked. It is the very important fact that *no individual can ever pay the debt for another*. Theologians have made the terrible blunder of ignoring this fixed and immutable law of Nature. They have built up their theological dogma of the vicarious atonement in contravention of the law of karma. If Jesus could pay the debt of a single other individual by his death on the cross, then the great law of justice itself becomes inoperative. By that very fact, the Creator would annul his own law. Even if Jesus were himself the incarnated Creator, and if he should take upon himself the sins of mankind, the entire scheme of justice would collapse, and the old plan of animal and human sacrifice would be justified.

At best such a doctrine is a virtual acknowledgment that the Creator was disappointed in man's conduct. After man had created a debt which he could not pay, the Creator himself had to pay it for him. But to whom did he pay it? Who held the mortgage? To say that he paid it to himself makes the death of Jesus on the cross no more than a grandstand play or a bid for public sympathy. To say that he paid it to the devil exalts that worthy to the status of an equal partner in a questionable transaction. It makes the Creator an absurd actor, obliged to make the best of a bad muddle. To say that he paid the debt to the law of justice itself is but a subterfuge of words.

The whole dogma is built up on the old rule of sacrifice and substitution, which was but a trick of the ancients to try to escape the legitimate consequences of their own actions. By that means they only deluded themselves into thinking that they had escaped their karma; but as a matter of fact, they greatly added to their karmic burden. Sacrifice is a very old and almost inseparable con-comitant of the slowly awakening consciousness of the inviolabil-ity of the karmic law. They knew they had to do something to escape the consequences of their moral debts, but they didn't know what to do. The whole scheme rests upon the assumption that God and the devil are running a dual empire: the devil in the ascendancy most of the time in this world, the Lord himself being but little more than a nominal sovereign obliged to keep up appearances under an embarrassing situation. If the Jews, and particularly St. Paul who created the Christian theology, had been well informed on the immutable law of karma, the idea of the vicarious atonement would never have been dreamed of. It is directly opposed to the eternal law of justice which runs through-out Nature.[1]

---

5. Reincarnation Explains Much

If karma and reincarnation are a little difficult to understand, especially among Western people to whom the whole idea is

---

1. It may be stated here that Saints can and do take upon themselves karmas of their disciples in certain cases. This is, however, possible only in the case of those whom they took into their fold while they were in the physical bodies and does not apply to those who lived either before or after them. This privilege is exercised by the *living* Master only.

rather new, on a little reflection it will be found the only rational explanation of some of the most complicated problems of life. For example, why does some useless old man linger on for years, a burden to himself and everyone else, while a beautiful child, full of promise and joy, has to die suddenly? Only karma and reincarnation offer any satisfactory explanation. To explain it as the inscrutable decrees of a deity, arbitrarily interfering in the affairs of human life, is to invite despair and unbelief. As a matter of fact, the parents are to understand that the child, due to his own past karma, was from the very beginning allotted just that brief span of life and they must be thankful that the child was 'loaned' to them for that brief period. The child, due to its own karma, had been allotted just that length of life and no more. That time being finished, it had to go. Its short life was only one scene, just a brief appearance, upon the stage of its career. This little act had to be played. It was also one episode in the life of the parents. That much of karma in the lives of both parents and child had to be paid. When it was paid, there was no further need for the child to remain there, any more than an actor should remain on the stage when his act is finished.

Again, why do some people enter this life with such terrible handicaps, while others, apparently less worthy, are born in the lap of fortune? Why are some children born with superior intelligence, while others are hopelessly dull? Why are some born with criminal tendencies, while others come into life with a lively sense of purity, justice and love? These and a hundred other questions press themselves upon us all, and they have no answer, except in the scheme of karma and reincarnation. This is not the first life of all of those people, and so each one enters this life bringing with him all of his inherited tendencies—*sanskaras,* the Master calls them.

Each one comes with a definite program outlined for him, according to his past record. This is his fate karma. That program he must carry out. When the last act of that program has been performed, the scene closes. The end comes. It must come. Moreover, the end cannot come until the last act of his preordained life has been performed. He then passes to another life. There again his future is assigned to him on the basis of his own earnings. In this manner every individual marks time in the grand calendar of the ages. The only thing that can ever bring this monotonous routine to an end is the meeting with a living Master. When a man has this opportunity, it implies a good fate karma and that the supreme crisis of his long career has come. His deliverance is close at hand.

If a student feels inclined to ask why all men have not the opportunity to meet a Master, the answer is again, their karma. They have not earned that privilege. (No man can meet a Master until he has earned the right.) And when they have earned the right, there is no power in the world that can keep them away from the Master—not even the stormy waters of seven seas. There is no injustice in this thing. Never mind if you think some who never meet the Master are much better people than some who do meet him. We have not sufficient data to judge who is most worthy.

If some people are favored in India, while so many good people in Europe and America have no such opportunity, it is because these people in India have earned the right. God only knows how many long and weary ages they have waited and suffered and worked, only to be born here with but little of this world's goods, and even poor mental equipment, yet with hearts filled with love, ready to follow the Master with no misgivings, no mental pulling back. They may have nothing else, many of them. They may be poor and ignorant, but they have much good karma, and so they find themselves at the Master's feet. On the other hand, a man in Europe or America may have great intelligence, wealth and position, yet his karma of past lives may not have entitled him to meet a Master in this life. That is why they do not meet him. It is not because they live so far away.

It may be asserted without qualification that if a thousand men and women, or even one alone, in America were fully prepared to meet a Master, they would find him, even if he had to come across the seas to them. When any man or woman has earned the right to stand before a Master, there is no power in the universe that can keep him away from the Master. The two must meet. But in every case it is good karma that brings the soul to the Master. It is well known among advanced students of the occult that

When the chela is ready, the Guru appears.

We may be asked, what is the final goal of good karma? The answer is that it will bring the individual to the Master. That is the extreme good fortune, the very highest reward of good karma. His early liberation from the wheel is then assured.

However, reason as we may, the final and *only conclusive proof* of the doctrine of karma and reincarnation comes when one enters the inner worlds and there beholds its operation for one-self. It is then not a question to be settled by academic disquisitions, by logic or beliefs. Like all other teachings of the Masters, this is founded upon observation and personal experience, upon sight and hearing, upon positive knowledge. These things are as well known to the Masters as are the common phenomena of wheat growing or house building. They behold them in operation, and therefore they need not guess.

When anyone enters the higher fields of knowledge, he is able to watch the operation of karma and reincarnation. With clear vision he is able to see its application to others as well as to himself. At that stage every one is able to see clearly his own past lives. He distinctly remembers them. It is then that he *knows* that he has lived before, and he knows just where and when he lived. Also, he knows his karmic earnings and losses. He can see exactly how the law of karma and reincarnation works out in his long succession of lives—how he came and went, times without number, always bringing with him his unsettled accounts. He remembers just how he suffered or enjoyed, according to his debits and credits. He knows that always he had to pay, pay to the uttermost. The great law is then no mere theory to him.

6. What Happens After Death

After a person dies, he or she is taken by the messengers of death to the subtle regions where Dharam Rai, 'the righteous judge', sits enthroned to judge every individual according to his deserts.

In the Christian lands these messengers of death are very appropriately called the Angels of Death or the Dark Angels, for dark indeed they are, but in India they are called Yama Dutas or the messengers of Yama, the king of the dead. This judge is always in court to take care of all comers—no long waiting, sitting in some jail cell.

No one ever questions the judgment. No comment is made, no long-winded oratory for the defense, no pretended righteous condemnation of the prosecution. The prisoner himself makes no complaint and asks no favors. He knows he is getting justice and consents to the judgment. He is then taken to the region or condition where he has earned his residence, be that good or bad. He remains there for a fixed time according to the judgment just rendered and handed down to him. After that period has expired, he is returned to this world or some other world to begin a new life. This is the routine procedure. He may enjoy a rest in some heaven or paradise, some pleasant country, perhaps many times more beautiful and delightful than any portion of this world. There he may remain for one year, a thousand, or a million years, all depending upon his karma. The higher he goes, the longer the period of his residence there.

But if one's life has been of a lower order, he may be taken to some purgatory or reformatory, often called a hell—there to endure the punishment earned by him during his lifetime. If his life has been one of gross misdeeds, of cruelty and greed, of murder and robbery, of slander and debauchery, he cannot escape the legitimate results. He must meet the appropriate punishments. But there is one feature about all such punishments that must be understood—they are remedial and not vindictive. They are intended for his good, to produce a reformation of character. And they are not eternal. But the law is inexorable; each one must get just what he has earned and just what is needed to impress upon his inmost consciousness that 'crime does not pay'.

Dante's Inferno is not all imagination. In the lower subtle regions are many sections adapted to serve as reformatories and training schools for evil-minded individuals who have passed on after leading lives of wickedness. In those regions all souls must meet the just rewards of their deeds. There is no possible escape. These purgatories may be severe or mild, according to the earning of the individuals who go there.

The hell of the Jonathan Edwards type is a horrible finality. Happily that doctrine is now almost a thing of the past. It is no longer used to threaten and horrify sensitive children to make them obey. It is said that actually at times people in the church of Edwards would involuntarily catch hold of the benches to keep from slipping into hell, as it was so vividly portrayed by Edwards in his sermons. But of course, such teaching is supported by the Bible, and we cannot blame Edwards. He was conscientious—I used to preach it myself, but I noticed that not many people ever took it very seriously. Now the inclination among religious people is to expurgate their religion of all sorts of hells. That is going to the other extreme.

The problem must be met and rationally solved. Facts are facts, no matter whether they are agreeable or not. We must face them. And the Masters know the proper solution. They know that all souls meet in the next life exactly what they have earned, and there they must face their karmic debts and pay them. If they have filled their minds with evil, that evil must be eradicated in some way. Infinite love holds onto the erring one and takes measures to reform him, to purify his mind and bring him up to a higher plane. How else can it be done if not by a course of remedial and disciplinary punishment and training? But when his period of training and discipline is over, he is free to work his way to higher planes and better conditions. Having been duly impressed with the evil nature of his former conduct, he will not readily return to it.

When a man begins the next life, he enters it chastened and humbled, more inclined to mercy and good deeds. He then has an opportunity to make good karma. In going to those disciplinary regions, there is no such thing as despair, no hopeless finality. There is kindness even in such punishments, kindness and infinite love. The punishment is for the good of him who endures it. If he had not earned it, he could not have been called upon to endure it. The Supreme Father never forsakes an erring soul, not even in his darkest hour.

After his period of discipline is over on the subtle planes, he may be required to reenter earthly life in some lower form, to finish up his karmic schooling. If he has lived his earthly life on a very low plane, in degradation and shame, he may be obliged to come back in some animal form, bitterly humiliated and chastened. But in any case that soul, that tiny spark of the Infinite Light, is never extinguished. It is simply obscured and humbled. The mind is circumscribed and limited to suit the limitations of the animal brain. When he returns to the human plane again, the mind is naturally expanded to suit the new brain. In the animal brain we may say the mind is simply darkened, imprisoned, and its light obscured.

Each tiny bit of mind-stuff, drawn from the universal mind, is just what that individual needs for the normal expression of his life in the body he has. The same mind goes with each one through all of his karmic career, but in each body it is obliged to adjust itself to the instrument it has. In the brain of a dog, for example, the mind is circumscribed and limited. It is cramped into such narrow confines that it cannot exercise its full capacity. But as soon as it takes human form again, it automatically expands to its full expression as a human. When the mind of a higher level man is liberated from the narrow limits of the human brain, it is then expanded to its full powers of expression upon a higher plane.

Students often ask: What is the explanation when one person suffers injustice at the hands of another? The answer is that there is no such thing as innocence suffering injustice at the hands of another. Let us explain: It only appears so because we cannot see the entire drama at one glance. We see only isolated acts, unrelated episodes. It must be remembered that this law of karma is universal. In every case a soul gets exactly what it has earned, no more and no less. There is no such thing as innocence suffering at the hands of tyranny or cruelty. Do not accuse the Creator of mismanagement of his affairs. What *seems* injustice in so many cases is only an appearance. How do we know? Because on the inner planes those who are qualified can observe the working of the law.

If not in this life, then in a previous one, that 'innocent' person had done something to earn exactly what he is now getting. If he had not earned it, he could not now get it. It is impossible that anyone should suffer an injustice, though it often appears as if one is suffering the grossest injustice. But as said before, that is because we see only an isolated act of the entire drama. Whatever one gets, he has certainly earned in some period of his long career.

When someone imposes upon another what appears to be an injustice, and looked at from all aspects of the affair known to us it is an injustice, we know the recipient has earned it at some time, somewhere—yet that does not excuse the one who inflicts the apparent injustice. He may be ever so guilty. Even if he is administering a just punishment to the other, it does not excuse him for the act. He should rise to a higher law and give out love and kindness instead of an eye for an eye—if he did so, he himself would earn good karma. But this way he incurs further obligations which he must pay at some later date.

It is injustice from the standpoint of the man who inflicts the injury. Nevertheless, he may be returning some act of injustice or injury which he suffered in some previous life. This actually happens in many instances. These transactions are often extremely complicated from our limited viewpoint. But if the actor had returned good for evil instead of stern justice, he would himself have fared much better in the long run. In no case is a man justified in injuring another, even if he has been injured by the other. In no case is anyone *justified* in returning evil for evil; but in every case the wrongdoer must suffer for his evil conduct, even if the suffering must come by what is called an act of God, like a storm or railway accident, where no one individual is responsible. (A storm may come and blow his house down and break his bones; karmic debts are paid that way very frequently.)

The moral responsibility of a bad act is in no wise lessened because his victim had earned the ill luck far back in some unknown past. Bear in mind that there is always an automatic execution of karmic debts. It must come, and it generally comes without the conscious participation of the parties concerned. Only one who has inner vision can see its workings.

7. How to Do Karmaless Actions

There is one more extremely interesting phase of karma which ought not to escape our attention. We have now seen how it binds us. We shall be interested to know if there is any possible escape from creating karma, even in the case of disciples of the Master.

There is no escape from karma once it is created. When the debt is incurred, it must be paid. But there is a way of living without creating karma at all. We have already said that all living beings create karma by every act of their lives. The Gita says that inactivity itself creates karma, and no one can escape it. But there is a way. What is that way? *By dedicating one's life to the Master.* The Master himself is karmaless. He has met and satisfied all of his own karma by the aid of his own Guru. After that, he rises above the action of the karmic law. He is no longer subject to that law because he has risen above the plane of its action. He is free from the laws of all regions where karma operates. He can never again be bound by that law. All work which he does is now done in the name of the Sat Guru whom he serves, seeking to please him only. He has no desires of his own. He does nothing without the full approval of the Supreme, and all he does is constructive. If he made any karma at all, if such a thing were possible, it would be good karma, and good karma elevates one. But the Master has already attained the supreme status. How can he go higher? Hence karma could have no effect upon him.

Now, if the Master's disciple wishes to escape the creation of karma of any sort, let him act in the name of the Master. So long as he does that, he will not create new karma, because he is acting solely as the agent of another, and always the principal is responsible for the acts of his agent. But he must do this not merely in a ceremonial way but with his entire thought and soul in it. In deep earnest let him do all things, every detail of his life, *in the name of his Master.* This will, per necessity, oblige him to do only what he thinks his Master will approve of. When he approaches a task or a proposed act, he will remember that it is to be done in the name of the Master. He will fix his mind on the Master, and then in love and devotion he will do the work as a genuine service to the Master, and in his name. He will remember that nothing is his own. All belongs to the Master because he has dedicated all to the Master—even his mind and his body, as well as his property. So he must use them all as if he were using the property of another, and use them exactly as he believes the owner would like to have him use them.

Everything then is used only in the service of the Master. Even the eating of one's own food is to be done as an act of service to the Master. Your whole life belongs to the Master and is to be spent in his service. Then you eat in order to keep the body in good condition, that it may go on rendering good service. There is a very meaningful sentence written by Guru Nanak, which says:

> Body, mind and wealth; give all to the Guru; obey his commands, and reap the reward.

If the critic objects that this is going too far, that it sounds like a scheme to get the disciple to give up his property to the Master, let him know that the Master never under any circumstance takes over the property of a student. No Saint or Master ever accepts a penny from his disciples. The Master accepts the disciples' money just as he accepts the disciples' mind and body, as a gift of love and trust. Now the Master holds a moral title to them; the student goes on using them just as he did before, but he uses them in the name of the Master, who is now the real owner. They are used for a noble service and cannot be used for any selfish or unworthy purpose. If he is about to commit an unworthy act, the student will remember that his mind and body are the Master's property and he cannot use them improperly. So this is a protection for the disciple.

But the main point under consideration here is that if the disciple uses his mind and his body and his wealth all in the name of the Master, he is not creating any karma. Essentially it is the

KARMA AND REINCARNATION

Master acting and not the disciple. The disciple is only the agent of the Master. So long as he is acting sincerely and wholeheartedly as the agent and disciple of the Master, it is really the Master who is acting. When our lives are sincerely dedicated to the Path, we give up all to the Guru and we think only of doing his commands. Jesus said:

> If ye love me and keep my commandments, then are ye my disciples indeed.

And this is so regarding the disciples of any Master. Inayat Khan, a noted Sufi, says:

> Give us all you have, and we will give you all we possess.

And in that saying there is much wisdom and a great promise. It means that if the disciple gives up all—mind, body, wealth and soul—to the Master, the Master will in return give the disciple such wealth as no king ever possessed. The Master will give him riches that surpass all else on earth, and in exchange for the surrender of himself to the Master, he will gain a freedom that makes him master of a limitless empire. It is not that the Master wants the disciple's mind or body or property. It is for the benefit of the disciple alone that the Master asks him to dedicate all to him. Such a gift on the part of the disciple generates more love in the disciple and enables the Master to do more for him, and at the same time it protects the disciple from making mistakes.

All this means that the big 'I' must be eliminated from the disciple's innermost thought. Humility and love must take its place. Perfect devotion to the Guru will lead you into the Light. The supreme advantage in following the Guru is that you will never make mistakes, for he knows what is best and correct in every possible emergency. In no sense is the personal liberty of a disciple ever circumscribed or limited by surrender to the Guru. The disciple is more free than ever before. He has no more fear of anything. He goes where he pleases and does what he likes with the most perfect assurance.

Here is a divine paradox—by surrendering all to the Guru, you gain your liberty. By giving everything to him, you gain everything. Only that man is free who walks behind the Guru. Only that man is free who always does the will of the Master. For the will of the Guru is the will of the Supreme Father. And that is really the secret of this whole matter. The Master is the representative of the Supreme. By following him, we follow God.

It may be well to note here that there are two different administrations of karma—that of Kal and the other of Dayal. Guru and Dayal are the same, and both refer to the Supreme Being, the Lord of the infinite universe. Kal is the Lord of karma for this world and all regions up to the second—Trikuti. Karma is administered by him to the great bulk of humanity. In fact, in case of all who have no Guru, they follow the routine outlined above, and karma holds sway over their lives from age to age. From the wheel of karmic destiny there is no escape, except when one meets a living Master. But the very moment a person takes Nam from a Guru, that is, becomes a disciple, all his karmic accounts are transferred to the Guru's keeping, automatically passing from the hand of the Negative Power. After that, the Guru, working under the directions of the Supreme Positive Power, administers the karma of his disciple. From that hour forward, Kal, or the Negative Power, has nothing to do with his accounts and has no power or control over him. The agents of death cannot approach him, nor can he ever be called into the courts of the Dharam Rai for judgment. His destiny in this life and in the next rests entirely in the hands of his Guru. The Master then administers the karma of his disciple just as he thinks best for the disciple.

8. Karma and the Vegetable Diet

It is well known that the majority of the Indian population do not eat meat. (The Moslems and a few modern Hindus do eat it.) This is not altogether because they cannot afford meat. Most of them object to it because it involves the taking of life. Back of that objection is the law of karma, which has been familiar to Indians for many thousands of years. Saints and their disciples do not eat meat, fish, eggs or any sort of animal food, for the same reason. It involves the slaughter of animal life, and that means the assumption of karmic debts. Let us now see how it works out both in theory and in practice.

In the vegetable there is but one active *tattwa*, or elementary condition of matter. That is *jal*, which means 'water'. It refers to the liquid state of any substance. In the insect there are two active tattwas, *agni* or 'fire', and *vayu* or 'air'. Agni refers to the resolving state, or heat; it means a transitional state of matter. Vayu refers to the gaseous condition of matter. In the birds there are three active tattwas: jal, agni and vayu. In the higher animals there are four active tattwas, *prithvi*, jal, agni and vayu. But in man, and in man alone, all five tattwas are active. As a matter of fact, all five tattwas are in everything in the world, but they are not active. *Akash* is the last one, which is active in man alone.

Now, the law by which we are governed is this: The greater the number of active tattwas that are combined in the living individual, the higher he is in the scale of evolution and also the greater the responsibility involved in killing that individual—hence, the greater the burden of karma assumed in killing. But since man has to eat something in order to continue his life here, the ancient Sages and Masters selected the *least* harmful substances, that is, those things in the killing and eating of which there is the least karma to be assumed. They decided on vegetables; no animals at all. Of course, there is some karma to be assumed in eating vegetables, as there is life in them too. But in the vegetables there is the lowest form of life, and hence the least karma involved. This is the chief reason why the Saints do not approve of killing and eating animals.

The second reason is that the eating of animal food interferes with one's spiritual refinement. It drags a person down toward the animal plane. It is a fact that so long as one eats animals, he will be more or less like animals. It is unavoidable that we should become like what we eat, just as we become like that of which we constantly think. We must absorb its qualities to some extent. How could it be otherwise? That is but common sense, and I believe most people will agree to it. It may be tested by anyone. A heavy animal diet will always awaken the animal passions and drag one's thoughts down to the animal plane. The same is true of eggs. The reader may test this for himself. Everybody knows that eggs are often used deliberately to stimulate the animal passions. The worst animal-man I ever knew made it a habit to take daily from three to six glasses of sherry wine, into each of which he put one raw egg. But the disciples of the Saints have as their chief aim and effort in life to rise above the animal plane and to unfold their spiritual powers. Hence they must not eat that which will pull them down to the animal level.

Another reason is strictly one of sanitation and health. An animal diet is a filthy diet. It fills the body with impurities, the purine group especially—uric acid and other by-products of animal-food digestion. All these bring on their train of evils, rheumatism, mental dullness, heaviness and laziness, appendicitis, etc. The refuse in the intestinal tract from animal foods develops soluble poisons that are themselves deadly, and if a person goes on manufacturing and absorbing them, he will certainly develop nervous disorders, auto-intoxication with its train of evils, and an early death or an enfeebled, decrepit old age.

But the student of the Masters wishes to keep his body in as perfect a condition as possible. This is one of the oft-repeated commands of the Master. Then it stands to reason that he must select the purest and least harmful foods available. This means a diet of vegetables, fruits, grains and nuts, and all dairy products.

Students of the Masters are strictly enjoined not to indulge in intoxicating drinks. This is because, in addition to creating bad karmas, it confounds the intellect, vitiates judgment and almost destroys discrimination. Under its influence, one may do things which result in a heavy karmic debt that can only be wiped off in several incarnations besides bringing shame and dishonor here. Both body and mind suffer—the resulting mental slavery being a great impediment in the way of spiritual practice.

9. Reincarnation and Social Reconstruction

Connected with this great fact of Nature is a problem of vital interest to society in general. It is this: Reincarnation and karma offer society a sound basis upon which to proceed in dealing with all sorts of human irregularities. They give the courts a clue to the problems of the criminal. They offer a working principle in applying the law of justice to all offenders. And what is of still more importance, they suggest how society may greatly improve itself by establishing a more healthy environment for its unfortunate members. And lastly, they offer a most salutary suggestion as to the best methods of education and the building of character.

The first suggestion offered is that the weak, the criminally inclined mental children in grown-up bodies, must all be treated more as patients for the physician rather than as victims for the hangman. They are not fully responsible, not in the later stage of their degeneracy. Many of them have long since passed the status of personal responsibility. Then is the time for society to step in and apply the methods of a father, to the end that his son may be restored to normal health. Society should never be frightened at the word *nepotism*. Let hide-bound conservatism talk. What is wrong if society does play the part of grandfather to a weak member of its family. It is far more humane than acting the part of the savage executing a weakling. So much the more credit to it. It is certainly more to the credit of the social order to play the part of a grandfather than to revert to the law of the jungle. The one method is the crown of civilization, while the other is only an anachronism in the long struggle for the survival of the fittest. It is simply a lingering remnant of barbarism.

All systems of education should be so adjusted that the weak shall be made strong, even as a weak muscle is strengthened by exercise. The right sort of impulses must be encouraged, while all destructive tendencies may be checked by a rational application of science. There should be an *applied science of ethics* as well as of agriculture.

Sympathy should take the place of vindictive punishment,

the aim being to restore the individual to a state of health and normality. The purpose should be always to change him into a good citizen. But it should be known to all by this time that no one has ever yet been made good by punishment. The universal experience of criminal institutions is that the criminal comes out more hardened than ever, and more criminally inclined. He feels he now has a real grievance against society. If in rare instances a man comes out of prison with a reformed character, it is because of his own inner nobility, and the reform has been fostered in himself in spite of his prison career. His better nature has found time to assert itself in spite of the hardening tendencies of prison life.

A knowledge of reincarnation will make a great difference in our treatment of both men and animals. It will teach us that we are all bound up in one karmic bond. We cannot then mistreat animals, neither can we go on killing and eating them. Knowing that we are all in one common brotherhood, this great truth will inspire more love and kindly consideration toward every living being.

All these points will be clarified in our understanding if we remember that this is not our first and only life here, nor will it be our last—unless we meet a Master. This understanding will help the courts and the educators. It will show them how people bring with them into this life all sorts of tendencies and inclinations not otherwise to be accounted for. These qualities must then be dealt with on a rational basis, keeping in mind that the ultimate aim is to eliminate the destructive tendencies of delinquents instead of trying to destroy the delinquents themselves. Society must endeavor to develop constructive ideals and build character. Only in this way can society build for itself a structure worthy to be called a civilized state.

Civilization and governments have changed from age to age, in each age taking shape to correspond with the inner development of its citizens. Not only do the Saints teach that there was a Golden Age from which the human race has descended, but they point out the more important fact that such descent has been marked by a gradual degeneration of mankind from their pristine glory; also, that this degeneration has resulted in establishing

different sorts of governments and totally different social orders.
The Mahabharata (*Santi LIX: 14*) says:

> At first there was neither state nor ruler; neither punishment, nor
> any body to administer it. The people used to protect one another
> by or through innate righteousness (dharma) and a lively sense
> of justice.

It is a fact which must sooner or later be acknowledged that
kings, rulers, courts, judges, priests, policemen, lawyers and legal
punishments are all marks of racial degeneration, and not indices
of a high degree of civilization as many fondly believe. We would
much like to discuss this subject more fully, but this is a statement of Santon ki Shiksha and not a treatise on education and
government.

All the sacred literature of ancient India teaches that kings,
states and civil laws came about because of the degeneracy of
mankind. Of course, this is a new idea to the West. But the West
may do well to ponder over it. As evil tendencies became more
and more manifest in society, some regulations had to be adopted
to protect society. Then a system of laws was worked out to suit
the conditions. Manu became the great lawgiver for India as
Moses was for the Jews. Laws were made suitable to the people
and the times. A definite *Danda* was established. In *Manu Samhita (VII:14–32)*, the Danda is set forth as the concrete will of
God, the foundation and support of society. It is the cornerstone,
the pillar of the state.

It is an old trick of priests and kings to teach the mob that
whatever they give out is 'the will of God'. It makes a better impression. Danda serves the will of God by restraining the evil tendencies of men, protecting the weak, and to some extent developing the higher impulses by inculcating higher ideals. It then aids
all well-disposed people to establish a wholesome swadharma in
their own lives. If a state or an individual is governed by this fundamental Danda, it must follow the divine law.

The most successful stroke of the statesman was to make the

people accept their laws as identical with the divine law. If a state is once established upon the supreme Danda, it is in a position to carry out the will of the Supreme. This was really the underlying principle upon which kings used to claim their 'divine rights'. But that was a misuse of the whole idea of Danda. The real Danda could be only a righteous law. The real Danda had in view just as much the 'divine rights' of the people as it had the 'divine rights' of kings. Over this bar of divine rights even the king could not trespass.

We cannot fail to make note of the fact that as the human race entered upon its decline in civilized standards, there was a transfer of the center of government from within man to enacted statutes—in other words, from moral standards deeply embedded in the inner consciousness of the people to laws written in books. When the time came that the fundamental Danda was no longer in the hearts of the people but in books, then the decline of civilization had already set in. When the time comes, if it ever does, when fundamental law will again become established in the public conscience, enacted statutes with courts, judges and prisons will pass away as useless adjuncts of a more sane government.

The *division du travail* of which Durkheim speaks is a commonwealth in which every citizen shares in the general responsibilities and rewards of good government. And this is the only stable, as well as the only just, government—be that government either monarchy or democracy. This was the sort of government Manu had in mind as well as Plato. But their ideas found a different expression in different times and among different peoples. It may be said also to embody the highest ideals not only of Plato and Manu, but of Moses, of Karl Marx and of Eugene Debs. Modern socialism is only a phase of the old, old struggle toward the realization of a civilized government. We believe that when this long struggle, worn on to its final conclusion, has reached its ultimate solution, society will finish up just where it began in the Golden Age—with no government at all, except that which has its fundamental Danda in the hearts of the people.

Most modern writers fail to call attention to the gradual

change in governments and social orders to the progressive degeneracy of mankind. They keep thinking too much of our ascent from the jungle beast. And they are right as far as they can see. But there was a period of descent, long ages of descent, before the comparatively modern era of ascent began. That earlier period the evolutionist cannot see, for he has not sufficient data at hand. It is only the great Masters who are familiar with that period. When the Golden Age had long passed, and the Silver Age also, the Copper Age witnessed many degenerative changes. Kings and priests and manifold weaknesses made their appearance. Slowly then came the Iron Age, marking the lowest ebb in individual and social degeneration. It was during that period that modern laws, governments and social regulations began to appear. The anarchist is quite correct *in theory*. But for anarchy to prevail with social equilibrium, it would be necessary for the whole race to become ideal citizens, individually governed by the fundamental Danda. Their swadharma must come from a pure heart and an all-embracing love. Unfortunately, that condition does not now prevail. But it will prevail, if ever the time comes when all men, having first deeply fixed the Great Law in their hearts, shall set out upon the Path of the Masters. Shall we dare hope for that?

Coming back now to our starting point, the establishment of the principles of Santon ki Shiksha, with full knowledge of the whole scheme of karma and reincarnation, must clarify and rationalize all philosophy. Upon this new interpretation of fundamental law a new state and a new social order will be established in which every man, woman and child will receive the best sort of treatment and protection, looking in every instance to their ultimate good, and the keynote of that philosophy will be love. And the Path of love is the Path of the Masters.

Last of all, knowing the law that every man must reap what he sows, and that he can never escape the law, no rational being will go on ruthlessly mistreating his fellow beings and indulging himself in vile passions. That would be equivalent to suicide. No man in his right mind will injure himself. This great science of the Masters teaches us that to injure another person is only another form of suicide.

10. Karma and the Nature of Evil

Karma is bound up with all forms of sin and evil, as well as of righteousness.

SIN—RIGHTEOUSNESS—KARMA

These three cannot be separated. Both sin and righteousness create karma. It may be of use to give a little more careful study to these three. In the sacred literature of India, *dharma,* 'righteousness', is doing right, obeying the law, and this means doing 'what is to be done'. *Adharma,* 'unrighteousness', is disobedience of the law of dharma. The same teaching runs through all religions. The Law of Moses, the Eightfold Path of Buddha, the Will of Allah—in fact, the commandments of God. No matter by what name the system may be called, they are all the same. Finally, to do whatever is written in the law is regarded as righteousness. To disobey is sin. But nowhere is it told exactly what sin and righteousness are, *per se.* And that is because all people go by a book of laws. No one except the Masters has attempted to tell what the substance of evil is or the essential content of doing right. When the time comes that mankind will look within their own souls for the fundamental law, and not in a book, all of these difficulties will be avoided.

Just why it is that certain conduct is wrong and forbidden, and why certain other conduct is good, can be known only from the teachings of the Masters, for no one else has ever told us. This is going to the bottom of the problem, but it has not been done in any religion. They simply write down their commandments in a book and assign penalties for their violation. Nearly all of them sum up the matter by saying: "Do the will of God." And when we come to a little closer investigation of the matter, we find that the commands of the lawgiver are assumed to be the will of God. Who is to tell us exactly what the will of God is? Of course, the priests and the prophets and the kings. But if we challenge their credentials to speak for God, they call us bad names. Ask them just why any given thing, like stealing, is wrong, and they will give you many reasons, but not the fundamental reason. Ask one of them why adultery is wrong, and he will tell you—because it is forbidden in the Ten Commandments or some other book of law. And that is as far as he can go. What constitutes good conduct? What constitutes bad actions? No clear conception of the fundamental nature of these transactions can be gathered from the literature.

But in all discussions which claim to be of a scientific character, these deeper problems must be met. Otherwise we shall only cloud our subject, ending just where we began, in a maze of meaningless words. The science of the Masters is able to offer an exact definition of all terms relating to the science and to reach down to the very inmost substance of the questions under discussion. For that reason we are endeavoring to give underlying principles here rather than superficial definitions or rules. The reader may then make his own rules and laws. The first of these fundamental principles is that which explains what is fundamentally evil or wrong. It is as follows:

Whatever pulls one's mind down from the center is wrong; whatever raises it is right.

This principle may be elaborated to suit the reader. Another guiding principle is:

To keep on the path of spiritual progress the mind must be maintained at its center behind the eyes; any action pulling it down from there retards progress and can, therefore, be called wrongdoing.

We must not forget that the doer is not the only one to be considered in any study of right and wrong conduct. The doer and the recipient both must be considered. If a certain act has the effect of delaying anyone else on the Path of spiritual liberation, then that course of action must be considered wrong. The simple sum of the matter is that no one is to be impeded on his way to the

Light. Any given act that has the effect of helping another party in his spiritual progress is to be considered good. The ultimate effect upon the higher interest of all concerned must be the prime consideration.

Do not be misled by that old but erroneous maxim—the greatest good of the greatest number. That is one of the most unfortunate slogans that ever gained recognition. It sounds plausible but it is utterly misleading. That saying has been used for centuries to justify murder in the name of society. Nothing can be moral or good if a single individual has to be sacrificed to gain it. Who is going to make good to the victim? Who shall compensate him for the deprivation of his natural rights? If a man misuses his liberty or his privileges, he may forfeit that liberty or those privileges, but by no means or upon any sort of pretext should he be deprived of his life. Society can take away a man's liberty and society can restore it. But society cannot restore one's life. Moreover, such a sacrifice is not necessary to protect society.

Last of all, what is evil itself? We believe there is no better definition than that given by some discerning students of both East and West, who say: Evil is only a lesser good. In other words, there is no such thing as evil *per se*. Perhaps a clearer expression of the same truth may be found in the statement: Evil is but a shadow, a lesser light. The shadow well illustrates the nature of the thing that troubles us so much and about which we talk so much and know so little. Let us analyze it.

A shadow is simply less light, nothing else. In total darkness there is no shadow. Total darkness is nothing. Neither is there shadow in the perfect light. But if some obstruction shuts off a portion of the light, then we have shadow. There is a spot or surface where there is less light than that which shines upon the surrounding region, and that is a shadow. The final conclusion of the whole matter is that just as shadow is a less light, so evil is a lesser good. We feel some pain in the lesser good because we crave the perfect good. A misguided ego thrusts itself into the foreground and obstructs the perfect light. Just how this works out in detail, I think may be left to the reader. It will not be difficult to follow it.

It is a logical corollary that *the cure of evil is unobstructed light*. When this occurs, as in the case of the Master, then all evil vanishes.

---

11. Love, the Passkey to the Kingdom

One of the most amazing and thought-provoking of all phenomena in the work of the Masters is the gathering of the simple and the lowly at their feet. How have they managed to find him when so many millions of 'the best people' of the world have failed to do so? How have they come, these who understand so little? Whatever moved them to seek spiritual liberation when they scarcely know any more than to eat, sleep, breed, and work a little? It is doubtful if many of them even know what they seek. What inner urge has brought them on such a strange quest? The flame of intelligence in their brain is so very low. Herein is a divine mystery. Read slowly and carefully the following suggestion, lest you miss the main point:

The key to this mystery is the great mercy of the Supreme; that and *the great love of these people*. Remember that the best thing in the world is not a matter of superior brains. We need not set ourselves upon a pedestal because we have more intellect than some others. I once knew a strange couple—a man and a dog. The dog was one of the most lovable and loving of animals. But the man was an ordinary reprobate. To see these two together and witness the unselfish devotion of the dog, it was not difficult to say which had the superior soul. In like manner some of the poorest and worst-looking specimens of human beings may have superior souls.

We should remember that no one can come to the Sat Guru until his good karma brings him. So these poor souls must have a lot of good karma, even though appearances may not indicate it. Their good karma was not utilized to purchase worldly position and wealth, but it was applied to secure something vastly more important—the *darshan,* 'meeting and beholding', of the Sat Guru face to face. They come not with good bodies and prosperous environments, but with an inheritance of infinitely greater value—a love, a capacity to love, like that poor dog, an inheritance which brought them directly to the Master's feet. They had but one idea; namely, that a loving Master would take them up out of the miseries of this world. That idea was all they required. They did not need to know anything else. Even though they did not have any of this world's goods and came as the humblest of mortals, very great is their good fortune. *To find one's way to the Guru is far better than to be born an emperor.*

But look at these people! Do they appear as if fortune had smiled upon them? Some of them have misshapen bodies; some are poorly developed, have distorted features; some with faces but little more than half-human, drawn and haggard, weary and old-looking at the age of twenty. If old in years, the poverty and misery of centuries is stamped all over them. Ask them a question which requires a little intelligence to answer, and you get only a blank stare. What has become of the light which distinguished them from the brute? How like Millet's "Man with the Hoe"! Edwin Markham should be here to paint a word-picture of these people.

But Markham blames the tyranny of governments for that slanted brow and extinguished light. This is wrong. Every man has made himself just what he is, in spite of the mistakes of governments. Poor as these people appear, they are among the luckiest of men. They have come up out of the darkness to be enfranchised sons and daughters of the King of kings. They have hit upon a direct route to the palace of their Father. And what has brought to them such good fortune? Their love. Again you will ask: How have these poor and lowly ones come to the Sat Guru, when so many millions of the world's greatest and best, with keen critical minds, care nothing for the Master? Or if they do care, they seem to have no opportunity to meet him. How has this paradox of life come about? Mercy and love—the mercy of the Supreme and the love of these lowly ones. A capacity to love is a nobler quality than the capacity to rule. These poor people have nothing else, but they are rich in love.

While you travel about in your beautiful cars, these humble

people trudge along over dusty highways, weary of limb, bearing their roll of bedding and a morsel or two of food. Two, three or four days, some of them walk determined at any cost to see their beloved Master. Some of them cannot afford even a third-class ticket, but they are determined to be at the monthly satsangs and sit before the Master. Today they sit in one grand concourse, perhaps twelve thousand. Here these poor and lowly mingle with the rich and the educated. I watch them. Suddenly that dull face loses its blankness. A flash of light changes the whole countenance. They smile; the whole face lights up with joy. They fold their hands. *The Master has come.* They gaze at him with rapt attention. Their whole being is agitated, joyous. It is their Sat Guru, the light of the world! That is love, adoration, devotion! No matter how poor they came into the world as men, now they are multimillionaires in love.

We know that *love is the passkey to the kingdom of heaven.* It may be that the conduct of some few of these people may turn out to be a trifle shady at times. But after all, they are but 'little children of the law'. Always there is that two-sided aspect of character. And it is very difficult to eradicate, even among the highest types of men. The other aspect is made up almost entirely of a great love. Humble and simple, only little children in mind capacity, they have nothing to block their way to the Master, like the worldly wise have. Jesus said: Unless men become as little children, they cannot enter the kingdom of heaven. *Love* and *faith* and *humility:* these virtues they have, these poor and lowly ones. And yet they are only little children in mind.

Love will admit you to all heaven-worlds. Love is the golden coin current in those worlds. That sort of love has brought these people to the Master. It has opened to them the doors which ever remain closed to the selfish and the vain. They may be beggars in rags here, but over there they are princes of the realm.

How great a thing is love! I think no man can write it down. No man will ever understand it until he himself arrives in the kingdom of love. If our good karma, running through a thousand centuries, should bring us nothing more than a capacity to love, then it were not in vain to suffer and toil up the long steep grades. The

love of the humblest soul is so great a thing that it exalts and en-
nobles not only that individual himself but everyone else in the
world. The whole of human life upon the planet is exalted, and to
some extent purified, by the love of one noble soul. If it were not
for the love that is in the world, the entire fabric of human and
animal life would crumble into darkness and chaos. Every person
who loves even a little in purity and unselfishness contributes that
much toward the elevation of the whole of humanity.

The question is often asked: When all the mists have cleared
away, when one of these poor and lowly shall stand side by side
with the man of great intellect and learning upon the bright shores
of Sach Khand, what will be the difference between the two?
What advantage will the man of learning have over the other? The
answer is—*none at all.* His intellect has never taken that man to
Sach Khand. Intellect will never take anyone to the higher regions. Love and love alone will do it—love and the help of the
Master.

Mind goes only to the second region and is there discarded as
a thing of no further use. When the soul of this poor stupid beggar,
stripped of its rags and its poor mental equipment, shall stand by
the side of an Emerson or a Plato on that fair shore, there will be
no difference at all between them. Both are drops from the same
Infinite Ocean. And that entire Ocean is love. Nothing but love.
Pure spirit and pure love. There is not a single drop of mind in all
that Ocean. There is no intellect there—nothing of the ordinary
earthly man, except spirit—only pure soul and a boundless love!

Chapter Eight

THE EXISTENCE OF HIGHER WORLDS

1. A New Concept of the Universe

TO the Oriental mind, there is nothing new or startling in the idea of higher or inner worlds. The people of the East have been accustomed to such ideas for almost countless centuries. Neither do they question the ability of a man to enter those finer worlds during his lifetime. He simply has to be qualified under a Master who has himself accomplished the task. The East has had such ideas, and many of its mahatmas have worked them out in individual experience during untold thousands of years. And not only have they worked out those ideas in practical experience but they have reduced those experiences to an exact science. This was done ages before the first pages of history were written.

The Sanskrit technical terminology of this science bears silent witness to its authenticity and something of its venerable age. In this volume many Sanskrit terms have been used, and such use could not well be avoided. This is to be regretted in some respects. Many people object to the use of Sanskrit in a book printed in English. But they do not realize the difficulties involved in trying to do without it. Would you try to write a book on medicine without using Latin and Greek words? In a work which deals with a science more accurate and exacting than that of medicine, we cannot dispense with technical terms. In that ancient language are many terms giving the minutest shades of meaning to almost every psychological and spiritual experience possible to man. This is conclusive proof that psychology and spiritual experiences had been reduced to a science when Sanskrit was a spoken language in its formative periods. Today Sanskrit sustains the same relation to spiritual science as do Greek and Latin to medicine or any of the other physical sciences.

But it is the very idea itself which concerns us most at this time. I remember as a young man it took me four or five years to develop the ability to entertain the idea of inner worlds, or the finer worlds above the physical, and of the possibility of actually learning anything reliable concerning them. Due to my old orthodox training, the very idea itself was almost beyond me. It all appeared to me the most visionary dream, fantastic, the rankest folly of a biased mind. But in the East it is not so and never was, so far as we know. They have always had the idea.

Meditation and seeing and hearing of things within oneself, trance, *samadhi*, leaving the body and going out to travel in higher and finer worlds, are all to the Oriental mind quite normal ideas. The actual accomplishment of such things has generally been left to those who are specially qualified. The Masters, however, tell us that the Way is open for any man to do these things if he will train himself for them. To the West this entire subject is still more or less bizarre, abnormal and fanciful. Such things are often attributed to some mental peculiarity or to some pathological state of brain and nervous system. The practical Western man regards such things as produced by a morbid state of mental excitation, more or less unwholesome. Of course, they do not concede that such experiences can be reduced to a science. This is unfortunate for the West itself. Kipling may have been right when he said:

East is east, and west is west, and never the twain shall meet.

But it will be a fortunate day for both East and West when each shall impart to the other the vast wealth that is in them both; when the West shall give to the East its magnificent scientific spirit and method, its marvelous achievements in manufacturing, in commerce and industry, and above all, its splendid and masterful forward movement in all things that make for material betterment. It will be an equally happy day for mankind when the materialistic West shall imbibe from the East its scientific method of mental and spiritual demonstration. The psychology of the Orient is just as much needed in the West as the science of the West is needed in the Orient. Today the West thinks it only has a psychology. It doesn't even think it has a science of the soul.

But the point we wish to emphasize here is the importance of the Oriental view in regard to spirit and mind. The very idea of 'going inside' of oneself and there seeing and hearing things called occult, or experiencing a state of superconsciousness resulting in a super-refinement of mind and soul, are all difficult for Western thought. This is because the whole subject is new to the West. It has never been a daily routine among us as it has been in the Orient. Long before the days of Herodotus, or even of Manu, the subject was familiar to every child in the East. Among us such notions, even today, are limited to men and women who are generally called impractical dreamers or visionaries.

It is also a fact of history, though almost universally ignored, that all religions in all ages have had their own methods of silent meditation and of going inside and developing inner experiences. And they have all achieved something along these lines. Out of those experiences the various religions themselves have sprung up. Devotees of every religion in the world have, to some extent, tapped the fountains of the inner life. This is true in Christian history as well as in all other religions.

Among most modern Christians, the method of going inside has been lost, just as it has been lost among the followers of all other religions. It is only the Saints of the East who have kept alive this knowledge and transmitted it as a pure science. However, isolated experiences are to be met with here and there among the devotees of all religions; but they are more or less sporadic and uncertain, both as to method and results. There was no system of teaching everyone how to do it. Mankind, in the great mass, have almost forgotten that they have souls or, more accurately speaking, are souls.

Let us never assume that civilization itself is the cause of the diminution of such experiences. It is rather a terrible loss which civilization has imposed upon itself through ignorance and self-indulgence. Civilization is suffering from overemphasis upon material values. But when a civilization arises which understands both material and spiritual values, and combines the two and carries them forward side by side, a real civilization will be born to supersede the present.

2. Quotations From Prominent Christians

To support the statement that some forms of concentration and inner experience have been practised by devotees of the Christian religion, we wish to give a few statements taken from the history of saintly persons of Christianity. They are all the more valuable because they coincide exactly, so far as they go, with the inner experiences of the Saints and their disciples of today. The following are a few accounts taken almost at random from *Mystic Experiences of Medieval Saints*.[1]

(1) Vision of St. Francis Xavier:

> After this prayer I once found myself inundated with a vivid light; it seemed to me that a veil was lifted up from before my eyes of the spirit, and all the truths of human science, even those that I had not studied, became manifest to me by an infused knowledge. This state of intuition lasted for about twenty-four hours, and then, as if the veil had fallen again, I found myself as ignorant as before. At the same time, an interior voice said to me: "Such is human knowledge; of what use is it? It is I, it is My love, that must be studied."

How truly this corresponds to the Masters' experience as far as these experiences of the Christians go! But of course, the Masters go far beyond this experience into worlds far more vast, into riches of the spirit immeasurably greater.

---

1. R. P. Aug. Ponlain, S. J., *Mystic Experiences of Medieval Saints* (Kegan Paul, n.d.). Translated from the French, *Des Graces d'Oraison.*

(2) Vision of St. Ignatius:

As he was going to pay his devotions at the church of St. Paul, about a mile out of the town of Manrea, and was sitting on the banks of the Gardenera, his mind was suddenly filled with a new and strange illumination, so that in one moment, and without any sensible image or appearance, certain things pertaining to the mysteries of the faith, together with other truths of natural science, were revealed to him, and this so abundantly and so clearly, that he himself said that if all the spiritual light which his spirit had received from God up to the time when he was more than sixty years old could be collected into one, it seemed to him that all of this knowledge could not equal what was at that moment conveyed to his soul.

This experience is also identical with that of every student of the Masters who enters upon the threshold of the astral zone. Note the 'enlightenment' of Gautama Buddha so loudly proclaimed to the world. Yet thousands of the great Masters and their disciples have had similar experiences since then. It is a common experience here on the banks of the Beas River in this good year of 1939. What a pity that these good men and women of the medieval ages did not have the method of the Masters, so that they might have gone forward with their inner experiences instead of being limited to a single sporadic flash of the inner light. Under a real Master this power may be developed so that those experiences may be repeated at will and then one goes far beyond them.

(3) Vision of Herman Joseph:

And as he stood there praying, he was suddenly raised above himself in such a wonderful manner that he could not afterwards account for it, and the Lord revealed to him the whole beauty and glory of the firmament and of every created thing *so that his longing was fully satisfied*. But afterwards, when he came to himself, the Prior could get nothing out of him than that he had received such an unspeakable rapture from his perfect knowledge of the creation, that it was beyond human understanding.

This also accords fully with the experiences of the Masters

and their disciples. They sit in meditation with mind 'one-pointed' at the inner center, fixed upon the Supreme Lord and the higher worlds; then the light comes, and with it their inner longings for light and understanding are perfectly satisfied. Great joy fills their whole beings.

But there is one important point which we ought to mention here. It is said in his experience that "the Lord revealed to him. . . ." This takes the matter out of the category of scientific experiment and makes it depend upon the grace of the Lord. But the Masters know that such experiences are available to anyone who knows the scientific method and devotes himself to the practice. Those medieval devotees simply stumbled into these experiences through their extraordinary love and devotion. How much more they could have done if only they had been familiar with the proper method! Besides, then they could have repeated those experiences any day and hour they chose.

(4) Vision of St. Benedict:

He saw a light which banished away the darkness of the night— upon this sight a marvelous strange thing followed. The whole world, gathered—as it were—under one beam of the sun, was presented before his eyes. For by that supernatural light, the capacity of the inward soul is enlarged. But albeit the world was gathered together before his eyes, yet were not the heaven and earth drawn into any lesser form than they be of themselves, but the soul or the beholder was more enlarged.

This is a fact of common experience among disciples of the Masters. The entire universe seems to stand directly before the beholder, and whether the universe itself is brought in to lesser space or the capacity of the beholder is enlarged, the effect is the same. The vision appears quite normal.

(5) Experience of Santa Theresa:

When our Lord suspends the understanding and makes it cease from its actions [by this she means that the normal activity of the mind is brought to a standstill, made motionless], He puts before it that which astonishes it and occupies it; so that without making any reflections [without reasoning things out] it shall comprehend in a moment more than we could comprehend in many years, with all the efforts in the world.

The disciples of the Master know that in a single moment of inner illumination vast stores of knowledge are received, running through years and ages of our time, and including many worlds. Also, in one instantaneous flash one may receive a complete vision of historical events stretching over months and years. Again Santa Theresa says:

> In an instant the mind learns so many things that if the imagination and intellect spent years in trying to enumerate them, it would be impossible to recall a thousandth part of them. Although no words are pronounced, the spirit is taught many truths. If, for example, it beholds any of the Saints, it knows them at once, as well as if acquainted with them for years.
>
> There appear to me two things in this spiritual state [inner raptures]: *the longing to see God,* obscuring all else, which might even endanger life itself, so intense is the desire; the other is an excessive gladness and delight, which is so extreme that the soul appears to swoon away and seems on the verge of leaving the body.

Now let the critic explain how such an intense longing for God can be generated by an hallucination, a thing which the individual never felt, nor even thought of, in his normal state of consciousness. The Masters know that such longing is induced by coming into closer rapport with God during samadhi. There is an affinity between every soul and the Deity. In samadhi, when the world is shut out, God attracts the soul with great force, due to the natural affinity. The Masters say that if a person were cleansed of his earthly attachments, and all of the coverings were removed, the soul would go up to God like a skyrocket. Nothing could hold it back. The soul is drawn to Him as an iron filing is drawn toward a great magnet. It is the love of the soul set free from the bonds of matter. The Masters say that if a soul, untrained and undisciplined for such experiences, were to be suddenly transported to one of the higher regions, there to come near to the throne of the Supreme Father, the upward pull upon that soul would be so strong that its physical life would be terminated at once. It could not endure it and remain in the body.

(6) Angela of Foligno says:

There is nothing then that the soul understandeth or comprehendeth to be compared with the rapture to which she can inwardly attain. For when the soul is lifted up above herself by the illumination of God's presence, then she understandeth and taketh delight and resteth in those good things of God that she can in no wise describe, for they are above the understanding and above all manner of speech and above all worlds. But in these the soul swimmeth in joy and knowledge!

It is the common experience of devotees of the Masters that they do really "swim in joy and knowledge!" It is also their common experience that they cannot put into words their experience. These are above all manner of speech. There is yet one feature of these inner experiences, just as she says, which astonishes the devotee. It is the fact that they transcend all other experiences of one's life in the depth of their joy and the sublime radiance of their light. Again she says:

And I was so full of charity [love] and with such joy did I have understanding of the power and will and justice of God, and not only did I have knowledge of those things about which I had enquired, but I was also *satisfied with regard to all things*. But this I cannot make known in any words whatsoever; for it is wholly above nature.

How will the materialist explain such marvelous flooding of the soul with love, such love and joy, if they are derived from an hallucination? If they are so derived, then it were well that all mankind should live in a perpetual state of hallucinations. Let the critic explain how such vast stores of knowledge can come from a pathological state. If, as we know well it is possible, a man may enter samadhi an ignoramus, and come out a sage, it were well that all men could suffer such 'intoxication of the cerebrum' for the whole of their lives.

(7) Marina de Escobar says:

> When in a deep ecstasy, God unites the soul suddenly to his essence,
> and when he fills her with his light, he shows her in a moment of
> time the sublimest mysteries. And the soul sees a certain immen-
> sity and an infinite majesty—the soul is then plunged, as it were,
> into a vast ocean which is God and again God. It can neither find a
> foothold nor touch the bottom. The divine attributes appear as sum-
> med up in one whole, so that no one of them can be distinguished
> separately.

Those who would attribute such experiences to mental
aberrations, let them explain how such majesty, such love, such
joy, such numberless wonders never before seen or even heard of,
quite unknown to these saintly Christians during the whole of
their earthly lives, can all be laid before the soul so suddenly. It is
well known and universally recognized among medical specialists
and psychologists that in all pathological psychoses nothing new
or totally different from the patient's former experiences can be
introduced into the dream or hallucination. Yet in nearly all of
these spiritual illuminations, the experiences transcend all sights,
sounds and ideas ever before had by the subject, and not only
that, but they go beyond anything known or experienced by any
person on earth during his normal life. The soul is lifted up into
superconscious states utterly unlike and beyond anything ever before known or even imagined. And then, with them all, a great joy
is felt such as no earth-limited mortal has ever felt. Again this
same good lady says:

> After some very thrilling inner experiences, she exclaimed to God:
> "Lord, how incomprehensible are thy judgments! Who shall un-
> derstand them?" And then God answered: "The little and the
> humble of heart, those who have left all for me, and who seek only
> to please me."

This sounds almost like an echo from the Gita. It is also a
paraphrasing of the words of Jesus, and it is in full accord with
the fundamental teachings of the Masters.

(8) Brother Giles of Assisi says:

> After asserting that *faith is converted into knowledge* by inner experiences, and being asked by a priest how he could then sing the "Credo" at High Mass, *he replied by singing in a loud voice: "Cognosco unum Deum patrem omnipotentem!"—I know the one God, omnipotent Father. . . .*

In other words, he declares that he no longer believes, but he knows. And this knowledge is always based upon inner experiences—mind you, not upon feeling, which is always of doubtful and uncertain value—but upon sight and hearing on the inner plane.

---

3. Inner Experiences Analyzed

In this hypercritical age, when materialistic science dominates the public thought of the West, there is a tendency to attribute all inner experiences which are out of the ordinary to the imagination, or to some pathological condition of the brain and nervous organism. But after reading the above extracts—which in the main, as far as they go, coincide with the experiences of the Masters and their students—let us ask one or two pertinent questions.

It will be admitted by psychologists that all experiences due to pathological conditions or to abnormal imagination, superinduced by suggestion or autosuggestion, must fall within the range of that person's past experiences, or of suggestions made to him or within his inherited tendencies. He can never see, hear or otherwise experience anything totally foreign to his own past history or to some combination of such experiences. Nothing entirely new can be introduced into the experience.

After reading the accounts of these inner experiences, as above cited, let us ask how we are to account for such vast and sudden increase of knowledge never before possessed or even heard of by the individuals, or even known to any of their ancestors. Also, how are we to account for such intense joy, the like of which no mortal ever feels in a lifetime of usual routine? How are we to account for a vision of things, of beauties and glories, such as no mortal ever saw on this earth—things which cannot even be described in human language? These and many other points involved may well be considered by the investigator.

The Masters teach that such experiences are superinduced by reality, in actual worlds lying on a plane higher and finer than our earth, planes quite beyond the grasp of material science. They are just as real, however—aye, much more real—than the routine phenomena of earthly life. When a soul, even in the smallest degree, separates itself from this dull earth, it rises into realms of beauty, joy and light which it never before imagined. And with that holy vision comes an understanding so all-comprehensive that the soul is lost in wonder.

The soul, contemplating this Path, should let the very idea of inner worlds and inner experiences of supra-mundane reality sink into his consciousness. Let him remember that our common everyday worldly sight and worldly understanding are at best only feeble reflections of the sublime reality which lies out there in an endless series of finer worlds. Then let him hold fast in his mind the practical fact that such higher and finer worlds may be entered and possessed by the student while he still lives in his present body. Let us not sell this birthright for a mess of pottage.

Those devotees of the Church have been able to do no more than to enter the outer borderlands of those higher worlds, while the real Masters pass at will above those borderlands and go on up to the supreme heights. And they do all of this by a definite scientific method, while religionists are working under a great handicap because they have no well-defined method. Most of them just 'happen onto' their experiences by force of their love and devotion but without knowledge of the Way. Also in marked contrast with these sporadic and haphazard experiences of the religionists, the Saints and their disciples have complete control over their inner experiences, being able to come and go at will, to remain on those upper regions as long as they wish, and return to them whenever they desire. This is a vital difference.

4. Inner Experiences of Mediums

The whole world is more or less familiar with that class of phenomena known as Spiritualism. It is manifested through mediums. The inner experiences of mediums must be noted here. Many prominent men and women have lent themselves to the most searching investigations of these experiences. The world is full of mediums and half-mediums of all grades and conditions, some good and some questionable. Some of them produce the most astounding phenomena, while others turn out to be little more than pretenders. Taking the genuine productions of mediums, let us analyze them very briefly in the light of the Masters' knowledge. They alone know the facts, and it is highly important that some of those facts concerning mediumistic phenomena should be told.

In the first place, mediumship is a misfortune. It is not a gift, as some claim, nor is it a development. It is a misfortune. Its processes are destructive to the best interest of the medium. It is closely allied to hypnotism—a destructive psychological process, destructive to both victim and operator. No matter if it is used to try to cure disease. It is nevertheless destructive. The net results are a distinct moral and psychological loss to both parties. Mediumship is a species of hypnotism performed by disembodied spirits upon the sensitive medium. Even so-called automatic writing and allied phenomena, which are believed by Spiritualists to be quite free from all hypnotic obsession, are nevertheless a partially subjective process. If practised for a long time, they lead to complete obsession. Mediumship is a breaking-down process, never developing or up-building. The medium always remains under the control of her guides. She can see nothing, hear nothing and do nothing, except just what her controls wish her to do. She is in no sense an independent actor. She is only their 'instrument'. The underlying principle of evil in the processes of mediumship and hypnotism is that no person can be controlled by another intelligence without injury. Therefore, no one should ever be subjected to the control of anyone else. The only way that any intelligence can ever develop itself is to have freedom to assert itself.

Secondly, the results of mediumship are not always reliable or dependable. They may or may not be true experiences. Her messages may or may not be based upon facts. Her predictions are not reliable. Sometimes they come true, but more often they do not. The writer is speaking here from abundant experience with mediums of all sorts.

Thirdly, the medium's guides or controls are generally of a low order of intelligence, often from the ranks of the worldly minded and passionate mob, but seldom of any high order of intelligence or moral character. This is a lamentable fact now becoming more and more recognized by all who visit the séances of mediums. If some dear relative or noble character of history is supposed to be one of the controls, it is never certain, but the medium is being imposed upon even if she herself is not trying to impose upon her sitters. She is not in a position to detect the fraud because she can see only what her guides wish her to see.

And last of all, the mediumistic contacts are all on the subtle planes below the astral, sometimes much below, where only a lower class of spirits are to be contacted. There are many subplanes far below the true astral zone, and it is to some of these that most people pass immediately after death. There they linger for their allotted time. The pure astral plane is very high and refined when compared with the lower regions, and it is only a very high class of people who go there at the time of their death. This fact may be understood when it is known that most of the founders of world religions, great yogis and mahatmas known to history, are still within the limits of the astral regions, and up to this day have not been able to go beyond them. If they cannot go further than the astral plane, how can we expect an ordinary man or woman to go beyond them?

Vast multitudes which no man can number, of all sorts and conditions of souls, inhabit those planes and subplanes lying between the earthly and the pure astral. Most of them will never see the astral until they return for a new birth, and then practise concentration under the direction of a Master.

It is no small achievement to attain the pure astral region. Its capital is the famous city of 'the thousand-petalled lotus'. Mediums talk of the astral plane, but as a matter of fact very few mediums, if any, ever get a glimpse of the pure astral regions. Have you ever heard of a medium who even claimed to have seen 'the mountain of Light' called the Sahasradal Kanwal? I have never known one who had even heard of it. That is proof positive that they had never entered the astral zone. If they had, they could not fail to mention this, the most conspicuous feature of all astral worlds. Their fields of observation lie far below the astral—in one or more of the numberless subplanes, some of which are only a fraction above the earth plane, barely invisible to the physical eye. Roaming about through these subplanes are that vast multitude of souls whom we speak of as 'earthbound'. Out of that number a few appear to men occasionally as ghosts.

It must be kept in mind that higher level spirits will never take any part in the practice of mediumship. They know it is not a wholesome thing. Besides, they live on a plane far above and beyond anything ever contacted by mediums. We must never believe their stories when they tell us that some great historical character, a fond father or a mother or some world benefactor, has come to hold communication through a medium, or to act as a guide or control. If we accept 5 percent or even 10 percent of mediumistic revelations as genuine, then all the rest may be set down as rubbish. In any case, it is not a wise thing to indulge in the practice of mediumship or even to attend their séances. There is a far better way of approaching the higher world—a saner and safer method. The way of mediumship is the way of subjection, of degradation.

But the way of the Masters is the Way of independent development, of soul culture and of spiritual mastership. It is the only right way, and it is the only possible way—except that of the yogi—to go beyond the lowest subplanes of the subtle worlds. The yogis may go to the pure astral, but only the Saints, the Masters, go to the higher regions of pure spirit.

5. Inner Experiences of the Masters

Now, what is the difference between the inner experiences of the mediums and those of the Masters? All the difference in the world. While those of the mediums are destructive and subjective—i.e., controlled by others—the inner experiences of the Masters are constructive; and they are always under the control of the Master himself. The Master is never controlled by anyone. What he sees and hears, he sees and hears by his own powers and in his own right. He does not need or accept the help of anyone. He rises freely and by his own powers to any one of the subtle planes or worlds whenever he so wills. When he has arrived there, he goes about at will, explores those regions to his own satisfaction and returns to the physical plane whenever he wishes. Moreover, while sojourning in any of those higher regions, the Master is acknowledged lord of those regions; and he does this because he represents the Supreme One wherever he goes, and he has all powers to go where he pleases and do what he wishes.

If the Master wishes to leave this earth plane, he simply sits down and concentrates, and by his own will leaves the body and goes up to whatever subtle world he may wish to visit. Arriving there, he visits with the inhabitants there, looks over the country, and then returns here when he chooses. The going and the coming are not difficult for him—no more than stepping from one room to another here. And he remembers his experiences while up in those higher worlds, although it is often very difficult for him to tell about them on account of our lack of sufficient language and mental imagery. Thus the Master goes and comes at his own will and keeps in touch with any and all of the higher worlds, just as he may wish to do. When his work here is finished, he simply steps out of his body and leaves it.

Chapter Nine

THE MICROCOSMIC CENTERS IN MAN

1. Man Himself a Microcosm

THIS part of our subject has been purposely left for special consideration. It might have been made a subdivision of the constitution of man, a division of psychology. But it is so very important that we wish to give it more emphasis.

A very comforting fact known to the Masters is that the Creator has so constructed man that he is able, when properly informed and trained, to place himself in conscious communication with the entire universe. At first thought, this would appear but a flight of fancy, but it is literally true. It can be done. This is so because of the way man has been constructed. And this is why we speak of man as a microcosm, a little world. He is in fact a replica of the entire universe of universes on a very small scale, and for that very reason he is able to reach consciously the entire universe lying outside of himself. It is because he has in himself a definite something which bears a special relation to every separate part of the outlying universe. This is a marvelous thing. It is so very wonderful that we approach it with deep reverence. Men do not ordinarily imagine that they are so remarkably endowed. They feel themselves to be shut off from the rest of the universe—those vast unknown regions inhabited by numberless hosts of beings like ourselves or superior to us. But it is nevertheless a fact that we may get in touch with the whole of that outlying universe if we choose to do so.

And as said before, in order to fit us for such conscious communication, we have been organized, put together and adjusted by the Creator so as to constitute a small universe within ourselves, with certain parts or centers which correspond with certain portions of the outlying universe. Hence man himself, taken as a whole, is a true microcosm, a little world or universe. We are indeed "fearfully and wonderfully made." We need not go into detail here. The student may do so if he likes. Let this be his clue: Every individual part of man, of his physical or astral or causal body, holds a definite relationship with some particular part of the outlying universe. This is the key. This relationship is the key to all possibilities. In every man there is a center more subtle than the physical, invisible to the physical eye, which is so adjusted that it may serve as a means of communication with a corresponding section of the macrocosm, the great world. And this is our opportunity, our one and only means of contacting those subtle worlds. If we had not these centers within ourselves, we could never know that those regions existed. Every student would do well to pause here and think. For the sake of emphasis, let us repeat a portion of what we have just said. The whole thing must be made so plain, so clear, that no one can fail to comprehend it.

Microcosm means 'small world', and *macrocosm* means 'large world'. Man is the microcosm, and inside of man are several other still smaller microcosms, each one of which has a definite relation to some portion of the outlying universe. We are not isolated from the big world as we feel ourselves to be. We have the ability, when our faculties are awakened, to actually hold conscious communication with the most distant heavens, to explore the utmost regions of space. This applies not only to all physical worlds of starry galaxies, but to all the astral and the higher spiritual regions. There is no limit. What marvels are in man! How little does the average man realize his noble inheritance!

The entire existence of man is wrapped up in a larger being. He himself is but a cell in the body of the cosmos. Yet, taken as an individual, man is a small universe. More accurately speaking, man, all within himself, is a cluster of universes. Take his nervous system alone, for example. Dr. Alexis Carrel says that the cerebral substance contains more than twelve thousand million cells. These are associated several trillion times in a manner most complicated by means of fibrils. Every smallest particle of this vast system works in harmony with every other part, so that the entire mass behaves as one single unit. And this complicated system of brain and nervous threads is the instrument of thought on the physical plane of consciousness.

But Dr. Carrel is not aware that the marvelous play of thought is upon a plane just above the physical and can be seen by a finer instrument of vision. He knows it cannot be seen with the physical eye. If only he could weigh thought with his laboratory scales! But there is a way for him to actually see thoughts. The Masters see them. The dynamic energy of thought is derived from a source which cannot be standardized in the laboratory. Yet the working of thought forces is plainly visible to the Master, even to many who are not Masters but who have awakened this faculty.

Dr. Carrel speaks of the mind as "the most colossal power in the world." And in this he is in perfect accord with the teachings of the Masters. Little do men suspect the 'colossalness' of that power. Yet the great scientist asks with simple naiveté if thought is produced by the cerebral cells, like insulin from the pancreas. Of course, he doesn't understand the mechanism of thought because he has no knowledge of the constitution of man above the physical plane. This is a pity, for such a great student of Nature would go far on the Path if he once gave himself to it. Could such a colossal force, as he declares mind to be, arise from the physiology of the brain? That noble scientist has, we believe, one foot upon the doorstep of the temple of wisdom. Many other earnest students are timidly approaching that temple. They have reached the limit of present ability in material research, and so they stand amazed, wondering if there may not be something beyond the reach of their material instruments, something which transcends in value all that they have thus far achieved.

Man is indeed the microcosm, complicated and wonderful in structure. In him lies hidden the sum total of all universes. How true it is that the greatest study of mankind is man! The pity is that so few have ever taken the advice of the sages. If, as scientists say,[1] the average man of today does not use more than one-millionth part of his brain cells, it is equally true that man has not yet explored a millionth part of those numberless worlds which lie out before him, to whose riches and beauties he is still a stranger. But he may make such explorations if he finds the method.

As intimated above, man is not only a living microcosm, related to the whole vast universe, but he is himself a whole system of universes. Each cell in his body is a still smaller universe, and each atom in each cell is a still smaller one. Note the nucleus of each atom, surrounded by its electrons. The relative distances between those electrons, when compared with their sizes, are quite as great as those between any central sun and its planets. Thus the body of man is a vast and complicated system of universes, even millions of universes, clustered together in a single unit. And at last, this single unit itself is but an electron in the great microcosm of the heavens. Man is indeed a complete replica of the vast system outside of himself. In that fact lies a great hope. It is a gracious promise.

This marvelous microcosm has been offered to the soul, not haphazardly, but so scientifically adjusted that he may take hold of it and through it come into possession of his noble inheritance. He can do this by the study of self, not by dissecting the body of his colleague. He must go inside of himself and see what is there. This will awaken all his sleeping faculties and liberate his latent powers. Doing this, he will then come into conscious touch with the entire system of worlds, both physical and subtle, filling endless space. The exact process by means of which this is to be accomplished will be revealed by the Master to each of his students. The Master himself has accomplished this stupendous task, and he is now in a position to guide others who wish to do the same thing. Most men are entirely ignorant of this great gift with which a benevolent Nature has endowed them, but every one may become conscious of it if he wishes to and will take the right steps. He has only to look for a living Master to open the Way for him.

---

1. Alexis Carrel, *Man the Unknown* (New York: Harper, 1935).

The important point for us now is that because of this marvelous construction of man himself, he is able to open conscious communication with the entire universe of worlds, both physical and spiritual. This any man may do, if properly guided, and if he is willing to do the work required. It is simply the method which he needs, and that he can get only from the living Master. *Each and every man, when properly trained, is able to detach himself from the physical body while still living in that body in perfect health, and then travel to all parts of the outlying universe.* Everyone has this ability whether he is conscious of it or not.

During long ages and many successive births in regions of coarse matter, the majority of men have lost the knowledge of how this is done. They have now to relearn the lost art from the Master. They may regain all the forfeited prerogatives. The inner faculties must now be reawakened and their proper functions restored. As the physical brain is in touch with all parts of the body through its nervous system, just so there are in the astral body certain important centers by means of which the intelligence may get in touch with the entire astral world. In like manner, other centers act as points of departure for communication with their corresponding higher and finer worlds. This contact is established, and the proper centers awakened, by means of *concentrated attention* at the point or center chosen under the direction of the Master. And this is the secret of all yoga, the objective of all occult exercises. By concentrated attention at any given center, the consciousness is awakened at that center, and from there the awakened consciousness moves upward toward those subtle worlds which are correlated to that center.

2. The Microcosmic Centers

Beginning from below, the microcosmic centers are:

(1) The *mul chakra*,[1] called also the *muladhara* or the *guda chakra,* and the *Chardal Kanwal.* This first chakra is situated near

1. *Mul,* 'root', and *chakra,* 'wheel'. *Guda* means 'rectum', and *Chardal Kanwal* means 'the lotus of four petals'.

the rectum. It governs elimination. These centers are shaped somewhat like the lotus flower, more or less round, and the number of distinct parts are spoken of as petals. This lowest one has four petals, the higher ones increasing in number. It is an interesting fact that these body chakras taken together have exactly fifty-two petals, corresponding to the fifty-two letters in the Sanskrit alphabet, and each petal gives out a sound, a distinct musical note, corresponding to one of the Sanskrit letters. These sounds can be heard by any person whose finer sense of hearing has been awakened. He can then see these chakras and listen to their sounds. It is claimed that these fifty-two sounds comprise all the sounds which can possibly be made by the vocal organs of man. They say that the ancient rishis, listening to those fifty-two sounds, fashioned a character for each one, and that is the way the Sanskrit alphabet came into existence.

(2) The second chakra is called *indri chakra*,[1] or *linga chakra*. It is also called *Shatdal Kanwal.*[2] It is situated near the sacral plexus and it has six petals. It has to do with reproduction.

(3) The third chakra is named *nabhi chakra.*[3] It is also called *Ashtadal Kanwal.*[4] It is situated at a point near the solar plexus. It mostly has to do with general nutrition.

(4) The fourth center is the *hrida chakra.*[5] It is also named *Dvadasdal Kanwal.* It is situated near the cardiac plexus and it has twelve petals. It has relation to the general circulation of the blood and breathing, so far as the heart is a part of the breathing apparatus. (This function is not yet recognized by physiology, but we know that if it were not for the heart, the oxygen inhaled by the lungs could not be conveyed to the whole body.)

(5) The fifth center is the *kanth chakra.*[6] It lies near the cervical plexus. It has to do with respiration. It is also named the *Shodasdal Kanwal*, the lotus of sixteen petals.

(6) The sixth center is called *Dodal Kanwal*, the two-petalled

---

1. *Indri* relates to 'sex', and *chakra*, to 'wheel'.
2. *Shat*, 'six', and *Kanwal*, 'lotus'.
3. *Nabhi*, 'navel'.
4. *Ashta*, 'eight'.
5. *Hrida*, 'heart' and *Dvadas*, 'twelve'.
6. *Kanth*, 'throat', and *Shodas*, 'sixteen'.

lotus. It is situated back of the eyes on a level with the lower part of the eyeballs, but exactly in the center of the brain cavity at a point in the subtle body corresponding to the position of the pineal gland. That is the seat of the mind and soul. That is the center of control over the body. All centers below this one are subordinate. All 'deities' or forces which are said to govern the body are themselves subordinate to the mind and spirit of man, which reside at this center.

Just above this center is another center, called *Chardal Kanwal,* whose function is to supply the fourfold antashkarans (mental faculties) of the mind with faculties of action. These four faculties are manas, buddhi, chitta and ahankar. Each of the petals of this lotus has its own sound, and these four complete the fifty-two letters of the Sanskrit alphabet. This is the lowest of the six centers in Anda and lies nearest to Pinda.

Just above the antashkaran four-petalled center, comes the *tisra til,* the third eye, at which point the Master teaches us to concentrate all attention when we meditate. Thus the soul resides permanently in Dodal Kanwal, the highest center in the Pinda, and from this center the concentrated attention is fixed on the tisra til center, skipping the antashkaran center. The attention in this manner crosses the line between Pinda and enters Anda, whence it departs on its upward journey. Tisra til is also called *shivanetra,* 'the eye of Shiva', and *nukta-i-saveda,* 'the black point'. In the system of the Masters, all concentration is begun at this point and is held there until ready to go higher. All the lower centers are disregarded. This is one of the fundamental differences between the system of the Masters and that of all yogis following the Patanjali method. Thus the Masters actually begin their work where the other systems leave off, for few, if any of them, go above this center. While the Masters know of the lower chakras, they disregard them as unimportant.

There are many centers still higher in the brain, each corresponding to a region in the higher worlds. There are twenty-two important centers in man's subtle body, besides almost numberless smaller ones which may be likened to the smaller nerve ganglia in the body. They all have a certain function. But in the system of the Masters we are not much concerned with more than ten or twelve of these centers.

We have given the six centers in Pinda, the body below the eyes, not as a part of the Master's teachings but as a study. This is because so many yogis emphasize these and use them. But the Masters do not use them. They begin their concentration at tisra til, and from there they go on up. If one begins there, the next station above tisra til is Ashtadal Kanwal, the lotus of eight petals, and then the next above that is the true center of all the astral worlds. Its name is Sahasradal Kanwal, and this is the first of the great regions traversed by the Masters on their upward journey. At this point almost all the yogis stop, many of them fully believing that they have attained the highest. But it is, in effect, the starting point of the Masters on their upward journey toward the Supreme Region. That lies eight distinct stages above—or seven, exclusive of Sahasradal Kanwal.

Sahasradal Kanwal lies just below the Brahm Lok of the Hindus, known in the technical language of the Masters as Trikuti. That is the second stage in their Path. But to the ancient Hindus and the Vedas, that is the end of all, the residence of the Supreme God. In the science of the Masters, Brahm is known as the Negative Power.

3. The Meaning of Going Within

One point may be mentioned here to avoid confusion. The Masters and their students often speak of 'going inside'. They speak of worlds inside man's body. They speak of going inside in order to begin their upward journey, and that this going inside is accomplished by concentration at tisra til. All this, if not properly understood, may be confusing. We must know exactly what is meant by 'going inside'. Many prophets, including Jesus, speak of the kingdom of God which is in man. These expressions need not cause us to wonder if they are understood. They do not mean that there are actually worlds or kingdoms inside of man's body or brain. If these teachers had that in mind, then we would know of a certainty that such worlds were only creations of a fertile imagination. But what is meant is that those other and higher worlds are gained by first withdrawing the attention from the outer world and then centering it within oneself.

In the case of the Masters' system, the attention is centered at the tisra til. When such concentration has been gained, the attention is all inside. The whole of the mind and soul have left the outer world and gone inside. Only the inner worlds exist for us, the outer world having been completely shut out from our consciousness. Then we go on holding our attention at the inner center. Slowly and gradually the soul and mind gather all their forces at that inner center and, finally leaving the physical world entirely, penetrate through some inner aperture and enter a higher region. We may call it a higher dimension. At that moment, the soul passes through the inner 'gates of light' and steps out into a new world. Those higher and finer worlds, which occupy limitless space to the uttermost bounds of the universe, are then spoken of as 'inner worlds'. They are the worlds 'inside of man'. They are so referred to because one must first go inside, take his attention inside, in order to reach them. This is then a convenient method of referring to these finer worlds.

4. The Release of the Kundalini

Since this matter has become so well known and so generally discussed by all writers on occult themes, it appears needful to mention it here in order to explain why the Masters do not deal with it in particular. It has long been regarded by students of the occult sciences as unwise and even dangerous to write down or in any other way reveal to the uninitiated any of the secrets of the inner Path. It is today regarded among yogis as a breach of trust, a violation of one's personal responsibility. Hence the yogis are very reserved about imparting their secrets until after the most rigid trials and tests. And indeed that is the only safe and sound course on the path of the yogis. But this precaution does not apply with equal force to people, or about secrets, on the Path of the Masters.

Those who work under the Patanjali system of yoga must beware. Why? Because the yogi's path is beset by many pitfalls, while that of the Masters has no dangers unless a person turns deliberately to wickedness after his initiation. And the Path of the Masters is safeguarded by its very own nature.

Let us illustrate. Under the Pranayama exercises, the Kundalini is released or awakened from its dormant state in the indri chakra or *swadhistana* center. It lies near the sacral plexus and is associated with the function of reproduction. It is the creative center in man. This Kundalini is said to be a great power. When awakened by the proper exercises, this force rises through the central canal of the spinal cord known to anatomists as the sixth ventricle; but to occultists it is the *Sushumna* path with two smaller canals, one called *Ida,* on the left, and the other called *Pingala,* on the right. When the Kundalini rises to the brain, fully aflame, there is a series of important changes which take place in the consciousness, especially in the feelings and emotions. The individual is 'on fire', so to speak. He has also a very great increase of powers—powers over the forces of Nature and powers over other people. If, however, that individual has not been properly prepared for these changes by a rigorous process of training in self-control and mind purification, the results may be disastrous. Even insanity or death may follow.

But no such difficulties can possibly attend the practice of the system of the Masters. Why? Because the science of the Masters does not permit the awakening of the Kundalini until the disciple has gained self-control and mental purity. It cannot be done until that inner cleansing has taken place. This is a vital point. In the system of the Saints all development is attained by a natural, slow growth and reconstruction. It is not a forced process; and for that reason it sometimes takes longer to see the Light on this Path than upon that of the yogi. But in the long run, this Path of the Masters leads upward by a much more rapid climbing than can possibly be done on the yogis' path, and it leads to heights never dreamed of by the yogi.

The student of the Masters unfolds his powers as easily, as naturally as a flower opens its petals to the sunlight. This Path may therefore be followed and its exercises may be practised by anyone from childhood to old age. But this work must be done under the supervision of a living Master. That must never be forgotten. If anyone presumes to go his own way alone, even with this book as his guide, he is foredoomed to failure. If you have all the knowledge in the world and have not a Master, you have nothing.

But let no man think that because the Path of the Masters is slow and comparatively easy, the final results will be less than those to be attained by the more difficult path of the yogis. The contrary is true. The Path of the Saints includes in its accomplishments all that any system has ever promised or attained, and then goes far above and beyond anything ever dreamed of by ancient yogis. It is well to repeat here for emphasis that a good yogi is one who has gained the first region on the Path of the Saints. This is the pure astral. It lies above the sun worlds and the moon worlds of the yogis and the rishis. The Sahasradal Kanwal center is sometimes called the lightning world by the Vedic writers.

A real Saint or Master is one who has attained the fifth region, called Sach Khand, four distinct regions or universes beyond the highest achievements of the yogi. The Saint has also corresponding increase of powers and understanding beyond those of the yogi or the rishi. The Masters gain all that is ever accomplished by the more laborious and even dangerous method of the yogis, and they gain it in much less time. After that they go on up to heights never dreamed of or imagined to exist by any of the old yogis or Vedantists. If any man feels inclined to doubt these statements, there is a way to prove them. Come to a living Master and test the truth of them for yourself. The way is open and an invitation is hereby extended to any honest investigator.

Seek, and ye shall find; knock, and it shall be opened unto you.
(Matthew 7:7)

Chapter Ten

MENTAL PREPARATION FOR
THE GREAT WORK

1. A Flawless Morality

THAT every man must come to this work "duly and truly prepared, worthy and well qualified" is a primary fact. If he is not so prepared in his heart, he need not come. Neither money nor power, nor worldly honors nor position nor learning, will avail him anything. The inner preparation simply must be made.

Let us now examine briefly what that preparation consists of. By the phrase 'flawless morality' is meant that he must be on the level with his fellowmen; he must be honest, sincere, truthful, just and kind. He must be unselfish in his relations and dealings. He must never live off others if he is able to work, and this applies to women as well as men. It applies to everybody. One must earn his own living if that lies within his power. He must always seek to do whatever service he finds at hand to do. He must use his wealth, if he has any, to do good, and never for selfish gratification. He must lead a simple, straightforward life, and become a noble example to all others. He must be chaste, both in mind and in practice. Even in the marriage relation, he must not be given to over-indulgence of his passions. In other words, he must be what the world generally calls a good man, not given to any form of self-indulgence. And when he has attained that much, he is ready for the next step on this Path.

It is quite useless for any but men of good intention to approach the Master. Yet there is encouragement for those whose past has not been up to the standard. A man may have had a checkered career, even a criminal record. Many of the best men of history cannot boast of the most exemplary conduct during the first period of their lives. But the point of supreme importance is *their present attitude of mind*—that and their present conduct. If they have definitely left behind them all shady paths and now stand firmly upon a platform of righteousness, determined to live properly in the future, they are suitable candidates for Nam, provided they have a deep and abiding desire for the Master and his Path. This desire is taken for granted in all who seek the initiation. As to whether one is ready for the initiation or not, that can be determined only by the Master himself. But in actual practice, among people of a high order of intelligence, it seldom happens that anyone applies who is not fit for the Path. If they are not ready, they will not knock at the door. Even Jesus said:

> Knock, and it shall be opened unto you.
> (*Matthew 7:7*)

All students will do well to remember that we are not to expect perfection of any beginner. That were to turn the whole process around. Perfection comes of long practice on the Path, and not at the beginning. Therefore, it is a great mistake to demand that a person shall have perfected his life before he applies for initiation. He seeks the initiation that he may perfect his life as a disciple of the Master. A starving man does not wait until he is strong before he takes food. He takes it in order to get strong.

2. The Next Step Is Viveka

This is really the first step on the Path of the Masters. For a genuine morality, a well-ordered life is taken for granted as the primary consideration and as a foundation upon which to become a disciple. But in becoming a disciple or in approaching this Path the first requisite is *viveka*. This means right discrimination. It takes in a broad field. Simplified, it means that one is to use all of his intelligence properly. He must think out things thoroughly, especially regarding this Path and his own spiritual interests. No one is to advance blindly. He must think long and deeply. He must carefully discriminate between that which is good and what is less good, between the true and the false, the useful and the useless.

While too many books usually confuse the student, yet one must read all that is available which promises to help make the Path clear. Underlying the entire problem will be found certain great universal truths and principles which should be learned well and kept always in mind. Great general truths help one to decide a multitude of details. Get a firm grasp on a few fundamentals, and then use them in deciding all else. All this and more is included in the technical term *viveka*.

A few fundamental principles may now be offered. But first of all, keep in mind that a well-established morality is the foundation upon which we build; without that we cannot even start. But assuming that, we must now begin a very thorough exercise of the rational intelligence in order to determine just where we stand relative to this Path. If it will not stand the most searching inquiry, it is not worth our time. Explore its depths, examine every philosophical principle and compare the principles of this science with all others, and then draw conclusions on the basis of facts and sound judgment.

The first general principle to be examined here is that which is couched in one of the oldest classical sentences known to the Vedic literature. It should be of immense value to any student of philosophy. In Sanskrit it reads:

Ekam sat vipra bahudha vadanti.

Translated, it means: 'That which exists is one: sages call it by various names'.

This was written by a great rishi, probably ten thousand years ago. It has run through all Indian philosophy, and it has profoundly modified the thought of all thinkers. It teaches that there is perfect unity in the Supreme One. It teaches also that there is perfect unity in all life in the entire world. All that lives is one life, one in essence, permeated and vitalized by the one universal Being. It is in that Universal One that all things live and move and have their being.

If Hindu philosophy had never done anything else than give to the world this one sentence, it would have justified its existence. Out of it has developed the modified monism of modern thought. Until we see nothing in the world but the Supreme One as the soul and life of all, every sort of evil will continue to beset our path. We shall make much of distinctions. We shall continue to set ourselves apart from all other beings and develop selfishness. It is only in the great Universal One, in the Spirit Infinite, that we come to realize that we are all one in interests with a universal kinship. Until we see the Infinite Good everywhere, even in evil, this perfect unity will not exist for us.

More important than all else, the very heart of this doctrine of universal unity is love. That is, the whole infinite universe is held together in one bond, and that bond is love. If we can bring ourselves to a full realization of this great fact, then we are ready for the Path. If we come to know that the Infinite One, all beings of this world and ourselves, all make up one Being, that Being governed by the great Law of Love, then we are ready to go forward with faces to the light.

Side by side with this noble concept is another Sanskrit expression, which in a general way supports the same fundamental idea. It sums up in three words the entire philosophy of our kinship with all that lives. It forms a rational basis for a universal love. It lays the foundation for a common interest and a universal brotherhood, including all living beings. It is:

Tat Tvam Asi

It means: 'Thou art that', and has a twofold practical meaning. First, it teaches that this individual is that individual. This is not nonsense. It means that every individual is so closely akin to all others that no real distinction can be made between them. In a very real sense each one is identical with every other one and they are all of the same divine essence.

Secondly, this Sanskrit epigram means that each individual is the Supreme One. There is no essential difference then between the Supreme Good and the individual man. They are one spirit, one essence, and we should regard ourselves as living a part of the infinite life and as expressing divinity in every act of our lives. The man is just a spark from the great central sun, but identical in substance. There is a time in the upward journey of the students of the Masters when they behold the majestic beauty and grandeur of one of the greatest Lords of the upper worlds. His name is Sohang. When the student beholds him, he is amazed to find himself in such perfect oneness with that wonderful soul. At that moment the consciousness comes to him with overwhelming joy— "I am that!" This is the real meaning of the word *Sohang*. As the student advances upward on this Path, he has an increasing consciousness that he is himself one with the Supreme One. This is pure Santon ki Shiksha, but it finds an echo in the Vedas.

This doctrine of universal oneness, and founded upon it a universal love, is probably the most important philosophical principle that enters into the mental preparation of the student for this Path. If he can accept this and make it a part of his thinking in all of his relationships, he is ready to go forward. His viveka is already accomplished.

As a part of one's searching discrimination, he should be acquainted with the four modes of mental action. He will then be able to see clearly what must be done to handle any situation. From then on, he can act always with clear-cut understanding. They are: (1) *Scattering,* running out after all sorts of objects, pleasures, works, friends, properties, etc. This is the way the mind acts most of the time. For a student of the Masters this is one of the most troublesome qualities, and it must be overcome before concentration can be effected. (2) *Darkening,* dullness, laziness, then injury, evil of all sorts, ending in destruction. (3) *Gathering,* striving to overcome the scattering and darkening tendencies and reversing the processes, and beginning to gather the mind at one point. This is the first step toward concentration. The beginning is made by confining the attention to one thing at a time, then selecting a center of attention. (4) *Concentration,* the one-pointed form of mental action which, when perfected, leads to samadhi. It is only the superior soul, after long practice, who attains the fourth form of mental action. But that is the goal for all who enter the Path of the Masters. Out of that the genius is born, and the crown of all genius is Mastership. Those who seek to enter this Path must decidedly bring the mind under such discipline as to rid it of the first and second forms of its habitual action completely, and then gain the third and fourth forms.

3. The Christ Attitude of Mind

His whole life being one of devotion and service, Jesus is a very inspiring example to anyone approaching the Path of discipleship. It is well that we seek to find out his mental attitude toward the whole of life, and especially toward the kingdom which he asserted lies inside of man. His life indicates the Way of discipleship. If one tries to live and think like Jesus, he will thereby fit himself to enter the Path of the Masters.

The very core and substance of the teachings of Jesus is love to God and man. If one has not this love, at least to some extent, it is quite useless for him to approach the Master. Jesus said so beautifully:

> By this shall all men know that ye are my disciples, if ye have love to one another. (*John 13:35*)

And so this is really the supreme test of discipleship—*love for all that lives*. We have already given some of those great philosophical principles of oneness upon which to base a universal love.

The amazing love which so characterized the life of Jesus is well emphasized in Pascal's *Mystere de Jesus*. "I have loved thee more than thou hast loved thy defilements," said Christ to Pascal.

Truly this sort of love is characteristic of the genuine Master. If the Masters did not love us better than we love our defilements, there would be but little hope for any of us. This is the love of the Master which passeth all human understanding!

Finally, when Jesus was undergoing his long fast, he bravely resisted temptation, showing the most splendid loyalty and the highest type of manhood. The disciple entering this Path must always maintain such a mental attitude in the presence of temptation. He must never waver or weaken in his love or his loyalty.[1]

4. The Gita Ideal of Discipleship

Lord Krishna, in the Gita, has given some of the finest ideals of discipleship to be found in all literature. If anyone approaches the Path of the Masters in the mental attitude taught by the Bhagavad Gita, his success will be assured. Read them over, these exalted statements, and imbibe them, live them, make them your daily bread, and you will surely approach the light on swift wing.[2] To the student who wishes to enter upon this Path, we believe there is nothing better as a mental preparation than the ideals set forth in the Gita. They offer an ideal not easy to acquire, but by persistent effort one can attain it. Then he is qualified, in fact he is duly and truly prepared, to begin his upward journey.

But the student must know that this attitude of mind, no matter how exalted it may be, is not itself the final goal. It is not the ultimate means of ascending the ladder of attainment. That alone will never carry anyone to the spiritual heights. That is one fatal mistake that many have made—believing that the cleansing of the vessel was equivalent to filling it. They read the Gita and other books, imbibe many of their sublime precepts, and then sit down contentedly to imagine that they are well on the Way toward the goal. This is a delusion. Those books and ideals will never lead anyone to spiritual liberty. The reason is that they can never take

---

1. For the essential substance of the teachings of Jesus, the reader may refer to Chapter Two, Section 18.
2. See Chapter Two, Section 10.

the place of a living Master. The ideals, even if thoroughly assimilated, only serve to cleanse the vessel, to prepare the mind for something real. The student is just then ready to begin the Great Work. When that preparation is made, the living Master will then give to the student the nectar of immortality, which is to fill the vessel anew after its cleansing.

If the disciple has attained the mental attitude suggested above, he is then ready for his initiation by the Master. If he does not attain this attitude until after his initiation, he must certainly attain it before he can advance very far on the inner Path.

5. Vairagya, the Next Step on the Path

It is our conscientious aim not to confuse the student with too many technicalities or details. We wish to so emphasize the essential points that they may be readily grasped and never forgotten. Hence, many things which are interesting and good must be omitted. The bulk of Indian literature is full of such things. But the great mass of it is more or less confusing, except to the pundits who have spent their lives in its study. Even they do not all agree. Happily, most of it is not at all essential on the Path of the Masters. It is more or less like a great storehouse of curious antiques. So let us stick to the essentials.

Vairagya is the next important step in mental preparation for the Path, after viveka has been well done. We believe the viveka through which most Western students pass before arriving at this Path includes a search, often a very long one, through the literature of nearly all the occult movements of modern times as well as the sacred books of the East. Before arriving at the Master's feet, we generally make our way through whole libraries of books on all sorts of themes. When we have gone through them all, and finally come to realize that they do not offer the ultimate solution of our problems, we come to the living Master. It is only then that the dove finds rest for her weary wings.

Even after coming to the Master, many students keep on reading every sort of book they can get hold of on similar subjects.

This is partly from habit, partly from desire to find a more perfect clarification of their own thoughts. Some books help and some do not. But up to the present, almost no book has been prepared in English which gives any satisfactory exposition of the Santon ki Shiksha. Before taking up the real work of the inner Path, the student will do well to seek a clear understanding of the essentials of the Path, what it is and what he is to gain by it, what to do and what not to do. He should imbibe and assimilate the ideals of the great Masters, so far as he can, and his higher intelligence should be so far satisfied as to place himself gladly under the directions of the Master. Ideals are of much greater value than detailed plans and working rules.

Having the mind saturated with the highest ideals, and fully satisfied as to the underlying principles of this system, he is then ready to proceed to get some actual experience on the Path. At this point, his next step is what Masters and pundits call vairagya. This means the *mental detachment* of oneself from the external world. This is real vairagya. It does not in any way teach or imply that one should physically detach himself from the world. He need not leave his family or society, his public or private duties. The Masters never teach that sort of vairagya, although it has been followed by many yogis.

It must be kept in mind that the Path of the Masters is not that of yogis. The Masters do not encourage asceticism among their disciples. Detachment, as taught by the Masters, does not imply austerities. Vairagya means that one is to detach himself in his affections, in his innermost feelings and interests. Essentially, this means that one is to cease to identify himself with his possessions and environment. He must not make them the substance of his life and thought. In other words, he must always keep his own independence of them. And this applies to one's own family as well as to all else.

This, however, does not mean that one is not to love his family, but he can love with detachment. One may love while keeping his own independence. Then, if he loses them, which is always a possibility, his life is not utterly wrecked, and at the same time he is able to make progress on the Path, knowing that is of more importance than family, friends, or all worldly possessions. A man must remain in the world so long as he has a single duty to perform, but he is not to love the world. He must not become so bound up with duties, family or worldly interests that he forgets his more important interests. He should never forget that one day he has to leave family, friends and all possessions. And he knows not what day he will be called upon to leave them.

He must leave not only his wealth and loved ones but he must leave his own body. He can take nothing with him, except his inner possessions. Material things and people all belong to the passing show. They all have but a temporary interest. They are not his own, and his attachment to them is only temporary. He must regard them not as his own but as loaned to him for the day, the moment, that he may both serve them and use them. This is vairagya in the real sense of the term. The deeper meaning of vairagya is very beautifully borne out in some of the quotations from the Gita, as given in Chapter Eleven, Section 10 of this book.

One word of caution must be uttered here. The student who gains the attitude of mind outlined above and who detaches himself from the love of the world, must never assume an attitude of self-righteousness and set himself up as something above others. He may not regard himself as having attained, while he looks down upon all others as his inferiors. This would automatically defeat his aims and nullify all progress made. He must always keep his ahankar, 'vanity', subdued, and he must allow the sweetest charity and humility to have full sway over all his thoughts and actions.

It is a principle of Nature that whatever we desire or love begins at once to travel toward us, unless a stronger force from a different direction draws it away. Attention and love are the means of connecting us with objects external to ourselves. When we are bound to objects of desire, they tie us down to them and to the world. How can we get up again? By vairagya, 'detachment'. By desire, we are bound to objects of desire. This is why the complete detachment of the mind from every worldly object is necessary if we are to enter upon the upward Path. That detachment avoids bondage to the world and its objects of sense desire. This is why we should not love anything with a desire to possess it. The moment we do that, we enter the first stages of slavery. This applies even to wife or family as well as to worldly goods. But as said before, this does not exclude love of family.

A 'detached devotion' to family may not be so easy. But it can be acquired. We believe that a 'detached love' is a much higher and nobler sort of love than that which demands possession, and then that possession goes on to self-identification with the objects of one's love. When such identification takes place, one is completely 'lost'. He is not himself anymore, and he is even less able to serve the objects of his affection while he is a slave to them.

We must not even desire to get rewards for our services. So long as a man craves rewards, he is bound to those rewards, and yin quo (karma) is his Master. This is the sage advice of the Tao. By all means, he who seeks liberation must cultivate complete detachment from all objects of sense, and he must harbor no desire for them. He must hold no concern at all about the rewards of his actions. He must attain that state of mind which is *like the sun, shining upon all alike, yet asking nothing in return.* This is what the Master really does. And this is our ideal. The soul lives forever by *giving,* not by receiving. This is the grand paradox. You get most by giving most. Conversely, by receiving much you impoverish yourself. By selfish accumulation you become bankrupt. Therefore, detach yourself from all that is perishable and from all thoughts of love for them. *To give and give only, never once thinking of rewards, is the beginning of immortality.*

No man becomes a Kakusha or a Buddha or a Tathagata or a Bodhisattva by fleeing from pain or by seeking comforts and sense pleasures, or by flattering attachments with worldly people; neither can they attain to such degrees by self-immolation. Serene detachment is the last step in the separation of the self from worldly bonds before entering the pathway to liberty. But when a disciple has attained this sublime degree of self-detachment from a corrupt and illusory world, he must still continue to regard his less fortunate fellows with loving sympathy in which there is no taint of vanity or self-righteousness. All Masters have taught:

Man shall not glory in his own enlightenment while he looks down upon others struggling in pain and ignorance, holding himself upon a pinnacle of self-righteousness or vainglory. One's true self includes the whole of life, and the wrongs of all others are your own guilt. *Do not blame men when they err, but purify your own heart.* Do not get angry when the world forgets the Way and ceases to abide by the law, but look for the fault in yourself. *The root of all evil is in yourself.*

This is a very high standard, no doubt. But it is true vairagya. It is an excellent preparation for the Path of the Masters.

6. The Final Destruction of Desire

The last step in the attainment of perfect vairagya is to get rid of desire itself. This is where many noble men and women have failed, even some great yogis. They could not get rid of desire itself, even after they had separated themselves from all connections with the world. But real vairagya is not attained until all desire itself has been overcome. This is perhaps the most difficult of all undertakings. Desire has been declared by all Indian pundits, yogis, and other Indian scholars generally, to be the greatest evil that besets a disciple on the Path of spiritual attainment. Their universal verdict is that desire must be gotten rid of at all costs. The yogi seeks to gain peace of mind, true *shanti,* or *santosh,* by getting rid of desire.

This is surely a shortcut to wealth. If one wants nothing, he has everything. When the great prince Siddhartha went out to seek the way of deliverance from sorrow, he came to the conclusion that desire was the cause of all sorrow. That is one of his 'fourfold noble truths'. From the days of Buddha to the present, the prevailing teaching in the Orient has been that desire is the cause of all sorrows and other ills of man. Hence, the cure of all ills is the destruction of desire. But just how to accomplish this stupendous task has been the big question of the sages. Desire has been pictured as a wild beast roaming the country, seeking whom it may devour. It is our worst enemy, the chief instrument of the mind to bind us to this material world. Desire draws us to objects of sense. *The senses overwhelm the mind and the mind enslaves the soul.* Following desire, the mind goes on creating karma and entangling itself in the net.

Desire never ceases its demands. It doesn't let a man rest, day or night. It follows him into his inner chamber and torments him in the midst of his prayers. It never relents, nor does it ever slacken its chains or cease to apply the lash, even though its poor victim lies weak and spent upon his deathbed. Even then, a desire to live, that overwhelming *trishna,* still holds on to its victim. When all other desires are subdued, even the last remaining wish to continue living in this world is a chain on the spirit. That also must be overcome, and in its stead, a happy surrender to the Master, that he may do as he wishes, should possess the whole consciousness.

The soul, or the mind wrapped in its desires, forgets the fact of *anitya,* the impermanence of all things earthly. He imagines the passing show to be the ultimate reality. He forgets all real values and grasps at the shadow. Always that black and ominous cloud hangs over us, that archenemy of the human race—*avidya,* 'ignorance'. When ignorance darkens the intelligence, then desire creeps up and makes its demands. *Raga* (or kama) 'desire', is always followed by her brood of evil passions, *dosha* (or krodh), moh, lobh and ahankar. They all aid each other in enslaving man.

Now, the paramount question is, how shall the student get rid of desire? The whole world is full of lectures on the evils of desire, but none of them gives any clear or certain recipe for getting rid of it. Only the Masters have the cure. In a word, the Masters get rid of desire by placing before the mind something which has greater attraction. If the student objects that this is not getting rid of desire at all, but is simply substituting one desire for another, then we shall cheerfully agree with him. It is quite true. But the word *desire,* as we use it in this discussion, refers to that attraction which the mind holds for things and sensations of a worldly sort, for things which belong to the animal plane, which hold us upon that plane and monopolize our attention there. Therein lies the evil of desire. Our business is to rise above the world of sense, the world of lower desires. If we are to enter the Path of the Masters, it is absolutely essential that we detach ourselves from sense objects and from all desire for them. We may go away from the things themselves, but that is not getting rid of them. If we do not get rid of the desire itself, we are no better off than at first.

If we can fasten our attention to something which is not of the sense world, something which is imperishable, something which instead of binding us here actually liberates us from this bondage, draws us in the opposite direction, and takes us up to liberty and immortality, then that thing becomes our chief good. A desire for that is not an evil. It is our very salvation. The evil lies not in desire, *per se,* but in the nature of what is desired. This distinction is often overlooked by Orientalists as well as Western students. How can the mind conceive the desire for a good thing to be an evil in and of itself? The good or the evil lies in the direction toward which a desire pulls us.

Let us illustrate. Place upon a table some iron filings, and a small magnet close to them. The filings will move toward the magnet. But if you place a larger magnet on the opposite side of the filings, they will ignore the small magnet and move toward the larger one. It is the old problem in physics—the stronger of two forces must prevail. Now if we go back to our problem of desire, we shall see that the same law operates with equal precision in the realm of mind. The strongest attraction will always prevail. There can be no exception to this law. It is universal, or it would not be a law of Nature. What then is the student on the spiritual Path to do to get rid of the desires which he does not wish to cherish? There can be but one way to get rid of them—manifestly, to set before the mind something which can outpull the lower desires. They must be overcome by a stronger force, acting in the opposite direction. There can be no other way.

The task can never be accomplished by negation. Suppose one of those iron filings had intelligence enough to say, "I will not yield to the pull of the magnet." Suppose it should say to that attraction, "Leave me alone." Do you think the attraction would cease? Never—because it is acting in accord with a universal law. The attraction can be neutralized only by a stronger pull in the opposite direction. An airplane goes up into the heavens. Does the attraction of gravity cease to act upon the plane? By no means, but the downward pull of gravity is neutralized by a greater pull of the engine in the opposite direction. The case is precisely the same in the mental world. The only way to kill an unwholesome attraction is to establish a desirable one in the opposite direction.

If this law in psychology and ethics could only be grasped by the general public, and its principles applied to individual and social problems, it would revolutionize society. And this is the teaching of all great Masters. They do not waste time and effort in lecturing their disciples on the evils of unwholesome desires, but they at once place before the disciple something to take the place of the lower desires, something which lifts the soul and the mind upward instead of pulling it downward. And that is the crux of the whole matter. This is where the Wisdom of the Masters excels. It holds the only effective cure for all human ills arising out of lower desires. It places before the tempted individual something which will tempt him with a greater force in the opposite direction.

7. That Which Kills Desire

There is but one thing known to human experience which will destroy all lower desires. That is *the Audible Life Stream*. It is the supreme instrument of deliverance from bondage. It is the one means of detaching us from worldly objects that perish, and of lifting us up to liberty and light. This Life Stream is placed before us by the Master and we are invited to make use of it. This has been the one remedy in all ages of the world for the cure of worldly desires. We shall attain perfect vairagya only when we enter into that divine Stream consciously.

At first we have to content ourselves solely with controlling desires; but controlling and destroying are two very different things. We may refuse to yield to the pull of desire and go on doing what we know is best. This is temporary mastery. Even if we cannot destroy it at first, we can subdue it, hold it in check and refuse its demands. This we may do, provided bad habit has not destroyed or weakened the will power too seriously. Then, by centering our attention upon that which is within us, following the Master to those higher and more attractive worlds, there we contact that Life Stream in its fullness and its maximum power. When that is consciously entered, when we hear its heavenly music and feel its overwhelming attraction, then we automatically forget all else. The lower attractions cease. We have no desire for anything else. That Current absorbs our entire being. We go with it, hoping never to be separated from it for a single moment.

To help us up to that point we have the Master himself. We see him; we learn to love him; we come to delight in following him, for we know that he is leading us toward the Fountain of Life. As the love for the Master grows, the pull of worldly attractions slackens until by and by it is no longer difficult to deny all lower desires and follow the Master to the inner regions. There the great Life Stream is contacted, the soul is merged into it, and after that there is no more difficulty with desires. They simply disappear, swallowed up in the great Stream. Liberation is then an accomplished fact. As soon as a person becomes one with that luminous Reality, all his problems are solved. He is a free man.

Let us understand this crucial question. How to destroy evil desires? It can never be done by negation. And yet negation is the method employed by 99 percent of the human race, by parents, by teachers, by reformers, by the courts. They all forbid things. They tell people what they must not do. They write in their laws, "Thou shalt not." A few understanding ones offer something better to attract the minds of the disobedient. But the goal can never be achieved by negation. We must always set before the mind something which has a greater power of attraction. If all men could realize the folly and emptiness of worldly sensations, they would then be ready for the Master and for the great Reality —the Holy Shabd. When the attraction for that great Reality becomes dominant in one's life, then all lower attractions cease. And this is the end of desire. It is the beginning of immortality.

The world rushes madly along, the vast majority driven under the lash of one or more of the passions, urged on by desire, hungering and thirsting after the things of sense. This is surely a spectacle to make the gods weep. This is the fatal disease of *karma bandhana*—bondage to works, bondage to pleasures, bondage to a thousand things of sense. Habitual yielding to kam, to objects of sense desire, creates heavier bondage and at the same time it further inflames the desires. The individual sinks deeper and deeper into the mud and mire of sensualism. How shall he ever escape? By attaching himself to a power that is mightier than all sense desires—the divine Bani, the life-giving Stream. The student can do this only by the aid of the Master.

Such a man is in a position analogous to that of a motorcar stuck in the mud. It is unable to extricate itself. But when it is attached to a powerful truck which stands on firm ground, it can be pulled out of the mud at once. In like manner the soul may attach itself to the Master, who is himself free from all bonds and is endowed with power unlimited. The Master unites the soul with the Audible Life Stream. Now the entire process is reversed. Instead of going on down deeper into the mud, he begins to climb toward the higher ground of light and liberty. He now has the power to rise, for in the Life Stream is power abundant.

This is the Shabd Marg, the Way of emancipation. The whole situation of the mind and senses is well illustrated in an analogy taken from the Upanishads:

Know the soul as the rider, the body as the chariot, the *buddhi* (intellect) as the charioteer, and *manas* (mind) as the reins. The sense organs are the horses, and the sense objects are the roads over which the chariot runs. The soul, joined to all of the above, is the experiencer.

This condition of slavery to the senses is well developed by one of India's best writers, Sri Aurobindo Ghose. He says:

There are two possibilities of action of the intelligent will. It may take its downward orientation toward a discursive action of the perceptions and the will, in the triple play of *prakriti* [material Nature], or it may take its upward and inward orientation toward a settled peace and equality in the calm and immutable purity of the conscious, silent soul, no longer subject to the distractions of Nature. In the former alternative, the subjective being is at the mercy of the objects of sense; it lives in the outward contacts of things. That life is the life of desire. The senses, excited by their objects, create a restless, or even a violent, disturbance, a strong or even a headlong outward movement toward the seizure of those objects and their enjoyment, and they carry away the sense mind, as the winds carry away a ship upon the sea. The mind, subjected to the emotions, passions, longings, impulses, awakened by this outward movement of the senses, carries away similarly the intelligent will, which therefore loses its calm discrimination and mastery. Subjection of the soul to the confused play of the three gunas of prakriti, in their eternal entangled twining and wrestling, ignorance, a false sensuous objective life of the soul, enslavement to grief and wrath, and attachment and passion, are the results of the downward trend of the buddhi—the troubled life of the ordinary unenlightened, undisciplined man. Those who, like the Vedevadins, make sense enjoyment the object of action, and its fulfillment the highest aim of the soul, are misleading guides.

The opposite course of action, as said above, is to join one's whole being to the self-active, all-embracing Power, under the directions of a living Master. From this karma bandhana, from this bondage of works and enslavement of passions, nothing in the universe can ever free a soul except the living Master and the Life Current.

Chapter Eleven

THE AUDIBLE LIFE STREAM: THE SOURCE OF ALL BEING

---

1. The Central Fact in Santon ki Shiksha

THE Audible Life Stream is the cardinal, central fact in the science of the Masters. It is the keystone of the arch. It is the cornerstone of the structure. It is the structure itself. And it is the Path of the Masters. One might say that the Master and the Life Stream constitute the Path of the Masters. The great spiritual Current is not only the central fact in the science of the Masters but it is the supreme fact and factor of the entire universe. It is the very essence and life of all things. It is perhaps less known than any other important fact of Nature, yet it is the one determining factor of all Nature. That is indeed a pity. This great truth or fact is significantly spoken of in the first chapter of the Gospel of Saint John:

> In the beginning was the *Word*, and the Word was with God, and the Word was God. The same was in the beginning with God. All things were made by him and without him was not anything made that was made. *(John 1:1–3)*

Here it is definitely stated that something which is called "Word" is identical with God, the Creator.

Although not at all understood by the Christian church, this statement is an important announcement of the stupendous fact of the Audible Life Stream. It is often called the Sound Current, but that is not a good name for it because it is not sufficiently definitive. The Indian name is simply *Shabd;* meaning 'sound', but that is not definitely clear. There are many sounds. *Logos* was the Greek term used by the Neoplatonic school, whose masters were familiar with portions of the Eastern Wisdom. *Logos* means 'the divine Word'. It is this divine current, wave or stream going forth from God himself and flowing throughout the universe. It is not only an emanation from God but it is God himself.

When any man speaks in this world, he simply sets in motion atmospheric vibrations. But when God speaks, he not only sets in motion etheric vibrations, but he himself moves in and through those vibrations. In truth it is God himself that vibrates all through infinite space. God is not static, latent: he is superlatively dynamic. When he speaks, everything in existence vibrates, and that is the Sound, the Shabd; and it can be heard by the inner ear, which has been trained to hear it. It is the divine energy in process of manifestation which is the Holy Shabd. It is, in fact, the only way in which the Supreme One can be seen and heard—this mighty, luminous and musical wave, creating and enchanting.

Now, this great fact of Nature, so little known to either ancient or modern thought, is the vital substance of the science of the Masters. It is cardinal and central in all their teachings. It is the one thing which distinguishes Santon ki Shiksha from all other sciences or systems. It is the very foundation of the Masters' system of yoga. It is the key to all of their success in unfolding their spiritual powers and controlling their minds. It is the one sign by which a real Master may be known and recognized from all others. No one is or can be a genuine Master unless he teaches and practises the Audible Life Stream, because it is impossible for anyone to become a spiritual Master of the highest order unless he consciously utilizes the Life Stream to gain his development.

2. Names of the Supreme Logos

The supreme Logos is commonly called Sound Current in India, among those who speak English. But the best translation which we have been able to discover is 'Audible Life Stream'. This appears to carry its deeper meaning and is more comprehensive and inclusive. It is, in fact, a stream—a life-giving, creative stream— and *it can be heard.* The fact that it is audible is extremely important and that idea must be conveyed, if possible, in any name that is applied to it. This Current or wave contains the sum of all teaching emanating from God. It is his own Word. It includes everything that God has ever said or done. It is God himself in expression. It is the method of God in making himself known. It is his language. It is his *Word.*

This Sound sometimes is called *Name;* in Sanskrit or Hindi, *Nam.* But in English we are not accustomed to put so much meaning in the word *name.* It is only correct if we understand that *Name* or *Nam* stands for all that the Supreme Being is. It is just another way of saying *Word,* and Word is what God says. It is equally what he does. It is the whole of the Divine Being in action. To distinguish God in action from God as divine Essence, we call him Shabd or living Word. The name of anything or anybody is the sound symbol which stands for the reality itself. The name conveys to thought everything which belongs to the reality for which it stands. When the Master is said to 'give Nam' it means that he gives the Current, the reality for which Nam stands. He literally gives the Audible Life Stream itself. (Just how the Master can give it is discussed in Chapter Twelve, Section 4.)

This divine Nam, Sound, or Word, stands for all that God is or has ever said or done. It includes all of his qualities. As said before, it is the only way in which the universal Spirit can manifest itself to human consciousness. So when the Supreme Being manifests himself as Sat Nam in Sach Khand he there becomes fully personified, embodied, and brings into manifestation all of the qualities of deity. As Sat Nam he becomes personal Creator, Lord, God and Father. There be becomes the Fountain out of which the Audible Life Stream proceeds. This Stream may be perceived and heard by all who participate in it throughout all worlds. It may be seen and heard by such as attain an awakened consciousness under the training of a Master. When a man hears it, he hears God. When he feels it, he feels the power of God. This Shabd is, therefore, the Divine Being expressing himself in something that is both audible and visible. This Current must not be understood to be like a river running in one course. It is more like a radio wave flowing out in every direction from the grand central broadcasting station. In fact, it comes from the supreme creative center of the universe of universes.

This wave has two aspects, a centrifugal flow and a centripetal flow. It moves outward from the central dynamo of all creation, and it flows back toward that dynamo. Moving upon that Current, all power and all life appear to flow outward to the uttermost bounds of creation, and again upon it all life appears to be returning toward its source. It is the latter aspect of it with which we have to deal mostly.

Upon that wave we have to depend for our return to our original home. When the Master makes the connection or, as we say in radio, "tunes us in," it is then that we begin our homeward journey leaving all perishable worlds behind us.

This Word is called Nada (pronounced *Nad*) in the Vedas. In Vedanta, sound is always spoken of as creative. Sound, or anything that sounds, is the creative energy. It is referred to as the Nada Brahma, meaning the primal Word of Brahm. By this Nada Brahma all creation was brought into existence. The whole of the visible and invisible universe is the manifestation of this primal Nada. The Nada is the grand symphony out of which all other symphonies flow. It is the primal music of the universe. Every musical cord of this world is an echo of that primal cord. It is the Vadan of the Sufis and the Shabd of the Hindus.

But all Sufis do not distinguish between the primal Word and the manifest word, between the original music and its echo. They are not able to point out the difference between the *dhunatmak* sound and the many *varnatmak* sounds. While we may truly say that all music in the world is a manifestation of the original symphony of the primal Vadan, yet there is a difference between them, a very important difference. The all-creative Nada is that Sound out of which all other sounds arise, while at the same time its heavenly strains linger in all material worlds as echoes of the original melody. It is only these echoes that we hear when we listen to a great orchestra produced by man. Those who love music should remember that they are listening to the distant echoes of the infinite chorus of the universe every time they hear a musical sound upon this plane. But we should always take care to distinguish between the echo and the original. The original cannot, however, be heard by the physical organ of hearing. A finer sense must be developed for that.

This Nada is *Shabd* in Hindi. It is spoken of as the *Shabd Dhun*, 'the melodious sound'. Again, it is called *Akash Bani*, 'heavenly utterance'. Kabir Sahib speaks of it so beautifully as "the pure white music." All Muslim Saints generally refer to it as *Sultan-ul-Azkar*, 'king of the ways', *Ism-i-Azam*, and *Kalma* or *Kalam-i-Ilahi*. It is also called *Surat Shabd Yoga, Anand Yoga* or *Anahad Shabd*, and *Anahad Yoga*. So it has been called by many names in many languages. It is "the still small voice" and "the voice of the silence." It is the same divine sound wave, no matter by what name it may be known. Let no one say it is not a sound because it cannot be heard by the physical ear. The radio electromagnetic waves cannot be heard by the physical ear until they are converted into atmospheric vibrations by the receiving instrument; yet when they are traveling through space they are just as truly sounds. The Shabd is in any case a sound because it can be heard by a finer ear attuned to its higher vibrations.

This Divine Logos is the real 'Lost Word' of the Masonic Order. It is that Word for the restoration of which every Master Mason is taught to look forward into the future ages. Those 'future ages' have now arrived. That 'Lost Word' is now in the mouth of the true Sat Guru, or Master. He is the real Master, compared to whom all other masters are only substitutes, just as the word they give is only a substitute for the true Word.

The real Master now awaits the opportunity to restore the Lost Word to the fraternity. But it remains to be seen if they will open their ears to it. If they can receive it now, "on the five points of fellowship," it will mean a new birth to the fraternity. They need no longer content themselves with the substitute, because the original dynamic Word is now available. They have only to indicate their readiness to receive it. That priceless treasure is now ready for them. But their representative must present himself before the Grand Master of Masters in a manner similar to that of every candidate who knocks at your doors. He also must be prepared in his heart, divested of all rags of self-righteousness; he must come knocking at the door as a poor blind candidate seeking the light. Do not forget that just as in your lodges, it is only the Master who comes out of the East, who is able to give this Word. But your master can give only the substitute, while the real Master is prepared to give you the original Word, which was lost to the fraternity in past ages.

Let us repeat now that the future ages referred to, and for which you have been so long waiting, are now here. Will the brotherhood listen to the challenge of the Master who bids them come and get the Word? In the great drama of the Third Degree almost every precept of the Path of the Masters is foreshadowed. The ritual makes you a substitute master. But the Great Work of the real Master makes the candidate a real Master. This takes place when he has absorbed the Lost Word into his very being and becomes one with it.

The Lost Word is now found again, and it is the Life Stream, the audible Word so emphasized by all the Saints.

3. What Is the Audible Life Stream?

It is not easy to explain exactly what the Audible Life Stream is. It cannot be defined or explained in words. This is so because it is beyond the capacity of any language, and it is also beyond the capacity of this writer. We have never known anyone who could put it into words, because language is limited. If we could summon all the languages ever spoken by man, extracting from them their utmost powers of expression, it were a vain effort even then

to undertake to describe and explain this primary fact of Nature.
It is a story which is never told because it cannot be told. It is a language which has never been spoken or written. It is the ever-living
melody which cannot be recorded on bars and spaces. Its notes
are beyond the strings of any earthly instruments. Its inspiring
chorus rings through every chamber of the soul, but there is no
way to convey the idea to other people who have not heard it.

Its glorious light cannot be pictured on canvas. One sees its
feeble reflections in the morning sky or that of the setting sun, or
in the silvery moon. But its colors are quite beyond the comprehension of any mortal artist; while in its pure state, above the regions of matter, it simply blends into one infinite perfection which
no man can describe, except to say with Soami Ji, "It is all love!"
It is the dhunatmak Word of those regions where language is
useless. It is the smile of the lover which finds its home in the
heart, but cannot be expressed in words. When it is heard, the enchanted listener is silent and filled with a great joy.

Stated in the simplest words we can employ, the Audible Life
Stream is the Supreme Creator himself vibrating through space. It
is the wave of spiritual life going forth from the Creator to every
living thing in the universe. By that Current he has created all
things, and by it he sustains them. In it they all live and move and
have their being, and by that same Current they will ultimately
return to their source of being.

Try now to get a picture of that Luminous Reality, the Grand
Orchestra of the universe. Its heavenly strains are not only filling
all interstellar space but they are ringing with far more enchanting music through all the higher worlds beyond the utmost bounds
of the physical. The higher we go, the more enchanting the music.
In those higher worlds the music is less mixed with matter, and so
it is not dulled. After passing the third region on the Path of the
Masters, this sublime chorus becomes so overwhelmingly attractive that the soul grows impatient to go on up. He is absorbed in it.
He lives in it day and night. It is his life, his joy, his spiritual food.
There is not a cubic millimeter of space in existence which is not
filled with this music. Sweeter and sweeter its heavenly strains
vibrate through every living being, great or small, from world to

world, and from universe to universe. Its life-giving melodies may not be consciously heard by those who are not trained to catch them, but there is not a living being in all creation which does not derive its life from this Current. All joy that has ever thrilled a living soul has come out of this Divine Harmonic. How great is this Luminous Reality!

If you still think much of the word *religion,* then you may say that this Current is the only real religion. Or better, it is the giver of all genuine religion. It is the one and only thing in the world which actually binds men back to God. That is the meaning of our word *religion*—something which binds the soul back to God. Without this Stream, nothing could live for a single moment or even exist. All life and all power come from it. From the crawling ant to the thunderbolt, from the tidal wave to the solar cycle, every manifestation of dynamic energy comes from this Stream. From the burning orbs of the Milky Way to the flicker of a candle, all take their light and energy from this grand central power. The pull of gravity, the flash of lightning, the building of thought-forms, and the love of the individual soul—all come from this Current primordial.

That which physical science calls energy, which the Orientals call Prana, is only a manifestation of this Life Stream, 'stepped down' to meet material conditions. Like electricity in the air, it is omnipresent. It is also omnipotent. In it lies all energy, either latent or dynamic. It only awaits the proper conditions to express itself as dynamic force in one form or another. It has many forms of expression, most of which are not yet known to physical science.

Of course, it has to be stepped down, and at each step down it takes a different character or quality to which we give names if we can demonstrate them at all. Science has not yet discovered most of them. But every force known, from primal energy called Prana down to electricity and magnetism, are all modified forms of the same eternal Current. Its stepping down is necessary to serve the common cosmic and human needs. But at last it is all one force. It is the Supreme One, manifested and manifesting.

The tremendous heat, energy, and light of our sun and of all suns are all derived from this Stream. Every ray of light in the universe is a phenomenon of this infinite stream of light. Upon its power hangs every star in its orbit. Not a single rose may bring forth its buds without this power, and no little child smiles without manifesting this power. If we speak of attributes, let us speak cautiously. Who can comprehend it or assign qualities? Who can analyze it? But we know from its manifestations that it has at least three very wonderful attributes:

Love—Wisdom—Power

And the greatest of these is love. It is believed by some to be quite true if we say that this Self-Luminous Reality has but one attribute—*love*. And this would coincide perfectly with the teaching of Jesus when he said, "God is love." What more can be said? God is love and love is God. They are the same and they are identical with this Life Stream. The theme is too deep for words. Language fails us. Thought itself is lost in a blaze of light! And that light is the Audible Life Stream—the one Self-Luminous Reality!

4. The Life Stream Can Be Heard

We come back now to that particular phase of the Audible Life Stream which concerns us most—the fact that it can be heard. This is an amazing thing, marvelous to contemplate! This idea is so utterly new, to the Western world in particular. It amounts to the most important discovery of modern thought, and yet it is not a modern discovery. It is a fact of Nature well known to Masters during the most remote ages. It is the loss of this important knowledge that has left most of the world in spiritual darkness. From age to age, the great Masters come to revive this knowledge, after materialism has obscured it.

As said before, it is not heard with the physical ear. But it can be heard, and everyone has the capacity. It only requires the development of an inner and finer organ of hearing which every person possesses. It is developed under the instructions of a living

Master. This fact of hearing the Sound is our supreme joy, for it points directly to our ultimate spiritual freedom. The Masters teach their students exactly how to develop this inner hearing. After that, the Life Stream can be heard as distinctly and perfectly as we can hear anything on this plane by means of the physical ears.

If it be true that no man has ever seen God, it means that he has not seen him with the physical eyes. Yet on the inner and higher planes of seeing and hearing, God may be both seen and heard. To accomplish this marvelous achievement, it is necessary to seek first a living Master and then place ourselves under his instructions. You must then succeed. God is seen and heard by all initiates of a living Master who devote themselves to the practice as given by the Master. This is one of the demonstrated facts of the science of the Masters. It is not theory. It is a fact of experience verified over and over again many thousands of times. There are many people personally known to this writer who have demonstrated this fact in their own experiences. God is seen and heard by all who try according to the method of the Masters. They cannot fail if they do the work.

This creative Current, filling all space, may be likened to the electromagnetic waves of the radio. The receiving set is the human body, more accurately, the astral body within the physical. The receiving set, standing on your table, simply has to be 'tuned in' in order to receive the music. Each individual man or woman is a receiving set. As soon as he is tuned in by the Master, he is ready to receive "the pure white music" spoken of by Kabir. It then remains only to keep the instrument in proper order to go on enjoying this melodious Bani. Of course, but few get the music at once after their initiation. It takes a little time to develop the inner hearing. The entire body, and more particularly the mind and astral body, must be cleaned and purified, and then attuned to the higher vibrations. After that, the music comes clearly. When one begins to hear it, he is filled with a great joy; for there is nothing in the world to be compared with it.

The full chorus of a Handel, the sublimest strains of a Wagner, are all dull when compared with this Bani. If we put into one composition all the values of a Bach and a Beethoven, let the harp and the violin, the pipe organ and the flute, combine to interpret the music of all the masters of music, even then you could not produce one minor chord of this sublime enchantment. It takes possession of the soul of the hearer; it recreates him, and then he finds himself a citizen of a new world. The attractions of sense disappear. He is exalted. His heart is purified and his mind is renewed. He lives anew. He has become immortal. How can the shadow of death ever cross his path? He has definitely entered the Stream of Everlasting Life!

When it is time for him to leave the body, he goes as one who throws off an old garment. Upon the divine wave he ascends to the bosom of God. No sorrow of earth can ever again submerge him. He rises above all turbulent waves of passion, as a man mounts the sky in an airplane, while the floods of muddy water roll by beneath him. He rises triumphantly above every evil. One can never again be unhappy after he has once participated in this life-giving music. Long after the melody itself is shut out by attention to things of this world, the joy of it goes on ringing through one's entire being. But the same ringing delight may be heard again any moment that the student wishes to listen to it. He has only to sit down, withdraw his attention from the outer world, and concentrate a little.

From the sacred hour when the student hears this music, he is never again alone or lonely. He may wander far from home or friends, but he is never lonely. In a true sense he enjoys the companionship of God himself. The Supreme One is always present with him, playing for his delight the grandest chorus of the universe! Its sweet tones are calling him, tenderly calling him back home. And he longs to be on the way.

5. The Sufi Idea of the Divine Vadan

The Sufis are divided into two classes—the *Ulvis,* who know of and often hear the primal music, or at least they did in the early days, and the *Siflis,* who have lost all knowledge of it or perhaps never had it. The latter class now speaks of 'the Heavenly Symphony' in figurative language, like Rabindranath Tagore trying to explain the rhapsodies of Kabir Sahib. Having no understanding of the inner symphony, they fix all attention upon its outward expressions in the manifest universe. Doing this, many of them become great lovers of music, and sometimes they are great musicians. They love the harmonies which the physical ear can hear, but they have lost the greater harmonies of which these lower sounds are no more than a feeble reflection. At any rate, if they know of them, they do not speak of them publicly. They speak much of the outer music, however.

One noted Sufi, Hazrat Inayat Khan, says that the physical universe is all music, that it is all a manifestation of music, and that *it was created by music.* How true this is, although he does not himself seem to understand the full significance of his own statement. He intends his words to be taken figuratively, when in fact they should be accepted in the most literal meaning of the words themselves. The universe was literally created by the great Shabd, the primal music of all words. This divine symphony or chorus is everywhere in all men and in all things. Indeed the whole universe is one grand Vadan. He agrees with Vedanta that the universe was created by the Nada Brahma, and this is exactly what all the Masters teach. But Inayat Khan does not realize how much he misses by looking to the manifest universe for his great Vadan instead of looking inside for it. Doing this, he has to be contented with the reflection, the faint echo, of the pure original melody.

But the great Masters make contact with the pure primal Current itself and thus enjoy the most perfect satisfaction, being absorbed in it. That creative primal music is vibrating through all the universe, and it may be sensed to some extent by many of the finer types of men and women. And this is why some of them become very great lovers of music. The greater the refined sensibilities of any person, the nearer he or she is to the primal Current. It permeates everything, as said before, from rosebud to star, and it is the life of everything. But this varnatmak music, so deadened and dulled by contact with matter, is not to be compared with the original. That original is the only genuine Vadan, the Audible Life Stream.

An extremely interesting Sufi effort to interpret the Surat Shabd of the Masters is the following extract[1] by Hazrat Inayat Khan. It shows how this central idea of the great Shabd has taken hold of all mystic thought, even if it is not clearly comprehended.

"Abstract Sound is called *Saute Surmadi* by the Sufis. All space is filled with it. . . . It was the *Saute Surmadi,* the sound of the abstract, which Mohammed heard in the cave of Gar-e-Hira. Moses heard this very sound on Mount Sinai. . . . It was heard by Christ when his Heavenly Father manifested to him in the wilderness. Shiva heard the same *Anahad Nada* during his *samadhi* in the cave of the Himalayas. The flute of Krishna is symbolic of the same sound. This sound is the source of all revelation to the Masters. . . . Whoever has followed the strains of this sound has forgotten all earthly distinctions. . . . The sound of the abstract is always going on within, around and about man. Man does not hear it as a rule, because his consciousness is entirely centered in his material existence. . . . In comparison to it, the sounds of the earth are like that of a whistle to a drum. When the abstract sound is audible, all other sounds become indistinct to the mystic.

"The sound of the Abstract is called *Anahad* in the Vedas, meaning unlimited sound. The Sufis' name is *Surmadi,* which suggests the idea of intoxication. The word *intoxication* is here used to signify upliftment, exaltation, freedom of the soul from its earthly bondage. Those who are able to hear the *Saute Surmadi* and meditate on it are relieved from all worries, anxieties, sorrows, fears and diseases; and the soul is freed from captivity in the senses and in the physical body. The soul of the listener becomes the all-pervading consciousness. Some train themselves to hear the *Saute Surmadi* in the solitude of the seashore, on the riverbank, and in the hills and dales; others accomplish it while sitting in the caves of the mountains, or when wandering constantly through forests and deserts, keeping themselves in the wilderness apart from the haunts of men. Yogis and ascetics blow *Singhi* (a horn) or

---

1. Hazrat Inayat Khan, *Mysticism of Sound* (California: Hunter House, 1979). Chapter 8.

Shankha (a shell) which awakens in them this inner tune. Dervishes play *Nai* or *Algoza* (a double flute) for the same purpose. The bells and gongs in the churches and temples are meant to suggest the same sacred sound, and thus lead a man toward the inner life.

"This sound develops through ten different aspects, because of its manifestations through ten different tubes of the body. It sounds like thunder, the roaring of the sea, the jingling of bells, the running water, the buzzing of bees, the twittering of sparrows, the Vina, the whistle, or the sound of *Shankha*, until it finally becomes the *Hu*, the most sacred of all sounds. This sound *Hu* is the beginning and the end of all sounds, be they from man, bird, beast or thing. A minute study will prove this fact, which can be realized by listening to the sound of the steam engine or of a mill; the echo of bells or gongs gives a typical illustration of the *Hu* sound.

"The Supreme Being has been called by various names in different languages, but the mystics have known him as *Hu* (Arabic), the natural name not man-made, the *only* name of the Nameless, which all nature constantly proclaims. The sound *Hu* is most sacred; the mystics of all ages called it *Isme-i-azam*, the name of the Most High, for it is the origin and end of every sound as well as the background of each word. The word *Hu* is the spirit of all sounds and of all words, and is hidden under them all, as the spirit in the body. It does not belong to any language, but no language can help belonging to it. This alone is the true Name of God, a Name that no people and no religion can claim as their own. This word is not only uttered by human beings, but is repeated by animals and birds. All things and beings exclaim this name of the Lord; for every activity of life expresses distinctly this very sound. This is the Word mentioned in the Bible as existing before the light came into the world: 'In the beginning was the Word, and the Word was with God, and the Word was God'.[1]

"The mystery of *Hu* is revealed to the Sufi who journeys through the Path of Initiation. Truth, the knowledge of God, is termed by a Sufi *Hak*. If we divide the word *Hak* into two parts, it becomes *hu-ak*. *Hu* signifying 'God', or 'Truth', and *ak* in Hindu-

---

1. John 1:1.

stani meaning 'one', both meanings together expressing one God and one Truth. *Hukikat* in Arabic means the essential truth, final reality. *Hakim* means master and *hukim* means knower; all of which words express the essential characteristics of life.

"*Aluk* is the sacred word that the Vairagis, the adepts of India, exclaim as the chant. In the word *Aluk* are expressed two words, *Al*, meaning 'from', and *huk*, 'truth'; both words together express God, the source of all truth.

"The sound *Hu* becomes limited in the word *hum*, for the letter *m* closes the lips. This word in Hindustani expresses limitation, *hum* means 'I', or 'we', both of which words signify ego. The word *Humsa* is the sacred word of the yogis which illumines the ego with the light of reality. The word *Huma* in the Persian language stands for a fabulous bird. There is a belief that if the *Huma* bird sits for a moment on the head of anybody it is a sign that the person will become a king. Its true explanation is, that when man's thoughts so evolve that they break all limitations he becomes as a king. It is the lack of language that it can only describe the Most High as something like a king. It is said in the old traditions that Zoroaster was born of a *huma* tree. This explains the words in the Bible: 'Except a man be born of water and of the Spirit, he cannot enter the kingdom of God'. In the word *huma*, *hu* represents spirit, and the word *mah*, in Arabic, means 'water'. In English the word *human* explains two facts which are characteristic of humanity—*hu* means 'God', and *man* means 'mind', which comes from the Sanskrit *manah*, mind being the ordinary man. In other words, *Hu*, God, is in all things and beings, but it is only man by whom he is known, or who is capable of knowing him. *Human*, therefore, means the God-conscious being, God-realized, or the God-man. The word *Humd* means 'praise'; *humid*, 'praiseworthy'.

"*Hur*, in Arabic, means 'the beauties of the heavens'.... *Ahura Mazda* is the name of God as known to the Zoroastrians. In this first word, *Ahur* suggests *Hu*, upon which the whole name is built. All of these examples signify the origin of the idea of God in the word *Hu*, and the life of God in everything that lives.... *Huva* is the origin of the name of Eve, symbolic of manifestation

of deity in womankind. . . . The words found in the Bible—*Eloi,
Elohim,* and *Alleluya*—are all corruptions of the original word
Allah-hu.

"The more a Sufi listens to the *Saute Surmadi,* the sound of
the abstract, the more his consciousness becomes free from all the
limitations of life. The soul then floats above the physical and
mental planes without any special effort on man's part, which
shows its calm and peaceful state. A dreamy look comes into his
eyes and his countenance becomes radiant. He experiences the
unearthly joy and rapture of *Wajad* ('ecstasy'). When ecstasy
overwhelms him, he is neither conscious of the physical existence,
nor of the mental. This is the Heavenly Wine, to which all Sufi
poets refer, and is totally unlike the momentary intoxications of
this mortal plane. A heavenly bliss then springs in the heart of a
Sufi, his mind is purified from sin, his body from all impurities,
and a pathway is opened for him toward the worlds unseen; he
begins to receive inspirations, intuitions, impressions and revelations, without the least effort on his part. He is no longer dependent upon a book or a teacher, for divine wisdom, the light of his
soul, the Holy Spirit, begins to shine upon him."

Of course, the Holy Spirit referred to just above is the divine
Vadan, the Audible Life Stream.

It is indeed quite refreshing and inspiring when one can enjoy
the harmonies of this world, can feel in his innermost consciousness the divine melodies that float like the whispered words of
God through all space. But the grandest of them all is the Anahad
Shabd. The gentle echoes of that sublime music are floating
through all lower worlds. They are but the whisperings of the real
music, the supreme Vadan. But we lose much if we are limited to
these echoes, however sweet they may be. We should not fail to
grasp the primal Current from which all other music is derived.

But this primal Shabd can be heard only by going inside, and
that again requires a Master to lead the way. The vibrations of the
outer world may be sensed only while the genuine primal Current
may be actually heard by the finer sense of audition. This inner
music is so enrapturing, so captivating, that all who hear it become exceedingly joyous, so much so that they often forget all

else; and then they are drawn upward with such force that the whole physical world becomes unreal and uninteresting. By the power of this music a man is literally pulled upward toward the highest heavens whence that music has descended. And so this becomes the chief means of deliverance from this world and its sense bondage.

6. The Only Means of Spiritual Liberation

The Masters all teach that there is no other means of spiritual liberation except the Shabd. Without actual, conscious participation in the Audible Life Stream, no one can ever escape the net of karma and reincarnation or ever become free and happy. If anyone feels inclined to deny this statement, ask him if he is himself free and happy, or if he knows anyone else who is. Ask him if he knows of any other way a man can free himself. Ask him if he is master of his own body or if he has conquered the last enemy, death. If he is honest he must say no. But all of this and much more is accomplished through the divine wave of spiritual power which we call the Shabd. Hence all the Saints lay the strongest emphasis upon this great Reality.

In fact, without this Life Stream, no Saint could ever manifest upon this earth, and hence the whole world would continue to sit in darkness through endless ages. No soul can ever escape from this dark material world without conscious participation in and a personal relationship with the Current. He should knowingly merge himself in that Life Stream, and upon it he will rise to liberty. It cannot be done in any other way. By this Stream alone one is enabled to transcend all lower regions and rise to the highest heavens. This stupendous fact having been proved by the Saints—and they have demonstrated it times without number—they offer that Path, that Fountain of Life, as the only actual means of spiritual liberation. Saints *know* that there is no other way. By other means men may advance some distance toward the light. Without a perfect Guru, and through him attaining conscious union with the Audible Life Stream, no one may hope to go further than the first region of light, commonly spoken of as the astral plane, possibly a little beyond that in a few rare instances. Then they are confronted with such insuperable difficulties, such gigantic obstacles, that they simply cannot go further. The Guru is then the absolute *sine qua non* of further advance.

This Path is known as *the Royal Highway* of the Saints, *el Camino Real*. It is the only Path that leads to spiritual light and complete emancipation. This is the gospel of the Life Stream. He who drinks of this Stream can never thirst again, but in him is a well of water springing up into life everlasting. This was the water of life which Jesus offered to the woman at the well of Sychar, of which, he said, if she would drink, she would never thirst again.

Truly, when one begins consciously to participate in this Life Stream, there is in him a well of water ever springing up, sufficient to supply the whole world. There is a Fountain which cleanses him, and then goes on giving life to every soul who comes in touch with it. It purges both mind and soul, making them whiter than snow. It is the real nectar of immortality. It flows on forever, a healing Stream for the nations. He who drinks of it will never again go about the world seeking food for his spirit. He will not look elsewhere for the light. A man in the broad sunlight will not go about seeking a candle. It is the medicine which cures every sickness. It is the one remedy which the great physician, the Master, offers for the relief of all ills. It is the universal elixir, the solace of all. It soothes away pain and gives rest to the tired. This is indeed the true light which lighteth every man who comes into the world. It is God, the Supreme Father. It is Wisdom, Power and Love. And this is the Audible Life Stream, known and practised by all of the great Masters of the East during untold ages of time.

7. New Birth Through the Shabd

It may be of interest to the student who was brought up in the Christian faith to know that Jesus himself very definitely mentions the Sound Stream and teaches that the new birth is to be attained by means of it. This is exactly what is insisted upon by all great Masters. Jesus himself says it can be heard, and yet the Church has entirely lost the meaning. In the first chapter of the Gospel of Saint John, it is called *the Word,* through which all creation came into existence. If only the Christian disciples had once grasped this fundamental fact and held on to it, it would have meant a very different history for the Church. But unhappily the real meaning which Jesus had in mind was wholly lost. In the third verse of Chapter III, Jesus speaks of contacting the Current, and of actually hearing it. Then he distinctly says the new birth is attained through it. All of this is exactly in line with the teachings of the Masters. But it is a pity that the Churches have never understood this reference of Jesus to the most important experience which can possibly come within the range of human life. To the Church this new birth is a mysterious operation not in the least comprehended. In some way it is supposed to be performed by the Holy Spirit. But the exact process is quite unknown to them. The Masters alone can explain this statement of Jesus, for the Masters alone know exactly what the new birth consists of.

Bear in mind that birth means bringing out into the light. Jesus says:

> That which is born of the flesh is flesh; and that which is born of the
> Spirit is spirit.   (*John 3:6*)

Holy Spirit, Spirit, and Shabd—all mean exactly the same thing. Then in the eighth verse, Jesus clearly mentions actually hearing the sound of the Spirit which gives the new birth. He says:

> The wind bloweth where it listeth, and thou hearest the sound there-
> of, but canst not tell whence it cometh and whither it goeth: So is
> every one that is born of the Spirit.   (*John 3:8*)

In this manner Jesus makes it very definite that just as the body of a man is born from woman, body from body, so the spirit of man is born, brought to light out of the dark womb of matter and its foul corruptions through the action of the Divine Spirit in the form of the Audible Life Stream. We know that it was to this Life Stream that he referred because he so definitely says it can be heard. When that birth takes place the soul actually hears the Sound just as definitely and distinctly as he can hear the rustle of the wind in the tall pines. But as no one can tell exactly where the wind comes from, so no one can tell where that inner Sound comes from, nor where it is going.

It would be difficult to make a more definite confirmative statement in support of the Audible Stream than this one of Jesus, and yet the theologians have never had the remotest idea of its meaning. If they had ever grasped this one fundamental truth, the whole theology of the Church would have been different. There is no new birth without this Holy Shabd, and there is no such thing as contacting the Current until one has first found a real and a living Master to 'tune him in' with it. So there is the entire matter in a few words. In the Bible, wherever the term *Holy Spirit* is used, it refers to this Sound Current and nothing else. It cannot possibly mean anything else. If it is a thing of spirit and if it is to be heard, as Jesus so distinctly says, then the spiritual Sound Current is the only thing to which it can possibly refer.

The much-discussed Holy Trinity of the Church is nothing more nor less than the gracious Trinity of all the great Masters— the Supreme Father, the Master and the Shabd. These are literally and exactly the Father, the Son and the Holy Spirit. It is much to be regretted that the Church itself never knew the real meaning of the Trinity, about which so many of its debates have raged and books have been written since the days of Athanasius down to the present time. If rightly understood, there is no difficulty at all in the idea of these three in one. The Supreme Father is the Universal One. The Master is a man who has made himself one with the Supreme Father, and the Shabd is the Supreme Spirit in process of manifestation throughout the universe. The Master is now the representative and the spokesman of the Supreme Father on this earth plane. He is the real Son of God. All Masters are real Sons of God. In fact, all men are, but the Master is a perfected Son. There is not the slightest philosophical difficulty in this concept. It is a sublime reality.

Had the disciples of Jesus finished their training and become one with the Life Stream—in other words, if they had themselves become Masters—the whole course of history might have been very different. But instead of that, their Master was snatched away from them by death before their course of development had more than fairly begun, after which the pure spiritual science which Jesus taught was soon obscured and lost. With that vanished among Christians the last remnant of knowledge concerning the Audible Life Stream. The history of Jesus and his teachings were covered up in a mass of dogmas and superstitions.

In the second chapter of the Acts of the Apostles an account is given of what happened on the day of Pentecost. They heard a sound "as of a mighty rushing wind" and then they saw lights, like "tongues of fire" sitting upon the heads of the apostles, and then they "were all filled with the Holy Ghost" (the Sound Current), and they began to speak in foreign tongues. Now this is a phenomenon which may happen, and often does happen, with disciples of any great Master. But it is an experience which comes in the very beginning of their development.

Often it is as if one is standing between two buildings, and then a sound comes like that of a train rushing by, heard for a moment and then vanished. This is something like the "rushing mighty wind" spoken of in the Bible. Other sounds are heard from time to time—eight or ten of them. All these sounds are heard before the true Shabd is heard. Again, one of the lights seen by all students of the Master appears much like the "tongue of fire" spoken of in the New Testament. Later the student sees many more lights and hears much more of the heavenly Bani. As a result of these experiences, the disciple is filled with increased light and power. Among other things, he is *able to understand all languages*. He understands them all, as if each one was speaking his own language. This is the universal experience of students of the Masters and is encountered in the first region on the Path of the Saints. Everybody understands the language of all others no matter what it may be. To become "filled with the Holy Spirit" is simply to hear and participate in the Audible Life Stream and to become absorbed in it, to become one with it. In becoming one with it, the student comes into possession of many of the higher powers of that Life Force.

8. Shams-i-Tabriz on the Life Stream

In the writings of all the Saints there is frequent mention of the Life Stream. Kabir sings of it in rapturous strains. In the Granth Sahib, the Holy Book of the Sikhs, there is frequent mention of it. Every Saint who has written anything at all has spoken of the Holy Shabd as the chief thing of importance. In the *Sar Bachan* of Soami Ji there is constant reference to it. We cannot reproduce the writings of the Saints here. They would not mean so much to the Western reader as they do to the Indian student. But we wish to mention one in particular who speaks so delightfully of the Audible Life Wave, corroborating the words of Jesus and of all other Saints. This is Shams-i-Tabriz, a Persian Saint of the later Middle Ages. It is difficult to say which of the two, Kabir Sahib or Shams-i-Tabriz, speaks more lovingly of the Life Stream. Their songs are most inspiring. Tagore has translated many of the songs of Kabir; but himself having no knowledge of the Life Stream, he does not seem to have grasped the real significance of Kabir's teachings.

The following was translated from the Persian by Judge Munshi Ram and Professor Jagat Singh[1] and was arranged in its present form by this writer, great care having been taken to preserve its original meaning. It is full of beauty and rapturous appreciation of the heavenly Bani.

> To me came the Sound incomparable, which comes
> Neither from within, nor from without.
> Neither does it come from the left, nor from the right,
> Nor from the back, nor from the front.
>
> You will ask then, whence does it come?
> It comes from the direction you are seeking to go.
> You will ask then, which way shall I face?—
> The side from which the bridegroom cometh.

---

1. He became the appointed successor of Maharaj Sawan Singh.

> That direction whence ripeness comes to fruit;
> > That direction from which stones become diamonds.
> Be silent and listen to the five sounds from Heaven,
> > The Heaven which is beyond all senses and directions.

> Every moment of life this wondrous Sound
> > Reaches down from the courts of Heaven.
> Fortunate above all the children of men
> > Is he who hears its enchanting melodies.

Speaking in the identical poetical spirit of that same Sound incomparable, Jesus says it may be heard in the direction whence the wind blows:

> Verily, verily, I say unto thee, Except a man be born again, he cannot see the kingdom of God.
> *(John 3.5)*

And this is one of the greatest sayings ever uttered by Jesus or by anyone else. In order to see the inner kingdoms of light, a man must be born or brought to light by that Stream whence all power flows. That Stream is inside of man himself, as the kingdom of light is within man. For this very definite reason Jesus says, as do all Masters, that this kingdom of heaven is within man. One has to go inside to get at it. That kingdom may be entered and explored only by the light and the power of the divine Bani, which is also within man. Yet all the world is busy seeking it outside of man. Even the very nature of that kingdom is a dark mystery to most people. They have only the haziest notion of it. But that kingdom is no allegorical, imaginary or metaphorical kingdom. It is real, concrete. It includes vast and numberless worlds of inconceivable splendor and beauty. And all of this kingdom, or more correctly speaking, kingdoms, are consciously entered and enjoyed by the Master and his disciples. To make the momentous discovery of those higher kingdoms, man must go inside, must enter a plane of higher consciousness and higher dimension. This means that he must withdraw his attention from the sense world and lift his consciousness to a finer world. All of this he does with the aid of the Audible Life Stream and the Master. Hence its vital importance in the scheme of the Masters.

In every age of the world, time and time again, the Saints have repeated those significant words of Jesus:

> Marvel not that I said unto thee, Ye must be born again.
> *(John 3.7)*

When the soul is connected with the Life Current at the time of his initiation by the Master—when he is 'tuned in'—it is the supreme moment of his 'new birth'. But the completion of that birth is usually a slow process, a very gradual coming into the light. The Master often refers to the physical birth of the individual as more like a death because it involves going down into darkness. When the soul leaves any of the higher regions and comes down to the physical, it means descent into darkness. But the real birth takes place when one is connected with the great Luminous Reality, and by its regenerating action is brought into the light. This is the new birth spoken of by Jesus and all other Masters.

9. Science of the Masters—In Six Words

We believe that the entire essence of this science may be summed up in six words. Each word is a gigantic pillar of light. These six words, expressing three great truths, are subjoined to give expression to the greatest system of Truth ever revealed to the consciousness of man. They are like the three great mountains in Trikuti, which grouped together form one gigantic mountain of light. These three truths are so vital and so central, that if we should forget all else, remembering them only, we would still possess the essence of Santon ki Shiksha. These three great facts stand out in letters of light at the very entrance to the Royal Highway of the Saints. They constitute the triple beacon of light to guide every soul on his way to freedom. They offer the basic concepts of the teaching of the Masters. They give the vital substance of this book in six words. They should be on the walls of the home of every student in blazing letters. They are:

Sat Guru—Shabd Dhun—Jivan Mukti

(1) Sat Guru, *the Master,* the Saint,

(2) Shabd Dhun, *the Audible Life Stream,* the melodious Sound, the Sound primeval,

(3) Jivan Mukti, *spiritual freedom here and now,* meaning perfect liberation during this lifetime.

Let us now take careful note of the relationship existing between these three. The three are absolutely inseparable. This is one of the most important points to be kept in mind. You simply cannot have any one of them without the other two. This is a sacred mystery—all of them or none. And there is no possible exception to this rule. There is not only a definite rule that one must have them all or none, but there is a very definite order in which they must come, and this fixed order cannot be changed. Their sequence is fixed by an immutable law of Nature; it admits of no variation. It lies not in the power of any man to modify this law and this sequence. *The Sat Guru must come first.* The Shabd Dhun comes second, and then comes Jivan Mukti. This is the order established by Nature or God. No man can alter it.

All men wish liberation, or what theologians call salvation. Their sort of salvation is, however, a very different article from that of the Masters. The salvation of the Masters is liberation from the wheel of transmigration, from the ills of this life or of any life. And last of all freedom to live forever in some heaven of unalloyed bliss. This is salvation as it is generally understood by the students of this Path. It must never be confused with the theological salvation of the churches.

Suppose now that people know nothing at all about the Shabd Dhun, and they object to the idea of a Master. Yet they would like to be spiritually free. Well, they simply cannot get Jivan Mukti, and there is no help for it. You may sit on the fence and weep all the days of your life, but nothing can be done for you. You may call upon all the religions known for help, but you will get nothing. You may pray to all the gods on record, and they will not hear you. It remains a stern fact of Nature that no man has ever gained or can gain freedom from the ills of this life and escape the uncertainties of the next life until he has the good fortune to meet a living Master. If he has not that good fortune, he simply must return again and again to this life until he does meet a Master. That is the sum of it and that is final. Without the help of a Master no one can ever gain permanent release from this wheel of birth and death. His eternal and monotonous awagawan must simply go on until the time arrives when his good karmas bring him to a Master, with his mind prepared to follow Him. Why? Because, as said before, these three links in the golden chain of salvation are absolutely inseparable.

No one can possibly gain spiritual freedom except by and through the Shabd Dhun, and no one can possibly get that Shabd Dhun without first placing his life in the hands of a Sat Guru. On the other hand, if you do get a Sat Guru, you cannot fail to get Jivan Mukti, or redemption. And this is because the Sat Guru never fails to connect his disciple with the Shabd Dhun. And so, having both Sat Guru and Shabd Dhun, one cannot fail to get spiritual freedom, which is here called Jivan Mukti. Let us repeat the fact here, that these three can never be separated—never under any circumstances. And we must not forget that the Sat Guru comes first. It is a natural and logical conclusion, therefore, that the first duty and most important concern of any mortal in this world is to find a true Sat Guru. If you fail in that one regard, your life is a failure, no matter what else you may gain.

Here then is the formula: First find a real Sat Guru who can tune you into the Life Current, the melodious Dhun. Then take hold of that Current, merge yourself into it. Listen to its enchanting melodies, feel its gracious uplift, experience its cleansing powers, float upon it upward and onward to the city of freedom. After you have once passed the outermost frontiers of the material and impure worlds, when you have actually entered the regions of pure spirit and have grown godlike and fit for the highest regions, you will never again return to these lowlands of birth and death. You have attained Jivan Mukti—life everlasting. Therefore, let these three great truths be engraved upon your waking consciousness and upon your subconsciousness—think always on these three—*Sat Guru, Shabd Dhun and Jivan Mukti.*

To put the matter in a little different way, there are three things of supreme importance to anyone contemplating this Path. They are *the Sat Guru, the Satsang and the Audible Stream.* Of course, the Sat Guru comes first; but when the disciple comes to the Sat Guru, he must attend Satsang. That means he must converse with the Sat Guru, listen to his discourses, and so get full instruction. He may or he may not attend public meetings. The point is that he must see enough of the Master to become well informed as to the great truths of this Path.[1] This prepares the student for entering upon the Path. After that, he is ready for the initiation which brings him into vital contact with the Life Stream. It is taken for granted that if he once comes to the Sat Guru, he will sit in Satsang and listen to the instructions of the Guru. Hence we say, three things a man must do—he must find a Guru, he must attend Satsang, that is, inform himself as to the Path, and he must consciously enter the Life Stream. To put it in another way, three things a man must have—he must have a Sat Guru, he must have the Life Stream, and he must have spiritual liberation.

---

1. All this implies the possibility of every seeker reaching the Master in person. Such personal meeting is not always necessary. The present Master has representatives abroad who can initiate seekers with his approval.

Chapter Twelve

THE GREAT WORK OF THE MASTERS: WHAT THEY ACTUALLY DO

---

1. The Scientific Yoga of the Saints

THIS chapter brings us to the very heart of our theme. What are the Masters doing for their disciples on this Path? We have now to point out first the particular method by means of which the Masters reach their goal, and when that is done our work will be finished. The Saints have a definite work to perform, and we shall call that their *great work*. There is no greater work known. Let us now try to see just what that work is. The Saints have no secrets to keep from the world which the people of the world could possibly use to their own advantage. Anything which would do the world good, the Masters will never keep from the world. The difficulty now is, and has always been, that many of the teachings of the Masters cannot be appreciated by all and cannot be used by them. If some things are not told here, let it be known from the start that those things which are withheld would be of no use to anyone who is not an initiate of a Master.

Otherwise the Masters are quite ready and willing to lay their treasures before the whole world and invite any hungry soul to help himself. But let no one blame the Masters if they withhold certain things for which the world at large is not ready and which they could never understand if given to them. One reason this book is written now, at the express command of a great Master, is to give to all who may possibly be able to recognize their value, some understanding of the priceless truths of the Masters of all ages. The ancient screen of profound secrecy is now removed. There is no longer any need for such secrecy. It was not many centuries ago when no Saint could speak openly, except at the peril of his own life. Moreover, the Masters do not teach Pranayama, or any other system fraught with dangers, to the ignorant. The method of the Saints is so safe in itself that no harm can result by giving it out to the whole world, provided they would not abuse it and misuse it. But this can never be ascertained in advance, if the teaching is given out indiscriminately. If everything were written down here, it would only cause confusion and misunderstanding. There are certain detailed instructions available to initiates only, and even they can make no good use of them except by the help of the Master.

Before offering the yoga of the Masters, it might be well to call attention very briefly to the other systems of yoga which have been practised by students in the East. They are all interesting but we do not need them—the system of the Masters is complete. But it is good to know about them. Below is a brief description:

(1) *Hatha Yoga.* This aims at the control of the mind and acquisition of the *siddhis,* or what are called psychic powers, chiefly through *asana,* or physical postures and exercise such as control of the breath. The asanas undoubtedly give a very beneficial effect upon the health, and are believed to bring the vital as well as the mental processes within the control of the student. Hatha Yoga has also been defined as the union of the sun and the moon.

(2) *Raja Yoga.* This does not follow the rigorous discipline of the Hatha Yoga, but seeks to concentrate and still the mind by easy and natural methods of mental discipline and control. The emphasis in Raja Yoga is upon the mind rather than the body.

(3) *Ashtang Yoga.* This is a comprehensive scheme of yoga training. As its name implies, it consists of eight elements, the first five of which—*yama, niyama, asana, pranayama, pratyahara*—refer to the body. The last three—*dharana, dhyana* and *samadhi*—refer to the mind. The aim of this school is to merge the soul into God or the universal soul. Pranayama, chiefly consisting of breath

control, and by that means the control of the Prana, plays a very important part in the scheme.

(4) *Laya Yoga. Laya* means 'absorption', and Laya Yoga consists of the absorption of the mind in the astral light. This is generally achieved through the practice of *mudra*.

(5) *Karma Yoga.* This is essentially the yoga of action. It enjoins upon its followers the necessity of doing one's duty, whatever that may be, but without fear of blame or expectation of rewards. The essence of Karma Yoga is the ideal of duty well done and the spirit of detachment. It rejects the idea of renunciation and insists upon playing one's part to the fullest extent without looking to the fruit of actions.

(6) *Bhakti Yoga.* This is the yoga of devotion, and it appeals most of all to people of the emotional temperament. It discards all rites and ceremonies and seeks union with the Master or the Lord through the force of love only.

(7) *Mantra Yoga.* This system aims at the acquisition of psychic powers and spiritual or astral regions by constant repetition of certain formulas which are supposed to set up particular vibrations, especially when repeated with the mind fixed upon certain centers. The formulas, as such, are believed to have an efficacy of their own.

(8) *Sahaj Yoga.* This is the Surat Shabd Yoga, the central theme of this book—the system of the great Masters. As said repeatedly in these pages, this is the essence of them all. It contains the best in them all, but it was not taken from any of the others. The yoga of the Masters is the oldest of all systems. From age to age the different yogic methods have been derived from the yoga of the Saints and changed, in many cases, to suit their own ideas. But the yoga of the Masters cannot be changed, except at great loss. Various sects have from time to time adopted methods of their own because they had lost the original system of the Masters. This fact accounts for the variety of systems in vogue in India during the last few thousand years. But the system of yoga as taught today by the Saints is the one which has been taught and practised, without modification or alteration, during the tens of thousands of years since man first began his career on this planet. It is

now in order to present that system of yoga in as much detail as we are permitted to give it.

The scientific yoga of the Saints is really one of the most vital portions of their science. It is that to which all else leads, and after all else has been assimilated and all other preparations are made, it is this scientific yoga which is to lead the student to the full realization of all that he is expected to gain by this science. As is so often said in these pages, the system of the Masters is not a religion, nor does it interfere with any man's religion nor seek to undermine it. Whatever he may have that is good he keeps, and this adds to his treasures. This much may be accepted without question. It does not seek to uproot or supplant any religion. The inner experiences to be gained on this Path far excel in value any experience to be had from the practice of any religion. But at the same time, it does not interfere with any man's religion. It does not touch religion.

The system of the Masters is called Sahaj Yoga. It is the yoga that opens the doors of the supreme regions. It is called also the Surat Shabd Yoga. This is the yoga which is carried on by means of the Life Stream. In this science it refers to a definite system of exercises worked out by the Masters, by means of which the student is to attain conscious union with God. It is also called Sound practice, because it consists mainly of following the inner Sound. This is the one point which distinguishes the yoga of the Masters from all other systems. This is the supreme test which must always be kept in mind while studying all other systems. If this Sound practice is not a vital part of them, then they are not the system of the great Masters and they are limited. Let this be made very emphatic, for many people insist that one system is about as good as another since all are intended to lead to the same goal. But as a matter of experience, they do not all lead to the same goal. Far from it. No other system leads to the goal of the Masters, the highest regions in existence. Besides, you will generally find that the person who says that one religion or one system of yoga is just as good as another, is himself practising none of them.

Let the investigator understand that the master or the so-called master who does not teach and practise the science of the

Audible Life Stream, is not a Master of the highest order. Nor does his system lead to the highest achievements. Every real Master in all history has taught and practised the yoga of this Life Stream. It could not be otherwise, for this is the system established by the Creator himself. He who knows nothing about it is ignorant of the most essential and elementary facts of all yoga. This system of the Saints admits of no alterations, substitutions or subtractions.

Students of Indian yoga in general agree that most or all of the old systems are very difficult, requiring much time, rigid asceticism and great self-abnegation. And this is true of them all. Indeed, the path of the ordinary yogi is a rugged one. But the method of the Masters is not the way of the yogis. It never has been. Before there ever was a yogi's practice, the science of the Masters was known and practised among men. But the exact method of the Masters has, from time to time, become obscured or even lost in times when real Masters were few or unknown to the general public. Then, trying to substitute for the Path of the Saints, yogis developed methods of their own. The two systems then have been running along parallel courses throughout history.

Not only are the methods of the yogis different from those of the Saints, but their final objective is different. Most of the yogis, even the best of them, know of nothing beyond the astral plane, commonly termed Turiya Pad, with the possible exception of a very few who may go to Brahm Lok. There they are automatically stopped unless they have a Master who himself goes further. Stopping there, most of them believe that they have attained the supreme heights. There they accept the Brahm of that region as the Supreme God. But the great Masters go so far above and beyond Brahm Lok that when they reach that region, they have only fairly begun their upward journey. While most of the yogis and imperfect masters regard Brahm as the supreme deity, the Saints know that Brahm is only a subordinate in the Grand Hierarchy of the universe. While the *Om* of the Vedas and the Gita is regarded as the most sacred word in all Hindu philosophy because the Hindus believe it to be the sound symbol of the Supreme Being, the Saints know that it belongs to one of the lower Lords. He is himself a created being, subject to the same laws of all created beings and must carry on under the wishes of the Supreme Sat Purush. He is by no means the ultimate Purushottam.

The yoga of the Saints accomplishes that which the yoga of the Vedantists can never do. It is therefore vastly more efficient. Moreover, it has been adapted to the needs of the modern man. This is its great glory. It is modern in method and yet it meets all the requirements of all ages. In every age of the world, the Saints have used a system exactly suited to the needs of the people and the times. People change to some extent from age to age, and so the Saints give them, in each age, exactly that system of yoga which is best suited to their requirements. But the yogis hold on to their archaic systems which are now out of date and wholly unsuited to the average man of this age. The nervous constitution of the modern man is somewhat different from that of the men of ten thousand years ago. The yoga of the Masters may now be practised not only by the ascetic but by all men in all walks and conditions of life, while carrying on their routine duties at home. This makes it a universal science. No possible harm can result from its practice, provided one does not degenerate into evil practices while he is pretending to follow the Path of the Masters. Against such a possibility every student is warned. You cannot mix the Path of the Masters and the shaded way of evil.

2. Demonstrating Truth for Oneself

The yoga of the Saints utilizes and embodies a system of scientific demonstration, offering the most positive proofs of all that is claimed by any religion; and then it goes far beyond them all. Now, on the face of the matter, why loiter along with uncertain systems, even admitting all the good they claim, if you can have a system that positively offers all the good that is claimed in all other systems put together? This is because it is a universal science and in it are universal possibilities. It includes them all and then goes far beyond them all. This is not simply an idle claim. It is a challenge to all men to prove the claim for themselves.

This system does not leave the disciple with blind beliefs, nor does it limit him to faith alone. We know of no religion which even claims to offer anything more than a system of teaching which must be accepted on faith. But by the method of the Masters, one gains the most positive knowledge and so becomes absolutely certain of his ground. Not only is this degree of certainty absent from all religions, but it is not believed by them to be possible in the field of religion. In this manner, religion deprives itself of the one and only thing which could make it worthwhile—actual knowledge. Yet knowledge is the only genuine appeal to modern intelligence. The world is no longer interested in finespun theories.

It must be admitted by thoughtful students that all elements of the many world religions are of doubtful value, except their ethics, for the very good and sufficient reason that they are dependent upon ancient books and metaphysical speculations. This takes the matter out of the category of knowledge, and so robs it of its chief value. Beliefs and speculations offer a very weak support for the hope of immortal life. But if any system is able to make scientific demonstration the basis of its conclusions, that system will be delivered from all handicaps. And that is exactly what the science of the Masters does. It is in this respect that the Wisdom of the East differs from all other religio-philosophical teachings.

It is this scientific method which the Masters now offer to the world, and this constitutes their unique gift to mankind. When people are ready to accept the scientific method of the Masters, religion as well as philosophy will be delivered from its habit and its handicap of fruitless speculations and blind beliefs.

If any man feels inclined to challenge the Masters to prove that they are able to demonstrate such high and mystic truths, then let that man come into the laboratory of the Master and make the demonstration for himself. That is exactly what the Master invites and prefers. The Master will gladly give him both the method and the materials with which to make the demonstration. And in passing, I may say freely that no man has ever yet failed to make this demonstration for himself who has undertaken the demonstration according to the method given him by the Master.

3. What Does This Science Offer?

If we refer back to a careful study of all world religions and philosophies, we shall see at a glance that they all talk much about 'realizing God' and gaining 'salvation'. But if you ask them just how they are to accomplish all that, they will reply, in substance, "Believe the book and follow the priests." To state the matter a little more accurately, we may say that all human hopes and efforts center about three things:

(1) self-realization or self-knowledge
(2) God-realization or knowledge of God
(3) entering the kingdom of heaven either in this life or in the next.

It is only the Masters who show how this is to be done *in this life, here and now*, while all religions point to the hope of it after death. Of course, the end and purpose of all of this is individual well-being. We call it happiness. Now, these three are the very things which the science of the Masters offers to the devotee, but the method by which the Masters propose to accomplish that great work is entirely different from that of any and all religions.

We may then ask, how do the Masters propose to place to one's credit such inestimable treasures, such kingdoms of wealth? The answer is, by their scientific method of yoga, their system of exercises by means of which they open the treasurehouses of the universe. When these treasures are presented to the disciple, he experiences spiritual realization. And this includes both self-realization and God-realization. It includes all of the values of any religion and much more. He gains entrance to the kingdom of heaven, here and now. While he may continue for a time to sojourn here, he is at liberty to enter and explore the greater kingdom and return to this plane whenever he wishes, any day, even many times a day.

This spiritual realization frees the disciple from the age-long coming and going, and from the pains of the eternal wheel. It makes him a Master not only of himself but a master over all the forces of Nature. He has mastery over those passions and all antagonistic forces and influences which tend to pull him down. He is really free. From the status of a poor blind beggar, he becomes king over limitless empire. From a common sinner, he becomes a Saint. It relieves him of all sorrows, worries, doubts and fears. It endows him with amazing powers and all-comprehensive knowledge. He is emancipated and filled with unutterable joy. What more can one ask? And yet the system of the Masters accomplishes much more than all of this. To understand it, one must experience it. No language can describe it.

If some skeptic feels inclined to say that the science of the Masters cannot offer so much because his own studies and experiences do not substantiate such claims, then I must refer him to the principles of his own science. It does not become a real scientist to say that anything is impossible. He will acknowledge this principle. In this age of scientific demonstration, the 'impossible' has been accomplished so may times that even the scientists themselves have grown more humble. If the claims of this science are doubted by the physicists, it is because they are not familiar with this science or its methods or possibilities. They have no idea what it can do. It is true that science tries to adhere to ascertained or ascertainable facts of Nature. And in this, it is quite right. But even the best of scientists cannot always say in advance exactly what is ascertainable and what is not. If they insist, as they generally do, that whatever is done must be in accord with natural law, the Masters will agree right gladly. Nothing can ever be done which is contrary to the established order of Nature. But there may be a vast field of natural law which is, as yet, quite unknown to the scientists.

I sit here in my room and look away to the towering summits of the Himalayas. Their snow-covered peaks look majestic in the morning sun. I am told that science is able to calculate the exact heights of those peaks without actually climbing them and measuring them. Suppose that I assume an air of wise incredulity and say, as our ancestors would have said in the distant long ago, that no man can perform such feats. How can anybody tell the height of a tree without measuring it? And further, suppose I say to one of these coolies working in my garden, that men have actually gone above the highest peak of those mountains in an airplane. He will probably look at me as if he doubted my sanity. So it may be regarding many of the achievements of the Masters.

It may be stated emphatically that whatever the Masters do, they do it not by the violation of any natural law but by working in harmony with the law. It must be remembered, however, that the Masters are superscientists. They have knowledge of laws which the physicists have never discovered. Their field of operation is not limited to the narrow range of the physical plane. It is, therefore, more in accord with the scientific spirit of this age, if the reader will agree to hold the matter of spiritual demonstration under observation, and in the meantime try to go ahead and conduct the experiment. That is all that the Masters ask. They ask no blind beliefs. They ask no more than is required of any man who proposes to build a bridge or make a chemical analysis. In every scientific experiment, one must accept something as a working hypothesis. He is then ready to proceed with his practical demonstration. In the process of the demonstration, he gains definite knowledge.

No man ever gained spiritual freedom, power and happiness by a process of logic, by *a priori* ratiocination, by metaphysics, by reading books or by listening to lectures. Yet these are the methods employed by the majority of mankind. The Masters solve all their problems by a scientific method as exact and exacting as mathematics. They get their information not by analysis and synthesis but *by sight and hearing*. Even after they have proved a proposition, they establish no authority except that of truth itself. Authority hampers truth, it throttles free investigation. Authority is an enemy to progress. The Masters have no infallible dictator to pronounce dogmas *ex-cathedra*. This science makes *personal experience* the final and only court of appeal. Its processes are simple and direct. They can be understood by the most ordinary intelligence, and for that reason the intelligentsia need not become offended at them. Hence this is a universal science available to all classes of every nation and people in the world.

Nearly every people and every religion known to history has had some sort of yoga, i.e., some form of meditation or spiritual exercise. These range all the way from the most elaborate ritual to the most simple prayer. For example, note the experiences of the Christian mystics quoted in Chapter Eight, Section 2. It is well known that nearly all of the church fathers, early and late, had their own systems of meditation, and they got results which were highly valued by them. Gibbon reports a certain abbot of Mount Athos of the eleventh century commenting on a system of meditation, as follows:

> When thou art alone in thy cell, shut thy door and seat thyself in a corner; raise thy mind above all things vain and transitory; recline thy chin on thy breast; turn thy eyes and thy thoughts toward the middle of thy belly, the region of the navel, and search the place of the heart, the seat of the soul. At first, all will be dark and comfortless; but if you persevere day and night, you will feel an ineffable joy and no sooner has the soul discovered the place of the heart, than it is encircled in a mystical ethereal light.

This, of course, shows that they had knowledge of how to go above the lower chakras.

Maurice Philipps, a Christian, says:

> We have followed the stream of Aryan religious and speculative thoughts, in all of its ramifications, through the mantra, Brahmana, and Upanishad stages, noting its descent. We have considered the Hindu Aryan conception of God, their speculations on the creation of the world, and their notion of the origin, nature and destiny of man, in each of those stages. We have pushed our enquiries as far back in time as the records would permit. And we have found that the religious and speculative thought of the people was far purer, simpler and more rational, at the farthest point we reached, than at the nearest or latest in the Vedic age. The conclusion, therefore, is inevitable, viz., that the development of religious thought in India has been uniformly downward and not upward—deterioration and not evolution. . . . We have seen further that the knowledge of the divine attributes possessed by the Vedic Aryans was neither the product of intuition nor experience, but a survival, or a reminiscence. We are justified, therefore, in concluding that the higher and purer conceptions of the Vedic Aryans were the results of a primitive divine revelation.

This points exactly and very definitely to the earlier times in those far-off ages when the "divine revelation" spoken of here was given out by the Masters. It has always been the rule of history to see that divine revelation obscured in later periods. The Saints have in every age called attention to the Path, the Way to the kingdom of God. But no sooner do they pass from the stage of action upon this plane than the people drift away from the Path. Their work deteriorates in the hands of their followers. This is a pathetic aspect of all history.

Asceticism is one of the regrettable features of modern degeneration and is a radical departure from the pure teachings of the Path of the Masters. It has been practised by men of nearly all countries and religions in the mistaken notion that it will aid them in acquiring spiritual perfection. Buddha practised it in extreme forms until he almost lost his life, and when he gave it up, his old friends condemned him. Medieval Christians practised it. Vast numbers of Indian yogis have practised it, and many are doing so today. But the Masters have never taught asceticism, and they do not teach or practise it today.

The Path of the Masters is for all mankind and, as such, it must be available to all men in all walks of life. Of course, we are not to condemn anybody for practising asceticism, even in its extreme forms, if they choose that way. It is their business and they mean well. They are seeking desperately for their release from material bonds. But they seek that release in the wrong way. They do not know the rational Path of the Masters. We admire their courage. We often feel humbled in their presence. When a man is willing to leave home, friends and wealth, and at times even a kingdom, and go into the jungle, there to endure all manner of hardships, and suffer cold, hunger, and be isolated from all that the world loves, when he does all of this in pursuit of a spiritual ideal, it means that he is far above the ordinary man. It indicates a genuine nobility that is highly commendable. It is God-like; it is the very cream of nobility and the essence of greatness.

When the great Buddha was a poor hungry beggar in pursuit of his spiritual objectives, his true nobility stood out far more than it did when he was in the midst of his father's royal splendors.

When Jesus, who might have commanded any army—so great was his mental energy—walked the dusty streets, tired and hungry in order that he might carry the bread of life to the multitudes, his greatness eclipsed all the splendors of Rome. When a man gains such self-mastery that he can sit for hours, or even days at a time, upon a block of ice, we must admire his courage, even if we do not approve of his method. It indicates a greatness of spirit and a strong power of will. This sort of thing requires a heroism far greater than that which impels a man to sacrifice his life on the battlefield. We must admire that man's devotion to his own ideals. And we must love him for showing what a man can do through mental discipline. The true yogis have done much to bring light and hope to a dark world. I would count myself fortunate to be permitted to sit at their feet if I had not a real Master whose spiritual greatness eclipses that of all yogis.

4. The Surat Shabd Yoga

This is the genuine yoga of the Masters. It is this for which we have been getting ready in all of the preceding pages. The reader will now refer back to Chapter Ten, in which the mental preparation for this great work was discussed. Read it all over again and then meditate upon it long and deeply. When he has adopted all of that into his innermost thinking and then made it a part of his life processes, he will be ready for the actual work of this Path. The practice of this Surat Shabd Yoga is the great work of the Saints. It is that for which all men have been born into the human body. It is the supreme duty and privilege. It is the one work without which no man can ever escape the ills of this life and return to his original home. It constitutes the great work of the Saints. Let us now give it the most careful consideration.

The very first step on approaching this Path is *to get the initiation from a living Master,* a genuine Sat Guru. This point we have so often emphasized, but it cannot be overstressed. It is absolutely necessary. Without the initiation, one may as well stop before he begins. He will get nowhere on the Path. He may gain a little intellectual understanding of the principles, but that will do him but little good. Then supposing that he has the initiation, he has not to learn a lot of rules and regulations; he has not to study any rituals nor to read any books—not even this one. He may read only to get his mind clear on certain principles. That is all. He has now first and foremost to get down to work on the exercises.

He must select a suitable room, as completely as possible excluded from all noise and all sorts of interruptions. At fixed hours he is to sit in meditation, as prearranged, with body erect and comfortable. The posture used in the East is given to him at the time of his initiation, but he probably cannot endure that position if he is a Westerner. He will sit in a comfortable position, as he may select. The main point is that he is to keep his mind on the center in the head. If he is in pain from a cramped position, he cannot concentrate. His attention is then fixed upon a point inside of his head, called *tisra til*, meaning 'the third eye'. This is between the eyes and on a level with the eyebrows. He may simply think of this center, imagining himself to be there. The attention is to be held at this point continuously and without wavering. No thought of the outside world is to be entertained, nor of any past experience, event or person. Perfect concentration at this center is the objective. It is the all-essential. The mind must be held still at this point. Make the mind perfectly motionless. Do not think at all, except of the Master, at this inner center. All other mental activity is to cease. The mind must be held perfectly quiet, but it must hold to the center. If any thought at all is to be allowed, it must be only of the Master and what is inside of the center. All of the mind and soul are to be gathered at this point. Remember that the mind and spirit are scattered all over one's body. But they must now be gathered and concentrated at this one point in the head. To make this concentration perfect is the first great task to engage the attention and effort of the devotee. Compared with that, nothing else in the world is to be considered of any importance at all.

Just how all this is to be done to the very best advantage is told to the disciple at the time of his initiation. Details of the process cannot be given here; they are given at the time of initiation. This is not because the Masters are not willing to give out these precious secrets. They would be glad to give them to every man and woman on earth if only they could use them. But they could not make use of them. Those secrets would be of no value to the uninitiated. Absolutely none. They would only confuse him and possibly lead to serious mistakes. Only after one has found a living Master and had the initiation are these secrets of any value to him. After that, they are priceless. In this book our aim is to give the student a definite outline of the general principles of the Masters' science. It is not intended to do away with the need for a Master. That would be the utmost folly.

Before beginning his exercises, the disciple is presumed to have gained perfect viveka; that is, he is supposed to have considered the matter thoroughly from the intellectual aspect of the subject. His mind is presumed to be convinced and in full accord. He should be satisfied that he is on the right path, that he is adopting the right method, the best there is. He must be satisfied that this is the path for him. Also, he should fully accept his Master with complete confidence and trust, with readiness to follow him at all costs.

He must never for one moment presume to set up his own ideas as superior to the instructions given by the Master, even in the smallest details. If he could know better than the Master in any detail, then he would have no need for a Master, nor should he think that general instructions given to others by the Masters do not apply to himself. The science of the Masters is universal. It applies to all with equal force. He must never imagine that any particular instruction given by the Master is not so important as it is held to be. That were to make a grave error. The Master gives no instructions that are not important.

Then one should follow the Master implicitly. If a student objects that this is giving up his own individuality too much, this point may be illustrated. A man is to make a long journey by ship. Now his first business concerning that trip is viveka—the best way to go. That is, he must select his ship and his route.

When he has done that, his discrimination ceases. His independence of choice is now narrowed down. He has delegated his independence. The captain of his ship is now in command. When he steps aboard that ship, he is no longer able to exercise the freedom of choice he once exercised. He must henceforth obey the captain and follow the regulations laid down for the government of that ship. He does that voluntarily and solely because he has once for all decided that the ship will take him to his destination. The situation is much the same in the journey we are to make with the Master. He is the great captain, and to go with him we must obey him.

This much being determined, he embarks upon his journey. He is also presumed to have gained vairag, complete mental detachment from the love of the world and all sense objects. A man simply cannot take this world with him on his journey to higher worlds. In his innermost thoughts, he must be detached from the bonds that fetter him. He is then ready to proceed.

When he has done all of the above, and properly seated himself for the allotted time to be given to the exercises, he begins on *simran* (*smarana*). This means the repetition of certain things given by the Master, which we may call 'key notes', for want of a better term. The object of simran does not involve any idea of charms or words of magical powers. It is simply a method of helping the mind to come to complete rest and remain at rest in the given center. Simran is used by all the world in one form or another. It simply means concentrating the attention upon one thing, then going over and over it, until it is made a part of the very fiber and substance of one's being. It is only in this way that success can be attained.

Since the student is now to enter the inner worlds, he fixes all attention upon that which is inside and which belongs to those inner worlds. When the mind wanders away, the repetition of those key notes will bring it back to the center. The outer world is to be completely forgotten. Any means which may be adopted to that end may be helpful. But the Master gives us the best means. No man can improve on the Master's method. It is a method that has been proved and tested for untold thousands of years. No man can enter those higher worlds so long as his mind lingers upon things of the outer world. Hence the Masters speak of closing *the nine doors* of the outer world. The nine doors referred to are:

> the two eyes,
> the two ears,
> the two nostrils,
> the mouth,
> the sex organ,
> the rectum.

These are the chief means of holding communication with the outer world. All these must be closed—that is, all attention must be removed from them.

When all the outside world has been shut out, even in our innermost thoughts, with attention fixed upon the inner center, then we begin to concentrate at that center. All the powers of both mind and soul gather at that inner center, and as a result the bodily extremities become feelingless. We lose all feeling or sense of the life and existence of the body. We forget it. The entire being now moves toward the center and the inner worlds to be invaded.

When every ray of attention is inside, concentrated at the proper center, with no wavering thought lingering outside, then the student is in a position to get results. He must get results. He cannot fail to get them. He will at first experience flashes of light or hear sounds—perhaps both. But no matter what he sees or hears, he should not allow his mind to wander from the center. In other words, he must never go out after any sound or sight. Let them come to him at the center. If you leave the center, you will lose the lights and sounds also. By and by, with the gathering of all the life currents of the body at the center, the powers of the mind and soul will greatly increase.

When this concentration has reached its maximum within the ability of the individual, the soul has sufficient force to penetrate *the tenth door*. That is an opening in the subtle body near the middle of the forehead. At first, one only looks out through this door. But by and by he goes out through it and leaves the body completely. He then steps out into a new world which he never saw before. This new world will probably be some subplane of the astral zone. It is a new dimension to us. Let us call it the fourth dimension, if you wish; yet the term has but little meaning.

There is in the greater universe an almost endless series of sets of three dimensions, one above the other, reaching up to the highest worlds. Each set is separated from the one just above or just below it by the differences in the substances, the fineness or coarseness of particle and the different rates of vibration. These differences make one set invisible to people living in another set, because the eyes of people inhabiting one region will have a limited range of vision, making it impossible for them to see a region much above or much below their own region, to which they have been adapted. This is the reason we cannot see the astral worlds by or through our physical eyes. But with the astral eyes, we can see on that plane just as well as we can see on the physical plane with the physical eyes. So with the still higher worlds. With each higher world, or set of dimensions, the light and the beauty increase materially; also the happiness of the inhabitants.

At the sublime moment when the disciple steps out into the higher world, he begins to realize that he has acquired a vast increase of powers, as well as joy. It appears to him, and it is a fact too, that he can do almost anything he may wish to do. Not only has he increase of powers, but his knowledge and understanding have expanded proportionately. At this time, the whole material universe appears as an open book to him, and all dark mysteries have vanished. In other words, he finds himself in possession of all knowledge of these lower worlds. He now knows them and he has power over them. From here on up, each world gained gives one complete knowledge and power over the world below him.

The disciple is now free to proceed on his way to still higher zones. He may not allow himself to be unduly detained in order to enjoy the new world he has just entered. He must proceed. Between the physical and the pure astral planes, there are many subplanes. Vedantic pundits speak of the sun-worlds first. Then come the moon-worlds, and after that, numerous subzones and finally what Vivekananda calls the lightning-worlds. This corresponds to the plane of the Sahasradal Kanwal, as it is known to the Masters. It is commonly referred to as the astral region. It is full of light and is very beautiful when compared with this world. It is that region which is commonly considered by many yogis as the supreme heaven. That is as high as they are able to ascend, as a rule. The Lord of that region they regard as the Supreme Being. The Saints speak of him as Kal Niranjan, while most Hindus think of him as Brahm, the Supreme God. He is, in fact, regarded as the Supreme Being by nearly all religions. This is because they know of nothing higher. It is only the great Masters who know of the higher regions and the higher deities, going on up to the Universal One, out of whom all others come.

At a point between the sun-worlds and the moon-worlds and the pure astral zone, the disciple of the Master enters a zone called Ashtadal Kanwal. At that place something happens which changes the whole course of his life and also his method of procedure from that point on. It is the meeting with his own Master in his 'Radiant Form'. This is the Master's Nuri Sarup or 'light form'. It is the Master, his own Master, appearing just as he does in physical life, except that his body is now much more beautiful and full of light, brilliantly illumined. The Radiant Master then and there receives his disciple with much love, to the great joy of the disciple. From that moment on, the two are never separated throughout the journey to still higher regions. Of course, this Form is always with the disciple from the moment of his initiation, but the disciple cannot see him. But from here on, the disciple can see the Master on the inner planes as well as the outer.

At this time another new feature enters the journey of the student. A new stage marks his career. So far his success has been only partial, but very great. He has accomplished much, but he has only fairly begun his upward journey. Up to that time, he has been doing smarana, repeating the key notes. And that has given him fair concentration. But from now on, he will discontinue the smarana. He will not need it. He now has the presence of the Master whom he may behold constantly. This is called *dhyan*. This sight inspires much love and adoration. It is the most perfect dhyan and it is more effective than smarana for concentration. In fact, at all times, even before the disciple goes inside, his best possible exercise is to look steadily at the Master's form, and particularly his eyes. If one will take advantage of every moment to look steadily, with no shifting of vision, right at the Master's eyes, he will find himself concentrating and going inside quicker than any other way. This is one very great advantage a disciple has in being personally near the Master. So we now have smarana and perfect dhyan. These are two of the essentials in the exercises.

At this point something else of great importance happens. You will contact the Audible Life Stream perfectly and consciously and its music will begin to work changes in you. You get a little of it before this point, but here you get it more perfectly. Here it begins to fairly enchant you and to pull you up with increasing attraction and power. You will find yourself listening to it with rapt attention and deep delight, completely absorbed in it. You will never wish to leave it, or to miss a single note of its marvelous strains.

Of course, your upward progress will be much accelerated from here on. It is said that the student who reaches this point may consider that one-half of his work is finished for the whole of his journey. While formerly you had to exert your will to hold your attention upon the focus, now you will find it equally difficult to withdraw your attention from it. The Master and the divine Bani are so extremely attractive. You will most ardently wish to go on forever looking at the one and listening to the other.

You will now go with the Master into the Capital, the great Sahasradal Kanwal. It is the center of the astral worlds. It is the famous city of the 'thousand-petalled lotus'. It is a marvel of light and beauty, which I think no one has ever attempted to describe in much detail simply because it is beyond human language. One thousand and one gorgeous lights (one large central light, and one thousand small ones clustered about), each light of a different tint, and all clustered together somewhat in the form of a gigantic lotus flower. It is sometimes called "the mountain of Light." It is in fact the real powerhouse of the physical universe. From that gigantic dynamo goes forth the power that creates and sustains the entire creation below it, galaxies after galaxies, without end. Further than this we may not here attempt any sort of description. He who arrives there will see it. Then let him try to describe it.

Entering that region, the disciple will be so overjoyed that he will wish to remain there forever. Living in that region are to be seen many millions of the best men and women known to history, even founders of world religions, sitting and enjoying their meditation or walking about amidst the beauties and splendors of that region. Much as we would delight to go on with our descriptions of this and still higher regions, we must stop here. We could not describe them if we would, and would not if we could. That concerns only those students who have made progress up to that point. Its knowledge does not belong to one who is still confined to the earth plane, nor would it do him the least good if given to him.

5. The Technology of This Yoga

It has already been said that a good moral life is the very first prerequisite to becoming a disciple of the Sat Guru. This may be called the yama of this Path, or the dharma. In the language of Muslim Saints it is called *shariat,* the law of life, that which is to be done or ought to be done. All this is taken for granted, even before one starts on the Path of the Masters. Of course, every student must be well grounded in the fundamental laws of righteousness. He must also practise the real dharma in all his life. Without it, he cannot even make a start. Sitting in the proper position, with mind detached from the world, is the asana of this Path. There is no pranayama in this yoga, as it has no place in the system of the Masters. Fixing the mind at the prescribed center, bringing it to one point, is the dharana of the yogis of Patanjali. Of course, this has to be done if one is to go inside. Beholding the Master with loving gaze, either in the physical form or the Radiant Form, is the dhyan of this Path. This has to be done in any case. But in this yoga, smarana comes first, before dhyan. Then after smarana and dhyan comes *bhajan,* a form of exercise not known to any other system. It consists of listening to the Sound, the Audible Life

Stream. The reason that no other system has this is because they know nothing of the Audible Stream, the Shabd Dhun. Thus they miss the most vital thing in the whole process.

All these things enumerated above lead one up to samadhi, to actually going inside and stepping out upon the astral regions, as suggested above.

The highest form of samadhi is *Nirvikalpa*. This is gained by disciples of the Master when they enter the Third Region. It is there that they behold themselves as pure spirit, after leaving behind all material coverings. But this stage is never attained by the ordinary yogi. His so-called Nirvikalpa is on a much lower plane, is a negative state and is not real Nirvikalpa at all. It is only a reflection of the real. All the rest of the terms used by yogis are descriptive of so many mental states experienced on the astral plane or on some plane below that. But the most important thing about all yogic systems is the complete absence in them of all knowledge of the Shabd and reliance upon it for entering the higher regions. Without it, no one can advance very far on the inner Path.

This then, is the system of yoga as taught and practised by all Saints since the beginning of time. We have given only a few hints of it, so that the general reader may not be wholly in the dark concerning it. Further details cannot be given to the general public, but will be given by the Master to all whom he initiates. Of course, in undertaking this system of practice, the mental preparations discussed in Chapter Ten are supposed to have been gained as completely as possible. This preparation should, in fact, be acquired before one comes to the Master or seeks initiation. If it is not gained before the initiation, it certainly must be done afterward. But now, out of great mercy and kindness, the Saints usually give the initiation first, so that it may help the weaker ones to make better progress in self-preparation. It is a fact much to be regretted that some students misuse this very great privilege; that is, some of them get the initiation and then lapse into idle indifference—either that or they look to the Guru to do it all for them. In this way many spend the whole of their lives making practically no headway on the Path. And yet, even if some of them do fall by the way entirely, they will do better in the next life if they have to return here due to their own lack of effort.

It may be mentioned, by the way, that the great Masters say but little about the technical terms used to designate the several steps on their Path. They generally tell their students in the plainest, simplest words just what they are to do. Interest in technical terms is limited mostly to scholars. But as this book has been undertaken to give the teachings of the Masters in a scientific statement, it has been thought best to give the more important technical terms used by scholars, and then explain their meanings, so that the scholarly student may have no difficulty in placing the system in its relation to all other systems. This science of the Masters is far and away the Master's system. This scheme takes the student, stage by stage, from the earliest beginnings on the occult Path up to the highest, the supreme goal; and by virtue of that progress, he passes from the status of an ordinary man to the "sublime degree of a Master-man."

Many subdivisions could be made in this scheme, but it is not deemed wise to confuse the study with too many unimportant details. Let it be repeated here also that this system of yoga is not to be undertaken without first getting the initiation from a real Master. If you try to make use of it without a Guru, you will be sure to fail, and besides, you may run into unforeseen difficulties. Either with or without this book, no one can ever make his escape from the net of karma until he places his destiny in the hands of a living Sat Guru.

6. Passing "The Gates of Death"

It will be apparent to the careful student that this system of spiritual exercises, taught and practised by all the Masters, carries the student actually through "the gates of death." After that he enters regions above the play of death, as we know it. He is also able to return to this plane, at will, retaining perfect memory of all he has seen and heard. This is one of the minor achievements of the student. The samadhi of this science takes the student through and beyond death. Of course, this solves once for all the most serious problem which has ever confronted the human race—the problem of death and what lies beyond it. This fact of experience has not remained wholly unknown to the world's greatest thinkers. Plutarch, for example, said:

> At the moment of death the soul experiences the same impressions, passes through the same process as those who are initiated into the Great Mysteries.

This is the exact teaching of the Masters and it is the common experience of all initiates who make some advance on the Path. But instead of the ancient initiation by means of which the neophyte was merely shown a momentary glimpse of something above and beyond the physical world, the Masters initiate students into the Path and give them the method by means of which they can go and come at will between this and higher worlds. This is what is called dying daily, or *dying while we live*. It is a part of the daily routine of advanced students. The student leaves his body much in the same way a dying man leaves it, except that the student does it voluntarily and the process is always under his own control, and he can come back into the body any moment he wishes to return. Otherwise, his passing out of this body is practically the same as that of the dying man. He thus learns what death means, and also what lies beyond death—even becoming acquainted with the future home to which he is to go when he finally leaves his body. He may also converse with friends who have long ago left their bodies.

This masterful achievement cannot fail to interest the student since it solves the gravest problems of life and destiny. This is one phase of the great work of the Masters. They have broken the seal of death, and so to them and their students there is no more death. And all of this is positive knowledge, not speculation or guess. Neither is it interpretation of any book. All the world, the Western world in particular, has been accustomed to think that no man knows or can know what lies beyond the portals of death. They assert, with apparent finality, that death lands us upon some mystic shore from "whose bourne no traveler ever returns." Of course, a few assume that death ends the individual career of man. But these need not concern us here. They will learn their mistake in due time. It is time that men cease to think of death in such a gloomy mood. In fact, there is no death at all. There is simply a shifting of the scenes, an awakening in a new world.

Death is a glaring deception. The Masters and thousands of their students know precisely what death is and what lies beyond it. They know it is only an appearance. They have themselves 'crossed the Great Divide' many times, and they can tell us all about it. But they find it difficult to get people to believe them. The whole world has for ages shuddered at this ominous but inevitable fate which hangs over us all. They dread it because they do not understand it. It is like a child crying at the darkness. It is afraid because it cannot see what is there. People fear death because they do not know what it involves.

In spite of the general ignorance on the subject, the Masters know what death means, and they are ready to impart their knowledge to all who will listen to them. Not only are they ready to impart their knowledge concerning the matter, but they are ready to show the investigator just how he may acquire the same knowledge.

The Masters and many of their students pass daily through "the gates of death" and hence they know all of the problems connected with the matter. They have explored worlds upon worlds beyond the gates of death. All of this they do in full consciousness as a direct result of their practice of Surat Shabd Yoga. The Master leaves his body at will in almost exactly the same manner as the dying man leaves it. This has been said many times. It is repeated here for the sake of emphasis. The idea is not easy to put over. But as said before, the Master has complete control over the process and may return at will, while the ordinary man in death is a helpless victim of the process. The Master never loses consciousness, and when he returns to his body he has complete memory of every experience he had during his absence from the body. Of course, this is a bold achievement, the most marvelous of all achievements of man. But the beauty of it is that this accomplishment lies within the power of any man. He requires only the knowledge of how to go about it, and then a little application to the task.

After one is able to leave his body voluntarily, there is not only no death for him in the ordinary sense of some dreadful catastrophe, but there is not even a moment of unconsciousness or a shadow of darkness. One steps out of this body at will and in full possession of all of his faculties. He knows exactly what he is doing and remains always in full control of the process. Is this not an accomplishment worthy of any man's effort? Of course, the Master and all his disciples leave their bodies when the time comes for them to go. But when that time comes, they go as they did before, only at that time they sever all connection with the body and discard it finally. Then they go as liberated souls rising on wings of power and delight. They simply step out of their bodies and go, as one would step out of a close, stuffy room into a beautiful garden.

When the Master leaves the physical plane, he goes where he wishes, for he is Master of all higher regions. If he pauses on the astral plane, he there uses his astral body. If he goes on up to the causal plane, he functions there in his causal body. And if he goes up to the third plane he discards all bodies, and from there on up he acts as free spirit, unlimited and unhindered. As pure spirit, he knows all things by direct perception without any sort of instrument of contact, such as he was obliged to use on all the lower planes. The dying man, of course, breaks all connection with his body when he leaves it; but the Masters, when they leave the body as a part of their daily work, leave a sort of connection with it so that they may return to it at will. This connection is poetically called in the Bible "the silver cord." We read:

> Or ever the silver cord be loosed, or the golden bowl be broken. . . .
> (*Ecc. 12:6*)

That is never broken by the Master or his disciple, until they are ready to leave the body for all time. Then they of their own will break the silver cord and pass on up to perfect freedom. And this is all there is to that much dreaded thing that men call death.

Now, *after death* what happens? Where do we go and what happens to us? To answer this question, we have divided mankind into four distinct classes or groups; and the reason is that each of these four groups meets with a different sort of experience after death.

(1) The first class includes *all who have no Master,* or Sat Guru. This, of course, takes in the great bulk of mankind. All of these are obliged to meet the emergencies of death unsupported, unescorted, absolutely alone and helpless under the law of their own karma. They are now to receive payment in full for what they have earned in their life just finished. Of them the messengers of death ask not when they shall come, neither do they listen to their cries of distress. They operate under the orders of their master, the Negative Power, whose duty it is to administer absolute justice with no favoritism. As we all know, this class includes the vast majority of mankind. No matter to what religion they may belong, no difference between king or peasant, no matter how good or how bad, all alike must face 'the dark angel' and follow where he leads. They must go when the hour strikes, whether they are ready to go or not. Their individual wishes are not consulted. There is no remedy, no escape. No man can stay the hand of death when the inevitable moment arrives. All must face death alone and meet its issues.

Let no one imagine that his Lord of some past age will come to his relief at the moment of death. It is not so. His religion and the founder of that religion will do him but little good when he faces the Dharam Rai of that court to which he must go. That summons he must answer and there he must appear in person to answer the stern demands of the law—the law of karmic justice. Each and every soul of this class is escorted to the court of the king-judge, there to "give an account of the deeds done in the body," as the book says.

This accounting is not postponed until some future time when all mankind are called up and judged. Each one is judged immediately after death. There is no such thing as a general 'judgment day'. Every man's judgment day comes immediately after his death. That court is always in session, and before that judge there will be no 'attorney for the defense'. Each one is judged according to his own record, and the sentence is pronounced in strict accord with justice. But it is a justice in which there is no mercy or clemency of the court. From that sentence there is no appeal and no release on probation. If a person has been very bad, living a selfish life, indulging his evil passions, his sentence will send him to some region of remedial and disciplinary punishment.

This sentence is not final, like that of the orthodox hells. It is intended to purge that soul of his evil mind. He himself will know and fully approve of his own sentence, for he will know that it is exactly what he has earned. When the period of his discipline expires—which may be years, a century or a thousand years—he has another chance to make good. He returns to earthly life for another birth and another chance to create for himself better karma. The deep impressions of his bitter experiences will be retained, and he will bring them with him into the new life although he may not actually remember the details of it. Automatically he will then shun those paths of evil which formerly brought him to grief. In the next life, he is then sure to have a better record.

If one has lived a better life, he will be sent to a better environment, to some sort of paradise where he may enjoy the good which he has earned, there to rest and recuperate, so to speak, until the time arrives for him to return to earthly life once more. But in each and every case, one receives exactly what he has earned and in each case he must sooner or later return to be born once more on this or some other earth. If one has lived a very exalted and noble life, he earns thereby the privilege of a long sojourn in some region of pure delight, there to await his eventual return to earth. He may thus enjoy a thousand or a million years in some heaven; but as certainly as time rolls on, he must finally return to earthly life after his earnings have been spent. Thus each and every one must tread the wheel of birth and death, age after age, until his good karma eventually brings him to a living Master.

(2) The second class are *they who have had the initiation from a living Master,* but who have done but little or nothing in the way of spiritual exercises. A few may have actually indulged their passions in unworthy conduct. As a result, they have made

no progress on the Path. Yet they have a Master. What happens to them after death? In what respect do their experiences differ from the common lot of mankind? There is a very important difference. The Master meets them at death or a little before. That is, he makes himself visible to them and he notifies them that their time is up. They must go. They respond with joy. At least we have never known or heard of one who was not glad to go with the Master at the time of their departure, and that without hesitation. They fear nothing, have no regrets at having to leave their families or the world.

No matter if they live ten thousand miles from the Master in the body, he is there in a form visible to them, to receive them and go with them. He comes to them in his Radiant Form, the Astral. As soon as they leave the physical body, the Master himself takes them to that region or locality which they have earned. There he places them in a sort of training school where they make good progress under his directions. If they have done very wrong, the Master himself administers whatever punishment or discipline he may deem necessary. They then continue in their training school until the time comes when they are fit to go higher. But in no case does any disciple of a true Master ever go before the king-judge, nor does the black angel of death ever approach him at the time of death. He cannot approach a disciple of a real Sat Guru. The Master himself is there to take care of his own. The Master is always lord of the situation. There is no power above him. The Sat Guru is the embodiment of the Supreme One, and as such he has power to do whatever he likes, and no one can obstruct his path.

(3) The third class are *they who have made good progress on the Path of the Masters*, but have not yet attained sainthood themselves. All of this class know the day and the hour when they are to go, long before it comes. The entire process of death is under their control, and there is never a shadow of difficulty or distress during the process of passing. Neither do they lose consciousness for a single moment. They pass out of the body as easily as one would lay off an old garment. In their daily practice, they have already gone through that process many times, so the whole performance is quite familiar to them. Many times already they have

visited the region to which they are now to pass. It is just like going back home. The only difference between their former visits to that region and this final exit from the physical world, is that now they break the silver cord and release themselves from the body forever. Separation being now complete, they are free to go where they wish without bonds of any sort. They go directly to that region under the escort of their Master, where they are to abide for the time until they are ready to go higher. Of course, the Master is with them during all of this change. They make it in great joy and of their own free will. There is no compulsion. Of course, they have absolutely nothing to do with the dark angel or with the king-judge. Like the second class, they are taken care of by the Master. It is an occasion of joyful homecoming.

These two classes never return to earthly life again, unless it is so willed and ordered by the Master. Generally, they are taken on up, grade by grade, until they reach the highest. It is extremely fortunate for any student if he has been able to reach Sach Khand before he leaves the physical body. The way to this is open to all, and they can do it if they do the required work. But in actual practice, not a very large percentage ever accomplish so much. But in every case, disciples of the Master are saved from the monotonous rounds of reincarnation. Their dreary awagawan is finished.

(4) The fourth and last class are the Masters themselves. When the time comes that a Master wishes to leave his body for all time, he simply lays it down of his own will and steps out of it, as he has so often done before, only now he breaks the cord and discards the body as an instrument for which he has no further use. His disciples prepare it and take it to the funeral pyre. The entire process of his passing, as well as all circumstances connected with it, are under his own control, and there is never a momentary shadow of unconsciousness. He remains Master even through the process of his own death. The Masters are lords of life and of death, a truth so often emphasized in these pages. They may do exactly as they please at all times, and no one can interfere. After leaving their bodies, they rise at once above all physical or material worlds, above all lower heaven-worlds, and take up their residence wherever they may see fit, according to their duties and

responsibilities, entering upon their higher duties as these may have been assigned to them by the Supreme One.

It may be said in passing that the Masters do not generally remain in their physical bodies much, if any, longer than the usual time allotted to ordinary mortals. They generally let Nature take its course in all matters physical, although they have plenary powers to interfere with the usual routine if they saw fit to do so. It is not generally their plan to interfere. They could remain in their bodies for centuries or even thousands of years if they wished to do so, and deemed it wise. But as a rule they do not.

Many yogis have been known to keep their bodies for centuries, and any higher level yogi can do it. But yogis are not Masters of the highest order. The Masters observe the laws of this world, and carry on their work in harmony with those laws as closely as possible. Their work is strictly of a spiritual nature, and they do not wish to interfere with the rules governing a foreign country in which they have but a temporary interest. They come to this world for a definite purpose and they stick to that purpose and work as closely as possible. After all, what advantage would it be if they should live in the body for a few centuries or even thousands of years? They go on to a higher work, leaving their successors to carry on here. The Supreme Sat Purush does not wish to have one of his beloved sons remain here in this dark region, the nature of which is more like a prison. When they have finished the work assigned to them, they are welcomed home to enjoy their reward. It would be a very great sacrifice to remain here indefinitely. While they would be willing to make that sacrifice, yet the Supreme Father does not wish them to do so.

7. Evolution and the Final Goal

As to evolution itself, it may be said emphatically that the Masters do not endorse pure Darwinism, so far as it relates to the origin of man upon this planet. They do endorse the theory of evolution so far as it sets forth a method of progress for both the individual and the human race as well as for all lower forms of life. As a matter of fact, individuals may either progress or retrogress. History proves that conclusively, and I think no one will deny it. This fact holds true of all forms of life upon the planet. Evolution is only a process of Nature, a method or procedure. But the theory must not be overworked.

It is purely a gratuitous speculation to assume that because we can see an evolutionary progress throughout all departments of life, therefore man himself is an outgrowth—or an upgrowth—from the lowest forms. The evolutionist must not forget that retrogression is as much a fact of history as is evolution. It is just as easy to prove by history, geological and otherwise, that the human race, as we know it today, has descended from a superior race of prehistoric antiquity, as it is to prove that we came up from the animal level. As a matter of fact, neither one of these theories has so far been proved by geology or any other records. Anthropology has yet to write its first chapter of the history of mån. Ethnology has yet to trace man's kindred to the original family tree. In the meantime, the Masters know that the human race is not a product of evolution from the lower animals. It is a remnant from a race of super-men who once walked this earth as sons of God far back in the Golden Age. It has been the fault of the ultra-Darwinian school to overwork its theory. Evolution does not even claim to account for the origin of species. Why should it pronounce so dogmatically on the origin of the human race?

In every Golden Age, there has been one vital point of distinction which has set that age off from all other ages. That is its high degree of spirituality. Spirituality is in fact the very soul and substance of civilization. Every civilization in every age of the world, whether high or low, corresponds in exact ratio to its degree of spirituality. Nothing else can ever make a civilization. Mental superiority produces no real civilization. Culture, literature, art, do not make civilization. Refined tastes do not make civilization. There is a vast difference between esthetics and ethics. Even ethics, in its highest development, does not constitute civilization. *Love alone makes civilization,* and love is of the essence of pure spirit. Spirituality is always abundant in every Golden Age. That is what makes it 'golden'. If now the friends of man wish to inaugurate a new Golden Age, let them do something to promote love among all men.

It has been the tragedy of history that from age to age spirituality gradually declines. Man is thus moving toward the animal plane of life. When the world is young, like a young man full of the vigor of youth, sustained by a great spiritual power, electrifying and stimulating every higher impulse, the people live on a very high plane. What we call evil and sin are practically unknown. No evil can be experienced until the spirituality of the world begins to wane in a declining age, after the lapse of millions of years. Then the world again becomes old and depleted of its spirituality. As a result, all manner of evils beset it, affecting both the individual and the race, even the world itself.

This decline can never be prevented; for the cycle of the ages, the coming and the going of the yugas, is as certain as the revolutions of the planets in their orbits. It is just as inevitable as the old age of individuals. This decline runs on through all the successive ages, yuga after yuga, until the whole race, together with all other life upon the planet, reaches its lowest ebb of retrogression. At that time man is but little more than what we call a primitive savage, a brute in human form. Even that form itself is much changed and humiliated. All this degeneration is brought about through the destructive action of the five passions, which never cease their inroads upon the individual and the whole world in general.

There is always the ebbing of the tides. We must not overlook that. Periodicity is a law of Nature, just as much as the survival of the fittest. During the ages of slow decline, there is less effort to curb the passions, until at last they become dominant. Little by little men lose the light of understanding; they no more hear the inner inspiring Shabd, and then they lose all knowledge of the higher worlds. Materialism covers the world in a dark mantle, for superstition always follows upon gross materialism. First the mind becomes fiercely self-assertive, then dogmatically materialistic; and lastly, when learning dies out, it is followed by all forms of superstition. Men sink into stupid savagery. As conditions of life become more and more hostile to man's comfort and welfare, man's numbers decrease. Finally a mere remnant of the race is left, battling hard for its existence in a hostile environment. At this point the entire race is threatened with extinction. Then a peculiar thing happens. At the very moment when men are driven to the wall, compelled to fight for their very existence, that very struggle begins to lead toward their salvation.

As too much ease and comfort lead to degeneracy, so hard battle develops more sturdy qualities. The fight was forced upon mankind by its own degeneracy and inefficiency. But the fight, now having grown very keen, begins to awaken in man his higher faculties, new powers of thinking and acting, faculties which his degeneracy had dulled and deadened. And this is the turning point in the history of the human race. It is also the turning of the yugas or the ages. Timed to suit the struggles of man when he begins his fight for self-existence, there is an increase in the spirituality of the whole human race. This spirituality becomes the motive power of his newly awakened efforts. It is the beginning of a new era of evolution.

For ages the race has been moving downgrade, but now man begins his slow ascent. He begins to climb back toward civilization. At this point the evolutionist picks him up. The Darwinian thinks he has discovered an up-climbing animal. But, in fact, he has found a degenerate man. Instead of pitying him as a poor fallen specimen of a nobler race, he thinks of man as a freak come up out of the darkness by fortuitous selection. Darwinism claims that this brute man has ascended from lower forms; but the Masters say that he has come down from a long line of human ancestors reaching back to the Golden Age. But the silver note in the discord is the cheering fact that this degenerate specimen is now on his way up. This is acknowledged by the geologist and the ethnologist. In that concession we may take great comfort. No matter where he came from, he is on the royal highway of improvement. It will, however, require some time yet for him to regain his lost prestige.

Of course, this regaining of all that was lost will be accomplished through the process of evolution. Isn't this glory enough for evolution? But one thing the modern evolutionist does not know is the fact that the evolution of the race takes place under the impetus of an awakened spirituality. In other words, the age-long degenerative process will be reversed, and the human race will slowly retrace its steps back to the heights whence it has descended. It is a fact of great interest that the depletion of spirituality in the whole world runs parallel to the progressive degeneracy of mankind. Likewise, the evolution of mankind runs parallel to the fresh charging of the world itself with a new spiritual force. The beginning of the upward march of mankind is then due to two great factors—his enforced struggle for existence and the simultaneous replenishing of the world itself with new spiritual life. That these two events of such world-significance should occur at the same time is in the order of Nature, and belongs in the rhythmic cycles of the universe.

We believe, although I have never heard any Master say so, that the lowest ebb in the degenerative retrogression of the human race took place something like four hundred thousand years ago. Of course, that was some time before the beginning of this Kal Yuga, the Iron Age. But the first day of Kal Yuga, as the Vedic sages reckon time, found the human race decidedly on the upgrade. History shows that. For they say that Kal Yuga began only about five thousand years ago. From that time on, slowly, almost imperceptibly, the race has regained some portion of what it had lost. During all of this time there have been many shiftings and resettings of the surface conditions of the globe. At the same time numerous races of men have appeared and disappeared.

If the darkest period of human history actually occurred, as we believe, about the middle or latter half of Dwapar Yuga, the Copper Age, then the race has been slowly evolving ever since that time. That would fit in perfectly with the findings of scientific evolution based upon geological records, and the few fragments of prehistoric man which have been left. Now man must go on evolving until he reaches the noon tide of the next Golden Age. This will, of course, require some time. But signs of such an upward trend are not wanting. It is moreover our conviction, looked at from the viewpoint of the long cycles of time, that there will be a very rapid upward advance from now on. To support this view, one noted scientist has made the declaration that the world has made more progress in the last quarter of a century than it made in all the two thousand years before.

We need not worry about war clouds. Out of the jar and clash of conflict, a newer and better civilization will emerge. Let no faint heart imagine that civilization is to be destroyed. It cannot be done. Real civilization is yet to rise above the wreck of battle. The spiritual science of the Masters must yet point the way for the building of a new federation of man. Its leading economic principle will be that every man shall enjoy that which he has earned, and its fundamental law shall be the law of Love.

One sweeter note in that long funeral march of man's downward drift has been the constant presence on earth of the great Masters. While the great majority of the human race retrograded, a few always remained true to the precepts and practices of the Masters.

I can almost hear some Western critics say: "Why didn't the Masters take measures to prevent that downward drift of the people? The answer is that the Masters could not prevent it. It was a part of the order of Nature. It was on the program from the beginning of time. These ages must come, as they are ordained by the Creator. It is no part of the duty of the Masters to interfere in world processes. Their duty is to help individuals to escape from this melee of troubles. And one thing we should always keep in mind—the Supreme is in command in this world and he will manage affairs to the best advantage. We need not doubt it. Just as certainly as the planets move in their orbits, so surely will this world go on as the Creator wishes it to. No man or group of men can wreck the world. No nation or group of nations can wreck the world. No nation or group of nations can make the Creator's plans miscarry. It is folly to become an alarmist. And in all this confusion and strife, the Masters are doing all they can for the world, while their chief attention is centered upon the relief of individuals who are ready to make their way up and out of this world of conflict.

The world has never been without a living Master. A surviving remnant of the Golden Age has kept alive the fires of genius and spirituality, while the masses drifted away toward a state of animalism. It was there that Darwin found them, and it is not at all surprising that he failed to recognize in that fallen specimen any marks of his true ancestry. It was quite a natural conclusion that man had come up from below—that degenerate man. He certainly looked like it. And were not his animal kindred all about him to bear testimony against him? But even the most pessimistic evolutionist will agree that within the period of available geological records, man has made much improvement. That is surely encouraging. We may not be able to tell what direction the original man came from, but it is clear now which way he is going; and, after all, that is what concerns us most. So let us take hope. But all the while, let us not give to the theory of evolution too much credit for the upward trend of mankind.

Beneath all other impelling forces, spirituality is the primary cause. That, and that alone, is the driving force in evolution. A struggle for existence is one factor. But without a greater force within, men would not take so much trouble to preserve an existence that only brings them misery. The driving force in all evolution is the eternal flame that always leaps up to join its source. When the physicist and the ethnologist learn to recognize the spirit as an element, a vital factor in all their problems, they will discover the real significance of evolution itself. They will discover that in every living being, from tiny plant up to man, evolution means that the spiritual flame of life is struggling upward and onward toward its source of being, and this process and this struggle must go on until the last speck of dust returns to the central fires of Infinite Being.

The message of the Masters fills the world with hope, and at the same time it offers a rational foundation for such hope. It not only tells people what they should do, but it offers them a definite method of doing it. In the march of the ages, cycle after cycle, in every planet where human beings reside, the great Masters are the Light Bearers of that world. Until the end of the ages, they will remain the friends and saviors of those who struggle toward the Light.

> Be led from the unreal to the real,
> Be led from darkness to light,
> Be led from death to immortality.
>
> —UPANISHAD

THE END

Glossary

ADI GRANTH. 'Original scripture'; sacred scripture of the Sikhs. Contains the teachings of Guru Nanak, his successors and other Saints. Compiled chiefly by Guru Arjan, the fifth Guru in the line of Guru Nanak, about the year 1604.

ADI KARMA. 'Original karma', 'karma of the beginning'; not earned by the individual, but established by the Creator in the beginning. See also KARMA.

AGAM LOK. 'Inaccessible region'; the name of the seventh spiritual region. Agam Purusha, the form of the Supreme Being that presides over Agam Lok.

AHANKAR. 'I-ness', 'ego'; one of the five deadly passions (*kam, krodh, lobh, moh, ahankar*); also one of the four divisions of mind, whose function is to separate self and self-interests from all else. See also ANTASHKARAN.

AHIMSA. 'Nonviolence'; not hurting any living being, by either word or act.

AHURA MAZDA. The ancient Persian name for God, used in Zoroastrianism.

AKAL PURUSHA. 'Timeless being'; the One who is beyond the sphere of birth and death; used to designate the supreme Positive Power, as opposed to Kal, the negative power.

AKASH. 'Sky', 'ether'; the highest of the five elements, the primary substance out of which all material things were created. See also TATTWAS.

AKASH BANI. 'Sound or voice from the sky'; the heavenly music, Audible Life Stream, Shabd or Word.

AKSHAR. 'Indelible', 'cannot be erased'; imperishable; appellation for God. Akshar Purusha, the creative power; the Lord.

ALAKH LOK. 'Invisible region'; the sixth spiritual region, presided over by Alakh Purusha, a form of the Supreme Being.

ALLAH. The Arabic name for God.

ANAHAD SHABD. 'Limitless sound or word'; a name for the Word or divine creative power. Also called Anahat Shabd, 'the unstruck sound'.

ANAMI LOK. 'Nameless region'; the eighth spiritual region, presided over by Anami Purusha, Radha Soami, the Supreme Being.

ANDA. 'Egg'; the second Grand Division of the universe.

ANTASHKARAN or ANTAHKARAN. 'Mental organ', 'mind'; combination of the four faculties of the mind: *manas, buddhi, chit* and *ahankar*.

ARYAN PATH. The Arya Ashtanga Marg, or 'eightfold path' of Buddha.

ASANA. 'Posture'; in spiritual practice, a meditative pose, with body erect, mind in poise.

ASHTADAL KANWAL. 'Eight-petalled lotus'; the name of the center beyond *Tisra Til* (the eye center) where the disciple first meets the Radiant Form of his Master.

ASTRAL REGION. That part of the subtle universe which lies next above the physical worlds; the first spiritual region, Sahasradal Kanwal.

ASURA. 'Demons'. Asura Lok, the region of demons. In the oldest portions of the Rig Veda, Asura is used for the supreme spirit; later, *sura* came to mean 'gods', and *asura*, 'demons', 'enemies of God'.

ATMA or ATMAN. 'Soul', 'spirit'. See also PARAMATMA; JIVATMA.

ATMA PAD. 'Spirit world', referring generally to the astral plane or first region; more technically, refers to the third region, Daswan Dwar, where self-realization comes.

AUM. See OM.

AWAGAWAN. 'Coming and going'; refers to age-long cycles of births and deaths; transmigration, reincarnation. See also CHAURASI.

BANI. 'Voice', 'word', 'teachings'; the Voice or Word of God, the Audible Life Stream, the Shabd.

BHAJAN. 'Worship'; listening to the melody of the Shabd within.

BHAKTA. 'Devotee'; one devoted to the Master.

BHAKTI. 'Devotion'; devotion to the Master.

BHAKTI MARG. 'The path of devotion'; attaining salvation by devotion.

BHANWAR GUPHA. 'Revolving cave'; the name of the fourth spiritual region.

BIBEK. 'Discrimination'. See VIVEK.

BINA or BEEN. An Indian musical instrument whose sound is somewhat suggestive of the Sound in the fifth spiritual region, Sach

Khand. But that spiritual Sound is so wonderful it cannot be accurately described, as there is nothing in this world with which it can be compared.

BODHISATTVA. One who is on the way to attainment of perfect knowledge and has only a certain number of births to undergo before attaining the state of a supreme Buddha.

BRAHM. The ruler of the second spiritual region; regarded by many as the Supreme Being.

BRAHMA. God of creation in the Hindu trinity of creator-preserver-destroyer (Brahma, Vishnu, Shiva).

BRAHMACHARYA. The practice of celibacy, remaining continent.

BRAHMANDA. 'Egg of Brahm'; the third Grand Division of the creation, having four principal subdivisions besides many minor subdivisions. It extends from Trikuti up to Bhanwar Gupha.

BRAHMIN. A member of the highest of the four Hindu castes; a priest.

BUDDHA. The great sage, Prince Siddhartha of the Sakya clan. The preceptor of Buddhism.

BUDDHI. 'Intellect'; one of the four phases of mind. See also ANTASHKARAN.

CAUSAL REGION. That part of the subtle universe which lies above the astral world; Trikuti, the second spiritual region on the path of the Saints. The causal body or *bij sharir* ('seed body') corresponds to this region.

CHAKRA. 'Wheel'; the six energy centers in the human body, each of which looks like a small wheel, with parts that suggest the petals of a lotus. See also KANWAL.

CHAURASI. 'Eighty-four'; hence, the wheel of eighty-four, the wheel of transmigration. The name indicates the eight million four hundred thousand species into which the soul may have to incarnate, referred to as the eighty-four lakh species.

CHELA. 'Disciple'.

CHITTA or CHIT. 'Consciousness'; one of the four divisions of mind; the faculty of discerning beauty, form and color—also of remembering. See also ANTASHKARAN.

DAMA. Restraining or subduing the passions, curbing the mind.

DANDA. 'Stick', 'staff'; self-discipline; punishment; law of life.

DARSHAN. 'Vision', 'sight', 'seeing'; implies looking intently at the Master with a deep feeling of respect and devotion and with one-pointed attention.

DASWAN DWAR. 'Tenth gate' or 'tenth door'; the name of the third spiritual region. *Daswan,* 'the tenth', refers to the subtle opening in the head through which the disciple passes to higher planes.

DAYAL. 'Compassionate one'; a term for the Supreme Being, the positive and merciful power, as opposed to Kal, the Lord of Judgment, who metes out relentless justice.

DESHA. 'Country', 'region'; inner world.

DEVA or DEVATA. 'Shining ones'; personifications of the forces of Nature; gods, angels.

DHAM. 'Country', 'region', 'abode', 'place', 'home'.

DHARAM RAI. 'King Judge', the Lord of Judgment or Justice, Kal, who administers reward or punishment to the soul after death, according to its own actions during life.

DHARMA. 'Righteousness', 'duty'; moral and religious duty.

DHARMA MEGHA. A kind of *samadhi,* an absorption of the mind into the object of meditation, with complete detachment (*vairagya*) from worldly bonds, thus freeing the mind from all activity, inward or outward; such a person is said to radiate a light like a mantle of glory.

DHUN. 'Sound', 'melody'; the Shabd or Word, the heavenly music.

DHUNATMAK. The inexpressible Primal Sound, which cannot be written or spoken, nor heard with the physical ears; the inner music, which can be experienced only by the soul.

DHYAN. Inner contemplation. A special technique taught by the Saints in which the devotee contemplates on the form of his Master within.

DWAPAR YUGA. The Copper Age, the third yuga in the cycle of the ages, whose duration is said to be 864,000 years. See also YUGA.

GRANTH SAHIB or SRI GURU GRANTH SAHIB. A title of respect given by the Sikhs to the Adi Granth.

GUNA. 'Attribute', 'quality'; 'the three gunas' are the three attributes or qualities of *prakriti,* the primordial matter out of which the creation proceeds: *sattva* (harmony, serenity), *rajas* (action or activity) and *tamas* (inertia, darkness), whose source is in Trikuti.

GURU. Master, teacher; spiritual enlightener.

GURUMUKH. 'One whose face is turned towards the Guru'; one who has completely surrendered to the Guru; a highly advanced soul; a term sometimes used for the Saint or perfect Master.

GYANI. 'A learned person'; one who practises or walks on the path of *gyan,* 'wisdom'.

GYAN MARG. 'The path of wisdom', 'the way of learning'.

HANSA. 'Swan'; symbolic of purity, *hansa* is the name given to the highly evolved souls in the regions beyond Brahm; the unevolved souls are often likened to crows.

HATHA YOGA. One of the Hindu systems of yoga, which deals with the physical body only.

IDA. See SUSHUMNA.

JI. An honorific term added on to names, etc., to indicate respect and endearment; somewhat similar to 'sir'.

JIVAN MUKTI. 'Salvation while alive', spiritual liberation during this lifetime.

JIVATMA. 'Soul embodied in the physical form'.

JOT or JYOTI. 'Light', 'flame'; refers to the light of the first spiritual region, Sahasradal Kanwal.

KAKUSHA. A highly developed soul, one who has attained true knowledge.

KAL. 'Time', 'death'; the negative power, the universal mind, the ruler of the three perishable worlds (physical, astral, causal); also called Dharam Rai, the Lord of Judgment, and Yama, the Lord of Death. Kal's headquarters are in the second spiritual region, Trikuti, of which he is the ruler.

KAM. 'Lust', 'passion', 'desire'; one of the five passions (*kam, krodh, lobh, moh, ahankar*); any outward tendency of the mind.

KANWAL or KAMAL. 'Lotus'; a name describing the light emanating from the energy centers, both in the physical body and in the inner regions. See also CHAKRA; SAHASRADAL KANWAL.

KARAN SHARIR. 'Causal body'; also called *bij sharir,* 'seed body', because the seeds of all karmas reside in it; all such actions or karmas manifest in the lower bodies (astral, physical).

KARMA. 'Action'; the law of action and reaction; the debits and credits resulting from our deeds, which bring us back to the world in future lives to reap their fruits. *Pralabdh karma:* the fate or destiny we experience in the present life; the past actions that are responsible for our present condition. *Kriyaman karma:* the debits and credits created by our actions in this life, to be reaped in future lives. *Sinchit karma:* the balance of unpaid *kriyaman karmas* from all our past lives; the store of karmas.

KARAM KANDA. Rituals, rites, ceremonies and outward practices in the various religions.

KRIYAMAN. Karma created in the present life. See also KARMA.

KRODH. 'Anger'; one of the five deadly passions (*kam, krodh, lobh, moh, ahankar*).

KUNDALINI. 'Coiled energy' that is supposed to lie at the base of the spine, above the lowest *chakra;* when aroused, it rises up through the central canal of the spine, unwinding serpentlike; a practice to be shunned by satsangis.

LAYA YOGA. A form of yoga in which the disciple merges his individuality in that of the Guru or Shabd.

LOBH. 'Greed', one of the five deadly passions (*kam, krodh, lobh, moh, ahankar*).

MAGI. 'The wise men of the East'; priests·of ancient Persia.

MAHA. 'Great'.

MAHA KAL. 'The Great Kal', ruler of the upper part of Brahmanda.

MAHA NADA. 'Great music'; the inner music, or Audible Life Stream.

MAHA SUNNA. 'The great void'; the name given to the upper part of the third spiritual region, Daswan Dwar; it is a region of impenetrable darkness that can be crossed only with the Master.

MANAS. 'Mind', the faculty of receiving and tasting; the mind-stuff itself. See also ANTASHKARAN.

MANU. An ancient lawgiver who divided the people into the four castes.

MARDANG or MRIDANG. A musical instrument, resembling a long drum.

MARG. 'Path', 'way'.

MAYA. 'Illusion'.

MOH. 'Attachment'; worldly attachments or entanglements; one of the five deadly passions (*kam, krodh, lobh, moh, ahankar*).

MOKSHA. 'Salvation', 'liberation' from the cycle of transmigration.

MUMUKSHA. The state of being a *mumukshu,* or one who desires to attain *moksha,* 'liberation'.

MUNDAKA. The name of one of the Upanishads.

MUNI. 'One who hears or experiences'; a sage, holy man.

MURSHID. Muslim term for Master.

NADA-BINDU. 'Seed sound'; the Sound out of which all things grow.

NAM. 'Name'; the Shabd, Logos, or Word; the divine creative power.

NIJMANAS. 'The inner mind', corresponding to Karan Sharir, the causal body.

NIRGUNA. 'Without attributes'; appellation for God. See also GUNA.

NIRVIKALPA. 'Unwavering', 'concentrated'; a state of deep meditation or *samadhi* in which the disciple cannot distinguish himself from the object of meditation.

NURI SARUP. 'The light body', the Radiant Form of the Master, the astral form.

OM. The sound symbol of Brahm; Audible Life Stream or Shabd of the second spiritual region.

ORMUZD. The old Persian and Parsee term for God; an angel; also the planet Jupiter.

PARBRAHM. 'Beyond Brahm'; the regions beyond Brahm Lok.

PARAMATMA. 'The supreme soul' or God.

PARAM SANT. 'A supreme saint'; a Saint who has attained the highest region.

PINDA. The physical universe; the physical body of man; the name of the first Grand Division of the creation (Pinda, Anda, Brahmanda, Sach Khand).

PINGALA. See SUSHUMNA.

PRAKRITI. The essential nature of mind and matter, which projects itself in various forms of emotions and actions, and which also influences the various parts of the body; they are twenty-five in number and consist of five principal manifestations of the five elements or *tattwas* in the body.

PRALABDH or PRARABDH. The fate karma; our destiny in this life, created by actions in past lives, and upon which the present life is based. See also KARMA.

PRANA. 'Vital force, essence'; 'vital air'.

PRANAYAM or PRANA YOGA. Part of the Patanjali yoga system, which aims at controlling the *prana*, mainly through breath control.

PREM MARG. 'The path of love'; the path of the Saints.

PURUSHA. A male being; creative energy; man; the supreme creative power.

RADHA SOAMI. 'Lord of the soul'; the Supreme Being.

RAJAS. The creative or active *guna*, or attribute of Nature.

RAJA YOGA. A practice that deals with the control of the currents of the mind by increasing the power of the mind through contemplation and certain postures.

RAM or RAMA.   A name for God, also Shabd; the power that pervades
    everything.

RISHI.   'One who sees', 'enlightened one'; sage of ancient India.

RUPA.   'Form'.

SACH KHAND.   'True or imperishable region', the name of the fifth
    spiritual region or the fourth Grand Division of the creation.

SADHU.   'One who has controlled the mind', a Saint; technically, a
    devotee who has crossed the region of mind and matter and
    reached the third spiritual region; sometimes applied to one who
    has gained the second region also; generally, a holy man follow-
    ing a path of spiritual discipline.

SAHASRADAL KANWAL or KAMAL.   'The thousand-petalled lotus',
    the name of the first spiritual region.

SAMADHANA.   Deep meditation, superconsciousness; a state of rap-
    ture.

SAMADHI.   A state of concentration in which all consciousness of the
    outer world is transcended.

SAMHITA.   A code of laws, e.g., the *Manu Samhita*.

SANNYASIN.   One who has renounced the world, who is free from
    attachments.

SANSKARA.   Impressions or tendencies from previous births, early
    upbringing, traditions and social influences, which shape the basic
    outlook and behavior patterns of a human being.

SANT.   'Saint'; one who has attained the fifth spiritual region, Sach
    Khand; a God-realized soul.

SANT MAT or SANTON KI SHIKSHA.   'The teachings of the Saints'.

SAR SHABD.   'The essence of Shabd', the pure Shabd, free from mat-
    ter, above Trikuti.

SAT.   'True', 'real', 'everlasting'.

SAT DESH.   'True home', 'true region'; another name for Sach Khand,
    the purely spiritual Grand Division of the creation.

SAT GURU.   'True or perfect Master'; a true light-giver; a Master who
    has access to the fifth spiritual region, Sach Khand.

SAT LOK.   'True region'; another name for Sach Khand.

SAT NAM.   'True name'; the unspoken, unwritten Name or Word of
    God;   the Supreme Creator,   Lord of the fifth spiritual region,
    original source of souls; our true spiritual Father.

SAT PURUSH.   'True or eternal being'; God.

SATSANG. 'True company'; 'association with the true'; company of or association with a perfect Master is external satsang; association of the soul with the Radiant Form of the Master, the Shabd or Nam within, is internal satsang. The highest form of satsang is to merge in the Shabd; a congregation assembled to hear a spiritual discourse is external satsang; even to think about the Master and his teachings is satsang.

SATSANGI. 'One who associates with the true'; initiate of a perfect Master; technically, one who has reached the first stage.

SAT YUGA. 'True age', the Golden Age, the first of the four great cycles of time. See also YUGA.

SEVA. 'Service'; voluntary service to the Master or his disciples. Of the four types of *seva* (monetary, physical, mental, spiritual), the highest form is the spiritual—the meditation practice.

SHABD. 'Word', 'sound'; Spiritual Sound; Audible Life Stream; Sound Current. The creative power, the source of all creation, which manifests as sound and light in the spiritual regions. As the soul manifests in the body as consciousness, the Word of God manifests itself as inner spiritual Sound. It is the Word or Logos of the Bible; Kalma, Isme-i-Azam, Bang-i-Asmani, or Kalma-i-Ilahi of the Quran. It is the Nad of the Vedas; Nam, Ram Nam, Gurbani, Bani, and Dhun of the Adi Granth. It is called the Tao by the Chinese; Vadan and Saut-i-Surmad by the Sufis. The Zoroastrians call it Sharaosha, and it is known by many other names. The secret of hearing the Shabd within oneself can be imparted only by a true Master.

SHABDS. Refers to hymns, and chapters, paragraphs or stanzas of sacred texts such as the Sar Bachan, the Adi Granth, etc.

SHABD DHUN. 'The music of the word'; the Shabd, the Audible Life Stream, the Word.

SHABD MARG. 'The path of the word'; the path of Shabd Yoga, the path of the Saints.

SHAKTI. 'Power', 'ability', 'strength'; the highest form of maya, or illusion.

SHANKARACHARYA. A great commentator of the Vedanta Sutras and the Upanishads.

SHANTI. 'Peace'; peace of mind.

SHARIAT. Muslim code of life, religious law, justice; Quranic law and ritual.

SHIVA. God of destruction in the Hindu trinity of creator-preserver-destroyer (Brahma, Vishnu, Shiva); ruler of the heart chakra;

the dissolving force, governed by *tamas,* the attribute of inertia, darkness.

SHRADDHA. 'Faith', 'belief', 'reverence'.

SIMRAN, SMARANA, or SUMIRAN. 'Repetition'; repetition of the five holy names according to the instructions of a perfect Master.

SINCHIT or SANCHIT, The store of unpaid past karmas. See also KARMA.

SOAMI or SWAMI. 'Lord'; the Supreme Being; the Master; commonly applied to all spiritual teachers, and to *sannyasis* in particular.

SURAT SHABD YOGA. The practice of joining the soul (*surat*) with the Word (*shabd*) and merging (*yoga*) with it; once the soul merges into the Shabd, it is carried by the Shabd to its source, the Lord.

SUSHUMNA or SUSHMANA. The central current in the finer body, starting from the eye center and leading upward to the higher spiritual regions, located and traversed by means of the spiritual practice taught by a perfect Master; also known as Shah Rug. It is not to be confused with *sushumna* of the yogis, which is the central canal along the spine in the lower body and is to be ignored by sat-sangis. The current on the left is called *ida* and the one on the right, *pingala.*

TAMAS. The *guna,* or attribute, of dissolution, inertia, darkness.

TATHAGATA. 'One who has attained'; a name for the Buddha.

TATTWA. 'Elements', 'essence'; the five elements are present, to various degrees, in all living beings: *prithvi* (earth), *jal* (water), *agni* (fire), *vayu* (air) and *akash* (ether).

TISRA TIL. 'Third eye'; a point in the subtle body, between and behind the two eyebrows; the seat of the mind and the soul in the human body, and the point at which the disciples of the Saints begin their concentration, and from where they go up. Also called *nuqta-i-saveida* (the black point), *daswan* (the tenth door), 'the single eye'.

TITIKSHA. 'Endurance', 'patience'; power of enduring hardships with calmness and peace.

TRETA YUGA. The Silver Age, the second grand cycle of time, immediately following Sat Yuga. See also YUGA.

TRIKUTI. 'Three prominences'; the name of the second spiritual region; also called Brahm Lok.

TRILOKI. 'Three worlds'; the physical, astral and causal regions.

UPANISHADS. A collection of ancient Hindu scriptures.

VAIRAGYA or VAIRAG. 'Detachment', particularly mental detachment from the world and worldly desires; a state of mind—not to be confused with asceticism or physical renunciation of the world.

VAIRAGI. One who has attained detachment.

VARNATMAK. 'Describable'; that which can be spoken or written. See also DHUNATMAK.

VEDAS. A collection of ancient hymns sacred to the Hindus; Hindu scriptures.

VEDANTA. One of the six systems of Hindu philosophy.

VISHNU. God of preservation in the Hindu trinity of creator-preserver-destroyer (Brahma, Vishnu, Shiva).

VIVEKA. 'Discrimination'; searching inquiry, careful study, as the first step on the Path of the Masters.

WHEEL OF EIGHTY-FOUR. See CHAURASI.

YAMA. The Lord of Death, who takes charge of the uninitiated soul at the time of death.

YAM DUTA or DOOT. 'Messengers or angels of death'; the agents of Yama.

YOGA. 'Union'; spiritually, a system of practices by means of which the soul becomes one with God.

YOGESHWAR. 'A king of yogis', 'a supreme yogi'; one who goes to the second spiritual region, Brahm Lok.

YOGI. One who practises yoga and has attained some degree, probably the astral region.

YUGA. 'Age'; a great cycle of time. The Hindus divide time into four recurring cycles: Sat Yuga, the Golden Age; Treta Yuga, the Silver Age; Dwapar Yuga, the Copper Age; and Kal Yuga, the Iron Age, through which we are now passing. One thousand yugas make a Maha Yuga, or 'great age', which is equivalent to one day of Brahm.

Index

A

Action and reaction. *See* Karma, law of
Adi Granth Sahib, 135–36, 138
Adi karma, 252
Agam Lok, 207, 233
Agam Purusha, 221–22, 233, 234, 238–39
Ages, the four. *See* Yugas
Agnosticism, 214–16
Ahankar. *See* Ego
Ahimsa, 82. *See also* Virtues
Akal Purusha, 221–22
Akash, 77, 232, 310
Akash Bani, 372. *See also* Audible Life
    Stream
Alakh Lok, 207, 233
Alakh Purusha, 221–22, 233, 238
Alcohol, 269, 270, 311
Anahad Shabd, 383. *See also* Surat Shabd
    Yoga
Anami. *See* God, names for
Anami Lok, 207, 233
Anda, 202–03, 209–10, 233, 237, 345–46
Angel, 241. *See also* Messengers of death
Anger (krodh), 62, 64, 257, 271–74
    as mental illness, 272–74
    effect on concentration, 271
    minor aspects of, 272
Animals, 251, 286, 292, 294–97
Antashkarans. *See* Mind, attributes,
    faculties of
Anthroposophy, 104
Aristotle, 86. *See also* Greek philosophers
Asceticism, 406–07. *See also* Austerities
Ashtadal Kanwal, 154, 346, 413–14
Astral body, 248–49, 343. *See also* Finer body
    plane, 203, 249, 336–37, 385, 399
    region, 198, 349, 412–15
    vision, 412
Atman, 35–36, 150–51. *See also* Soul
Attachment (moh), 61–2, 256–57, 276–78,
    358–61
Attention, 146, 263, 345–47, 354–55, 359,
    362–63, 408–09, 410–11, 414
    withdrawal of, 390. *See also* Concentra-
    tion
Attitude towards life, 359
    ideal of Gita, 60–63
    example of Christ, 355
Attraction, law of, 363–64. *See also* Detach-
    ment
Audible Life Stream, Life Current, 30, 34–36,
    42, 49–50, 64, 66, 73, 108–09, 137,
    139–40, 145, 180–81, 186, 206–07,

283, 293–94, 364–78. *See also*
    Sound, Surat Shabd Yoga
    as creative force, 204, 252, 374–75, 379
    as cure for worldly desires, 364–66
    attraction of, 374, 377–78, 383–85
    connecting souls to, 186, 366, 391. *See also*
    Initiation
    listening to, 368–94, 404, 414, 416
    in the Vedas, 71–75
    other names of, 371–73
    same as the Word, Logos, 35, 49–50, 95,
    368–70, 386–88
Aurobindo Ghose, 71, 366–67
Austerities, 48, 179–80. *See also* Asceticism
Aversions, 290. *See also* Sanskaras

B

Baba Jaimal Singh, 190
Bani, 372, 377. *See also* Audible Life Stream
Belief versus knowledge, 183, 301, 401, 404
Bell sound, 73, 381. *See also* Sound
Bergson, Henri, 12, 19, 217
Besant, Annie, 105
Bhagavad Gita, 59–70, 356
Bhajan, 415. *See also* Meditation
Bhakti Marg, path, yoga, 76, 397
Bhanwar Gupha. *See* Fourth region
Bible, mention of the Word, Shabd in, 95, 98,
    368–69, 385–88, 390
Bigotry, 280–81
Bina. *See* Sound
Birth and death. *See* Wheel of eighty-four
Birth, new, 292, 391. *See also* Initiation
Birth, virgin, 170–71
Blame, 34, 42, 271, 361
Bodhisattva, 34, 360. *See also* Buddha
Body, human, 230, 247
    care for, 161, 179, 310–11
    fate of, 295
    service with, 307–08
    See also Astral body; Causal body; Finer
    body
Bondage, release from, 235, 362, 364–67.
    See also Liberation; Escape from
    passions
Brahm, 36, 181, 207, 239, 413. *See also* Kal
    Niranjan
Brahm Lok, 68, 71–72, 110, 126, 181, 237,
    399. *See also* Trikuti
Brahma, 239–40
Brahman, 72
Brahmanda, 203, 207–08

Brahmacharya, 66. *See also* Continence
Breath control. *See* Pranayam
Brotherhood, universal, 76, 93, 122
Buddha, Siddhartha, 21, 45–47, 272, 361.
    See also Bodhisattva
Buddhi, 81, 255. *See also* Mind, attributes,
    faculties of
Buddhism, 45–52

C

Causal body, 248–49, 289
Causal plane, 252
Cause and effect. *See* Karma, law of
Celibacy, 66. *See also* Continence
Chakras, six, 343–46
Charity, 360
Chastity, 282, 350–51
Chaurasi. *See* Wheel of eighty-four
Chela, 177, 301
Children, 291, 299
Chitta. *See* Mind, attributes of
Christ, as example of disciple, 355
    as son of God, 170
    teachings of, 86, 92–99, 385–86
Christian mystics, 327–33, 405
Christianity, beginnings of, 83–85, 89–92
Christian Science, 110–14
Civilization, 312–16, 326–27, 426–27
Concentration at the eye center, 78, 126,
    147–48, 271, 345–47, 355, 408–09,
    411, 413–14. *See also* Attention;
    Simran
    awakens consciousness, 343
    lack of, 271
Confucius, Confucianism, 31, 36
Consciousness, 219, 326, 343
Contemplation. *See* Dhyan
Contentment (santosh), 282, 361. *See also*
    Peace
Continence, 66, 79, 282
Copper Age. *See* Yugas
Cord, silver, 420, 424
Creation, order of the universe, 199–212,
    232–34, 237–41
    Vedic idea of, 77–78
    See also Higher regions; Universe
Creative energy, 370–71. *See also* Audible
    Life Stream
Creator, 220–24, 238–39. *See also* Sat Purush
Criticism, 162, 192–93, 272–75, 361
Current. *See* Audible Life Stream
Cycle of birth and death. *See* Reincarnation
Cycles of time. *See* Yugas

D

Darkness, 42, 98, 178, 211, 215, 319, 384, 391.
    See also Evil
Darshan, 108, 320
Darwin/ism, 425–30

Daswan Dwar. *See* Third region
Dayal, 309
Death, an illusion, 166, 418–19
    as experienced by Masters, 424–25
    at time of death, 209, 420–25
    judgment at, 301–306, 420–25
    See also Dying while living
Deception on inner planes, 148–154
Desire, 33, 61–62, 268
    cause of sorrow, 49, 361
    destruction of, 361–67
Destiny, 191, 287–88, 290, 293–94, 358–60,
    410
    seeds of, 248
Detachment, 32–33. *See also* Attachment;
    Attraction
Devas, 240
Devotion, 64, 307, 308, 322, 355. *See also*
    Love
Dharam Rai, 222, 301–02, 309, 421. *See also*
    Kal
Dharma, 35–36, 41, 317–18, 415
    path of, 63
Dhun. *See* Audible Life Stream
Dhunatmak, 371, 374
Dhyan, 80, 413, 415
Diet, 309–11
Direct perception, 81, 249–50
Disciple, 96, 116–17, 169, 190, 294, 306–09,
    402
    as agent, 307–08
Discipleship, ideal of in Gita, 69, 356
    of Jesus, 94, 355
Discrimination (viveka), 72, 81, 282, 353–54,
    409
Dissolutions, 68, 209–10
Divine Word, energy, 369. *See also* Audible
    Life Stream
Drug habit, 270
Dying while living, 96–98, 138, 334, 377–78,
    410–15, 418. *See also* Death; Going
    inside

E

Earnings, honest, 180, 350
Eddy, Mary Baker, 111–12
Effort, 356, 416
Ego, 93, 189, 256–57, 268, 278–81, 359, 382
    minor phases of, 280–81
Eightfold path. *See* Buddhism
Elements, five, 309–10
Enlightenment, 48, 272
Escape from passions, karmas, 32–33, 68,
    235, 239, 281–82, 290, 306, 316, 366,
    384–85, 407. *See also* Wheel of
    eighty-four; Bondage
Essene Brotherhood, 84
Ethics, 31, 49, 143, 426
Evil, 42–45, 162, 204–05, 211–12, 226–27,
    239, 271, 317–20, 361, 363
Evolution, spiritual, 107, 431
Evolution, theory of. *See* Darwinism

F

Faith, 72, 96–99, 178, 188–89, 322, 401
Fate. *See* Destiny
Fate karma. *See* Karma
Fault-finding, 179, 280
Feelings, unreliable guide, 101–102, 172, 174–75
Fifth region. *See* Sach Khand
Finer body, 166, 340, 342. *See also* Astral body; Body; Causal body
First region. *See* Sahasradal Kanwal
Five passions, enemies, 256, 266, 267–81, 362. *See also* Escape; Mind remedies for, 281–82.
Food. *See* Vegetarianism
Forgiveness, 282
Fortune, good, 392–93. *See also* Karma, good
Free will and karma, 235
Freedom, 117, 308–09. *See also* Liberation

G

Gita. *See* Bhagavad Gita
Gluttony, 270
God, 213–28
    definition of, 213, 376
    existence of, theistic hypothesis, 213–17
    non-existence of, scientific theory, 217–19
    names for, 221–25, 238–39, 380–83
God-realization, 29–31, 150–51, 211, 401–03
Gods, 221, 224
    definition of, 236
    possessing creative powers, 236
Going inside, 97, 146, 325–26, 343–47, 390. *See also* Dying while living; Meditation
Golden Age, 210, 242–43, 313, 426–31. *See also* Yugas
Grand divisions, hierarchy. *See* Creation, order of the universe
Great White Brotherhood, 105–07, 120
Greed (lobh), 257, 275
Greek philosophers, 8, 25, 40, 86, 104, 246.
Guide, spiritual, necessity of, 59, 188. *See also* Guru; Living Master
Gunas, 63
Guru,
    necessity of, 136–37, 169–70, 251, 384, 393–94, 417. *See also* Living Master; Master; Satguru
    administers karma of his disciple, 309
Gurumukh, 281–82
Guru Nanak, 135–36
Gyan Marg, 63, 72, 76. *See also* Yoga

H

Habit, 258–62, 267
Happiness, worldly, 22–24
    spiritual, 204, 206, 211, 402, 412
Healing, by mind, 111–14
Heaven, 203–04

Hell, 302–03, 422
Higher regions, planes, 97, 166, 177, 181, 196–212, 333–34, 411–15. *See also* Creation; Inner kingdoms; Regions
Hinduism, 59–83
    trinity of, 239–40. *See also* Vedas
Holy Ghost. *See* Audible Life Stream
Holy Spirit, 380–83. *See also* Audible Life Stream
Holy Trinity (of Christians), 387
Honesty. *See* Morality
Human form, purpose of human life, 407. *See also* Body
Humility, 93, 308, 322–23, 359
Hypnotism, 335–36
Hypocrisy, 275

I

I, I-ness, 255–56, 278–81
Idleness, 271, 416
Illumination, 81, 330
Illusion, 8
Immortality, 67–68
Impatience, 272
Impermanence of materiality, 362
Initiation, importance of, 137–38, 159, 191
    selection of disciples for, 190–192, 197, 232, 350–52, 391, 393, 407–09, 416
Inner experiences, knowledge, 97, 102, 140–42, 146–47, 219, 301, 324–38, 347, 376–78, 402–04, 412–13
Inner journey, path, 60, 186, 197–98, 249, 345–47, 413, 416
Inner kingdoms, worlds, 166, 346–47, 390–91. *See also* Higher regions
Inner music, 75, 137, 383–84
Insect, 292, 309–10, 397
Intellect, 5, 9, 81, 166, 255
Intuition, 81, 176–77
Iron Age. *See* Kal Yuga
Irritability, 272
Islam, 52–57

J

Jesus Christ. *See* Christ
Jivan Mukti. *See* Liberation
Joy, spiritual, 140, 331–34
Judaism, 123–35
Judgment. *See* Death, judgment at
Justice. *See* Karma, law of; Karmic debt and payment

K

Kabbalah, 126–33
Kabir, 56, 135, 372, 377, 389
Kal, negative power, 39, 42, 65–66, 154, 192, 221–23, 236–40, 266, 308–09, 346, 420–21. *See also* Brahm; Dharam Rai; Universal Mind
Kal Niranjan, 233, 236–40, 413
Kal Purusha, 222

Kal Yuga, 6, 191, 429. *See also* Yuga
Kam. *See* Lust
Karan mind, nijmanas. *See* Mind, higher
Karan Sharir. *See* Causal body
Karma, accumulation of, 252–53
    and diet, 309–11
    and reincarnation, 289–93
    fate karma, 298–303
    good, 300, 320–21
    law of, 33, 235–36, 283–89, 291–92
    three types of, 293
Karmaless actions, 305–09
    of Satguru, 306
Karmic debt and payment, 286, 294, 297–98,
        302–06, 421–22
Khan, Hazrat Inayat, 379
Killing, the burden of karma, 310
Kindness, 272
Kingdom of heaven (in Bible), 28, 57, 59,
        86–87, 92–94, 98–99, 402
Knowledge, 183–85, 401. *See also* Inner
        experiences
    versus belief, 102, 174–76
Koran, 56
Krishna, teachings of, 64–66
Kriyaman karma. *See* Karma, three types of
Krodh. *See* Anger
Kundalini, 79, 347–49

                        L

Lao Tse, 32–33
Laziness, 271, 354
Leaving the body. *See* Dying while living;
        Going inside
Liberation, spiritual, 69, 72, 109, 138–39,
        188, 193, 235, 277, 291, 384–85,
        392–94. *See also* Bondage
Life current, stream. *See* Audible Life Stream
Light, 385, 411
Light body, 248. *See also* Astral body
Lightning worlds, 412
Living Master, 36, 41, 102, 136–39, 167, 171,
        181–83, 214, 221, 298–303. *See also*
        Master
    necessity of, 56–60, 69–70, 72–73,
        98–100, 136–38, 173–74, 193, 198,
        282, 342, 349, 367, 376, 391–93,
        430–31
    as guide, 148, 186, 188–89
Lobh. *See* Greed
Logic, misleading, 214
Logos, 369. *See also* Audible Life Stream
Loneliness, 378
Longing, 72, 193, 211, 239, 330
Lord. *See* God
Lost Word, 372–73
Lotus, analogy of, 33
    microscopic centers, 343–49
    thousand-petalled. *See* Sahasradal Kanwal
Love, 75, 94–95, 143–46, 169, 207, 228, 241,
        308–09. *See also* Devotion

    as Audible Life Stream, 143, 145–46, 353,
        373–76, 385, 427
    detached, 358–60
    essence of religion, 141–46
    of Master, 96, 117, 160–64, 179, 187, 294,
        322, 413
    path of, 44, 316, 353–54, 355
    perfect, 144
Lust, 268–71. *See also* Senses

                        M

Magi, 85–86. *See also* Zoroastrianism
Maharishi. *See* Rishi
Mahatma, 105, 107–08, 157
    four classes of, 158
Mahavakya, 69
Mahabharata, 59, 314
Malice, 272. *See also* Anger
Man, real, 8, 230, 247–51
    as top of creation, 241. *See also* Soul
Manmukh, 281–82
Manu, laws of, 314–16
Marriage, 350
Masonic order, 132, 372–73
Master(s). *See also* Living Master; Path of the
        Masters; Radiant form; Saints;
        Seeking the Master
    as example, 161–62, 187
    as guide, 150, 186, 216
    classes of, 158
    departed, 137, 171–75
    duties of, 66, 122, 159, 185–87, 235
    follow laws of nature, 404, 425
    genuine, how to recognize, 159–64,
        175–81, 369–70
    human embodiment of God, 168–71
    meeting, 45, 177–78, 300–01, 320–21
    necessity of, 60
    perfect man, 159–60, 176
    qualities of, 160–63
    rules by love, 117, 179
    son of God, 170, 387
    speak from inner experience, 26–27, 166,
        194, 235, 338
    succession of, 59, 173, 243
    teachings of, 30–31, 48–50, 58–59,
        136–39, 180, 383–88
Mastership, 243
    indications of, 178–81
    successorship, 59, 60, 173
Materialism, 427
Maya, 186, 235, 256
Meat, 309
Mechanistic theory, 12–14, 216
Meditation, 180, 328–29, 398–99, 404–05,
        408–15, 417–21. *See also* Bhajan;
        Going inside; Simran; Sound
Mediumship, 114–19, 335–37
Melody, Divine. *See* Audible Life Stream
Messengers of death, 241, 301, 421, 423.
Method of the Masters, 213, 214, 218. *See also*
        Path of the Masters
Microcosm of man, 339–46.

Mind, 77–79, 249–82, 304, 341, 362. *See also* Buddhi; Five passions; Thoughts; Visions within
an instrument, 253–54
attributes, faculties of, 252–63, 267–81, 345, 354–55
cleansing, purification, 93, 143, 385
control, 109, 256–57, 262
creations of, misleading, 147–154
higher and lower, 250, 262–64
illness of, 272–75
power of, 257
Miracles, 78, 84–85, 180
Mohammed, 52–53.
Monism, 229–31
Monotheism, 41, 229–31
Moon-worlds, 127, 349, 412
Morality, 260, 350–51
Mormonism, 153
Muni, 158. *See also* Rishi
Mystic experiences of medieval Christian Saints, 327–34, 404–06
Mystics. *See* Masters

N

Nad, Nada-Bindu, 30, 32, 71, 73, 371. *See also* Audible Life Stream
Nam or Name, the Sound Current, 369–71. *See also* Audible Life Stream
giving of. *See* Initiation
Nanak, Guru, 78, 136–36, 190
Negative power. *See* Kal
Negativity, 211–12
Nietzche, 161, 163
Nine doors, 411
Nirvana, 33, 127
Non-killing. *See* Patanjali, yoga of
Nuri Sarup. *See* Radiant form

O

Om, 35–36, 66–67, 224, 399
One, oneness, 6, 74–77, 142–43, 223, 230
Origin, original home, 8, 186
Ouspensky, 155
Oversoul, 171

P

Pain, of world, 21, 25, 107, 239
freedom from, the Gita, 61–64
See also Suffering
Pantheism, 229
Par Brahm, 208
Paradise, 205, 290, 302, 422
Param Sant, 158–59
Parameshwar, 221
Parents, 291–92, 299
Parsees, 37. *See also* Zoroastrianism
Passions. *See* Five passions
Past lives, karma, 45, 299–302

Patanjali, yoga of, 67, 79–83, 198, 345, 348, 415
Path of the Masters, love, 30–31, 44, 60, 213, 316, 348–49, 355, 368–69, 399–400. *See also* Master, teachings of; Method of the Masters
distinguishing feature of, 368–69
failure on, 192
leads to immortality, 68
preparation for, 33–34, 360. *See also* Inner journey; Preparation
Paul, the Epistles of, 89
Peace, 62–63, 69, 361–62
Perfect man, 159–60, 176, 187
Perversions of mind, 257. *See also* Five passions
Philanthropy, 106
Physical body. *See* Body, human
Physical universe, 201–02, 210–12, 233
Pinda, 201–02, 210. *See also* Physical universe
Plato, 86, 104, 315.
Pleasures, worldly, 267–69, 365
Plutarch, 418
Polytheism, 229
Possessions, 358–60
Prakriti, 64
Pralabdh karma. *See* Karma, three types of
Prana, 77, 232, 375–76
Pranayama, 79, 198, 347–48, 396–97
Preparation, mental, 350–67
to enter the path, 177–78, 183, 394
lack of, 191–93
Primal Word, music, Shabd, 371, 379, 383
karma, 252
Primordial element, 204, 375
Procrastination, 277
Profanity, 272
Psychic powers, 396, 398
Punishments. *See* Karmic debt and payment
Pure spirit, 203, 247, 416, 426
Pure white music, 372, 377
Purgatories, 203
Purity, 93
through Shabd, 95
Purusha, 221. *See also* Soul
Pythagoreans, 86

Q

Qualifications of Saints, 136–38
Quarrelsomeness. *See* Anger

R

Radha Soami, 221
Radha Soami Dham, 207
Radiant form of the Master, 97, 150, 154, 177, 413, 415–23
Ramakrishna, 71. *See also* Vedanta
Reality, 6, 30, 282
Rebirth. *See* Wheel of eighty-four

Region of immortality, 205–08. *See also* Sat Desh
Regions, lords of, 75, 232
   creation of, 233. *See also* Higher regions
Reincarnation, 289–93, 298, 304, 422.
   See also Wheel of eighty-four
   of an initiate, 191
Religion, genuine, 140–42, 375
   defects, failure of, 29–30, 138–40
   love is foundation of, 142–45
Religious movements, 154–56
Repetition. *See* Simran
Requirements for the path. *See* Path of the Masters, preparation for; Preparation
Resentment, 272
Reserve karmas (sinchit), 293
Rishi, 158, 193, 198, 208, 237. *See also* Yogi
Rosicrucians, 105, 119–21

S

Sach Khand, 159, 197, 205–07, 238, 349, 370
Sadhu, 48, 158
Sahaj Yoga, 397–400. *See aso* Surat Shabd Yoga
Sahasradal Kanwal, 71, 202–03, 208–09, 337, 346, 349, 412–13
Saints, 157–59, 168, 206, 349, 384–85, 391.
   See also Satguru; Master
   mission different from mahatmas, 107, 109–10, 122
Salvation. *See* Liberation
Samadhi, 62, 80, 325, 330–32, 416, 417
Samhitas, 74
Sanskaras, 250, 290, 299, 422
Sanskrit alphabet, 344
Sant, 157
   Param, 158–59
Santon ki Shiksha. *See* Path of the Masters; Surat Shabd Yoga
Sat, 222
Sat Desh, 75, 204–07, 238
Sat Guru, 157, 159, 191, 198, 214, 294, 372, 392–94, 423. *See also* Saints
Sat Nam, 157, 222, 233, 370. *See also* Sat Purush
Sat Lok, 205–07. *See also* Master; Sach Khand
Sat Purush, 30, 161, 191, 204, 221–22, 233, 238–39, 400. *See also* Creator; Sat Nam; Supreme Lord
Sat Yuga, 310. *See also* Golden Age
Satsang, 181–82, 394
Science, limitations of, 165–66
Science of the soul. *See* Surat Shabd Yoga
Second region. *See* Trikuti
Seeking the Master, 24, 29–30, 176–78, 181–83, 357, 394. *See also* Master, genuine, how to recognize
Self, I-ness, 278–81
Self-realization, 8–10, 30, 76, 106–07, 402

Self-righteousness, 279
Selfishness, 33, 279, 280, 352–53, 360
Senses, sensuality, 64, 109, 255, 269–71, 362, 365–67. *See also* Lust
Service (seva), 307–08, 350, 360
Sex passion. *See* Lust; Senses
Shabd. *See* Audibe Life Stream
Shakti, 240
Shams-i-Tabriz, 56, 389–90
Shiva, 239–40
Siddhis. *See* Psychic power
Sight, inner, 403
Silver cord, 420, 424
Sikhism, 135–38
Simran, smarana, 410, 413–14, 415. *See also* Attention; Meditation
Sin, 317–18. *See also* Evil
Sinchit karma. *See* Karma, three types of
Slander. *See* Anger, minor aspects of
Soami Ji, 190, 207, 389
Sohang, 75–76, 354
Sons of God, 387
Soul, 82, 143, 191, 230–31, 241, 250–52, 262, 264, 322–23, 366. *See also* Atman; Man, as top of creation; Purush
   activates mind, 253
   attraction of soul to God, 330–31
   creation of, 238
   helplessness of, 265–67
   spark of the divine, 193, 354
Sound, Sound Current, 8, 73, 376–78, 380, 386, 388–90, 398, 404. *See also* Audible Life Stream; Meditation
Source. *See* Audible Life Stream
Space, 82
Spinoza, 76
Spirit, qualities of, 241. *See also* Soul
Spiritual blindness, 98, 183, 402
Spiritual regions. *See* Higher regions
Spiritualism, 114, 335–37
Steiner, Rudolph, 104
Stilling the mind, 408–09. *See also* Attention; Concentration; Simran
Struggle for spiritual freedom, 239
Submission. *See* Surrender to a Master
Subtle body, 249. *See also* Astral body
Suffering, 44, 49–50, 257, 288–89. *See also* Pain
Sufis, 38, 371, 378–84
   as Masters, faquirs, 158
Suicide, 23–24, 274, 316
Sun worlds, 127, 349, 412
Superstition, 428
Supreme Lord, Being, One. *See also* God; Sat Purush
   as Creator, 206, 220, 229–231
   chief attributes of, 219, 225, 228
   in the Master's form, 169, 228
Surat Shabd Yoga, 56–58, 68, 108–10, 372, 397–400, 407–17. *See also* Audible Life Stream
Surrender to a Master, 188–90, 306–09, 362

T

Talmud, 125–26
Tao, 32–37, 360. *See also* Audible Life
. Stream
Taoism, 32–33
Tattwas. *See* Elements, five
Tenth door, 411
Theosophy, 103–10
Third eye, 345–47, 408
Third region, 30, 203, 249, 416
Thoughts, thought-forms, 147–49, 258, 260.
See also Mind
Thousand-petalled lotus. *See* Sahasradal
Kanwal
Three worlds, 208, 222, 237
Time, 82. *See also* Yugas
Tisra til. *See* Third eye
Tobacco habit, 270
Torah, 125–26
Trance, 325
Transmigration, 294–97. *See also* Wheel of
eighty-four
Trikuti (second region), 126, 181, 207–08, 237,
252, 309, 346. *See also* Brahm Lok
Trinity, Christian, 387
Hindu, 239–40
Trust in the Master, 188–89. *See also* Faith
Truth, 69, 98, 168, 177–79, 368–69, 391–94
Truthfulness, 350–51

U

Universal mind, 208, 249, 252. *See also* Kal
plane of, 192, 203
Universal oneness, 222, 352–55
Universe, created and sustained, 375–76,
379–80, 414
four grand divisions, 201–05
hierarchy of, 232–41
See also Creation
Upanishads, 71–74, 76, 366

V

Vairagya. *See* Detachment
Vanity. *See* Ego
Varnatmak sound, 371, 380
Vedanta, 71, 371. *See also* Hinduism
Vedas, 70–83, 352–54. *See also* Hinduism
Vegetarianism, 309–11
Vina. *See* Sound

Virtues, 82, 225
the five, 282
Vishnu, 224, 239–40
Visions within, 148, 151–54, 327–33. *See also*
Inner experiences; Mind; Thoughts
Vitalism, 13–14
Viveka. *See* Discrimination
Vivekananda, 28–29, 71
Voice of the silence, 108
Voices, hearing, 148, 151–53
Vows, the four,
lacto-vegetarian diet, 309–11
meditation, 415–18
morality, 350–52
no alcohol, no habit-forming drugs, 270,
311

W

Wealth, 274–76, 307–08, 350, 359–60
Wheel of eighty-four, 32, 67–68, 268, 292–93.
See also Escape from passions;
Reincarnation; Transmigration
ended by meeting Perfect Master, 68, 235,
300, 393
escape from, 50, 309, 392–93
White Brotherhood, 105–07, 120, 389
Will, individual, 189
Will of God, 309, 317
Word. *See* Audible Life Stream

Y

Yama. *See* Messengers of death
Yoga, 157
of the Audible Life Stream. *See* Surat
Shabd Yoga
of Patanjali. *See* Patanjali
systems, 396–98. *See also* Gyan Marg
Yogi, attainments of, 66–68, 78, 109, 198,
347–49, 400, 425. *See also* Rishi
definition of, 157
practices of, 79–80, 399–400.
Yugas, 427–32. *See also* Golden Age

Z

Zarathustra, 37–42
Zend Avesta, 38
Zohar, 133
Zoroastrianism, 37–42. *See also* Magi

INFORMATION AND BOOKS
ARE AVAILABLE FROM:

The Secretary
Radha Soami Satsang Beas
P.O. Dera Baba Jaimal Singh 143204
District Amritsar, Punjab, India

CANADA

Dr. J.Khanna, 5550 McMaster Road, Vancouver V6T IJ8, B.C.
Dr.Peter Grayson, 177, Division Street S.Kingsville,
    Ontario, N9Y IRI, Canada

U.S.A.

Mr. Roland G.de Vries, 10901 Mill Spring Drive, Nevada
    City, Calif. 95959
Dr. Gene Ivash, 4701 Shadow Lane, Austin, Texas 78731
Mr. Roy E.Ricks, 651 Davis Street, Melrose Park, Ill.60160
Mr. Henry F. Weekley, 2121 N.Ocean Blvd., Apt. 1108E,
    Boca Raton, Fla. 33431

MEXICO

Mr. Jorge Angel Santana, Cameta 2821, Jardines Del
    Bosque Guadalajara, Jalisco

SOUTH AMERICA

Dr. Gonzalo Vargas N.,P.O. Box 2666, Quito, Ecuador
Mr. Leopoldo Luks, Ave. Maracay, Urb. Las Palmas,
    Qta. Luksenburg, Caracas Venezuela
Mrs. Rajni B. Manglani, c/o Bhagwan's Store, 18 Water Street,
    Georgetown, Guyana

WEST INDIES

Mr. Thakurdas Chatlani, 2A Gittins Avenue, Maraval, Trinidad
Mr. Sean Finnegan, P.O.Box 2314, Port-au-Prince, Haiti
Mr. Bhagwandas Kessaram, c/o Kiddies Corner, Swan Street,
    Bridgetown, Barbados

ENGLAND

Mrs. F.E. Wood, c/o Lloyd's Bank, 20 North Street,
    Leatherhead, Surrey

SWEDEN
Mr. Lennart Zachen Vintergatan, 15A I, 172 30 Sundbyberg

DENMARK
Ms. Inge Gregersen, Askevenget-15, 2830 Virum

HOLLAND
Mr. Jacob Hofstra Geulwijk 6, 3831 LM Leusden

WEST GERMANY
Mr. Rudolf Walberg, Falkenstr. 18, D-6232 Bad Soden/Taunus

AUSTRIA
Mr. Hansjorg Hammerer, Sezenweingasse 10, A-5020, Salzburg

SWITZERLAND
Mr. Olivier de Coulon, Rue de Centre, CH-1131 Tolochenaz

FRANCE
Count Pierre de Proyart, 7 Quai Voltaire, 75007 Paris

SPAIN
Mr. H.W. Balani, Balani's International, P.O. Box 486, Malaga

PORTUGAL
Mr. Alberto C. Ferreira, R. Machado dos Santos 20, 2775 Parede

GIBRALTAR
Mr. Sunder Mahtani, 5/5, Trafalgar House

ITALY
Mr. Ted Goodman, Via Garigliano 27, Rome 00198

GREECE
Dr. Constantine Siopoulos, Thrakis 7.145 61 Kifissia

CYPRUS
Mr. Hercules Achilleos, Kyriakou Matsi 18,
    Pallouriotissa-T.K.9077, Nicosia

WEST AFRICA
Mr. Krishin Vaswani, Vaan-Ahn Enterprises Ltd.,
    P.O.Box 507 Monrovia, Liberia
Mr. Nanik N. Balani, Kewalram (Nig.) Ltd.,
    P.O. Box 320, Lagos, Nigeria
Mr. J.O.K. Sekyi, P.O. Box 4615, Accra, Ghana

EAST AFRICA
Mr. Sylvester Kakooza, P.O.Box 31381, Kampala Uganda
Mr. Sohan Singh Bharj, P.O.Box 47036, Nairobi, Kenya
Mr. D.N. Pandit, K.Lands Limited P.O.Box 1000,
    Dar-es-Salaam, Tanzania
Mr. David Bowskill, P.O.Box 11012, Chingola, Zambia
Mr. Vernon Lowrie, P.O.Box 690, Harare, Zimbabwe

SOUTH AFRICA
Mr. Sam Busa, P.O.Box 41355, Craighall Transvaal 2024
Mr. R.Attwell, P.O.Box 5702, Durban 4000

MASCARENE ISLANDS
Mr. D.S.Sumboo, 9, Bis Harris Street, Port Louis, Mauritius

ISRAEL
Mrs. H.Mandelbaum, P.O.Box 2815, Tel Aviv-61000

U.A.E.
Mr. Chander Bhatia, Shabnam Trading Corp.
    P.O.Box 2296, Dubai

KUWAIT
Mr. & Mrs. Ghassan Alghanem, P.O.Box 25549, 13116, Safat, Kuwait

AFGHANISTAN
Mr. Manak Singh, c/o Manaco, P.O. Box 3163, Kabul

SRI LANKA
Mr. D.H. Jiwat, Geekay Ltd., 33 Bankshall Street, Colombo-11

NEW ZEALAND
Mr. Tony Waddicor, P.O.Box 5331, Wellesley St. P.O.,
    Auckland 1

AUSTRALIA
Mrs. Janet Bland, P.O. Box 3, Oaklands Park,
    South Australia 5046

INDONESIA
Mr. G.L. Nanwani Yayasan Radha Soami Satsang Beas,
    JL.Kelinci Raya No. 32A, Jakarta-Pusat
Mr. Tarachand Chotrani, 51, Dji. Bubutan, P.O.Box 144,
    Surabaya

SINGAPORE
Mr. Bhagwan Asnani, 1806 King's Mansion, Singapore-1543

MALAYSIA
Mr. N.Pal, c/o Muhibbah Travel Agency, Sdn.Bhd.,
    46 Jalan Tanku Abdul Rahman, Kuala Lumpur01-07

THAILAND
Mr. Harmahinder Singh Sethi, Sawan Textiles Ltd.,
    154 Serm Sin Kha, Sampheng, Bangkok-10100

HONG KONG
Mr. S.G. Dasani T.S.T. P.O.Box 96567 Kowloon

PHILIPPINES
Mr. Kay Sham, P.O.Box 2346 MCC, Makati, Metro Manila

JAPAN
Mr. L.H. Parwani, Radha Soami Satsang Beas,
    Semba P.O. Box 209, Osaka 541-91

*   *   *   *   *   *   *

FOR OTHER FOREIGN ORDERS WRITE TO :
Mr. Krishin Babani, Buona Casa Bldg., 2nd floor,
    Sir P.M. Road, Fort Bombay-400 001, India

Addresses changed since this book was printed :

BOOKS ON THIS SCIENCE

Soami Ji Maharaj
1. *Sar Bachan*

Baba Jaimal Singh
2. *Spiritual Letters* (to Huzur Maharaj Sawan Singh : 1896-1903)

Huzur Maharaj Sawan Singh
3. *Discourses on Sant Mat*
4. *Philosophy of the Masters (Gurmat Sidhant),* 5 vols. (an encyclopedia on the teachings of the Saints)
5. *My Submission* (introduction to *Philosophy of the Masters)*
6. *Philosophy of the Masters (abridged)*
7. *Tales of the Mystic East* (as narrated in satsangs)
8. *Spiritual Gems* (letters : 1919-1948)
9. *The Dawn of Light* (letters : 1911-1934)

Sardar Bahadur Jagat Singh Maharaj
10. *The Science of the Soul* (discourses and letters : 1948-1951)

Maharaj Charan Singh
11. *Die to Live* (answers to questions on meditation)
12. *Teachings of the Saints* (first Chapter of *Die to Live)*
13. *Divine Light* (discourses and letters : 1959-1964)
14. *The Path* (first part of *Divine Light)*
15. *Light on Saint Matthew*
16. *Light on Sant Mat* (discourses and letters : 1952-1958)
17. *Quest for Light* (letters : 1965-1971)
18. *Light on Saint John*
19. *Spiritual Discourses*
20. *Spiritual Heritage* (from tape-recorded talks)
21. *The Master answers* (to audiences in America : 1964)
22. *Thus Saith the Master* (to audiences in America : 1970)
23. *Truth Eternal* (a discourse)

Books about the Masters

1. *Call of the Great Master* – Diwan Daryai Lal Kapur
2. *The Living Master* – Katherine Wason
3. *With a Great Master in India* – Dr. Julian P. Johnson
4. *With the Three Masters*, 3 vols.– from the diary of Rai Sahib Munshi Ram
5. *Heaven on Earth*– Diwan Daryai Lal Kapur

Books on Sant Mat in general

1. *A Soul's Safari*– Netta Pfeifer
2. *In Search of the Way*– Flora E. Wood
3. *Kabir, The Great Mystic*–Isaac A. Ezekiel
4. *Liberation of the Soul*–J. Stanley White, Ph.D.
5. *Message Divine*–Shanti Sethi
6. *Mystic Bible*–Dr. Randolph Stone
7. *Mysticism, The Spiritual Path*, 2 vols. Prof. Lekh Raj Puri
8. *Radha Soami Teachings*–Prof. Lekh Raj Puri
9. *Ringing Radiance*–Sir Colin Garbett
10. *Sant Mat and the Bible*–Narain Das
11. *Sarmad, Jewish Saint of India*–Isaac A.Ezekiel
12. *Teachings of the Gurus*–Prof. Lekh Raj Puri
13. *The Inner Voice*–Colonel C.W. Sanders
14. *The Mystic Philosophy of Sant Mat*—Peter Fripp
15. *The Path of the Masters*–Dr. Julian P. Johnson
16. *Yoga and the Bible*–Joseph Leeming

Mystics of the East Series

1. *Saint Paltu*—Isaac A. Ezekiel
2. *Saint Namdev, His Life and Teachings*–J.R. Puri and V.K. Sethi
3. *Tulsi Sahib, Saint of Hathras*– J.R.Puri and V.K. Sethi
4. *Tukaram, Saint of Maharashtra*–C.Rajwade
5. *Dadu, The Compassionate Mystic*–K.N. Upadhyaya, Ph.D.
6. *Mira, The Divine Lover*–V.K. Sethi
7. *Guru Ravidas, Life and Teachings*–K.N. Upadhyaya, Ph.D.
8. *Guru Nanak, His Mystic Teachings*–J.R. Puri
9. *Kabir, The Weaver of God's Name*–V.K. Sethi
10. *Bhulleh Shah*–J.R. Puri and T.R. Shangari
11. *Dariya Sahib, Saint of Bihar*–K.N. Upadhyaya Ph.D.